ORSON WELLES

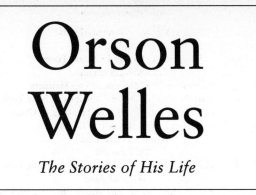

Orson Welles

The Stories of His Life

PETER CONRAD

ff

faber and faber

First published in 2003
by Faber and Faber Limited
3 Queen Square London WC1N 3AU

Typeset by Faber and Faber Ltd
Printed in England by Mackays of Chatham plc, Chatham, Kent

Photographs and illustrations courtesy of BFI Stills, Posters and Designs

Peter Conrad is hereby identified as author of this
work in accordance with Section 77 of the Copyright,
Designs and Patents Act 1988

A CIP record for this book
is available from the British Library

ISBN 0-571-20978-5

2 4 6 8 10 9 7 5 3 1

Contents

Preface

There are already half-a-dozen biographies of Orson Welles; this is not another one. Rather than telling the story of his life, I have set out to investigate the stories he told about that life.

The man was a myth: self-created, but all the same unable to enjoy sole ownership of himself. His persona compounded the roles he played – kings, despots, generals, captains of industry, autocratic film directors – and the more or less fictitious exploits with which he regaled other people or which they attributed to him. *Citizen Kane* was an early instalment of his autobiography, telling in advance the story of a life he had hardly begun to live. Welles – though he did not appear in the film about them – was all of the Ambersons, whose loss of magnificence rehearsed his own decline. Even his Harry Lime in *The Third Man* was a self-portrait, however indignantly he denied it. The Great Orson, as he called himself when performing in a wartime magic show in Los Angeles, resembled the great Gatsby, that fantasist who enacts a society's glorious and meretricious dreams. Gatsby, of course, is a fictional character, whereas Welles actually existed: who would have dared to invent him? And there is another crucial difference between them. Gatsby's greatness depends on the myth-mongering of strangers; Welles applied the adjective to himself, and he did so as a joke. Having manufactured his myth, he then punctured it, or took care to prove himself unworthy of it.

Some of the stories he told about himself derived from the literary works he adapted. Impersonating a series of archetypal figures from Faust to Falstaff, he did not so much act these parts as turn them into commentaries on himself. Other stories are hidden in books he wanted to adapt. A project like his *Heart of Darkness*, cancelled by RKO, took on other forms and infiltrated other films; the role of Kurtz gave Welles an opportunity for risky, fearful self-exploration.

The stories contradict each other. How could one man possess both the crazed mental ardour of Faust and the luxurious indolence of Falstaff? How did Welles get from the megalomania of Kane to the dejected, impotent idealism of Don Quixote? Despite these inconsistencies, each story corresponds to an aspect of Welles. The whole was enormous, and it consisted of the disputatious, inconsistent parts he played. In an interview with *Cahiers du cinéma*, he said that his Shakespearean films were made in 'moral CinemaScope'. They needed 'a larger screen', in order to exhibit the full range of human possibility or the variety of his own selves. He was forever adding to the total; he experimented with identities by performing. Lear asks to be told who he is, and the fool replies that he is Lear's shadow.

In his childhood, people acclaimed Welles as a boy wonder, a genius, which meant that they considered him to be 'sui generis'. Genius is required to be self-generating. But wasn't Welles, like all performers, impelled by the expectations of others, obliged to live out their dreams and – in due course – their nightmares? Grandiloquence was forced on him. He was required to be exemplary: he impersonated America in *Citizen Kane*, then did the same for post-war Europe in *The Third Man*. On the radio, Welles liked to say that he was the 'obedient servant' of his audience; he always played public figures, who by definition have little or no private reality. Rosebud, whatever it might be, is the one thing that Kane does not possess. Welles came to think of himself as the victim of a gift he had not asked for and could neither understand nor control. Hence his fondness for romantic poets like Byron and Coleridge, whose imaginative compulsion was a curse. Increasingly, he sought a reprieve by claiming that the praise for his creative powers was unmerited. He had duped his admirers. Couldn't they see that he was a fraud? Like all his stories, this one was self-tormentingly honest and also glibly false.

Jean Cocteau said that he preferred mythology to history because 'history begins in truth and ends in lies, whereas mythology originates in a lie and progresses towards truth'. Cocteau resolved the paradox by fabricating his own identity, and declared 'I am a lie that tells the truth'.

Many of Welles's statements in interviews were true lies of this kind; I have paid particular heed to two of them. In 1950 he did a quick round-up of his talents for a journalist from *Sight and Sound*, and said that he disliked acting, liked directing, but enjoyed writing most of all. His essays, journalistic articles, works of fiction and unproduced screenplays are an invaluable guide to his motives, too seldom consulted by critics. Possibly, like Coleridge, Welles took even more pleasure in talking than in writing, and despite his visual virtuosity, he complained that criticism of films concentrated on images and ignored content. He understood that photography is a means of writing with light; I have tried to decipher what he was writing about.

Talking to *Cahiers du cinéma* in 1964, he made a related decision about which of his identities mattered most to him: 'I am really a man of ideas – yes, above all else.' I have chosen to take him at his word. The man was himself an idea, or a succession of ideas, to which he gave flesh. Because he was a director who acted, the ideas that intrigued him were personae he tried on for size. Those ideas, of course, were not entirely his own: it has been fascinating to discover how much Welles owed – when he ruminated about myth, history and art – to favourite writers like Robert Graves, T. H. White and Isak Dinesen. But he always made deft, surprising, idiosyncratic use of what he borrowed. 'I guess,' he told *Cahiers*, 'I am even more of a man of ideas than a moralist.' He was happy for the ideas to lead him in unorthodox, illicit directions.

This man of ideas had ideas about everything. He was a bold, brilliant interpreter (or re-creator) of literature, who tested his critical ideas – about Shakespeare, Marlowe and Cervantes, or Melville and Mark Twain, or Conrad, Kafka and Dinesen – in performance. During the early 1950s he sought to book-end the entire European literary tradition by filming both Homer's *Odyssey* and Joyce's *Ulysses*. Though these projects came to nothing, conception mattered more to him than accomplishment. Once he had an idea, its execution was either impracticable or a dreary anticlimax. He eventually took to disparaging films because they were so encumbered by technology that the idea behind them was dead before it ever got to the screen. His mode, he thought, was the essay, visual or verbal, which sketched a possibility, then advanced to something else. He delighted in what Melville called 'the comedy of thought': its provisional nature, its inspired accidents, its lively refusal to reach an end, a stop, a conclusion.

With Welles, you are bound to think laterally or peripherally, because that is how his mind worked and how his career, which he was unable to plan, actually developed. Talking to Peter Bogdanovich, he regretted that the editors engaged by RKO to cut *The Magnificent Ambersons* had removed a discussion of olives, an exotic novelty served at the ball. The mystified comments of the guests on these hard, sour green things led nowhere, but their chatter, Welles said, gave density to the story; this was an example of what he called his 'marvellous mad digressions', true to the free-associating mental liberty he had learned, he told Bogdanovich, from Gogol's novel *Dead Souls*.

I have adopted a similar method, and my book progresses, as Welles did, by digressing. I have kept my stories, more or less, in chronological order. But Welles moved to and fro between simultaneous projects and competing identities; he had a multiplicity of lives, which proceeded along parallel tracks. Therefore, my chapter on Faust the magus, which begins from his production of Marlowe's play in 1937, looks forward to anticipate the meanings that magic later acquired for him, and the chapter on Kurtz considers the way in which, later in life, he used Conrad's character as a means of questioning and assessing the notion of greatness, that dangerous standard to which he felt himself accountable. In my chapter on Don Quixote, I have looked backwards, noticing the quixotic heroes who populated his work long before he began to make his film of Cervantes' novel.

When filming the stories of mythical figures like Falstaff or Quixote, Welles said his task was 'to make a world for them'. On stage, a character is self-sufficient, and can get by with minimal scenery. But a film requires the character to be placed in a context: the figure needs a landscape. Welles's Falstaff in *Chimes Midnight* flees from a brutal battle that represents the end of his smug, privileged society, and Quixote, in the film he never finished, trails uncomprehendingly through a country where the fire-breathing monsters are internal combustion engines, and where fighter planes not guardian angels streak noisily across the sky. I too have tried to make a world for Welles, or rather – since he moved between the American mid-West, New York, Los Angeles, Rome, Paris, Vienna, London and Madrid, with excursions to Brazil and the northern fringe of Africa – a series of alternating, interchangeable worlds.

Those contexts are intellectual not scenic; my purpose is to fill in the background to Welles's activities, or to uncover their subterranean implications. Behind *Citizen Kane* – thanks to the opening quotation from Coleridge's 'Kubla Khan' – lies the world of English romanticism, with its emphasis on the imagination's power to make dreams materialise. Welles, who called himself a latter-day Byron, felt he belonged in that exorbitant, self-dissipating culture. This account of the romantic Welles continues in a chapter that considers his enthusiasm for Robert Graves, the last and most stubbornly unrepentant of romantic poets, whose ideas about woman as a bewitching, demanding, deathly muse are anticipated in *The Lady from Shanghai*. Welles was equally at home in the Italian Renaissance, as his reference to Machiavelli and the Borgias in *The Third Man* and his performance in *Othello* proclaim; his ideas about this period, derived from the historian Jacob Burckhardt, amount to another appraisal of himself – a proud justification, and also a guilt-ridden reproach. The last of his imaginative resting-places was the Middle Ages. He saw Falstaff, by whom he meant himself, as a battered relic of a time he insisted on regarding as happy, merry, even paradisial. It was a fantasy, but it sustained him in the last part of his life.

Other worlds to which Welles adhered actually existed, waiting for him to annex them. In Brazil, for instance, where he spent several months in 1942, he found a society whose riotous carnival enabled him to cast off the puritanical, businesslike rigour of the United States. He lived briefly in Seville as a young man, later established a residence in Madrid, and chose to have his remains interred in Spain. The country gave him another compendium of national stories which he adopted as his own – stories about the anachronistic folly of chivalry, about lives gallantly risked in the arena and blood uncomplainingly shed on the sand: an education in idealism and tragic fortitude.

Determined to encompass the entire world, the American Welles joined east and west, just as the Europeanised Welles bestraddled north and south. From the career of Kane, the demise of the Ambersons and the journeying of O'Hara in *The Lady from Shanghai*, he constructed a biography of America that doubled as his autobiography. Living in exile as an honorary European, he tried to balance Nordic and Mediterranean mythologies: the energetic will of Faust and the sybaritic cynicism of the Archbishop in *Une grosse légume*, a little-known but revealing novel he salvaged from another unmade film.

Welles the aspiring intellectual began as an ideologue, for whom ideas served as incitements to action. From the mid-1930s to the late 1940s, as a political orator and a possible candidate for office, he explored the relations between performance and demagoguery. The idea of power had a treacherous attraction for him, especially if – as in *The War of the Worlds*, his alarming dramatisation of a Martian invasion, broadcast at Halloween in 1938 – it involved power over people's minds, a capacity to direct their dreams. The dictators who ruled the world during those years relied on Welles's own technological media to universalise the image of themselves and to insinuate their voices into every house and head. Was Welles himself, for all his liberal scruples, secretly one of them? He debated the issue in his script for *Heart of Darkness* and in *The Stranger*, where he plays a Nazi living incognito as a schoolteacher in sedate Connecticut. There is, Welles admitted, 'a fascist in each of us'.

For an actor, that was a shockingly literal confession: the fascist lived inside his body, and broke free in the wild-eyed violence of the scholarly Kindler in *The Stranger* or the sardonic, amoral grin of Harry Lime. Later, having lost the power that was lavished on him by CBS and then RKO, Welles suspected that his downfall might have been a moral boon. He had been saved from himself.

He continued to worry about the political and philosophical crises of his time. Discussing *Touch of Evil*, he said that it showed the fermenting decay of our species. Did humanity have a future in a society run by machines, or by mechanised men? In his film of Kafka's *The Trial*, the querulous individual is bullied by bureaucrats whose identity is corporate not personal, and menaced by a computer which, like one of Macbeth's witches, foresees his life and ordains its course. Both films were versions of Welles's own story, reflecting on his failed campaign to remain an individual while working on an industrialised production line; but in both he cast himself as the villain – a lawman who tampers with the law, a lawyer who operates against the interests of his clients. He was never sure whether to think of himself as a hero or as the monster who is due to be slain by the hero. Potentially he was both, which turned all the stories he told into fables of self-destruction.

Although he enjoyed the authority conferred on him by his looming body and his rumbling voice, Welles settled finally into a view of himself as an ineffectual creature: a magician whose art depended on deception and illusion. He thought of films as dreams, killed off by daylight. Images flicker like the light from the fire projected onto the faces of the dying Major in *The Magnificent Ambersons* or Falstaff at the beginning of *Chimes at Midnight*; then they fade. Some of Welles's best ideas disappeared into the air as he talked, describing films he was never allowed to make. The work he did complete was mostly taken from him and revised by producers and editors who eliminated and discarded anything they did not understand. He was reduced to smuggling ideas of his own into bad films made by others, in which he appeared to raise money. Ill-wishers were often to blame for his upsets and disappointments; it might also be true that he had too many ideas and, therefore, because he believed he could be everybody and do everything, dissipated himself rather than concentrating his energies. Or did he prefer incompleteness, like the romantic poets who have such an influence on *Citizen Kane*? To leave a work unfinished, or not to begin it at all, preserves the excitement of the first inspiriting idea that – like genius – emerges from nowhere.

To postpone completion was also a way of wishing that there might, after all, be a future: he made *Citizen Kane* in his mid-twenties, and suffered all his life from the shamed, fearful sense that the best was behind him.

For whatever reason, Welles left us only fragments of himself. I have tried to piece them together.

ORSON WELLES

Welles multiplying himself.

CHAPTER I

So Many of Me

Orson Welles was a metamorphic, even a metaphysical man. He staked out the limits of his identity and the extent of his ambition by comparing himself to both Christ and Lucifer. He claimed to resemble mankind's redeemer and also the rebel angel who brought about the fall of man: an artistic saviour and – since art is a reflex of the probing, dissatisfied mind – a damned soul. At other times he acknowledged an affinity to universal geniuses or world conquerors, to Leonardo da Vinci and Shakespeare, or Napoleon and Hitler. When he ran out of divine, infernal or superhuman prototypes, he called on forces of nature to explain himself. In the act of creation, he saw himself as an oil well disgorging black, muddy gold.

Awestruck colleagues were reminded of Niagara Falls, an earthquake, and a swampy, entangled jungle. Some observers considered him to be terrifyingly subhuman. To them, Welles in certain moods was an infuriated bull, a spouting whale, a rogue elephant or (thanks to his growling voice) a sea cow. He might have been a classical god, able to assume any or all of those forms. But he did not believe in his grandiose impersonations for long: the actor deceives everyone except himself. When not fantasising about global domination, Welles – in a stiller, smaller voice – admitted to being merely a fraud, a charlatan, a low trickster. Or was this another of his acts?

He made up myths about himself, and permitted others to add to their store, because there was no other way to account for such a self-begotten being. Once, trying to rid himself of all this accumulated lore, he claimed that his gigantism was forced on him by his bulk. 'I always have to be bigger than life,' he said. 'It's a fault in my nature.' In practice, he enjoyed his own excessiveness. He was an infant prodigy, who grew faster than others and eventually outgrew everyone else. Why shouldn't he also grow bigger, eating his way to dominance? His inordinate body fuelled him as he worked his way through a series of lives, which were inevitably punctuated by deaths.

The characters Welles played were all extensions of himself. Sometimes they represented eternal human types, like Marlowe's Faustus, Cervantes'

3

Don Quixote and Shakespeare's Falstaff. Their modern equivalents were self-invented legends like Graham Greene's Harry Lime and Joseph Conrad's Kurtz. The stories of Welles's life, which he started to tell in adolescence, cast him as the kind of hero who is deposited on earth to challenge prohibitions, to attempt the impossible, even at the cost of defying and offending God (which is why he adopted the devil as a self-image). His earliest heroes were demons of spiritual conceit, the arrogant offspring of Faust. Their dizzy rise, like his own, was followed by an equally steep fall. Later – chastened by professional rejection and disappointment, or perhaps wanting to be pitied and given a second chance – he felt entitled to incarnate downcast virtue. When he played Falstaff, he declared the character to be the epitome of unspoiled, unappreciated goodness. Sanctifying the old toper, he conveniently overlooked his greed and immorality. Was Welles himself a tragic hero, struck down for hubris? Or should we see him as a comic character, enfeebled by petty weaknesses?

Either way, Welles lived a life of allegory. The abundance of his talents made him, as his acolytes insisted, a Renaissance man, and he accepted the nomination when he played Faustus or Machiavelli's mentor Cesare Borgia. The fifteenth-century humanist Pico della Mirandola, in his treatise *On the Dignity of Man*, asked 'Who would not admire this chameleon?' Instead of the guilty, fallen miscreant chided by the Middle Ages, Pico della Mirandola saw the human being as a creature of wondrous mental dexterity, engaged, like the chameleon, in a playful, perpetual recreation of himself. But Welles was a Renaissance man born in the wrong century. He found himself in a modern, mechanised society where people were expected to be uniform and pliant, and his idiosyncrasy made him unemployable. Hyperbolic as ever, he sometimes wondered if he might be the last representative of the endangered human species. In other moods, he doubted that the chameleon deserved our admiration. Renaissance men, as he liked to point out, were wreckers and iconoclasts. All his life he suspected that his rampant, rebellious creativity was another name for destructiveness, and feared that it would impel him to destroy himself.

Although Welles acted, directed and wrote, the role to which he always returned was that of storyteller. At the beginning of his career he recited stories on the radio. He also acted them out – on stage, on film, and in life. He himself suffered problems of political conscience like Shakespeare's Brutus, and discovered the fatality of overweening ambition like Macbeth.

He uncovered other aspects of himself in Conrad's story about the depraved and demented imperialist Kurtz, in Melville's characterisation of Ahab the mutilated, self-scourging whaler, and finally in Cervantes' account of Don Quixote, a knight of unblemished if impractical faith. In 1950 he told the interviewer from *Sight and Sound* that he was sick of literary adaptations. 'I am only interested now in putting my own stories on the screen,' he said. But what else had he ever done?

Late in life, Welles occasionally gave reminiscential one-man shows, when he joked about the versatility that for Pico della Mirandola was the sign of the chameleon's superior nature. Jean-Luc Godard attended such an event in Hamburg. Welles began by enumerating his copious selves, and introduced himself as 'author, composer, actor, designer, producer, director, scholar, financier, gourmet, ventriloquist, poet'. He modestly left out the odd jobs he did on his own impecunious film sets, where, in case of need, he served as first cameraman, lighting designer, gaffer and sound mixer. He had also forgotten his work as a political columnist and his brief career as an expert on international relations, in which capacity he lectured about the fascist threat in 1945. Kenneth Tynan, telling a similar story about another such appearance, allowed Welles to add 'I also paint and sketch, and I am a book-publisher. I am a violinist and a pianist.' As if all of this were not enough, he might legitimately have listed the roles of bullfighter and – thanks to a rather wheezing pop record he made in 1984, the year before his death – singer. Oddly, in both accounts he omitted the role of magician, in many ways the closest to his heart. When performing tricks, he protested against reality's pro-hibitions and waived natural laws; at the same time, he archly admitted his own fraudulence and the illusoriness of all art. In the Godard version, Welles completed his personal inventory and then expressed surprise that so many people had come to see this polymorphous parade (though there were only three paying customers in the house). Tynan's Welles, more wistfully realistic, said to the audience 'Isn't it strange that there are so many of me – and so few of you?'

Micheál MacLíammóir, Iago in his film, did another quick head-count when introducing his account of filming *Othello*. He called Welles 'Movie Star and Director, Conjuror, Viveur and Philosopher of determination'. MacLíammóir's final compliment was sarcastic, since during their years of piecemeal work on the film Welles was chronically indeterminate and unreliable. But perhaps the accolade was justified. Welles was indeed a philosopher – a thinker obsessed by conjecture as well as conjuring, forever experimenting with new modes of vision and of self-presentation. Inside that bulbous body or underneath the billowing magician's cloak he wore, he found a thronging repertory company of characters. He played wise preachers and bloodthirsty warlords, liberal democrats and sadistic fascists, genuine wizards and phony enchanters. His progeny included a few romantic visionaries for whom the idea has become an unearthly ideal, and a single, bibulous clown who wisely eschews thought in favour of sensation. The costume party reeled, in a series of quick changes, through five centuries of history in as many decades, from a Renaissance intellectual like Faustus to a modern man like Harry Lime, who invokes the Renaissance spirit to justify his vicious, unfeeling egomania. The sequence of Welles's roles or the variety of his selves rehearsed the range of human possibilities. Great actors, as Hazlitt said, demonstrate to us 'all that we are, all that we wish to be, and all that we dread to be'. Welles made himself famous on the radio by playing a dematerialised detective known only as 'The Shadow'. Dramatising both the best and the worst of us, he was the imposing, ominous shadow we all cast.

Welles, acclaimed as a genius when scarcely out of his cradle, seemed predestined for a hero's life. Even his pets were an augury of the great achievements that seemed certain: at the age of six he had a dog, bigger than he was, called Caesar. Newspapers tracked his advance through adolescence with astonished headlines. 'I had no idea,' Welles laughed in the 1970s, 'what awaited me.'

For a while he did amaze and even terrorise America. In the first stories he told, he lived dangerously and enjoyed his unearned power.

In 1936, aged twenty-one, he staged an all-black *Macbeth* in Harlem, accompanied by a contingent of voodoo drummers from Haiti. Jazzing up the tragedy, Welles discovered the contagious madness of theatre.

In 1937, he ventured into political protest, condemning capitalism in his production of Marc Blitzstein's *The Cradle Will Rock*, an opera about predatory bosses and downtrodden harlots in a grim industrial outpost called Steeltown. When police prevented the show from opening, Welles staged a popular uprising, led a march up Broadway, and presented a single, impromptu performance in a rented auditorium. The walls of the city should have tumbled down, as if besieged by trumpets.

In 1938, he tried to topple New York all over again, sending Martians to atomise the skyscrapers in his radio dramatisation of *The War of the Worlds*. The city once more survived, and Welles at the end of the broadcast reminded the traumatised mobs of listeners that they were the victims of a Halloween prank. Popular fury was not appeased when Welles appeared before the press looking, as he said, like an early martyr. Ignoring his penitent air, the headlines next morning cast him, to his own gratification, as the ultimate evil-doer. 'I was Judas Iscariot,' he said, 'and my life was over.' He had begun to enjoy these periodic disasters, because they proved, at least for the time being, his capacity to recover from professional death.

A month later he began his series of radio dramatisations for the *Campbell Playhouse* on CBS. The overawed announcer introduced Welles as a mythical being, and told listeners to imagine a combination of Baron Munchausen and Alice in Wonderland: a man who was at once a vaunting fabulist and an ingenuous child.

Thanks to the reverence of his elders, Welles was granted freedoms which he promptly misused. In 1941, he came close to outsmarting himself in *Citizen Kane*. Ridiculing the press magnate William Randolph Hearst, his film denounced the national mania for acquisition and accumulation, and warned of the perils inherent in the new media of communication (which Welles himself so unscrupulously exploited). Hearst did not see the joke, and the film was nearly destroyed before it could be released.

As always after an attempted revolution, the world soon decided that it preferred the safe status quo. The providers of industrialised entertainment declared Welles to be unbankable. When he was still in his twenties, a steady descent into corpulence, shiftlessness and defensive irony began.

In 1942 he already had a reputation as a spendthrift and a playboy, misbehaving in Brazil and frittering away the budget for another unfinished film. In his absence, the studio slashed *The Magnificent Ambersons* and expelled the colleagues he had left behind from the premises. His career, to all intents and purposes, was already over. After the war, emerging from the Vienna sewers in Carol Reed's *The Third Man*, he came to personify the moral irresponsibility of the times. Harry Lime is a superficially charming devil, given power by his wit, guile and emotional nullity. Welles played the role without make-up, as if confessionally. In 1955, a comment made by a character in *Mr Arkadin* calls the hero – a piratical tycoon played, of course, by Welles himself – 'a phenomenon of an age of dissolution and crisis'. It was hard, by then, not to see Welles as just such a phenomenon. He was ruined by megalomania and self-indulgence, but had also been shrewdly disarmed by a society that reduced those who threatened it to harmless buffoons. Once the avowed enemy of commerce, he had become a professional celebrity, hawking his depreciated legend as a commodity.

Every few years, he persuaded producers to trust him with funds. In 1946 he made *The Stranger*, playing a Nazi living incognito in Connecticut. He unfairly discredited the film, perhaps to conceal the candour of its self-analysis. He also blamed the studio for chopping up *The Lady of Shanghai* before its release in 1948. Nevertheless, what remains is precious for its exposure of Welles's mad romanticism. Scrimping and improvising, he managed to film two Shakespearean trajedies, *Macbeth* and *Othello*. The first took three weeks to make, the second three years. The chaotic *Mr Arkadin*, known in some of its contradictory versions as *Confidential Report*, was his confidential report on his own lethal myth, an exercise in self-demolition. In 1958, thanks to Charlton Heston's intercession, he was allowed to write and direct *Touch of Evil*. It too was recut by the studio, which locked Welles out and ignored his desperate editorial memos.

For the rest of his life, he relied on European donors, who paid for literary adaptations: Kafka's *The Trial* in 1962, *Chimes at Midnight* – his own digest of Shakespeare's chronicle plays – in 1966, Isak Dinesen's *The Immortal Story* in 1968. In 1973 he pieced together an oblique autobiography, *F for Fake*. After this there were only schemes, dreams, projects that were cancelled or abandoned.

By the end, self-parody was his only reliable source of income. Not long before he died in 1985, he made a commercial for a brand of Japanese whisky. He began by introducing himself: 'Hello, I'm Orson Welles. I direct films, and act in them.' It was a depleted echo of earlier self-declarations. In the trailer for *Citizen Kane*, he calls for a light, like God when creating the world. He then has a microphone lowered into its beam so that he can talk about the film while remaining (again like the deity) unseen. In the whisky commercial, on the other hand, he has to face the camera and state his name and profession. It is painful to watch him displaying credentials that no longer carry much credence. His eyes wander evasively, he plays with his cigar and glances round a supposed movie studio that is nothing more than a shoddy mock-up. After uncomfortably telling the customers who he is, he pronounces the personal motto that is meant to double as a recommendation for the whisky: 'What we aim for is perfection.' Did Welles the film-maker aim for perfection? Then why did he leave so much of his work in such a painfully imperfect state? The change from first person singular to plural evinces his embarrassment. There used to be so many Welleses, but those prolific alter egos are now nowhere to be seen. Perfection may have been his aim, but – unable to follow an industrial formula like the whisky makers – he seldom, if ever, achieved it. Perhaps the aim itself was improper, inappropriate alike for artists and for human beings.

Renaissance man questioned God's existence and deified himself, only to discover, as Hamlet remarks after he begins to see through humanism, that we are merely a 'quintessence of dust'. In his script for *Touch of Evil*, Welles wrote a dismissive epilogue to this apotheosis of man. The comment, which concludes the film, also served as an obituary for himself. Playing the crooked police chief Quinlan, he slumps into a slimy, typhoid-infested creek to die. Someone asks Marlene Dietrich – who plays Tanya, the clairvoyant gipsy Quinlan once loved – what he was like. She shrugs: 'He was some kind of a man. What does it matter what you say about people?' She then walks away with a casual, uncaring swagger. Since he is a man, she expects corruption from him: our bodies degenerate, and so do our morals.

But her nonchalant verdict is too facile. We do need to know what kind of a man Welles was, because his combination of genius and folly made him an extreme yet exemplary case, as an artist and as a man; it does matter what you say about people, because in summing them up you try to arrive at a precise judgement of individuals who struggle against, or perhaps surrender to, an inimical world. Lives and deaths, whether of great men or of those whom no one but their families remember, are graphs of hopeful optimism and its dismaying limitation. Is defeat inevitable? Are compromises essential, and betrayal inescapable? Are talents just loaned or entrusted to you, rather than being outright gifts? Do they expire after a while? For how long, resisting the world's determination to be rid of you, can you go on reinventing yourself? And what is it possible to leave behind?

To tabulate someone's existence is a terrifying responsibility, which is why Dietrich's shrug spares both herself and Welles. That is also why the elderly Welles tried to avoid talking about his early films, refused to see them again, and even disliked looking at himself in the mirror unless he was rendered unrecognisable by a false nose. What can justly be said about a man who between 1936 and 1941 briskly revolutionised the arts of theatre, radio and film, but ended, in his last frustrated years, as a spokesman for cheap wine, lager, dog food, or any other product the advertising agencies asked him to tout?

We have a choice between tragedy or comedy. Welles himself was unsure which genre suited him. Was he King Lear, deposed and deprived of power by craven conspirators, or was he Falstaff, who settles for self-indulgence and relies, like an overgrown infant, on always being forgiven? Of course he was both. But he came to suspect – as life had its humbling, tragicomic way with him – that the clown might be a wiser, better, more loving and more admirable character than the wildly infuriated king.

As a youth, he possessed a compulsive, agitated ambition, which seemed to him, when he reflected on it, quite terrifying. In 1933, in an autobiographical play called *Bright Lucifer*, he allied himself with the infidel angel who challenged God. The hero Eldred Brand – a fire-brand, and a successor to the spiritually aggravated hero of Ibsen's *Brand* – happily inhabits an inferno of fumes, created by the cigars he is always smoking. One of his first theatrical roles was Marlowe's necromancer in *Doctor Faustus*, a man who satisfies his craving for knowledge and sensual delight by entering into a contract with the devil. Near the end of his life, Welles prepared an autobiographical film script based on the flustered, exhausting months in 1937 when he played Faustus while trying – against opposition from bureaucrats and a censorious government – to direct *The Cradle Will Rock*. In one scene, Welles imagined himself leading a gang of pursuers a merry chase on the *Doctor Faustus* set, using trapdoors for his getaways. The traps supposedly opened into the underworld; in fact they concealed a lighting grid beneath the stage. Disappearing, the young Welles tauntingly alludes to the story of another character with a magical talent for defying death and fortuitously reincarnating himself: 'Is he in heaven? Is he in hell? That damned elusive Pimpernel!'

Welles often sentenced himself to damnation. It was his way of beseeching us to intercede and vote for his salvation. In *The Stranger*, he is impaled on a sword gripped by a Gothic angel on a clock tower, and lurches from the top of the church. The next year he repeated the fatal plunge in Gregory Ratoff's film *Black Magic*, in which he played the diabolical hypnotist Cagliostro. Quinlan in *Touch of Evil* has less far to fall: he staggers for a few feet and then sloppily collapses into the murk, just as Lime in *The Third Man*, shot before he can climb up the ladder, tumbles into the tunnel of effluent. Comic characters, as Aristotle decreed, are ridiculous because they are ugly. We are dispensed from having to care about their mishaps, and can laugh at their sufferings with impunity. Lime still has the baby face of Welles the young archangel, but Quinlan is a gargoyle: only forty-three when he made the film, Welles self-mortifyingly imagined what he might look like after a few more decades of depressive overeating. Nevertheless, the sleek, smiling Lime is more monstrous than Quinlan, and Welles discovers a tragically warped idealism inside that comic mound of inert, sagging flesh. Quinlan infallibly identifies wrongdoers; a pity that he too breaks the law by planting the evidence needed to convict them. *The Magnificent Ambersons* likewise concludes with the 'comeuppance' of the callow, selfish George Minafer. If George were merely a comic character, we would gloat when he is brought low. Instead, we are startled into sympathy as he bends over his mother's bed and sobs in an agony of regret. And although Welles did not cast himself in his film of Booth Tarkington's novel, George was the role he played when he adapted the book for radio in 1938.

Despite Dietrich's terseness, the parting remarks of her character compress Mark Antony's eulogy for Brutus in *Julius Caesar*. The elements were mixed in Brutus, Antony says – and at this moment in *Touch of Evil*, Quinlan's cast-off body is about to dissolve itself again into the elements (gaseous air and expiring fire, baser earth and water) of which it was composed. Thanks to this chemical equability, Antony goes on, 'Nature might stand up, / And say to all the world, "This was a man!"' Welles had played both parts – Brutus on stage in 1937 (in a production whose title he tersely abbreviated to *Caesar*), then Antony on record a year later – so he might have been uttering these lines about himself. The tribute is reticent, even grudging. It refuses to talk about the singularity that is the boast of tragic heroes, who believe that their deaths will deprive the world of something irreplaceable. Brutus's lot is more common and communal, as is Quinlan's – or as was Welles's, if you think of him as a combination of tragic apostate and comic weakling, which is how he increasingly thought of himself: an unrepeatable individual who is, despite that, just the same as everyone else. Humanity is a species, and these are representative specimens.

Welles's weight, his height (he reminded MacLíammóir of a monkey-puzzle tree) and that resonant voice ensured that he was never average. He accepted an invitation to perform Arthur Miller's *Death of a Salesman* in Dublin in 1951, but reneged on the agreement. He did well to desist: it is impossible to imagine him as the crushed, shuffling Willy Loman, a tragic hero designed for a lowly democratic society. He played tyrants, cardinals, chief executives, never shopkeepers or commercial travellers.

In another Dublin project that did not come off, he even intended to black up to play a grandee of the jungle in Eugene O'Neill's *The Emperor Jones*. Welles believed that his body conferred a divine right on him. At his fancy-dress party, Arkadin, already huge, augments his volume with tails, a heavy cloak with a triple tippet, and a three-cornered hat: in a novel based on the film (published under Welles's name though he may not have written it), Arkadin is said to register an effect of 'deliberate massiveness'. In 1950, Eartha Kitt – tiny but lithe and huskily seductive – beguiled the Paris audience with her jazzy songs in Welles's adaptation of the Faust legend. He responded by upstaging her, completely obliterating her so that her voice, as she sang somewhere behind him, seemed to originate inside him. Had he gobbled her up?

François Truffaut in 1967 rightly considered the characters Welles played 'exceptional beings', but hesitated about judging them: Truffaut called them 'geniuses or monsters, monstrous geniuses'. Grandiloquent by nature, Welles did not share Bertolt Brecht's objection to the tragic ennoblement of man as Man. For Brecht, tragedy was the self-interested propaganda of a doomed aristocratic caste. But Welles at least sought to balance man's ennoblement with his debasement. He knew that the enthusiasm of the humanists had been disproved by modern history, which remorselessly dehumanised the world. Harry Lime, in the speech Welles wrote for himself to deliver high above the Prater in *The Third Man*, tries to convince his naive friend that the black dots scurrying below are expendable for a price. Nowadays, he says, 'nobody thinks in terms of human beings'. Welles both was and was not Harry. He made up the character's credo, and gave him house-room inside his body, but he was irritated when, during the 1950s, bands in nightclubs and restaurants quoted the zither music from the film as soon as he appeared on the premises. How could he have been so grievously misunderstood? In the speech that praises the amorality of the Borgias and mocks the pettifogging democratic Swiss for having invented nothing but the cuckoo clock, the Renaissance man made the first of many attempts to dissociate himself from the Renaissance.

From then on – whether evoking Merry England in *Chimes at Midnight* or reviving the Spanish version of that innocent, unfallen world in his film of *Don Quixote* – he tried to repatriate himself to the Middle Ages, before the Renaissance cult of individuality began to produce characters like Hamlet and Faustus or Machiavelli and Orson Welles. It was a startling act of cultural secession: halfway through the twentieth century, an American with impeccable liberal credentials became an apologist for feudalism. His change of allegiance counted as a wishful suicide – either despairing and embittered or humorously resigned, according to your choice; a morbid retreat into obsolescence or an act of self-rejuvenation. In 1905, an earlier passionate pilgrim from America, Henry Adams, wandered out of modernity into the twelfth century in his book *Mont-Saint-Michel and Chartres*. Quitting his own time, relieving himself of its anxieties and arid scepticism, he felt he had grown 'prematurely young', and noted that only 'old people . . . have the time to be young'. His exploration of Chartres, with its celestial glass, its all-encompassing arches and its inspiring spire, dramatised, as Adams said, 'the struggle of his own littleness to grasp the infinite'. The cathedral belittled and thus soothed him. Why bother to compete with the universe?

In *F for Fake*, made in 1973, Welles followed Adams on a pilgrimage to Chartres. The sight of the cathedral excuses him from the need to be ambitious, because man – 'unsatisfied, incomplete, overstrained' as Adams put it – can never supplant God. Chartres testifies, Welles remarks, 'to what we had it in us to accomplish'. Speaking in the plural, he is talking about mankind, not himself; speaking in the past tense, he admits that his own accomplishments, mostly incomplete, no longer matter. Tynan, reviewing Welles's performance as Ahab in his own adaptation of *Moby Dick*, lamented that 'everything he does is on such a vast scale that it quickly becomes monotonous. He is too big for the boots of any part.' But not even Welles dares to measure himself against the carved encyclopaedia of Chartres, that plenum of created nature. All his abundant selves are outnumbered and outlasted by the stone population of the porches. At dusk, he gazes at the façade and speculates about the anonymity of the craftsmen who constructed it. They were medieval artisans, not self-glorifying Renaissance artists; their example suggests to Welles that art, with its conceited quest for immortality, is at best irrelevant, at worst a lie.

Like the chameleon changing its colour to inky blue, Welles at the end of this trip to Chartres retreats to a respectful distance and serenely wishes himself out of existence. Both he and the cathedral fade to black as night falls. Then, after a momentary extinction, he reincarnates himself, and the film resumes.

The bear's son with Caesar.

Peter Pan

Joseph Cotten, noting Welles's evasiveness when questioned about his early years, remarked 'I . . . seriously doubt that he was ever a child.' It could equally well be claimed that – with his wide-eyed delight, his indiscriminate greed, his petulance when crossed, and his belief that his waywardness would always be pardoned – he remained an infant all his life. During his radio career, he gave gurgling, hiccuping voice to all five of the newly born Dionne quintuplets. When he dramatised *Huckleberry Finn* for the radio in 1940, he added a prologue in which he and Jackie Cooper quarrelled over who would play Huck; Welles, twenty-five at the time, deferred to the child star with sulky reluctance. Arrested development was nothing less than his right. As Baudelaire said, genius is childhood recovered at will.

In his screenplay for *The Cradle Will Rock*, Welles has Marc Blitzstein fondly call him Peter Pan, the boy who could never grow up. Graham Greene made a similar comment about Harry Lime – another of Welles's alter egos – in the novel based on his own *Third Man* script. Greene specifies that Peter Pan is a monster: Lime's childishness explains his moral anaesthesia. Taking up the idea in *The Cradle Will Rock*, Welles avoids Greene's accusation of cold-hearted brutality by prompting a maternal figure to indulge and forgive him. In the belated revision of his life, he assigns this role to his first wife Virginia, whom he married in 1934 and divorced in 1940. The script impels her to defend Welles against Blitzstein. She fondly notes that Orson 'was never young', which entitles him to a delayed childhood in the theatre. She then recites her own version of the titular nursery rhyme: 'So down will come cradle, baby and all . . .? Well, Orson is my baby. And this is his cradle.' For Blitzstein, the rocking cradle was a premonition of revolutionary storms, which would upset a lazy, parasitical social class. For Welles's version of Virginia, the cradle must never be rocked, so the prodigious infant can go on being pampered, praised and subsidised by his elders.

Cotten could not imagine Welles as an actual child, because the child is owned and defined by others, whose offspring it is. As Noël Coward announced when he said 'I am related to no one except myself', a genius emerges fully formed – but from where? At the age of thirteen, Welles claimed, he 'played Mary the Mother of Jesus', who brought to birth her own curiously engendered genius. He added that he was 'very good in drag'.

Conveniently, Welles lost both parents while still a boy. This enabled him to concentrate on manufacturing his own myth and devising roles for those parents to play in it. His mother died of hepatitis in 1924, not long after his ninth birthday. His father, a failed inventor and an alcoholic, died in 1930, his heart and kidneys worn out. Welles was away at school, having broken off relations with him. He told John Houseman, his partner in the Mercury Theatre, that his father had killed himself, and even helpfully identified the Chicago hotel from whose side entrance the body had been carried out; the story was not true. In a memoir written in 1982, he elaborated on the fictitious incident. Here he claimed that his father died after setting himself on fire. The flames allegedly derived from a cigar named Dick Welles in his honour: no such item ever existed. On other occasions, he said he was 'convinced . . . that I had killed my father'. The act, committed by making a wish, was essential for the genius, who is his own progeny: in art, as Picasso succinctly put it, one must kill one's father.

When Welles arrived in Hollywood in 1939, local wits disparaged the cocky prodigy who had come from nowhere by nicknaming him 'Little Orson Annie'. Though Welles may have relished his orphaned state, he made amends by casting both parents in *The Magnificent Ambersons*. The heartbroken parting from his own mother he gave to George Minafer – and he added an Oedipal confession, since the sexually jealous son has denied her the chance of happiness in a second marriage. If Isabel Minafer had remarried, it would have been to Eugene Morgan, who invents and manufactures automobiles. Welles liked to say, without justification, that Eugene in Booth Tarkington's novel was based on his father.

The stories Welles told often recalled his proud self-creation. In *Citizen Kane*, the mother expels her child into the world, refusing to let personal affection interfere with his destiny. Agnes Moorehead, as if anxious for the breach, reveals that she packed the boy's case a week before his departure. Charlie, thanks to her cruel renunciation, is raised by a bank. Moorehead had rehearsed this sacrifice in Welles's 1937 radio version of *Les misérables*, where she plays a brutish inn-keeper who willingly sells her foster-daughter Cosette to Welles's Valjean. The parting here is painless. 'Take her,' snaps Moorehead, 'keep her, carry her, stuff her, eat her, drink her, and be blessed by all the saints.' In *The Trial* – Welles's film of Kafka's novel, released in 1963 – Anthony Perkins as K resists the importunities of several would-be parents. He squirms as his landlady mothers him, embarrassed by her barely repressed eroticism, and he snaps 'I am not your son' at a paternalistic priest. His uncle proprietorially says, 'I'm the nearest thing to a parent and a father that you can lay claim to in the world.' K brushes him off all the same.

Welles's parents had at least named him before their tactful disappearance, but there were so many uncertainties and second thoughts attached to their choices that he could take sole responsibility for this aspect of his identity as well. The family's name in previous generations had vacillated between Wells and his own fancier, more quaintly olde English spelling. Orson was a Welles, though others cheekily misspelled him and in doing so pointed out how tenuous the distinction was. In 1940 he shared a radio interview in San Antonio with H. G. Wells, whose science fiction he had dramatised with such wicked freedom in his *War of the Worlds* broadcast. Wells had reportedly been outraged by the apocalyptic frivolity of the show; Welles – uncharacteristically nervous, relying on defensive verbal bluster – sounded as if he was expecting a rebuke from a disapproving ancestor. But the old man, seventy-four at the time of the interview, treated the young one as a truant child, and chucklingly referred to him as 'my little namesake'. Wells's cunning humour, by describing the overgrown Welles as 'little', waved away the intimidating disparity between their heights along with the difference in the spelling of their names. He challenged Orson to drop the supernumerary, affected 'e' in his surname, and said he could see no reason for it. More maliciously, the forger Elmyr de Hory in *F for Fake* paints a phony Picasso and affixes an exact replica of Welles's signature to the canvas – except that, surely intentionally, he spells the surname Wells.

To begin with, his name was George Orson Welles. 'I could have grown up George', he reflected during the 1960s, aware that names are prophetic and relishing the prospect of an alternative life. Or was that a life he was better off not having lived, since George is the name of his alter ego in *The Magnificent Ambersons*? In any case, his father soon capriciously decided that George was more suitable for a railway porter, so the boy was referred to by his middle name. But Orson contained uncertainties of its own. Welles pretended that it commemorated some remote Italian antecedent, who had been an Orsini. This gave him a personal stake in the Renaissance – in 1948 in Henry King's *Prince of Foxes* he played Cesare Borgia, with Tyrone Power as his cynical protégé Andrea Orsini – but there is no genealogical evidence for the fantasy, just as there were no grounds for the illegitimate Andrea's adoption of the noble Neapolitan family's name: in the novel by Samuel Shellabarger, which was the film's source, he is 'an Orsini unrelated to the Orsini'. The etymology of the word, however, has its own relevance. The original owner of the name is, as the self-made myth requires, a foundling, the son of an 'ours' (which means bear in French). The name comes from a late-medieval French romance about an abducted princeling raised by bears in the forest. However fantastical that story might seem, it suited the circumstances of nineteenth-century America: Herman Melville in his novel *The Confidence-Man* refers to the typical backwoodsman as a 'Hairy Orson', midway between Eastern culture and the shaggy, unkempt nature of the West.

Having given birth to himself, Welles could then discount genetic precedent and decide what he would look like. Physically, it was difficult to account for him or assign him to any recognisable type. He could migrate at will to another species: in 1961, when he played a stumbling, slobbering King Saul in a wretched Italian film called *David and Goliath*, a review in the *Daily Worker* commented that his make-up turned him into 'a Thing from the ancient world', as if he were now one of his own Martians. He was quite happy to present himself as a mystifying, unclassifiable object. In his film of *Othello*, he steps into his first close-up – black-faced, bearded, wearing a turban – just as Desdemona's father points a finger disgustedly at 'the sooty bosom of such a thing as that'.

MacLíammóir, fascinated by Welles, spent a good deal of time speculating about his origins. Could he be Swedish? Welles insisted, untruthfully, that he was a Latin through and through. So where did he get what MacLíammóir called his 'disconcerting Chinese eyes'? Welles capitalised on this feature by developing a lucrative line in Tartar or Mongolian potentates. In 1939, beginning to universalise himself, he played a Himalayan Raja in William Archer's melodrama *The Green Goddess*. Despite his European education, the Raja says that he belongs to 'the race of the Buddha', and believes that his merger of west and east has turned him into Nietzsche's 'man of the future – the Superman'. Zarathustra, after all, originated in Persia. These were heady notions for the young man who declaimed them, and the character was at once incorporated into his personal myth. Baffled by Welles's exoticism, MacLíammóir at least credited him with possessing 'American hands' that 'moved with a controlled abandon never seen in a European'.

In a 1968 interview MacLíammóir commented again on their first meeting, when Welles auditioned for his theatre company in Dublin. He described him as 'this brilliant – not necessarily an actor – but a brilliant creature'. Only later did he add 'Orson is a wonderful person.' A creature first, fitting into no known genus; a person second. Eartha Kitt, cast as Helen of Troy in Welles's play about Faust, chose her words with equal care when she described their first encounter. 'A huge domineering-looking hombre,' she reported, 'giant-stepped his way toward me.' A 'hombre' suggests somewhat larger than a man, possibly more animal than human, so Kitt goes on to compare Welles with the Brodbingnagians from *Gulliver's Travels*. Perhaps, again like a Martian, he emitted a force field dangerous to mere human life: she felt 'the electrifying waves of his personality hit me as he drew nearer', and when he shook her hand he seemed to have severed the nerve. She had met a monster, perhaps a mutant. Acting with him in his play, she had to utter a comment he had written about himself: 'I couldn't think that God would create a man such as you.' MacLíammóir, discussing Welles's audition in a 1961 interview, spoke about him with the same awe: 'No, I didn't "discover" him. He sort of revealed himself to me.'

Welles employed the freakish power of self-transformation about which Shakespeare's Richard III boasts: 'I can add colours to the chameleon.' In this line, the humanism of the Renaissance turns sinister. The actor, a professional dissembler, here exempts himself from emotional truth and moral accountability. Welles played Richard while still at school, and returned to one of the crookback character's scenes from *Henry VI* for a German tour in 1950. He would have noticed that the ill-formed Richard disgustedly imagines himself to be another Orson, an 'unlick'd bear-whelp, / That carries no impression like the dam.' His mother, pausing to curse him, archly enquires 'Art thou my son?'

Welles's self-generation made him think of himself as a freakish exception to biological rules. Playing Rochester in Robert Stevenson's 1943 film of *Jane Eyre*, he assures his fiancée Blanche that he is 'revoltingly ugly'. His face, masked by the smoke from his cigar, is contorted by self-dislike. He scowls, slurs his words, barks like his own mastiff, and provokes Blanche to call him a cur. Yet when he relaxes with Jane, he can look childishly wide-eyed and vulnerable. Here we can glimpse the combination of 'narcissism and self-loathing' which John Houseman, as puzzled and infatuated as MacLíammóir, found in him. In *Tomorrow is Forever*, directed in 1945 by Irving Pichel, he played another surgically constructed freak: a soldier whose shattered face is clumsily pieced back together, so that – although he looks to the rest of us like the inimitable Orson Welles – he is unrecognisable to his wife (Claudette Colbert) when he returns home.

The *Daily Worker*'s joke about the extra-terrestrial, unclassifiable Thing was not far from the truth. Welles was a Frankenstein who – operating on himself with the aid of putty, latex, sponge rubber, jelly and the other cosmetic aids which turned a twenty-five year old into the senescent Kane – doubled as his own monster. Frankenstein, like Faustus, is a scientist who challenges nature. He ignores the customary biological routine of procreation, and surgically assembles his monstrous offspring from bits of exhumed corpses. Here was another mythological figure who intrigued Welles. During his early years in Hollywood, he made a pitch for a filmed version of *Macbeth* which would, he told the studio, have hybridised *Wuthering Heights* and *The Bride of Frankenstein*, mixing Gothic weather and atheistic sorcery. When he eventually made his own *Macbeth* in 1947, it turned out to be something like that, with the stew-pot of the witches, inside which they mould a murky humanoid figure, as the laboratory of Frankenstein. And the alliance between the actor's invented faces and the undead creature sutured together on the operating table turns up again in *Mr Arkadin*, during a masquerade at the Spanish castle. Van Stratten, the con man played by Robert Arden, wonders why the guests have their heads encased in papier-mâché helmets, and asks 'What's with all these crazy Frankensteins?' The gigantic heads later appear discarded in the cloisters after the party: the bodies have wriggled out from inside them.

The revellers are 'cabezudos', or what the cinema – in an early term for a close-up shot – called 'Big Heads'. They perhaps reminded Welles of how much he dreaded close-ups, which enlarged his own already ponderous head and made him devise new modes of anatomical self-revision. In his film of *Othello* he performs one of the character's grandest speeches with his back turned to the camera. The critic Eric Bentley said that Welles did not act, he simply allowed himself to be photographed. But only if he couldn't help it: he preferred the story-teller's invisibility on the radio, or the director's unseen vantage-point behind the camera. He passed this personal scruple on to Arkadin, who refuses to be photographed. If menaced by a camera, he breaks both it 'and the head of the photographer'. Arkadin does not want to be exposed to others. Neither did Welles, who hid behind his infamous kit of putty noses. In 1981, on the set of *Butterfly*, Stacy Keach watched as he prised one of these off his face. It was exactly the same shape as the real nose underneath it – a diminutive mushroom, which Welles detested because he thought it looked infantile: it was the one part of him which had not grown up. Why, Keach wondered, wear a disguise if it duplicates your own features? But, for Welles, those sticky fortifications were like Arkadin's battlemented castle or Kane's NO TRESPASSING sign on the fence at Xanadu. They warned off impertinent observers, or attempted to do so. Engaged in 1953 by Sacha Guitry to play Benjamin Franklin in *Si Versailles m'était conté*, Welles arrived on set wearing a false cranium, a false forehead, the usual false nose and a pair of false eyelids, along with a padded belly and fortified legs. Guitry, confronted by this moving mask, had to ask 'Are you really Orson Welles?' The person inside the disguise agreed that it might have been fun to sign the contract and send someone else – unrecognisably encased in make-up – to do the day's work. At the end of the session, he removed his camouflage, revealed himself actually to be Orson, and said goodnight.

To manufacture himself as Welles did, and to go on fabricating new personae, counted as a magical feat. He had less interest in the humdrum, natural business of reproducing himself. In the course of three marriages he accumulated – like King Lear – a trio of daughters, but he had scant time for his offspring. An infant was a rival, monopolising attention and affection. Welles assigned the girls roles as extras in his films, according them unpaid bit parts in his own fictitious life. The first, Christopher, born to Virginia Nicholson (who declares in the *Cradle Will Rock* screenplay that Orson is her real baby), played Macduff's child in the *Macbeth* film. Welles altered Shakespeare's text so that, rather than ordering the slaughter of Macduff's family, Macbeth did the job personally. It is unsettling to watch Christopher, then aged nine, being killed by her own father. Rebecca – the child he had with Rita Hayworth, to whom he was married from 1943 to 1947 – carried a Venetian senator's train in *Othello*. His third daughter, Beatrice, was born a few months after his marriage to Paola Mori in 1955; early in their affair, Paola herself had played Welles's daughter in *Mr Arkadin*. Welles later cast Beatrice as Falstaff's page in *Chimes at Midnight*, again turning a child into a deferential attendant. Someone as autonomous and idiosyncratic as Welles could hardly tolerate the notion that a younger version of himself might one day take his place, so it may be fortunate that none of his children were boys. In *Citizen Kane*, he cursorily sentences Kane's only son and heir to death. The lad is seen beaming with delight at the political rally; he never reappears, and we are later casually informed that he and his mother were written off in a traffic accident. In an earlier version of the script, Kane's son is killed during a fascist uprising, and buried in the crypt at Xanadu. In neither case is he permitted to outlive his progenitor.

Welles came from nowhere, magically materialising out of the air which, as Hamlet remarks, the chameleon feeds on. In his production of *Doctor Faustus*, he hurtled into hell by way of an asbestos funnel in the floor, as if travelling through the birth channel in the opposite direction. Then he popped up again – whole once more despite his dismemberment by the devils – to take curtain calls. He was always experimenting with and fortuitously recovering from annihilation. In 1985, when he finally vanished after suffering a heart attack at home alone in the Hollywood hills, he preferred to leave nothing behind. Of course there were the films, but he refused to consider them as substitute offspring – and since most of them had been bastardised by studio interference, he partially disowned them. During a press conference at the Cinémathèque française, he insisted that it was vulgar to bother about posterity. You misunderstand the nature of life and time if you think you can defeat death and control the future by having children or (like Kane) amassing property or making art. A film for Welles, as he beautifully put it, was 'a ribbon of dreams': a fragile, windblown plaything, inscribed with images that fade in the daylight, no more substantial than the dust sifting from Yorick's skull.

Eartha Kitt solemnly referred to him as 'His Majesty Orson Welles'. John Huston once admired the figure Welles cut in a floor-length purple bathrobe: 'a regal colour, befitting Orson, and, sans crown, he was indeed majestic'. Enthroned at the Cinémathèque française in 1982, he was described by the journalist Michel Boujut as 'King Orson the First'. As Welles himself liked to say, he was the kind of actor typecast as a monarch.

He borrowed the notion from Kenneth Tynan's youthful study of heroic acting, *He That Plays The King*, to which – entreated by the worshipful Tynan – he contributed an introductory letter in 1950. His height, weight and reverberant voice conferred sovereignty on him. But though he often exploited his aura of dominance, he refused to be taken in by it, just as he laughed at the pompous balustraded staircase in the Amberson house and pointed out that these people had no 'royal progresses' to make up and down it. Editing the Christmas issue of French *Vogue* in 1982, he drew a caricature of himself as 'le roi du monde', looking grumpy and unregally shaggy. An unkempt white beard sprouts from beneath his crown. He grips a club instead of an orb, and a fulminating cigar replaces the customary sceptre. Though he slumps on a throne, weighed down by his pot belly, what world does he rule over? Welles knew that Hamlet, snarling about the actor who impersonates a king in his play within a play, meant to suggest that all kings are usurpers, like his murderous uncle – performers for whom royalty is imposture, affectation, consisting of a dusty robe and a tarnished crown. Welles saw his characters as ersatz kings, whose power is taken from them as we watch. Kane, he said in 1958, 'tries to become the king of his universe, a little like Quinlan in his border town', just as Harry Lime sets himself up as 'king of a world without law'. And their common presumption, he insisted, damages 'the whole tradition of liberal civilization'.

Only the child enjoys unqualified supremacy, and is guaranteed immunity from prosecution for the offences he commits. The spoiled infant, as Freud said, is treated – at least for a while – as 'His Majesty the Child'. Welles's first role on stage was that of a baby who is aptly nicknamed Trouble: he was three years old when his mother loaned him to the visiting soprano Claudia Muzio, who was singing Puccini's *Madama Butterfly* during a summer season at Ravinia, outside Chicago. Playing the geisha's son, Welles witnessed her ritual suicide, a sacrifice made by Butterfly to secure the boy's happy future in America. The story of the opera was folded into his mythical account of his own destiny. As a boy, he could fairly be called a 'princely terror', which is how the townsfolk refer to the ringleted George Minafer when he whips his pony down the main street in *The Magnificent Ambersons*. It was difficult for Welles to grow up, because he knew that he would never again enjoy the unanimous adoration which adults lavished on him during his first prodigious decade. Then the terms of his RKO contract spoiled him all over again, offering him complete creative control of the project which became *Citizen Kane*. The grown-ups soon withdrew their indulgence, which made Welles all the more determined not to graduate into their sober, cautious company.

This is why he was so touched by Antoine de Saint-Exupéry's *The Little Prince*, written during the author's American exile from occupied France. Soon after its publication in 1942, Welles prepared the script for a film of the book, which of course was never made. The fable must have seemed, like all his favourite stories, a kind of autobiography. On his extra-terrestrial travels, Saint-Exupéry's prince visits a king whose monarchy is absolute because the asteroid he squats on is so tiny that his ermine robe covers its entire area. Welles joked about his own status as a global – or at least globular – being in *The Man Who Saw Tomorrow*, a film about the prophecies of Nostradamus, which he narrated in 1981. In one sequence, he is ensconced at a desk in a library, seated behind a huge geographical globe. The circular earth is like an extension of his protuberant stomach; he seems to be nursing, or perhaps incubating, the world.

On his diminutive private star, the little prince can enjoy as many sunsets as he wishes in a day, simply by adjusting his angle of vision. Welles shared the prince's universality, and the stories he liked were about characters whose stamping ground was the entire earth: Phileas Fogg systematically circumnavigating the planet in *Around the World in 80 Days* (which Welles staged in 1946), Ahab more frantically pursuing the whale across two hemispheres in *Moby Dick* (which he also staged in 1955), or Harry Lime who recovers from his death in Vienna and resurfaces all over the map in a radio series that Welles narrated during the 1950s. But for Welles, globe-trotting required more of an effort than it did for Saint-Exupéry's prince, who only needs to move his chair. He was always rushing to catch plains or trains, generally with creditors or tax inspectors or irate wives and mistresses on his tail, and he often arrived at the airport or the station too late.

The smaller your planet, the more ubiquitous you can be. On earth, when Saint-Exupéry's prince arrives there, he discovers the relativity of an absolutism like his own, as Welles did when he was ejected into adult reality. Our world, the prince discovers, has 111 kings (not counting those who are black), each of whom considers himself omnipotent. A fox tells the little prince that all chickens look the same, and so do all men. On his asteroid, the prince cultivates a single, vain, capricious flower; on earth, he strays into a rose garden where all five thousand blooms are exactly alike. His flower's egomania used to seem absurd, but at least its preening preserved the sense of difference. Here below, the mass crushes the notion of individuality: this was how Welles came to interpret his professional setbacks, and in *The Trial* he presents the crowd's extermination of idiosyncrasy as the grim, inevitable edict of modern society. He liked the idea of royalty because of the privileges it entailed. You had the right to misbehave, and to compel service from your doting subjects (which is why he came to rely, when making his last, uncompleted films, on favours from the old friends and unpaid admirers who made up his cast and crew). The king in the *Vogue* sketch has forfeited his kingdom, but Welles reclaimed that lost autocracy by turning his film sets into principalities as quaintly or quirkily autonomous as Monaco or Lichtenstein or Luxembourg. His films function according to what Truffaut called 'the closed-universe principle'. Xanadu is just such a private world. Later Welles created a border town in and around the crumbling plaster piazza of Venice, California, in *Touch of Evil*, squeezed Kafka's bureaucratised city into the derelict Gare d'Orsay in *The Trial*, and for *The Immortal Story* conjured up the oriental colony of Macao using a square and a few adjacent streets in a Spanish village. Stepping onto a soundstage for the first time when he began work on *Citizen Kane*, he described it as the train set every boy dreamed of owning. It was also, if you retreat to the world of a somewhat younger child, a play-pen – a cushioned domain well stocked with toys, safely insulated by wooden bars like the forbidding fence around Xanadu.

The Little Prince was for Welles both self-vindication and self-criticism. It established his claim to superiority, while wistfully conceding that we are all no more than temporary kings. Shakespearean monarchs like to boast that they rule by divine right. Welles's grandeur bestowed the same supernatural aura on the characters he played. The tycoon's sycophantic secretary in *Mr Arkadin* says that, if his boss were to go waterskiing, he would resemble Neptune. Playing Arkadin, Welles does not risk himself on the water, but with his crimped wig, his bristling eyebrows, his beaked nose and the entourage of harlots who serve him as mermaids, he looks as if he could easily handle a trident. Critics paid him similarly pious compliments. His friend Maurice Bessy called his Falstaff 'jupitérien'. André Bazin said that Welles's plantation-owning patriarch in *The Long, Hot Summer* was, depending on your moral system, either 'Olympian or monstrous'. That choice defined the uncertain metaphysical territory within which Welles operated. Was he a god or an ogre, an overweight goblin? Is Peter Pan charming or repellent?

Deprived of a kingdom after his expulsion from Hollywood, Welles became a specialist in scenes of abdication. Playing Louis XVIII in Sergei

Bondarchuk's *Waterloo* in 1970, he limps laboriously down the staircase of his palace and is carted off into exile, frightened by the advance of Napoleon. His kings are unseated by rebels, his deities menaced by atheists. Godard rightly saw *The Magnificent Ambersons* as a Nietzschean film, summarising the philosophical assaults and social upsets that destroyed eternal verities at the end of the nineteenth century: he referred to its 'atmosphere of a twilight of the gods'. The Amberson mansion – its opulent Moorish salons deserted, occupying land whose value has dwindled, soon due to be subdivided into low-rent apartments – is a Valhalla that does not need to be put to the torch, as it is by Brünnhilde in Wagner's *Götterdämmerung*. It succumbs instead to the cold: by the end, Fanny (Agnes Moorehead) cannot afford to light the boiler in the kitchen.

As the militaristic Raja in *The Green Goddess*, Welles pointed to the sky and mocked the feeble defences of 'the Maharaja up yonder' who each night sends his legions of stars to stand guard. A European captive in Archer's play notes this sarcastic blasphemy: the Raja dislikes being subject to 'a still more absolute ruler'. Like Welles, the Raja measures himself against the universe. He despises its 'mere size', which believers call immensity, and declares himself more in awe of a mosquito. He swats one on his arm to prove his point. Welles – who was twenty-four when he played the role, first on radio and then in a Pittsburgh vaudeville theatre – made such bragging part of his own persona. In time, he came to recognise his error. The universe diminishes all of us, like Lime's dots. The best Welles himself could aspire to was mere size, the bulbous gaining of weight.

While Tynan merely paid homage to Welles as a king, Eric Rohmer bowed down to him as a god. For the young Rohmer, the delayed advent of *Citizen Kane* – not seen in France until after World War II – amounted to a cosmic thunderclap, generating a new world of creative possibility. It also resolved, for a while, the nagging modern problem of faith, since Rohmer, like Tynan, had found someone to worship. But, when he saw how Welles's career had gone astray after *Citizen Kane* and *The Magnificent Ambersons*, Rohmer wondered whether his obeisance had been misplaced. Should he turn 'to other gods'? In 1952, *Othello* reassured him. 'Our god,' Rohmer said, speaking for a multitude of admirers who were also desperately needy acolytes, 'was not dead.' Welles himself grew into the part. When he recited some biblical extracts in Ireland in 1960, a cheeky audience member asked how he liked playing God. 'He gets to win most of the time,' chortled Welles, who sometimes wondered whether God had decreed that he would end as a loser.

The insecure, perhaps unworthy divinity underwent many disillusioned deaths and miraculous revivals. MacLíammóir, when he first met the teenage Welles, felt that 'he was precisely what he himself would have chosen to be had God consulted him on the subject of his birth . . . He couldn't have done the job better himself, in fact he would not have changed a single item.' Tynan likewise called Welles a self-made man who fervently believed in his own maker. Yet in *Mr Arkadin*, Welles denies the divinity others wished on him. A god has no history and comes from nowhere. When Arkadin employs the sleazy opportunist van Stratten to compile a confidential report which will fill in a past he pretends to have forgotten, he goads the investigator to destroy him. Of course Arkadin intended to murder all those who give evidence about the foul sources of his fortune. But even if he had succeeded, he would still have exposed his own fraudulence. Tynan, who called *Citizen Kane* 'the biggest cultural event of my early life', viewed it as a 'solo performance', a demonstration of all-round genius. He was dismayed in 1971 when Pauline Kael's essay on the script convinced him that Welles had usurped credit for writing actually done by Herman J. Mankiewicz. Veneration, as so often in appraisals of Welles, gave way to disillusion. The god failed once more, and Tynan conceded that 'my earliest definition of art was based on a lie'. Welles expected and probably wanted to be unmasked, if only because the magician's triumph comes in his revelation that he has cheated us. Nevertheless, he dreaded the consequences of a process he had instigated. Having agreed to be interviewed by Peter Bogdanovich for an autobiographical book, he behaved towards his collaborator with all the defensive paranoia of Arkadin as he struggles to stay ahead of van Stratten. He called Bogdanovich an inquisitor, as if the questions he asked were a form of torture, or addressed him as 'Mr Hoover', on the assumption that he was snooping for the FBI.

Welles liked to see himself as the victim of betrayal – let down by false friends or dishonest business partners or untrustworthy women – but he usually provoked the breach for which he blamed others. How could he accredit a religion which had foolishly elected him to the office of god? Over and over again, he told the same story; he told it so often, with so many variants, that it amounted to a myth. Not quite the story of his life, it is more the story of how he tried to understand that life, with its great expectations and lost illusions. The situation is constant: a man sits in judgement on his friend, kills the thing he loves. Sometimes Welles played one role, sometimes the other. He had to be both characters, because the story was about self-examination and self-execution.

Brutus in *Julius Caesar*, which he directed in New York in 1937, is prompted by constitutional scruples to condemn and stab his friend Caesar. In the same year, Welles adapted Victor Hugo's *Les misérables* for the radio, playing the fugitive Valjean who is hunted by the detective Javert. At the barricades, Valjean has the chance to kill the captive Javert and to free himself from the infliction of the past. Instead he sets his persecutor free, and reveals both his current alias and his address so as to make Javert's renewed pursuit easier. 'I'll come for you,' promises Javert, almost tenderly. The journalist in *Citizen Kane* scavenges information which might help him to demystify the dead hero. When alive, Kane withstands the same harsh scrutiny from his friend Jedediah (played by Joseph Cotten). Like Valjean challenging or beseeching Javert to arrest him, Kane collaborates in his own arraignment. This is why, when Jedediah is too drunk to complete his harsh notice of Susan Kane's inept operatic début, Kane writes it himself. The review is now his verdict on his own folly. Before *Citizen Kane*, Welles wanted to film Conrad's *Heart of Darkness*, which he had already dramatised for radio. Here he would have played both the pursuer Marlow and the corrupt, crazed Kurtz, whom he pursues. He had done something similar in 1939 in his radio version of Agatha Christie's *The Murder of Roger Ackroyd*, where he contrived to be both detective and murderer. In one instalment of *Les misérables* he was both the real Valjean, now respectably living under an alias as the mayor of a small town, and a ruffian who is taken into custody because he fits Valjean's description: this enables him to cross-question himself at the trial. In a radio version of *Beau Geste* with Laurence Olivier, also in 1939, Welles managed to be at once a guilty fugitive and an innocent altruist, though on this occasion the two characters were one and the same. Beau runs off to join the French Foreign Legion, allowing his family to believe that he has stolen a priceless heirloom. But the crime to which he confesses is a self-sacrificing cover-up. To save the family estate, his aunt has already sold the sapphire to a Maharaja; he takes the blame for her action.

In 1953, Welles appeared in a segment of a British portmanteau film, *Three Cases of Murder*, playing a Tory grandee telepathically tormented by a Welsh socialist whose career he has wrecked. The low-born orator Owen invades Lord Mountdrago's dreams, watching as he attends a fancy reception without his trousers or cavorts with the marimbas in a sordid nightclub. A psychiatrist tells Mountdrago that 'We're all of us not just one self but many, and one of the selves in you . . . has taken on Owen's form in your mind to punish you.' The multiplying selves Welles liked to enumerate are now at war. Mountdrago, proud and ambitious, declares that 'Greatness is my aim' and insolently rests his feet on the despatch box during debates in the House of Commons: this is the Faustian Welles. But Owen, played by Alan Badel, 'a dreamer who lacks practical ability' and babbles of 'childish Utopias', is another Welles: the visionary, unwilling to compromise his artistic conscience. Mountdrago dreams that he pushes Owen under a train. But a derisive phantom pursues him, and he tumbles to his own death down a staircase in the Palace of Westminster. 'He came after me,' he says as he expires, and congratulates himself on having outrun Owen. Then he remembers that the demon is merely another aspect of himself, and admits that he has not escaped at all.

In *The Stranger*, Welles plays a Nazi who has gone to ground in a Connecticut town. He is tracked down by a reformed colleague from the Third Reich who wants to save him from the past, and by an investigator from a tribunal investigating war crimes whose aim is to prove his guilt. Generally Welles cast himself as the man on the run, but he could also play the dogged agent of the law, as if to establish the culpability of that slippery alter ego who wants to evade capture. When he adapted *Around the World in 80 Days* for radio, he took the part of the punctilious Phileas Fogg, who circumnavigates the earth for a wager. Staging the show as a musical with songs by Cole Porter, he changed to the stubborn, devious detective Fix, who tracks Fogg across continents and oceans, convinced that he has robbed a bank.

Variations of the same compulsory story – it is Welles's 'immortal story', comparable, in its inescapable human truth, with the Isak Dinesen fable he filmed in 1968 – crop up in later projects. Holly Martins (Cotten again) turns against his boyhood friend in *The Third Man*, and volunteers to shoot him. Iago, insidiously commiserating, betrays Othello. Hal frolics with Falstaff while planning to spurn him. As Quinlan in *Touch of Evil*, Welles is destroyed by the treason of a colleague who idolises him and whose life he once saved. The cop who sides with Quinlan's accuser suffers the agonised qualms of Brutus; twenty years after his early production of Shakespeare's play, Welles now plays the toppled Caesar. The connection is enforced when Janet Leigh, as one of Welles's incidental victims, mocks his accomplice Akim Tamiroff, a bumbling thug with an ill-fitting wig. She calls him a 'ridiculous old-fashioned jug-eared lop-sided Little Caesar': the emperor has shabbily mutated into a gangster. By 1967, Welles, having already played Brutus, Antony and Cassius, was ready to cast himself as Caesar in a projected film of the play, with Paul Scofield as Brutus. As usual, he could not raise money for this latest chapter in his Shakespearean autobiography.

F for Fake admits the personal relevance of the story. Everyone, in this teasing amalgam of documentary and playful fiction, betrays everyone else. Clifford Irving testifies to the deceit practised by the art forger Elmyr de Hory, while simultaneously preparing a deception of his own as he fakes the memoirs of Howard Hughes. Welles, who edited the interviews with the counterfeiters and contributed an ironic commentary on their careers, presents himself as the most consummate and cheekily unrepentant of fakers. The film begins with an exhibition of his magic tricks, which befuddle the brain by cheating the eye, and goes on to beg pardon for his mendacity.

To bewildered observers, Welles seemed mythological. Maurice Bessy described his Falstaff as 'tonitruant', another adjective too exalted to be translateable: his grumpy moods were the rages of Thor the thunderer. Bazin likened him to Jupiter, brandishing a ten-inch cigar instead of the god's usual accessory, a lightning bolt. But Welles knew that myths were fictions or, to use the harsher word he employed in his autobiographical film, fakes; and he also knew that this is why they are so valuable to us – an emotional solace and a brave proof of our capacity to overcome the discouraging facts of the world. In conversation with Bogdanovich, he sharply differentiated his own mentality from that of John Ford. He venerated Ford, and when preparing *Citizen Kane* he screened *Stagecoach* over and over to learn the craft of film-making. Yet he resisted any comparison between their separate visions: 'I'm interested really in the myth of the past, *as* a myth. Jack Ford is one of the myth-*makers*.' The remark is brilliantly and dolefully self-aware. Ford the patriot believed in the myth of the American West, and truly saw the cavalry as latter-day cavaliers, riding to the rescue of imperilled settlers. Welles viewed Ford's idealistic romances with bitter regret. His own cavalryman was Don Quixote, a chivalric hero defamed by his crassly unheroic age.

The terrain in which Welles set his films is mythological – the walled garden of fantasy in *Citizen Kane*, the sedentary, genteel mid-Western

America of *The Magnificent Ambersons*, the sensual tropics of *The Lady from Shanghai* – but the story he always told is about a paradise we have lost, or which maybe never actually existed. His narrated introduction to *The Trial* begins by noticing that 'Before the law there stands a guard.' He inserts a slight pause after the first phrase, just long enough to make you wonder whether he is referring to space or perhaps to time. Kafka's fable sets the guard in front of the gate that defends the citadel of law. Welles's voice seems to equivocate in uttering the line: he pines for a time before the law holds you hostage and makes you accountable for your deeds – the enchanted, amoral time of childhood. However, such nostalgic regret is illusory, like the reminiscences of the decrepit Shallow as he totters through the snow at the start of *Chimes at Midnight*: did he ever actually do all the madcap things he boasts of? The snow scene inside the glass ball in *Citizen Kane* only looks idyllic in retrospect, now that it is irretrievable. Would Charlie Kane really have wanted to live forever in blank, blizzard-stricken Colorado? Schoolboys run carelessly through the woods in *The Stranger*, unaware that they are crossing another polluted paradise. Beneath the leaves is a fresh, hastily concealed corpse. In *Touch of Evil*, a bleary neon sign in the crumbling arcade announces THE PARADISE: the Eden in question is a raucous dance hall. The bad-tempered 'roi du monde' in the *Vogue* cartoon is the king of a world he, like the rest of us, has lost. As Welles said of the mythical Merry England inhabited by King Arthur or Falstaff, it was a time that never was, and that nowadays 'only the oak trees and the flowering chestnuts remember truly'.

In July 1938, Welles and his Mercury Theatre colleagues began their series of radio programmes with an adaptation of *Dracula*. In subsequent weeks, he presented versions of a number of plays and novels that recurred throughout his life because they had a pointed private significance: *Treasure Island*, *Julius Caesar*, *Jane Eyre*. In the autumn, in three consecutive weeks, he presented *Around the World in 80 Days*, *The War of the Worlds* and *Heart of Darkness*. This was a triptych of self-portraits. First came Welles the world citizen, circling the earth as Phileas Fogg. Next, Welles the mischievous magus sentenced that world to death, admitting in an epilogue that the broadcast had been only a Halloween joke. Finally, playing Conrad's Kurtz, now recast as a fanatical fascist, he revealed another shadowed side of himself: the superman who, like Harry Lime, looks down with contempt on his brutish inferiors, and orders their extermination.

Welles subtitled the series *First Person Singular*, which was something of an understatement. His own parade of available identities, set free in the vocal metamorphoses of the radio programmes, made him a plural being. In 1954, Ben Hecht called him 'that Sousa's Band of an actor', who had so many voices that he could play every instrument in the orchestra. Welles proved Hecht's point in a segment of an abortive television programme he made in the late 1960s. Here, in a London street, he literally plays an uproarious one-man band, as well as a ribald costermonger and a stern policeman. In *F for Fake* he lends his voice to a bed-ridden art forger, supposedly the grandfather of Oja Kodar (who was Welles's companion at the end of his life). Kodar recites lines purportedly uttered by Picasso, berating the faker for having pastiched his work. She tells Welles that he is one of those who use so many names that they forget their own. Welles – pretending to repeat the conversation of a man who, as he soon admits, never existed – defiantly answers back: 'I, señor, am not *one* of anything. Like you, I am unique.'

This is an ambition he shared with a favourite fictional character, the opera singer Pellegrina Leoni from Isak Dinesen's *Seven Gothic Tales*. (Karen Blixen, who used the pseudonym Isak Dinesen for her fiction, felt she had encountered her own character in the flesh when she heard Maria Callas sing at Carnegie Hall in New York in 1959; the role was played by Kodar in *The Dreamers*, an unfinished film coupling two Dinesen stories which Welles worked on between 1980 and 1984.) Pellegrina, the exhibitionistic soprano, is 'indignant because it was impossible for her to perform two roles within the same opera'. Renouncing her career, she sets off to travel anonymously, and announces that henceforth 'I will be many persons.' Such feats were second nature to Welles. During his radio career, he would generally arrive in the studio just before transmission began, grab a script, and breathlessly ask who he was supposed to be. If the role happened to be that of the ninety-seven-year-old John D. Rockefeller, as it once was, he aged seven decades in the few seconds left to him. In his radio productions of Shakespeare, he took several roles in a single play. He recorded *Julius Caesar* early in 1938, playing Brutus; then he re-recorded it, now playing Antony, Cassius, and the narrator (always his favourite role, because the story-teller is the god who commands human lives and can terminate them). On that broadcast of *Dracula* in July 1938, he switched back and forth between three roles: himself as host, Bram Stoker's chronicler Dr Seward, and the vampire. He covered these transmigrations by warning listeners who he would be 'the next time I speak to you'. The cohabitation of these antagonistic characters is alarming; to be so many people is a haunted condition. By 1951, Welles was able to joke about this uncanny capacity for metempsychosis. He introduced each episode of the radio series about Harry Lime's posthumous adventures by asserting that Lime 'had many lives. And I can recount all of them – because I am Harry Lime.' And as everyone knew, Harry Lime was Orson Welles, who was the sum total of so many different people.

Uniqueness for Welles did not entail singularity. He was unique, as he said in likening himself to Picasso, without being 'one of anything'. He meant that he was multiple, a self-multiplier. He could whistle up whole anthologies of lives on a whim. His career got started thanks to this fantastical, fraudulent talent. Penniless in Dublin in 1931, he persuaded Hilton Edwards and MacLíammóir to hire him at the Gate Theatre by reeling off a string of fictitious triumphs on the New York stage, along with other far-flung exploits. 'I've toured the States as a sword-swallowing female impersonator,' he is alleged to have said. 'I've flared through Hollywood like a firecracker. I've lived in a little tomato-coloured house on the Great Wall of China on two dollars a week . . . I've eaten dates all over the burning desert, and crooned Delaware squaws asleep with Serbian rhapsodies.' His new employers later claimed that they didn't believe him, but calculated that anyone with such cheek must be a good actor.

For Welles this incident served the same purpose as myth, which exists, as the anthropologist Mircea Eliade has said, to account for creation, to relate 'how something was produced, began to be'. Some myths narrate the prehistory of the world; Welles here narrated his own prehistory, generating something out of nothing. An enigmatic remark in his script for *The Trial*, cut from the finished film, illuminates his reasons. 'This is,' the narrator says in the script, 'a story inside history.' No one would mistake Kafka's account of K's tribulations for the literal truth. Camouflaged as history, it tells a story that is actually a myth, a fable that purports to show how our paranoia begins. The film starts as K wakes up: as soon as we arrive in the world, we notice that it is thwarting and persecuting us. K feels guilty, even though he is innocent. The story inside the history could perhaps be called myth. Kafka does not need to specify what charge has been made against K: he is party, like all of us, to an original sin, and his arrest, as his landlady tells him, is 'something abstract'. Myth, describing the inception of history, necessarily recognises a loss, a lapse. Why does man, unlike his supernatural sponsors, turn out to be mortal? How do disappointment, disillusion and death come to invade the world? Because it ventures to answer such questions, Bronislaw Malinowski insisted in 1926 that myth is more than an 'an idle tale'. The responsibility of a myth, as Claude Lévi-Strauss argued, is to overcome intolerable contradictions, and it can hardly do so if it is constrained by facts.

All these complicated motives and shifty manouevres were present in Welles's backstage performance at the Gate. He often recalled his Dublin hoax in later years – for instance in *F for Fake*, where it serves to indict him as a faker. He reflected on it again in his screenplay for *The Cradle Will Rock*, where it becomes a moment of fatal, destructive hubris: he has his colleague Houseman call this a Faustian choice, when Welles – aged sixteen but pretending to be twenty-two – 'sold his youth for grown-up glory', and thereby sentenced himself to a 'delinquent adolescence' which, because he hadn't lived it at the right time, lasted until he died. Welles was always trying to identify the instant when his tragedy began, but it is hard to believe that he was genuinely repentant about hoodwinking Edwards and MacLíammóir. On the contrary, he enjoyed the success of this bluff. He knew the story would be retold by others, including its two victims, and he did not object if they amplified and altered it. MacLíammóir, after transcribing his speech, admits in a cheeky footnote that 'This is an almost totally inaccurate report of his monologue.' Why bother about accuracy, since Welles himself was so implausible? MacLíammóir gives him the mythomania of one of his own characters: here we have Othello bamboozling the Venetian senators, who are happy to believe that he has come across 'Anthropophagi, and men whose heads / Grew beneath their shoulders.' And MacLíammóir allows Welles to cap the recitation with a flourish of supreme effrontery. 'But I haven't told you everything,' he has Welles say at the end of the synopsis. 'No; there wouldn't be time.' A myth is a story open to supplements and extrapolations. MacLíammóir, attributing fanciful stunts to Welles, was following the procedures of Malory or Cervantes when they made up new stories about Arthur or Quixote.

Welles's fictional status intrigued and antagonised Hollywood during the months in 1939 and 1940 when he expensively juggled projects at RKO before settling down to make *Citizen Kane*. He arrived from New York wearing a beard, which he had grown to play Falstaff in *Five Kings*, his staged compendium of Shakespeare's histories, and which he

intended to keep for his role as Kurtz in the film of *Heart of Darkne*
The beard baffled clean-shaven Hollywood: what face or faces ...
behind it? In 1940, F. Scott Fitzgerald wrote a story for *Esquire* called
'Pat Hobby and Orson Welles', in which Hobby the washed-up screenwriter asks the studio bookie Louie 'Who's this Welles?' Louie succinctly
explains 'He's that beard.' They agree that his mystique is dependent on
his facial hair. A wig maker offers to supply Hobby with a beard of his
own. The demoralised hack agrees. He has come to think of the invisible,
unknowable Welles as a personal nemesis, who is taking jobs away from
him. Why not assume his identity? Freshly and fakely bearded, he
crayons the name of Welles in brash letters on a piece of cardboard,
places it on the windshield of his car, and drives through the studio,
where he is indeed mistaken for Welles. But he lacks the swagger to carry
off the imposture, and scuttles away to a bar. Hobby and Welles are Nick
Carraway and Gatsby all over again – except that this time the little man
refuses to believe in the great man's aura, and further cheapens it by his
impudent mimicry. A hanger-on called Mayzie Katz in Welles's screenplay
for *The Cradle Will Rock* associates him with Gatsby during a scene at
one of the parties he and Virginia gave for Manhattan celebrities at their
house on the Hudson River at Sneden's Landing. She remarks that Welles
doesn't seem to be attending his own party, just as Nick Carraway notes
Gatsby's detachment from the parties he throws for mobs of strangers.
'We think of him,' Mayzie remarks, 'more as a guest of honour.'

Welles initially invented himself, but he permitted others to share in
the process. The mythical man, like the celebrity, must consent to be a
projection of other people's desires or fears. In this, Welles himself
resembled Citizen Kane, who, as Jean Domarchi pointed out in *Cahiers
du cinéma* in 1958, has no interior life and exists only in the fantasies or
guesses of the other characters, whose versions of his story give them a
purchase on him. Kane may own the world, but they own a portion of
him. The character of Gregory Arkadin was also a collaborative creation.
It remains unclear who actually wrote the novel *Mr Arkadin*, published
in 1956. Welles's name was on the title-page, but he insisted – defensively,
or maybe arrogantly, as if he were bragging about the deputies and
dependents he possessed – that the author was Maurice Bessy. Then
when the book received fine reviews, he changed his mind and decided
that he might have written it after all.

Welles's deception of Edwards and MacLíammóir was a crucial
moment, because by improvising those anterior existences he devised a

hero's life for himself. He was summarising the kind of career through which characters swagger in primordial epics and folk tales. Such heroes are not gods, and cannot rely on supernatural powers; they must assert themselves by performing marvels – slaying ogres like Siegfried or St George or Jack the Giant-Killer, pulling swords from stones like Arthur. Or at least they must pretend to do so, since their status depends on fabulation, which we now call publicity. If their feats are dazing enough, they graduate to demigods. All the elements of this legendary narrative are present in Welles's stage-door fantasy, and in the related tales he told about his early years. The hero must first be abandoned by his family, sent out to fend for himself. Welles's mother and father died on cue. Next in the hero's itinerary come protracted voyages, wanderings in quest of adventure. Welles travelled to Japan and China in 1930, and in *The Lady from Shanghai*, playing a sailor, he alludes to his own supposed sexual initiation in the brothels of Macao. Everywhere the hero finds dangers to be avoided. Wanting to calumniate Welles before the release of *Citizen Kane*, Hearst's minions planted an underage girl in his hotel room; tipped off, Welles escaped entrapment. The allegorical story is supposed to end with victory over a monster, which occurs in Welles's mockery of Hearst.

If it all seemed like too much experience to be crammed into a single life, then Welles awarded himself extra lives. Like Arkadin, he rid himself of the past, or revised it as he went along, in order to make room for these fresh existences. The young Welles arrived in Dublin as a stranger, and further estranged himself by manufacturing those lurid younger selves. Melville's *The Confidence-Man*, which contains the reference to Hairy Orson, is about this kind of self-augmenting imagination, which is an American prerogative. The novel is set on a Mississippi steamboat whose passengers are all fakes, frauds, literally self-made men whose pasts cannot be verified. America itself, according to Melville, 'though always full of strangers, . . . continually adds to, or replaces them with strangers still more strange'. Welles's *The Stranger* might be a commentary on this alarming observation. Who exactly is the titular stranger in the Connecticut town? It could be the old Nazi colleague who comes to visit Kindler (the schoolteacher played by Welles) and is killed by him, or the prosecutor (Edward G. Robinson) who arrives on the same bus and passes himself off as a dealer in antiques. Surely it is not Kindler, now called Rankin. He is already respectably rooted in the place, and no one in town questions his cover story, because American memories are so short. In *Touch of Evil*, a sign at the entrance to the sleazy Mexican town shouts WELCOME STRANGER! One of the cosmopolitans in Melville's book, whose travels are as fabulous as the young Welles's or as spurious as Gatsby's affiliation with Oxford, comments that 'strangeness is the romance; it is what contrasts with real life; it is the invention, in brief, the fiction as opposed to the fact'. Hence Welles's blarney, which captivated the managers of the Gate, just as Othello's tall tales beguile Desdemona.

Welles's multiplicity hints at the mystery, confusion and possible annihilation near the centre of mythic stories and of myth itself. The anthropologist Max Müller, sceptically investigating mythology in 1897, defined it as 'a disease of language', the muddled product of polynymy. Because we have a bewildering variety of names for the same thing, one god splinters into many. Le Chiffre in Ian Fleming's *Casino Royale*, the character played by Welles when the book was filmed in 1967, is an example of such a plural person. His name is a symbol, and all his aliases, as James Bond learns, are 'variations on the words "cipher" or "number" in different languages; e.g. "Herr Ziffer"'. He turns up as a displaced person at Dachau in 1945, suffering supposedly from amnesia (which is Arkadin's convenient disability), and adopts the name Le Chiffre because he claims to be merely the number on a stateless passport. 'Nobody knows who he is,' says someone in the film of *Casino Royale*. 'Not even he knows who he is.'

Welles's synonyms also proliferated, which – according to Müller – is what you should expect from a god. Should we call our hero Orson or Orsini, Wells or Welles? Are Kane, Cain and Kubla Khan the same being, and is Arkadin – who may be named after Chekhov's feckless actress Arkadina in *The Seagull* – another alias? Is there an alliterative allusion to them all in the name of Kindler, the Nazi in *The Stranger*? A walking stick left behind in the cheap hotel incriminates Quinlan in *Touch of Evil*; the tottering Mr Clay in *The Immortal Story* supports himself on another stick. Do their canes turn these characters into Kane's coevals? Welles enrolled another of his archetypal characters in this punning company in *Moby Dick – Rehearsed*, his theatrical adaptation of Melville's novel. Here, Ahab the monomaniacal captain is played by the Actor Manager who runs the theatre: the dual role, of course, was Welles's. Because the play is a rehearsal, there's no attempt to duplicate Ahab's ivory leg, a replacement for the limb he lost to the white whale. To suggest its sound as it drums on the deck when Ahab paces, Welles directs the Actor Manager to tap on the floor with the 'cane' he carries. All Welles's supermen are kin, and the verbal clues that link them are his own exercise in polynymy.

Quinlan is 'some kind of a man', but there are many kinds – and they're all the same, moulded from the same malleable clay like Welles's putty noses, merging in 'the brain of this foolish compounded clay-man', as Falstaff says in the opening speech Welles gave him in *Five Kings*. A slippery shape-changer in Melville's *The Confidence-Man* paraphrases the prophet Isaiah: 'We are but clay, sir, potter's clay, . . . feeble and too-clinging clay.' Perhaps that inescapable, murky substance recalls Antony's remark, in his first scene with Shakespeare's Cleopatra, that 'kingdoms are clay'. If so, the 'roi du monde' is once more unkinged, and Welles's prolific creativity has resulted, as it often did, in an act of self-destruction. Because of its pile-up of variants, a myth, as Lévi-Strauss has said, is 'a picture of chaos'. That picture might be a portrait of Welles, whose false face in *Citizen Kane* was compounded of white modelling clay cast in plastic foam.

The Renaissance humanists saw mutability or plasticity as evidence of man's divine descent, as Pico della Mirandola proposes in one of his most puzzling formulations. 'He who cannot attract Pan,' Pico warned, 'approaches Proteus in vain.' This comment, which hints that the potency of the gods transcends the meagre singleness of human identity, has a teasing relevance to Welles. Of course he was protean, like Richard III who, after adding colours to the chameleon, boasts that he can 'change shape with Proteus for advantages'. Richard goes on to claim that he is more cunning than the murderous Machiavelli; the actress Lea Padovani – for a while Welles's lover, and also one of the three or four Desdemonas he used in his film of *Othello* – once bitterly likened him to Machiavelli. Her accusation was sharply pertinent, since Welles had played Cesare Borgia, Machiavelli's model of political duplicity, in *Prince of Foxes* during their time together. For her, the slipperiness of Welles was devilish rather than divine.

Certainly he attracted Pan, the forest god who is half man and half goat. Christ's appearance in the world supposedly ousted Pan: a deity who sponsored carnal revelry and riot was replaced by a chaste saviour of souls. But the censured pagan gods kept on returning. They did so during the Renaissance, and they had another comeback in the twentieth century. In 1902, E. M. Forster wrote *The Story of a Panic*, about some English visitors to Ravello chased through the chestnut woods by a wind which is a manifestation of Pan. The god is angry because a curate has declared him to be dead; his spirit enters a sullen schoolboy and ignites him, driving him to caper under the stars and babble poetry. At last the boy quits society and its strictures altogether, laughing as he disappears. The young Welles – who refers to himself as 'The Boy Wonder' in *The Cradle Will Rock* – might have been that inspired, uncontrolled lad, whom Forster calls Eustace.

MacLíammóir associated Welles with this maniacal condition when describing the way he gibbered and raved as Claudius in *Hamlet* in 1934: 'his horses panicked,' he remarked. The next year, one of Welles's first theatrical roles in New York was as a bankrupt tycoon in Archibald MacLeish's play about the stock market crash, called *Panic*. After his dramatisation of *The War of the Worlds*, referred to by later commentators as 'the panic broadcast', Welles became associated with this condition of numinous terror. He had another lineal connection with the horned mischief-maker. Pan's father, according to legend, was the trickster Hermes, otherwise known as Mercury, whose name Welles took for the theatre company he formed in 1937 and used for his radio broadcasts. The so-called panic broadcast was literally the brainchild of Mercury.

Once only gods could incite panic, which gives us an alarmed, elated awareness of the higher powers that can overturn our world. MacLeish's play demonstrated that, in modern society, the same contagious terror could be provoked by economic calamity. And, in his *War of the Worlds* hoax, Welles discovered the aptitude of the mass media for whipping up hysteria, like Pan causing cattle or Forster's genteel English tourists to stampede.

Because the god's influence was so pervasive, a mistaken etymology connected his name – which was actually a contraction of 'paon', meaning pasturer – with the word 'pan', meaning all. In 1926, Lawrence reported that Pan, expelled from Europe, had sought refuge in 'the young United States'. There he was reincarnated as Walt Whitman, who extolled 'the Allness of everything'. Reduced to an undercover affix, Pan made a further onward journey with Welles when he went to Rio de Janeiro in 1942 to make his film about the popular culture of the continent, which was meant to unify north and south. The preliminary title was *Pan America*, and the subjects Welles wanted to cover – jazz in the United States, bullfighting in Mexico, samba and voodoo in Brazil – in different ways showed Pan at his volatile, deranging work. For the segment on jazz, he hoped to engage Duke Ellington. Nothing came of that, though Ellington later wrote some songs for Welles's travelling production of *Doctor Faustus* in 1950. Eartha Kitt purred them with diabolical seductiveness, while Marlowe's rioting devils demonstrated the meaning of pandemonium. Ellington also included a sketch of Welles in the *Deep South* suite, performed by his band in 1947. The music is gruff, threatening, spook-ridden, as if remembering the witch doctors Welles said he consorted with in the Rio slums. The episode in question is called 'Hearsay', with Welles's name added in a subtitle. Certainly rumour magnified and mystified his activities.

Welles's creativity often made itself manifest in spasms of violence. 'Our world at the end: a new world!' cries the crowd in MacLeish's *Panic*. You can only make a new world if you first smash the pre-existing one. In 1848, at a dinner in Paris attended by Baudelaire, a rabid young radical drank to the health of Pan. When Baudelaire asked why, the enthusiast replied 'It's Pan who starts revolutions.' As a revolutionary, Welles, like Pan, was necessarily a vandal. Early on, he developed the habit of demolishing hotel rooms or restaurants. William Herz, a colleague in the Mercury Theatre, remembered an episode at the Ritz-Carlton in New York in the late 1930s, when Welles systematically trashed all the rooms on a floor. The manager next morning presented him with a bill for forty thousand dollars worth of damage. In December 1939 in Hollywood, he broke off his collaboration with Houseman by hurling dish heaters at him in Chasen's, incidentally setting the restaurant's curtains alight. He filmed himself in action when Kane meticulously tears apart the bedroom of the wife who has deserted him, or when his Lear – in Peter Brook's television production in 1953 – joins the rowdy knights in smashing Goneril's furniture.

These rampages were a complaint against the stubborn, resistant nature of reality. They allowed Welles to return to that malleable state before anything was fixed, before forms and rules were imposed on us – the time, yearningly hinted at in his narration for *The Trial*, before the law. Chaos is one name for this condition, and mess is another. 'You're a mess, honey,' says Dietrich when she first sees him in *Touch of Evil*. But the bloated body was the seat of his prolonged childhood, a cushioning defence he constructed around him, like Macbeth in his castle, Othello in his fortress or Kane in his private kingdom. Sooner this than reduction to a skull like Yorick or to skeletal emaciation like Shallow, Falstaff's companion. Richard III, called a 'lump of foul deformity' by Lady Anne, recognises the power that deformation or formlessness endows him with. He has arrived in the world shaped, as he says, 'like to a chaos'. But at least he understands the turbulence and treachery of that condition, and can destroy others by luring them into it. Though twisted and irregular, he is made of clay, which can be manipulated and remoulded. 'I'll frame my face,' he promises, 'to all occasions.' The body can be reframed too: hence, in *The Lady from Shanghai*, the crabwise gait Welles designed for the crippled lawyer Bannister (played by Everett Sloane), whose scaffolding of bones is held up by two sticks. On occasion, this versatile monster can bifurcate, pluralising the first person as Welles did. During the murder trial Bannister interrogates himself, and switches between the roles of attorney and witness as Welles had already done in *Les misérables*.

Chaos was Welles's working method. Houseman described his furious efforts to get their radio programmes written and rehearsed each Sunday in 1938. During the few hours before the broadcasts began, scripts were hurled together and then torn apart. Roles were reassigned among a gaggle of confused actors. Tempers frayed, coffee spilled, and the clock remorselessly ticked towards transmission. The 'minor drama' of whatever show it happened to be that evening was upstaged by 'the major drama of Orson's gargantuan struggle to get it on'. Houseman, dismayed by such unprofessional methods, still saw something sublime in that struggle, as if Welles were a tornado. Like a mythological hero, he grappled with capitalised cosmic foes: 'sweating, howling, dishevelled and single-handed he wrestled with Chaos and Time'.

But did he combat chaos, or was he chaos in person? Jorge Luis Borges, noting that there is nothing to unify the incongruous fragments that make up our picture of Kane, called this Wellesian alter ego 'a chaos of appearances'. With an equally telling choice of word, MacLíammóir in 1946 likened Welles's Dublin audition to a 'holocaust'. Before reading the suggested excerpt from *Jew Süss*, he flung a table, a chair and some books from the stage and ruined a display of plum blossom; he stirred up 'a violent cloud of dust, like a miniature sand-storm'. MacLíammóir and Edwards said a prayer in the hope that he would not tear down their theatre. Welles went on to give a demonstration of 'demoniac authority'; his voice was 'softly thunderous', his smile like 'white lightning'. MacLíammóir noted his 'chaos of inexperience', but called it 'a brilliant chaos'. Overawed, MacLíammóir is in the state of reverence defined by the philosopher Martin Heidegger, who claimed that 'chaos is the sacred itself'.

True to form, Welles's plots, whether tragic or comic, were chapters of accidents, with characters scrambling to keep up as things go wrong, frenetically improvising like Welles himself in the radio studio or on his film sets. In 1937, he adapted Eugène Labiche's farce *The Italian Straw Hat* for the Mercury Theatre, calling it *Horse Eats Hat*. A bridegroom's horse munches on the hat belonging to an older man's young and fickle wife. She insists that he abandon his wedding and find her a replacement, or else her elderly husband will become jealous. Joseph Cotten, playing the lead, swung from a chandelier, got drenched by an onstage fountain, and broke up the theatrical decor. It was the kind of action Welles adored: a chase or pursuit that races round in a circle. When the bomb in the car goes off at the start of *Touch of Evil*, the honeymoon of Vargas and Susan (Charlton Heston and Janet Leigh) has to be suspended: the plot is still that of *Horse Eats Hat*. Anarchism is chaos turned into a political ideology: it changes the world, as Welles did, by disrupting it. In *Citizen Kane*, a reporter is sent to investigate a possible murder in Brooklyn, and is told, if the missing woman's husband won't cooperate, to accuse him of being an anarchist. But Jedediah (Joseph Cotten again) defuses the insult and accepts it as a compliment. During the riotous party with the bordello girls, Kane calls him a 'long-faced, over-dressed anarchist', and he replies indignantly 'I am *not* over-dressed!' In 1941, just as *Kane* was released, Welles wrote a play called *His Honor, the Mayor* for a radio series dramatising the significance of the Bill of Rights. The mayor in this dour fable presides over a restive town in the hinterland whose electorate includes a single communist – eighty-seven years old and, therefore, no menace to public order. Yet when the old man (played by the indispensable Everett Sloane) has a chance to speak, he corrects the town's view of him and proudly proclaims himself an anarchist.

Welles eventually enrolled himself in the same party. He began as a liberal: his Brutus in *Julius Caesar* seemed in 1937 to be prompted by Welles's own civic conscience, resisting the totalitarian cult of the leader. In his 1940 radio version of *Macbeth*, he coughs and sputters in indignation as he comes to the end of the phrase 'the seed of Banquo *kings*!' The word is shocking, unspeakable. Fair enough to achieve kingship by merit, or by crime as Macbeth does, but Welles cannot tolerate the hereditary principle. By 1958, explicating his personal morality (and his political leanings too) in a French interview, he saw the world differently, and chose to emphasise his 'aristocratic and anarchistic' sympathies. The democrat who once proselytised for the New Deal had now spent a decade in Italy or Spain; Europe, older and wilier, taught him to mistrust American puritanism. Brutus's attempt to distinguish right from wrong no longer seemed so important. Calling such virtue sentimental and bourgeois, Welles said he preferred the haughty negligence of the aristocrat, who is more concerned with style than ethics. But why did he couple the aristocrat and anarchist? Because the courage he admired had an element of defeatism in it. The natural aristocrat exhibited grace under pressure, like Hemingway's bullfighter, and took care to be all the more graceful when the bull's horns gored him. Anarchism for Welles entailed an ironic indifference, even to your own survival. 'I believe,' he said, 'that you can judge men only on the basis of their behaviour in the face of death.' He cited Colette as a model of this moral bravura. When the Gestapo came to arrest and deport her husband, she didn't weep and wail like a sentimental bourgeois wife. Instead she told Willy 'Go with them quickly.' The gesture may have seemed heartless, but at least there was no mean calculation of interest or advantage, no effort at the emotional bargaining and blackmail which are bourgeois specialities. You have to die, so why not do so stylishly? This resigned wisdom coincides with the credo of Isak Dinesen, who in *The Dreamers* has the storyteller Mira declare that to love God 'you must love change, and you must love a joke, these being the true inclinations of his own heart'. Welles, a victim of change, chose to treat his professional disgrace as an existential jest. Truffaut said that what made Welles a liberal was his sad, smiling acknowledgement that nothing can be conserved. This included his youth, and his aborted or butchered films.

Perhaps Welles should have called himself a nihilist, since his anarchism tended in that direction. *Touch of Evil* begins with one explosive moment of annihilation, which liquidises a local political boss so that his remains (as Joseph Cotten, playing the forensic examiner, remarks when he arrives on the scene) can be strained through a sieve; *The Trial* ends with another, as a blast in a waste land eliminates Joseph K. In *The Lady from Shanghai* as well, the crazed Grisby (Glenn Anders) sweats on a cliff in Acapulco and imagines the searing, purgative heat which will be unleashed by the hydrogen bomb. Welles, as O'Hara, takes the aristocratic, anarchic view of this cosmic detonation. The world, he says, had a beginning once upon a time, so why shouldn't it come to an end?

Bombs show chaos theory in operation. They mobilise and energise inert matter. But once they blow apart the created world, it can be recreated in a new form, which was Welles's abiding aim. Chaos was therefore a state he longed for. An early version of his *Macbeth* film began in drifting Scottish mist while Welles, as narrator, explained that it was set 'between recorded history and the time of legends' – a time in which he too belonged, as a legendary being whose history was largely self-fabricated. He went on to prepare audiences for a religious war he had added to Shakespeare's text: a holy father wanders through the action brandishing a Celtic cross and attempting to repel the witches. 'Christian law and order,' he says in his narration, here confront the 'agents of Chaos, priests of hell and magic.' This is the perennial Welles plot, and it was also the story of his life – law and order at odds with chaos; bureaucratic caution versus the anarchy of art.

Welles's next Shakespearean character, Othello, reflects on the same metaphysical battle when he says that, if Desdemona should be untrue, 'chaos is come again'. For Othello, this return to chaos and violence is tragic, but Welles himself could see the comedy in it. Therefore, in 1960, ten years after his performances as Othello on film and on stage, he made a point of jocularly quoting this line in a very different context. In Anthony Asquith's *The V.I.P.s*, he plays one among an assortment of celebrities stranded at London airport. Welles's character, a harassed, improvident film director called Max Buda, is a caricature of himself with a Hungarian accent. He needs to get out of England to escape the taxes he owes, and is furious that 'chaos is come again' because of bad weather. Meteorologically, chaos manifests itself here in the same way as in *Macbeth*: the airport has been closed by fog, which – like those highland mists – is air that is no longer transparent, churned into an obstructive, unstable mess of molecules. As Rochester in Stevenson's *Jane Eyre*, Welles also hurtles out of thick fog on a rearing, snorting horse, and soon disappears again into that numinous gloom. As an agent of chaos, he appreciates chaotic, befuddling weather.

The Greek word for chaos overlaps with verbs meaning yawn or gape; it refers to a void and vacant state, a primeval emptiness. But Ovid in his *Metamorphoses* claimed that the cosmic maker went to work on this formless disorder, and drew from within it elements, determinate beings, and all our human, civilised systems of order and harmony. Welles first re-enacted that miracle, then confounded it. When he filmed *Macbeth*, he concentrated on the obscure, messy beginnings that are the material of myth. His witches resemble Ovid's cosmic maker, or Prometheus who moulded the first man from the mud of a river bed. In Welles's prologue,

44

they use the offal stewing in their stock pot as raw material for a manikin. They squeeze this creature of wet clay into shape, and set a coronet on its head. This plaything is their Macbeth, and they toy with it throughout the film. Then, at the end, they strike off its little head. Welles, rearranging Shakespeare's text, gives them the last words: 'The charm's wound up.' Their dabbling, devilish exercise in pottery sums up his personal story. We watch creativity in action, then we see destruction occur. Chaos comes again. The cycle continues, with new lives followed by new deaths. There were so many Welleses; he gave birth to all of them, and also killed them off.

Citizen Kane begins with genesis. A mouth in close-up whispers a word, like God giving voice to light. But the creator dies at that very moment, and his little world – a private universe inside a glass ball – smashes on the floor. Myths report on origins, so the mythmaker purports to know what happened before any of us existed. Everyone agrees that Kane said 'Rosebud', though none of the characters was present to hear him and they have no idea what the word means. Perhaps it evokes the mystery of growth, placed on show when a flower opens; at the same time, it links genesis with our genitalia, since Rosebud happened to be Hearst's pet name for the private parts of his mistress Marion Davies, parodied in the figure of Susan. The world emerges from nothing, and it returns there at the end of *Citizen Kane*. First that flurry of particles whips up a blizzard inside the glass dome; then the furnace in the Xanadu basement, its mouth agape like chaos, greedily consumes solid objects and subjective memories, as if in anticipation of the day when the earth will be judged by fire. Snow creates a white world, as innocent as a blank page or a strip of unexposed film. Cold causes things to solidify, confirming their form, which is why Kane's childhood is associated with winter. Fire undoes these preservative endeavours of imagination. In this crematorium, everything melts and merges.

Welles often reverted to the incident with the globe, which joins creation and annihilation. As Quinlan in *Touch of Evil*, he pauses during a quarrel with his colleagues to investigate a nest he finds on a window ledge of the hotel room. The nest contains an egg; matching it, a carton in the bathroom of the young Mexican's apartment holds two sticks of dynamite, which supposedly prove that Sanchez has blown up Linnekar's car. The pigeon which laid the egg is not around, and the dynamite, likewise, came from nowhere. Vargas notices the shoe box minutes before, and sees that it is empty. The props propose twin conundrums. Was the world born, or did it explode into being? Where do works of art come from? The egg and the dynamite bring together the opposed facets of Welles, since he – among all the people who swirl and mingle and argue in the cramped apartment or the hotel room, like flustered snow flakes in Kane's glass ball – is the only one who touches both of them. MacLíammóir enigmatically called Welles 'an eerie mixture of atomic bomb and keepsake album'. The egg is the album, vouching for his tender, regretful sense of the past, his conservation of childhood. The dynamite and the bomb store his terrifying energy. The opposites cannot exist without each other. Creativity requires destruction: this was the lesson of Welles's life. Eggs must be broken before birth, or even cookery, can occur.

Quinlan's egg is his equivalent to Kane's global receptacle, the sealed, inaccessible container for an individual's history. But whereas the dome contained the past, the egg's contents are the future. In it is packaged a generative secret, possibly a genius. The broken glass is an end, but the first crack in the shell should represent a beginning. Welles himself respected its fragile integrity, and in 1962 told an interviewer that he lied about himself on purpose, to guard his psychological sources: 'I'm like a hen protecting her eggs,' he said. In his script for *The Cradle Will Rock*, he went back to the idea. The title of Blitzstein's opera refers, in prophesying revolution, to a nursery rhyme in which the baby is ejected from its cradle, like an egg tumbling from the nest. Blitzstein warns Welles's wife Virginia to expect a showdown with authority, and she replies, in a curiously telling turn of phrase, 'I'm a grown woman; I don't live inside an egg.' Grown women do not inhabit eggs, they produce them inside themselves – and so do male artists, whether grown-up or not. But the egg in *Touch of Evil* shares the fate of the glass ball in *Citizen Kane*. Quinlan picks it up, with a charming infantile curiosity: only boys steal eggs from nests. Despite his wonderment, he handles it too roughly and, like the witches decapitating their home-made Macbeth, he breaks it. The unhatched life smears all over his fingers, and he wipes them disgustedly.

Still, this is far from being Welles's final version of that primal scene. His first film began with his own end, as Kane utters his last word and drops the glass ball. Welles was always endeavouring to escape from that early, voluntary extinction. He alluded to Kane's demise in *Touch of Evil*, and then in *The Trial*, as if running the film in reverse, he cancelled the obituary for himself. For his initial appearance as the Advocate, he lies bedridden in a dark room. As in *Citizen Kane*, a nurse enters. But instead of drawing a sheet over the face of her patient, she applies a hot towel to his head. He rears up, vociferously trumpeting, resurrected by his own efforts. Reports of his death are not to be trusted.

Like a storyteller revisiting and revising a myth, Welles returned to the episode once more in *The Immortal Story*. Mr Clay has a trophy which corresponds to both Kane's snowy ball and Quinlan's vulnerable egg. It is a shell, a conch, containing dead seas of memory. It is safer because it is hollow, dried-out: the life it once harboured, like the wet storm in Colorado or the embryonic pigeon, has long since departed. It sits on the floor beside Clay's chair when, the morning after he directorially stages the immortal story in his bedroom, he is discovered dead. But though it may have fallen from his hand, like Kane's most prized possession, it has not shattered. A thing of beauty survives, outlasting the breakage of so many lives.

Welles as Brutus the liberal confronting the fascists in *Caesar*.

CHAPTER 3

Everybody

At the age of nineteen, Welles did not quite know everything. Nor had he yet fully developed his capacity to become everyone. But he had already identified an artist to whose omniscience he deferred for the rest of his life. This was Shakespeare, the creator whom he thought of as a parent. Shakespeare, he believed, should belong to everybody, because the characters in the plays show us aspects of ourselves. And Welles himself, as he spent his life demonstrating, was all of those dramatis personae bundled into one. When he cast Eartha Kitt as Faust's eternal woman, she asked him what kind of person she was meant to be. 'All kinds,' he said. And how old? 'All ages.' Living when? 'All periods.' She was baffled by this mythic malleability; for Welles himself, it was self-evident. Or was he bluffing? Liev Schreiber – who played the young Welles in *RKO 281*, a film about the making of *Citizen Kane* – guesses that the clue to his character was 'deep fear and insecurity'. He struggled, Schreiber has suggested, to find out who or what he was, and hoped that by acting he would manage to define himself. Welles anticipated Schreiber's surmise when he made Arkadin (who of course is lying, like the actor he is) tell van Stratten 'I don't know who I am'; in the novel, the urgency of the statement calls for italics.

He began his self-examination by working his way through Shakespeare. In 1934, after his theatrical apprenticeship in Dublin and a season on Broadway, he returned to Todd School in Woodstock, Illinois, where he had been a pupil between 1926 and 1930. With his former teacher Roger Hill, he edited and illustrated performing editions of *Twelfth Night*, *The Merchant of Venice*, *Julius Caesar* and *Macbeth*. In 1939, when Welles performed these plays on the radio, the texts were reissued as *The Mercury Shakespeare*. But in 1934 they appeared under a more demotic title, as *Everybody's Shakespeare*. Welles wrote a brilliant prefatory essay in which he explained this populism, insisting that 'Shakespeare speaks everybody's language'.

Welles thought that the Elizabethan idiom should be instantly comprehensible to Americans because, as he argued in *Everybody's*

Shakespeare, England in the sixteenth century was 'waking up noisily and too suddenly into adolescence and bounding blithely into the sunny, early morning of modern times'. It was both a rousing patriotic plea and a bumptious self-advertisement. For England, read America; and for Shakespeare, read Welles, who was then romping through his own late-adolescent modern morning. In John Ford's *My Darling Clementine*, made in 1946, a drunken actor is detained in a saloon and forced to recite 'To be or not to be', accompanied by the bar piano, while a gang of outlaws fire bullets at his feet. Wyatt Earp rescues him and escorts him to the theatre. As he leaves, the indignant thespian sneers that 'Shakespeare was not meant for taverns'. Welles disagreed. The very rowdiness of the setting is Elizabethan; the Globe conjoined brothels and bear-baiting pits on the south bank of the Thames. Shakespeare's London, like Tombstone in Ford's film, was a wide-open town.

With typically breezy audacity, Welles contended that 'America was discovered . . . just so . . . we could have William Shakespeare'. He meant that the wealth of the colonies, percolating into London's theatres, made Shakespeare's career possible. But it was also true that – for this young man so aware of his own manifest destiny – America was discovered just so we could have Orson Welles. He had already settled on his conquistadorial mission, which he hinted at again in 1961 when describing the career of the 'Russian adventurer' Arkadin. He called Arkadin 'a barbarian in conquest of European civilisation', and said that only his morality, not his project, was detestable. The Russian accent was another disguise: Welles was an American adventurer, and the adventure involved peacably annexing the older civilisation. He began with its greatest writer.

What did England – 'learning to talk' thanks to Shakespeare's invention of language – have to say? Welles gave a digest in the opening sentences of his essay. 'Shakespeare', he said on Shakespeare's behalf, 'said everything. Brain to belly; every mood and minute of a man's season.' He added that Shakespeare 'speaks to everyone and we all claim him', though Welles himself had a more personal claim than most of us. Those first sentences were a prophecy, proved true over the next fifty years. It was as if Shakespeare had begotten Welles – spoken him into being, given voice to the perturbations of his brain and the rumblings of his belly, foreseen all his seasons, from his lusty spring in 1934 to the frozen winter of Falstaff in *Chimes at Midnight* in 1967. The plays were a personal itinerary, and a preview of his fate. The tone of the preface is infectiously enthusiastic. But when re-read after the end of

Welles's life, it acquires a prophetic doom. Given Shakespeare's oracular power, there was little left for Welles himself to say. Instead he concentrated, during all those decades performing and directing Shakespeare, on a search for the private nemesis lurking in the texts.

Between 1974 and 1979 he worked on an autobiographical documentary called *Filming 'Othello'*, in which – while convivially drinking with MacLíammóir and Hilton Edwards, and chuckling that they have all heard the chimes at midnight – he reiterated his conviction that Shakespeare was the greatest writer ever, and added that he was also 'the greatest man': the ultimate authority on what it means to be human. But this enthusiasm had a debilitating underside. In a French television interview with Richard Marienstras in 1975, Welles said that Shakespeare was 'the greatest man who ever lived', adding that, by contrast, the rest of us are just 'poor moles working away under the earth. All we can do is grab a little bit of him and nibble on it.' His words confirmed our reduced, belated, second-hand state of being. They recall Hamlet's comment about the noise made by the ghost of his father as it buries itself beneath the stage: he calls the spirit 'old mole' and asks 'Can'st work i'th'earth so fast?' But the wit of Welles's citation points to a possible recovery from our helpless dependence on Shakespeare. Though he may have said everything, we can appropriate his lines and make them mean new things as we speak them. Hamlet's Oedipal joke cheekily shows us how to free ourselves from ancestor worship: he wills the revered and perhaps resented father to die all over again, and wonders why he makes so much noise as he goes about it. Welles – the man who played kings not princes, and who therefore assured Marienstras that the ghost was the best role in *Hamlet* – chose to be the mole, and looked at the play from the animal's subterranean viewpoint. The mole, in Welles's version, now nibbles on Shakespeare, like the worms dining on the corpses of Polonius or Yorick. We feed on him and in the process absorb him into ourselves. Eating our way through his plays, we successively discover who we are.

Welles began declaiming some of King Lear's speeches at the age of ten, and was still scraping together finance for a film of the play when he died sixty years later. At school he played both Antony and Cassius in *Julius Caesar*. In Dublin in 1932, he was the ghost in *Hamlet*, doubling as Fortinbras; later he was cast in *Richard III*, *King John* and *Timon of Athens*. In 1934, back at Todd for a summer season with MacLíammóir and Edwards, he played Claudius in another *Hamlet*, then joined Katharine Cornell's troupe to play Mercutio and later Tybalt in *Romeo and Juliet*. The *Macbeth* he directed in Harlem in 1936 was followed by *Julius Caesar* on Broadway, with his first Brutus. In 1938 he recorded *Twelfth Night*, playing Malvolio (and also the actor Burbage, who converses with Shakespeare in a prologue written by Welles); recording *The Merchant of Venice*, he played both Shylock and the Prince of Morocco. He then mounted his initial version of *Five Kings*, the compendium of history plays that eventually became *Chimes at Midnight*. He was not yet twenty-five. Because the tragedies were the stories of his own life, he allowed himself to grow into them. He adapted *King Lear* for radio in 1946, once more prematurely playing the senescent king. In 1947 he returned to Macbeth, and next undertook Othello.

Trusting in Shakespeare's wisdom, he employed the plays as family therapy. In 1945 he tried to save his radio series and his current marriage, both of which had faltered, by suggesting that he and Rita Hayworth might perform a potted *Taming of the Shrew* on the air. The sponsor rejected his proposal; the series was cancelled, and so was the marriage. Nevertheless, Welles went on citing Shakespeare as the wisest of counsellors. In 1952 he played the rabidly jealous tycoon Sigsbee Manderson in *Trent's Last Case*, a British whodunnit. Because Manderson believes himself to be a cuckold, Welles had an excuse for reciting some of Othello's speeches and referring dismissively to his own recent performance on stage in London: he mentions seeing *Othello* at the St James's Theatre, says he didn't care much for the actor in the title role, but is glad that it prompted him to re-read the text. Planning to murder his wife's lover, Manderson explains to his victim that when a man has been made a fool of, life doesn't seem worth living. 'Shakespeare', he avers, 'knew that.' Later, forced to go on making a fool of himself on television to raise money, Welles tried, whenever possible, to sneak in a plug for Shakespeare, as if this might redeem him. In 1956, he performed his Las Vegas nightclub act in an episode of *I Love Lucy*, interpolating some Shakespearean soliloquies while he levitated Lucille Ball. In 1967, he and Dean Martin sang 'Brush Up Your Shakespeare', Cole Porter's duet for name-dropping gangsters from *Kiss Me Kate*, on a variety show.

No other actor or director can match this missionary zeal. Olivier started out as Katharine in *The Taming of the Shrew* at school, then forgot about Shakespeare until the end of his twenties. He then alternated with Gielgud as Romeo and Mercutio, and went on to play Hamlet, Sir Toby Belch and Henry V at the Old Vic. His Coriolanus, Richard III and Othello were grand, extravagant exhibitions of histrionic technique; otherwise he allowed Gielgud to be the Shakespeare specialist (and for that reason cast him as Clarence in his film of *Richard III*, playfully murdering him to dispose of his prior right to the throne). Yet, despite Gielgud's vocal authority, his range was limited. He was best as wistful introverts like Hamlet and Richard II or the repressed Angelo in *Measure for Measure*. He made four valiant attempts at Lear, convinced no one as Macbeth and Othello, and near the end of his career turned to Caesar and Prospero. Welles admiringly cast him as the dying Henry IV in *Chimes at Midnight*.

Both Olivier and Gielgud disparaged Welles's Shakespearean crusade. In 1951, Olivier acted as producer when Welles played Othello in London; gossips said that he did so in order to see Welles fail. Gielgud was taken aback by the prospect and said to Welles, on a rising arc of incredulity, 'You're doing Othello? on stage?? in London???' Welles may have lacked Olivier's athletic fury and Gielgud's lyricism, but he outdid them in effort, eclecticism and proselytising keenness. Olivier and Gielgud shared the roles of Romeo and Mercutio in London in 1935, while Welles had played a manic Mercutio and a blood-hungry Tybalt on tour throughout America and then in New York. If we believe Oja Kodar, he had designs on other roles in the play. Though she knew him only as an old man, she has attested that 'He was a great Romeo.' Having said this, she added enigmatically, 'And he was a great Juliet.' His extra-curricular addictions were Shakespearean: the Havana cigars he preferred were called 'Romeo y Julietta'.

Whatever the project, he always elicited parallels with Shakespeare. In 1958 he consented to include *The Third Man* in what he called his 'oeuvre'. (He was being interviewed in France, so the self-importance in the word was inadvertent.) The reason was that, having written much of Harry Lime's dialogue himself, he had now found a way of enlisting Shakespeare as a co-author. Lime, he said, was a close relative of the Bastard in *King John*. In Greene's *Third Man* novel, Holly Martins curses Lime after visiting the children's hospital, where he sees the victims of all that diluted penicillin: 'The bastard. The bloody bastard.' Welles, by connecting the two characters, suggestively filled in Lime's inner life, about which the film tells us nothing. Not coincidentally, he considered that 'all [Shakespeare's] interesting characters are bastards'. The Bastard in *King John* is a talented upstart, denied the throne by his irregular birth. Exclusion makes a satirist of him, and he castigates the self-seeking of the legitimate princelings. Lime has a similar scorn for the powers sanctimoniously quarrelling over a city they have carved up between themselves. In what the Bastard calls a 'mad world', where 'kings break faith upon commodity', why shouldn't he trade in black-market commodities of his own and rule Vienna from his hide-out underground?

In *Mr Arkadin*, Robert Arden plays van Stratten as an unpretentious grifter. In the novel, the character is more cultivated, and his familiarity with Shakespeare allows him to ask Raina why Arkadin guards her so jealously: 'What fun does your father get out of acting Othello to your Desdemona?' The suspicion of incest is uncomfortable, since Welles was sleeping with Paola Mori, who plays his daughter. If this triangle corresponds to the plot of *Othello*, then van Stratten's commission to demolish the great man's legend becomes more ethically dubious: he is Iago. In the novel, describing his grubby life as a smuggler in Marseilles, he remarks that 'I held only one joker, which was my U.S. passport.' Lecturing on Shakespeare in New York in the late 1940s, W. H. Auden identified Iago as 'the joker in the pack', the jester who brings the game to an end and demonstrates that social life is impossible unless each of us is permitted our disguises. At the end of the film, Arkadin momentarily resembles another of Shakespeare's existential gamblers, Richard III. His financial empire and the continued love of his daughter depend on his catching an overbooked flight to Barcelona; he offers fifty million marks to anyone willing to turn over their seat to him. Richard wants to trade his kingdom for a horse, which might have carried him to freedom. Arkadin looks to a more modern form of transport.

Melville strove to equal Shakespearean tragedy in *Moby Dick*. Welles, transferring the novel to the theatre in *Moby Dick – Rehearsed*, made its Shakespearean ambitions explicit by showing how a repertory company could assign its rotating stock of players to analogous roles. Welles cast himself as the Actor Manager, who also plays Ahab. He strolls on quoting a speech of Lear's, which he supposedly performed the night before. The actress cast as Pip the cabin boy (played by Joan Plowright in the 1955 London production) was his Cordelia – and the circle closes if we accept that in Shakespeare's theatre the same boy actor doubled as Cordelia and Lear's fool, because the mad Pip also tells Ahab uncomfortable truths. A company member identified as the Serious Actor, cast as Starbuck, wins this part because of his Shakespearean credentials: Welles's cast list specifies that he has already been Kent, Richmond, Iago and Mercutio. His function as Ahab's humane opponent and potential assassin aligns him with Kent, who is Lear's conscience, and with Richmond, who is Richard III's executioner. But his credits puzzlingly include Iago. Does that mean he is the grandiose hero's mean, self-interested adversary?

Early in the 1980s, Welles prepared a screenplay called *The Big Brass Ring*. It concerns a presidential candidate, Blake Pellarin (whose name also hints at Dinesen's Pellegrina, since both are variants of the word pilgrim). Pellarin's career might be ruined by his connection with a disreputable ancient mentor, a homosexual sage called Kim Menaker. This was the role Welles reserved for himself; the film remained unproduced because no currently bankable star would sign on for Pellarin. Though there are analogies with just about every previous Welles film, the central relationship evokes that between Hal and Falstaff – except that now Falstaff is the crown prince's former lover, as well as his substitute father and tutor. Welles drew attention to other analogies, calling Pellarin 'a sort of Hamlet' because he vacillates, unsure whether to go ahead with his presidential campaign. Menaker, briefing a reporter about his protégé, quotes Othello's overgenerous obituary for himself: 'Speak of him as he is, "nothing extenuate."' The erotic understanding between the two men is underlined when Menakar mentions Mercutio's phallic joke about 'the bawdy hand of the dial . . . on the prick' of midnight. Did Welles mean to imply that Mercutio is unrequitedly in love with Romeo, like Falstaff doting on Hal? Performance is a way of trying out such possibilities, seeing if they will play.

Welles's reading of the plays was unorthodox, always risky and sometimes risqué. It helped that he was American, and did not have to honour Shakespeare as a national bard. When Olivier played Henry V, Charles Laughton said to him 'You are England.' Gielgud could not match this heroic belligerence; even so, for him Shakespeare encapsulated Englishness, and in 1958 he took this insular gospel on a world tour in a Shakespeare recital called *The Ages of Man*. His source was an anthology of Shakespearean precepts edited by George Rylands in 1939. Rylands thought of the plays as ethical primers, enabling us to 'school our hearts'. Like a secular Bible, Shakespeare belonged 'at the bed's head'; in him the devout reader discovered, according to Rylands, 'the powerful and beautiful application of ideas to the question, How to live'.

Gielgud himself avowed that 'There are answers in this man Shakespeare to every contemporary question. There is religion without dogma, humour without mere facetiousness, tragedy without grotesque horrors, and a simplicity and knowledge of human nature unsurpassed.' After a war in which men had behaved inhumanely, and in a decade when machines were beginning to outstrip the mental as well as the physical capacities of men, Gielgud presented Shakespeare as the fundament of a hopeful new humanism. Welles's view was deeper, darker, braver than this. He found questions in the plays, not answers.

His 1934 essay implies that Shakespeare had written the story of Welles's life before he began to live it. But in which plays was his future hidden? Performance enabled him to explore aspects of his predicament, or to examine alternative selves. 'There is', he said, 'a villain in each of us, a murderer in each of us, a fascist in each of us, a saint in each of us.' Acting Shakespeare uncovered those potentialities. In 1951 he wrote a foreword to MacLíammóir's wickedly witty book about the filming of *Othello*. The Moor's 'free and open nature' invites betrayal; Welles, more guilessly generous than Othello, defended the satirical account of him written by his own Iago. He remarked that the book's portrait of him blended Caliban, Pistol and Bottom with 'an acrid whiff . . . of Coriolanus'. MacLíammóir treated him as a low comedian, since even Coriolanus is not tragic but titanically petulant. Welles's other Shakespearean parts exposed further aspects of his character. Macbeth the careerist killed more efficiently than Welles ever did, though for a while on the night of the *War of the Worlds* broadcast he had to consider the possibility that he might be a mass murderer: at one point, the panic was said to have claimed ten lives, though by morning it was confirmed that no one had actually died. As Brutus, Welles laid bare his political qualms. Archibald MacLeish said that this performance represented 'the bewildered liberal . . . in a world threatened by fascist destruction'. The corruption of Brutus's principles challenged Welles to reconcile his own liberalism with the professional autocracy of the director. Trying to raise funds for a film of *King Lear* in the 1980s, he underlined the similarity between his own fate and that of the disregarded king. Old men, he noted, were no longer venerated as sages, especially not in the youth culture of Hollywood.

Welles, who wanted Shakespeare to be everybody's, was himself that everybody. Not an everyman: the word implies an average man, whereas Welles was unlike anyone else. Instead he resembled the mythic hero in

Joyce's punning, babbling novel *Finnegans Wake*. Earwicker's initials are H. C. E., which stands for Here Comes Everyone who Haveth Childers Everywhere. In 1945 and 1946 Welles recorded an anthology of political orations, including an address by Pericles which defines democracy as 'the whole body of the people'. He managed to embody that polyphonic forum, finding voices to match the sober Thomas Paine and the incendiary Patrick Henry, the smilingly enlightened Jefferson and the weary Lincoln, Woodrow Wilson's high-mindedness and F. D. Roosevelt's call to arms: Welles was an entire parliament.

As Jaques says in *As You Like It*, one man in his time plays many parts. Welles played more than the rest of us, and often played them simultaneously. He learned how to do so from Shakespeare, whose people have a blurred consortium of selves. Sonnet 53 reflects on the puzzling plurality of character:

> What is your substance, wherof are you made,
> That millions of strange shadows on you tend?
> For every one hath, every one, one shade,
> And you, but one, can every shadow lend.

The androgynous loved one in the sonnets is the poet's 'master-mistress'. Welles, who encompassed both Romeo and Juliet, rejoiced in the actor's peculiar power to flout the dualism of nature, which restricts creatures to being either male or female. To be everybody entails possessing every kind of body (or at least both kinds). In 1945, along with his readings from political philosophers, Welles recorded a feverish nuptial episode from *The Song of Songs*, and turned the wedding night into a duet for one: altering his voice, he is both the virile, thrusting groom and the bashful, yielding bride. He quoted himself in his *The Cradle Will Rock* screenplay, declaring that there are '*three* Goddam sexes – men, women – and *actors*!' Like an alchemist or a magician, the gender-bending Shakespearean actor specialises in transmutation, the Protean talent that brings man nearer to the divine. Welles put the theory into practice in *One-Man Band*, in which he plays all the characters who populate a London street: among his personae here is a fat, frumpy matriarch of the slums with her hair in curlers, who empties her chamber pot on the itinerant musician.

Those strange shades can be moral opposites. At Todd, Welles acted the roles of Christ and Judas – though not in the same play. Later, such Manichean doubling-up became customary, since radio allowed his voice to escape from his body. In his 1938 version of *Oliver Twist* he was the ingenuous Oliver and Fagin, his corrupter. In *Treasure Island*, during the same season, he was the grown-up Jim Hawkins and also Long John Silver. In 1944 in *Donovan's Brain*, he played both halves of a divided personality. His accomplices were never quite so adept. Elaine Dundy, Tynan's first wife, was hired to play assorted female roles in the Harry Lime radio series. She varied her voice as much as she could, but once had to stop a recording to tell Welles 'I'm following myself on.' He demanded to know what had happened to the other actors; the producer pointed out that Welles had fired them all during a fit of pique at lunchtime.

He assumed that he could do everything himself. But you can only become everybody if, secretly, you are nobody at all. Welles understood the vacuity within Shakespeare's great characters: the lack of what we would call ingrained, inborn characteristics, which enables them to invent and reinvent themselves with such dazzling spontaneity. In his radio version of *Huckleberry Finn*, Welles played a fraudulent travelling actor, who specialises in Shakespeare. The man successively passes himself off as the French Dauphin, 'the late Charlemagne', and 'Looey the Seventeen', the rightful King of France. His colleague pretends to be a duke. On stage, the king is billed as Kean the Elder, while the duke is Garrick the Younger. Huck suspects them of having a sideline in 'the counterfeit-money business', but when some of the king's lies are exposed he cannot help admiring the Falstaffian resilience with which the rogue repairs the damage by producing a barrage of fresh fictions. Huck marvels that the king 'was actually beginning to believe what he was saying'. Fakers only want to deceive their victims; an actor is liable to deceive himself, grieving – as Hamlet says about the player-king – about a Hecuba he never knew. The king in *Huckleberry Finn* shares Welles's versatility, and plays Juliet in the balcony scene as well as Hamlet. But his grandest Shakespearean performance is the muddled, malapropistic oration he delivers at the funeral of Peter Wilks. He calls the deceased the diseased, and confuses obsequies with orgies. Such 'tragical mirth', as the rustics define it when announcing their play in *A Midsummer Night's Dream*, sums up the unholy hilarity of Shakespearean drama, where death is often a laughing matter. If you are nothing in yourself, how can you take anything seriously? The faker is an existential jester.

Shakespeare prompted Welles's permutations. He relished Shakespeare's double plots, which, like myth, examine variants of the same story.

'Gloucester', as he said in 1975, 'is a parody of Lear, and Falstaff's recruitment scenes are a parody of the struggle for power at Henry IV's court. Shakespeare loved to show the same thing twice, in a mirror image.' Welles's own mirrors do not simply duplicate reality; they multiply it, splitting faces into an infinity of facets, like the 'metamorphosing mirrors' described by René Crevel in the surrealist magazine *Minotaure* in 1933. Hence the hall of mirrors where the three characters in *The Lady from Shanghai* confront and destroy the images they have formed of one another by firing bullets into the glass.

Welles intended to play double roles in *Heart of Darkness* and in a planned *Salome*, where he would have been both Oscar Wilde and the sluggish, decadent Herod. Neither film was made; the only chance he had to duplicate himself was in Richard Fleischer's *Crack in the Mirror*, made in 1960. Here he played both a proletarian murder victim and the sleek, double-dealing lawyer who defends the murderers. A reviewer in *The New York Times* was grateful that Welles's first character died before the second appeared: how could the screen, even when distended by CinemaScope, accommodate two of him? He had more opportunity to be omnipresent on his soundtracks. He often dubbed films without the original actors, whom he could not afford to recall; like a ventriloquist, he bestowed his own voice on them. In *Mr Arkadin*, he is everybody: Bessy counted eighteen separate vocal impersonations. In *The Trial* there were eleven, including a moment when Welles mimicked the inimitable stammering of Anthony Perkins. In the Shakespeare films, his choices were self-conscious, extending the double plots to suggest startling affinities between unlike characters. In *Othello*, you can occasionally hear his voice emerging from the mouth of Robert Coote's Roderigo. It's an aural reminder that Roderigo is a gull like Othello, easily trapped by Iago. In *Chimes at Midnight*, Welles dubbed the officious, orotund voice of the sheriff who arraigns Falstaff at the inn after the Gadshill robbery: as in *Heart of Darkness* or *Around the World in 80 Days* or *The Murder of Roger Ackroyd*, he is pursuer and pursued, and triumphantly arrests himself.

In 1963, reflecting on the difficulty of casting *Julius Caesar*, Gielgud blamed 'the division of sympathy between the characters of Cassius, Antony and Brutus'. Welles solved the problem, on record at least, by dividing his own sympathies between all three. He had to do so, because they were components of his own psychodrama. Cassius is Welles the untrustworthy trickster, Antony is Welles the demagogue, Brutus is

Welles the worried liberal. He found different voices and identities for each of them, as well as for a fourth character, the narrator, who speaks the non-Shakespearean stage directions Welles wrote for himself.

As Brutus in his earlier, abbreviated recording of the play, he is grave, serious, but perhaps unselfaware. Brutus has no mirror, after all: recording is not a visual medium. Cassius offers to be his glass, but what he reflects back is a distortion. As Brutus, Welles's speech is measured, with caesuras and pauses carefully inserted to equilibrate his lines. His precise elocution sanitises the ugly words he has to use ('carve' or 'hounds') when discussing assassination. His speech justifying the murder in the marketplace is almost pedantically reasonable, and in the quarrel with Cassius he remains calm, indifferent to merely personal emotions. This is Welles as he might have liked to be: considerate, controlled, stoical.

In the second recording, where he plays both Cassius and Antony, we have two aspects of Welles as he actually was. His delivery of Cassius's lines is tense, barely suppressing his nervous anxiety. In the speech suborning Brutus, he emphasises the adjective when referring to 'my single self': this is another of Cassius's deceptions, since he, like Welles, is deviously multiple. Whereas Welles the narrator whispers information to indicate that his comments are not part of the play, as Cassius he mutters balefully, since the character is saying things he wants no one else to hear. The narrator is an omniscient eye assisting our ears; Cassius – more technically cunning, already an expert at employing the microphone – uses his ears in place of eyes, and when he recognises a colleague by identifying his voice in the stormy darkness, Casca says 'Your ear is good.' As Antony, Welles is a light, careless tenor. Caesar dotingly notes that Antony loves plays, revels long at night, and cannot be expected to get up early: here Welles indulges his own libertinism and, when rabble-rousing during Caesar's funeral, his showmanship.

The cohabitation of so many selves can sound like madness, as in the case of the scientist mentally overtaken by the brain of the dead Donovan in that 1944 show. Welles admitted as much in his performance as the persecuted Malvolio in his recorded *Twelfth Night*. Malvolio is locked in a dark room and quizzed by Feste the clown; Welles is both the victim and, as narrator, a neutral, unflustered commentator. His narration draws attention to the darkness of the scene, which even in the theatre makes it an aural, not a visual, experience. Feste, questioning Malvolio, also conducts a dialogue with himself, since he pretends to be Sir Topas the minister, who admonishes Feste while pacifying Malvolio. The stage directions in Welles's edition of the text specify that 'Malvolio's face turns towards each invisible voice'. The recorded scene is a vocal quartet performed by two actors: Welles as Mavolio and narrator, LeRoi Operti as Feste and Sir Topas. It is not surprising that Malvolio is confused and, finally, demented. In his own prologue to the recording, Welles as Burbage badgers Shakespeare (George Coulouris, who is Orsino in the play itself) to supply him with a new part. Will has promised him the tragic Hamlet, and he says that he does not want to be fobbed off with a comedy about twins. Burbage's bluster provides Welles with a good self-reflexive joke. Twins were a natural subject for him; he had even played quintuplets. On the radio, he regularly exhibited his talent for bi- or trifurcation. One plot in *Twelfth Night* is about that morphological mystery. Antonio, marvelling when he sees the twins Sebastian and Viola together in the final scene, asks 'How have you made division of yourself?' Although Welles played none of these characters, the question challenged him to account for the psychological fission that lay behind his performances.

Welles did more than act in Shakespeare's plays. He enacted them in his own life.

He did not quite traverse the seven ages of man enumerated by Jaques – infant, schoolboy, lover, soldier, justice, pantaloon, senex. With his button nose, he made an exemplary baby, even after he should have grown up. At Todd, he was a famously apt pupil. The next three phases were more problematic: as he told Bogdanovich, the beginning and the end of life are golden times, but 'middle age is the enemy'. Welles the compulsive philanderer was not much of a lover. He revered women but also feared them, as his treatment of Rita Hayworth in *The Lady from Shanghai* reveals. As for soldiering, he had no more liking for it than Falstaff did. His duelling in the *Macbeth* film is laughably clumsy; he shrewdly avoided the draft after Pearl Harbor. The role of the justice was even more inimical, though in *The Trial* he cast himself as the Advocate, a lecher who interviews clients from his bed. Justice was Welles's foe: he spent much of his adult life fending off law suits or wriggling out of contracts. He was spared the last two phases by his relatively early death, but from the beginning of his life Welles had tried to imagine the end of life and what followed it. Once at Todd he came to class as a hanged man, with a blanched face and a scarf serving as his noose. His first dramatic role in the 1938 Mercury radio season was the undead

Dracula. The actor enjoys more than one life, and can also venture outside or beyond life at will. In *The Third Man*, when Cotten tells him about Valli's arrest, Welles grins cherubically and asks 'What can I do, old man? I'm dead, aren't I?'

Welles refused to wait for the seven ages to unroll in proper chronological order. As Kent says of Lear, he 'usurped his life'. Precocity is a wanton rejection of childhood; it graduates through the stages of life too rapidly, and arrives prematurely at the end. Perhaps this is why Welles's Mr Clay in *The Immortal Story*, taken aback when his clerk quotes Isaiah, barks 'I don't like prophecies!' A prophecy forecasts what is to come, and functions as a sentence of death. To borrow the phrase of the fortune-telling gipsy in *Touch of Evil*, it uses your future up. Welles began mortgaging his own future while still a child. At the age of ten, he played the crabbed, wintry Scrooge in *A Christmas Carol* at school in Madison, Wisconsin. In Dublin, aged sixteen, he appeared as the sixty-year-old Duke in *Jew Süss*. It was at this time that he began smoking cigars: he thought they would lend him an air of mature gravity, and hoped that their smoke would hide his baby face. Back in New York, now aged nineteen, he turned himself into the financier McGafferty, supposedly in his late fifties, in MacLeish's *Panic*. He was twenty-four when he went on tour as Falstaff in *Five Kings*. His Hal, Burgess Meredith, was six years older than Welles's ancient reprobate. During the season of summer theatre at Todd in 1934 he made his first film, *The Hearts of Age*. It lasts four minutes, and skittishly abbreviates the ages of man. In it Welles courts his future bride Virginia Nicholson. Though she girlishly bestrides a hobby horse, she is made up as an old woman, with worry lines written across her face, and Welles her wooer – with a conical latex skull and the pointy pincers of F. W. Murnau's Nosferatu – plays Death. Welles interrupts his seduction to design and direct a hanging. Then he plays a dance of death on the piano, and leafs through jokey funeral placards to commemorate the corpse. He rejects REST IN PEACE and WITH THY GOD, deciding on a tablet that says simply THE END. It serves both as tombstone and title card, to conclude the ghoulish escapade.

Citizen Kane likewise begins with Kane's end. Make-up sessions lasting four and a half hours abridged the decades, adding fifty years to Welles's age. Pads of sponge rubber grafted Kane's sagging physique onto him. Seventy-two separate latex pouches and membranes were applied to his face, and lenses with rheumy fluid in them dimmed his eyes and made them watery. Faust asks the devil to prolong his youth; Welles, rather than cheating time, liked to demonstrate its swift, implacable course by jumping ahead of it. He made another premature, oblique effort to play Lear in 1957 when cast as a southern patriarch who presides over a civil war within his own family in Martin Ritt's film of William Faulkner's *The Long, Hot Summer*. Aged forty-two, Welles made himself up to look sixty-one, with inked eyebrows that seem about to melt in the swampy Mississippi heat, a tobacco-coloured complexion, and a voice like a catarrhal volcano. This impatient meddling with nature continued to fascinate him. In his 1958 television film, *The Fountain of Youth*, an endocrinologist touts an elixir that will supply an extra two hundred years of life, as opposed to the meagre twenty-four Faust gains by his pact. The medicine does not work, and decomposition resumes before the half-hour is up. In 1963, hoping to direct the segment about Jacob in Dino de Laurentiis's *The Bible*, Welles experimentally turned Keith Baxter into a nonagenarian patriarch with the aid of waxy artificial skin, false hair and some gloomy lighting.

Film is a time machine. It conserves the present but redefines it as the past, and can unreel towards the future with scary speed. Do these technical miracles mock our slow, shelving temporality? Welles, like Shakespeare's tragic heroes, brooded on the relationship between the brevity and haste of drama and the elongated narrative of our actual life. Hotspur in *Henry V* says 'O gentlemen, the time of life is short', and Macbeth, acting on the prophetic hints of the witches, finds 'the future in the instant'. Hamlet, by contrast, moves slowly, travels round in circles, tries to remain inert, and hopes in this way to defeat time; of course it catches up with him, and Laertes tells him 'in thee there is not half an hour of life'. This Shakespearean sense of our existential tempo informs *The Magnificent Ambersons*, linking social and personal history. A stationary, old-fashioned culture is destroyed by motorised modernity; individuals age, and stumble into an alien future like George (Tim Holt) as he wanders through a sooty, industrialised city he no longer recognises. Eugene (Joseph Cotten), inventing the motor car, is an emissary of that future, but he is wise enough to honour the past. In renouncing the widowed Isabel (Dolores Costello) because George, her son, objects to their romance, Eugene acknowledges that time, which seasons and matures people, must take its own time to do so. 'Forty can't tell twenty about this,' he says in his farewell letter. 'Twenty can only find out by getting to be forty.'

Long after finishing *The Magnificent Ambersons*, Welles planned to return to it and add an epilogue, in which seventy would tell forty about the extra trials that lay ahead. He wanted to amend the sudden, sweetened ending shot and glued on by the studio after he absconded to Brazil. Instead, organising a reunion of the cast, he would show the same characters thirty years on, and put the evidence of ageing on screen without recourse to latex. It was one more of his grand, impossible ideas. Time itself outwitted him: Agnes Moorehead, who played Fanny Minafer, was already dead. Devouring time created continuity problems for *The Other Side of the Wind*, a more or less confessional film about a film director (Welles's deputy, named Jake Hannaford and played by John Huston). He worked on the project whenever he could afford to between 1970 and 1976, but found it increasingly difficult to make the characters look consistent. Between bouts of work, the actors got fatter or thinner, changed their hair styles or lost their hair, mislaid or grew out of the costumes they had provided.

Welles's obsession with the ageing of man recurs in *The Lady from Shanghai*, and adds a tragicomic wisdom to the film's greedy, sordid manoeuvrings. His source was a novel by Sherwood King, *If I Die Before I Wake*, in which there is an intriguing exchange between forty and twenty. The crippled lawyer Bannister ogles the strapping young sailor he has hired: 'I'm forty-three. Forty-three! Do you know what I'd give to be twenty-six again, with a build like yours?' The film ignored this homosexual subtext, though Welles's script constantly harks back to the problems of longevity and survival. Bannister defends the sailor O'Hara (played by Welles) at his murder trial, but does so only to incriminate him. He promises to plead for a stay of execution, and has his own sadistic reasons for hoping that it will be granted: 'I want you to live as long as possible . . . until you die.' We are all on death row. O'Hara tries to jump the queue, and gobbles pills to execute himself. Revival is a fate worse than death. Cops trundle him around the room, as if exercising a corpse, and the judge orders 'Keep him walking.' Finally, after everyone else is killed, O'Hara accepts the life sentence which is our fate as mortal men. He vows that he will try to forget Elsa (Rita Hayworth), or 'maybe I'll die trying'. His last reflective monologue, as he leaves the hall of shattered mirrors and walks towards the ocean at daybreak, contains a peculiarly Wellesian formulation. 'The only way to stay out of trouble', he says, 'is to grow old.' What a life lesson! For most people, growing old involves sailing into trouble. For

Welles, whose professional and physiological troubles accumulated as he grew older, just staying alive proclaimed a victory over time, if only for the time being.

In the novel, Bannister says to the sailor 'Wasn't it Voltaire who suggested that we make love in our youth, and in old age attend to salvation?' Welles once more disrupted the sequence of the ages. Even as a young man, he worried about salvation. It was an inevitable consequence of the curiosity about perdition that made him leap ahead, in his performances, to an imagined dotage. One means of salvation lay in second childhood, or the protraction of irresponsible infancy. That is the disreputable charm of Falstaff. Anna makes the same point about Harry Lime in *The Third Man*. 'He never grew up,' she says, though the world grew up around him. Making a series of television programmes for Granada in 1955, Welles tracked down another elderly, incorrigible baby: Raymond Duncan, Isadora's brother, still a spry bohemian wearing a home-made tunic and sandals in a studio on the Left Bank. 'Unfortunately I'm not a beau garçon,' admits Duncan with a toothless grin. Welles asks him if he doesn't prefer 'things that have been used by life'. The wizened Duncan says that the public prefers fleshier, 'rounder, baby-looking faces'. Welles chortles with glee: 'So there's a little hope for me then!'

In another instalment of *Around the World with Orson Welles*, moving from Paris to London, he considered a more adult mode of salvation. He visits an almshouse in Hackney, where five widows in cardigans grow old gracefully. 'We're all true blues, all Tories,' insists one whiskery matron. Welles does his best to encourage some disgraceful behaviour, saying that he's heard about romps in the garden. 'Not half,' cackles one ancient nymph, 'we can kick our legs up!' She might be Mistress Quickly, arthritically capering with Falstaff. Then, in Chelsea, Welles interviews the scarlet-coated military pensioners at the Royal Hospital. Again like Falstaff when out recruiting, he takes some of the octogenarians to the pub, but the pints of beer he proffers do not unsettle their composure. 'Everything in decorum,' says one of them as he serenely reflects on the arrangements for his regimental funeral. Welles, touched, muses on the indignities of age, and admires the way the Hackney widows and the Chelsea soldiers have preserved an individuality that time usually erases.

Everett Sloane was only six years older than Welles, so that *The Lady from Shanghai* could hardly use the speech from the novel about age and its rancorous envy of youth. But Welles remembered it, and repeated it himself when time had confirmed its truth. The year before his death, he recorded a pop song with a soupy band and the dooh-waahing back-up of the Ray Charles Singers. He speaks his lines rather than singing them; in a doleful refrain, he tells the blithe chorus 'I know what it is to be young, / But you don't know what it is to be old.' For the sake of a rhyme, this melancholy wiseacre adds 'Time takes away – / So the story is told.' Half a century before this terminal, short-breathed ditty, he had given voice to a different notion of time. Every week on the radio from 1935 to 1938 he narrated *The March of Time*, a news digest in which time trod triumphally forwards, marching onwards and upwards as American optimism decreed. In *Citizen Kane* he parodied this programme and made it run back to front, as the newsreel called *News on the March* summarises the ages of Kane in reverse order, beginning with his death. Finally, in the song he recorded in 1984, he told time's true story: a painful dwindling or diminution, which ends by leaving you, like the old man at the end of Jaques' speech, 'sans everything', and demonstrates that your life, in Macbeth's words, signifies nothing.

There were so many Welleses that, somewhere inside himself, he could find an affinity with virtually anybody and everybody in Shakespeare's plays. His selves burgeoned, and so did each Shakespearean character. Because, as Welles believed, 'every single way of playing and staging Shakespeare – as long as it is effective – is right', such characters consist of the sum total of all possible interpretations. His 1934 essay included his own sketch of 'a thousand Shylocks', lined up in a kvetching, gesticulating procession that trails off into the distance, as if every unemployed actor in the world had arrived to wait for an audition at the stage door.

The characters were fractions of Welles, who admitted that any performance would be just a fraction of the character. Discussing Macbeth with Marienstras, he said that no one could play the whole man. Macbeth, he explained, is both a murderous brute and a refined, sorrowing poet. You need Olivier for the first part of the play and Gielgud for the second. There might have been some smug mental arithmetic at work here. Perhaps the body of Olivier plus the brain of Gielgud equals Welles. No, it is more likely that Welles was genuinely conceding the inadequacy of all three. None of us is a whole man (or woman); we consist of fragments. The principle explains his apparently indecisive approach to casting. Filming *Othello*, he got through four, perhaps five, maybe even six Desdemonas. He began with Lea Padovani, sacked her in favour of

Cécile Aubry, then when she walked out replaced her with Betsy Blair, who gave way to Suzanne Cloutier. Paola Mori appears in some of the long shots, and Gudrun Ure dubbed Cloutier's dialogue, so they should be included in the list. No single one could encompass all of Desdemona's contradictions, though each might represent a part of her.

One way of telling the story of Welles's life is to see him advancing or declining through three tragic prototypes. First is Macbeth the thrusting careerist, then comes Othello whose service to the state is undone by the shame and confusion of his private life. He ends as Lear, the ancestor who is unceremoniously bundled into obsolescence. Hamlet – the fourth of Shakespeare's tragic heroes – is oddly absent from the record. He circled around the role, playing Hamlet's father, his uncle, and his successor Fortinbras; then, just once, on the radio in 1936, he played Hamlet himself – or bits of him, since he had reduced the tragedy's four hours to thirty minutes.

He drew teasing attention to this omission or evasion when he recorded *Twelfth Night* in 1938. In his prologue, playing Burbage, he asks Shakespeare 'How is my dark, Danish, high-tragical Hamlet?' Shakespeare replies that he is still at sea, on the way to exile in England. He has been becalmed there for five weeks: Shakespeare is stuck, and is diverting himself with *Twelfth Night*. He fobs Burbage off with the role of Orsino, whom the actor mistakes for another character in *Hamlet*, perhaps one of Osric's relatives. Shakespeare explains the difference between Illyria and Elsinore. 'Anything but *Hamlet*!' rails Burbage, 'Leave comedies to Ben Jonson, and write me a death scene.' It is not that Welles was in any way incapable of playing Hamlet. Perhaps he avoided the part because of an uncomfortable self-recognition. He suffered from the malady that the Russian film director Grigori Kozintsev called 'Hamletism', an imbalance between thought and will. The man of ideas had too many ideas, and lacked the time or energy to follow them through. In 1928, MacLeish wrote his own version of the play, published as *The Hamlet of A. MacLeish*. Here Hamlet gives himself a dressing-down and resolves to:

> . . . play the strong boy with the rest of them!
> Be hard-boiled! Be bitter! . . . Sneer! Swagger! O be
> Hard!

It is timely advice, but a tough, efficient, Hemingwayesque Hamlet who went straight to work as a killer would not be tragic. Shakespeare's hero delays the mandatory action of revenge. He strays into time-wasting subplots, flirting with Ophelia, joking with Rosencrantz and Guildenstern, lecturing the players, fencing with Laertes. Welles too balked at completing the great work that was expected of him, because he doubted his own capacity to live up to the expectations of others. Like Hamlet, he resorted to a baffling diversification. He always had half-a-dozen projects on the go, and as a result he completed very few of them.

There might have been other, more privately distressing reasons for his reluctance. Freud had made it fashionable to treat Hamlet as an Oedipal neurotic; Olivier's *Hamlet,* in which his own performance was frankly incestuous, challenged Welles's *Macbeth* at the 1948 Venice Film Festival. (Irresolute as ever, Welles withdrew his own film from the competition, allowing Olivier to win.) Welles, like Kane, grieved, perhaps too tenderly, for his lost mother. The hero of Melville's novel *Pierre, or The Ambiguities* has a sickly infatuation with his mother, and for this reason tears up his copy of *Hamlet* because, as well as accusing him of ineffectuality, it shows him his 'loathed identity'. As if this self-recognition were not uncomfortable enough, the young Welles was also something of a wishful parricide. He allowed himself to articulate this motive indirectly when discussing other Shakespearean roles. Brutus, he thought, kills a father figure. He even suggested to Marienstras that 'Perhaps he was the natural son of Caesar'; he relished his own ingenuity by adding 'It's not in the text.' And he argued that Prince Hal has a choice between two fathers, Henry IV and Falstaff – though in this case Welles was not the ruthless son but the doting father whose heart is killed when Hal rejects him.

The Magnificent Ambersons provided Welles with a substitute for *Hamlet.* George, the role he played on the radio in 1938, shares Hamlet's Oedipal weakness, and in Booth Tarkington's novel he even quotes his 'mirrored princely image'. He repeats Hamlet's narcissistic lines about his mourning costume – ''Tis not alone my inky cloak, good mother' – and at the end, reconciled to the economic downfall of his dynasty, he remembers Hamlet's elegy in the cemetery and extends it to a democratic, irreverent America where historical memory is even shorter: 'Nothing stays or keeps where there is growth . . . Great Caesar dead and turned to clay stopped no hole to keep the wind away; dead Caesar was nothing but a tiresome bit of print in a book that schoolboys study for a while and then forget.' George, like Hamlet, has a tormented encounter with his mother in her bedroom, when he censures her sexual reawakening. But

Shakespeare's tragedy is mitigated and softened by Tarkington and Welles. On her deathbed, Isabel continues to play the nurturer: 'Darling, did you get something to eat?' she asks George. 'All you needed?' She then spectrally shimmers into George's hospital room, and her shade – by contrast with the father's retributive ghost in *Hamlet* – prompts a reconciliation between him and Eugene, whose romance with Isabel he had vetoed. That reported, invisible presence in the room goes beyond tragedy to the miracles which magically preserve comedy in Shakespeare's last plays: for instance, the resurrection of the maternal Hermione in *The Winter's Tale*.

Hamlet is the youngest of Shakespeare's tragic figures, Lear the oldest. Welles advanced from one to the other, from son to father. But even in later life, mixing up the ages of man as always, he did not abandon Hamlet. In 1975, in a breathtaking leap of imagination, Welles argued that 'Falstaff was a Hamlet who never returned from his exile in England, where he became old and fat.' The anxious, self-wasting thinker embeds himself in the body as if snuggling into a mattress, and realises that the better part of valour lies in self-preservation. Welles's Falstaff in *Chimes at Midnight* makes his first appearance in bed, snoring beneath the counterpane as he clutches his tankard. There, with luck, you can stay out of trouble, growing old, fat, and also wise.

Jean-Paul Sartre, lecturing in 1958 on the differences between theatre and cinema, inadvertently explained why Welles's Shakespearean films are so autobiographical. In the theatre, according to Sartre, we keep a judicious distance from the hero, whereas film persuades us that 'we are the hero, we are part of him', and his fate is ours. How much more so if you are both behind the camera and in front of it. Sartre, like Brecht with his salutary doses of alienation, disapproved of this subjectivity: 'In film nowadays, participation excludes observation and explanation.' He mistrusted close-ups, because they turn the fallible human individual into a superman. Welles – no less sceptical, though unencumbered by Sartre's Marxist prejudices – had a finer understanding of the medium and its cruel scrutiny of his face. This self-examination runs through his performances as Macbeth – on stage in Harlem in 1936, on record in 1940, then on stage in Utah once more in 1947 as a rehearsal for the film he made in 1948.

The Harlem *Macbeth*, with its jungle setting and its voodoo drummers, was of course an all-black affair, but when the unreliable lead actor, Jack Carter, dropped out for a while, Welles replaced him. In *The*

Cradle Will Rock screenplay, Carter resentfully calls this 'the first time a white actor in an all-Negro cast played Shakespeare in a black face'. For Welles, the white face under the black mask demonstrated the fraudulence of acting. It also points to the act of trespass involved when one person assumes the identity (and in this case the race) of another.

Shakespeare's play contains a stage direction that curiously anticipates the cinema. At the end, the conquerors are supposed to exhibit the heads of Macbeth and his wife, stuck on poles. This never happens in the theatre, and though Welles made a point of depicting it in the marginal illustrations for *Everybody's Shakespeare*, he skirted it in his recorded version, where the narrator announces that Macduff drags in Macbeth's body, rather than carrying on 'his cursèd head'. Somehow decapitation seems better adjusted to the cinema, whose early, ingenuous audiences often mistook close-ups for pictures of severed heads. In his film of *Macbeth*, Welles confronts this forbidden image. The witches behead their clay manikin at the end, which announces the same fate for Macbeth. We do not need to see this, because it has already been placed on show at the beginning, when Welles – adding to Shakespeare's text – elaborately stages the execution of the Thane of Cawdor, with flaring torches and dolorous drummers (as in Harlem). Cawdor is dragged up a craggy flight of steps to the block, and thrust to his knees before a sweaty, half-naked axeman. We next see his head impaled on a pole. In the distance, it shares the screen with another bodiless head, much closer to us. This belongs to Duncan, who ponders Cawdor's treachery and says 'There's no art / To find the mind's construction in the face.' Welles's composition – with those two faces, one separated from its body by the axe, the other by the viewfinder – gently corrects his statement. There is such an art after all, and it is called film.

Even so, Welles did his best to withhold his own face from this psychological X-ray, and as he begins Macbeth's 'Tomorrow and tomorrow and tomorrow', the camera drifts away into a drifting mist. The evasion pacifies his fear of delivering such soliloquies, but it also subtly shows the construction – or the breakdown – of the mind behind the face. The fog is Macbeth's thoughts, disintegrating as we watch. Everything in Welles's *Macbeth* is dissolute, halfway between solid and liquid states. The air is murkily condensed, or thick with smoke. Mud bubbles, and light itself 'thickens', as Macbeth says. Surfaces suppurate. The walls of the castle audibly and visibly drip. The rock face is slick; its vapour at one point gathers into an internal waterfall, in which Macbeth cools his seething head. The clay manikin made by the witches perspires or weeps or bleeds.

This is what Welles meant when he had a character in *The Other Side of the Wind* declare that Shakespeare invented the cinematic dissolve. Shakespeare's metaphors fuse inconsistent feelings, as when Macbeth on his way to kill Duncan couples murder and sex by likening himself to Tarquin creeping towards the room where he will ravish Lucretia. Or they create a communion between the unconscious minds of characters: Lady Macbeth imagines killing a child, while Macbeth speaks of pity as a protesting newborn infant. Welles found a way to film such associations of ideas. Voices dissolve into one another during the transition between scenes. Macbeth starts to recite his letter to Lady Macbeth, who is heard reading it out loud before she is seen; their brief duet establishes their collusion. A visual dissolve makes Macbeth's 'dagger of the mind' materialise, swooningly out of focus. As he approaches Duncan's bedchamber, the rugged walls swim and blur, and so does Macbeth himself, dissolving in a sweat. Cinematic images are insubstantial, transparent, merging or mutating at will. A ghost can be conjured up by smearing vaseline on the lens of the camera. When Macbeth believes he has seen the dead Banquo, his wife mentions an earlier hallucination, the 'air-drawn dagger' that led him to Duncan; at once Duncan himself blearily reappears. 'I see thee still!' cries Macbeth after the mental dagger, drawn on the air, vanishes. But he has not actually seen either the dagger or the ghosts. Instead he has pictured them, and the camera, as if located inside him, captures his flickery imaginings. Prowling through the castle, travelling in and out of gloom, it enables us to see in the dark.

The film opens with an abstract exhibition of these associative powers. The witches get straight down to their cooking, which in Shakespeare does not happen until the fourth act. Welles enjoyed this scene, and in his 1940 recording made the cauldron bubble noisily, with splashes as the offal is hurled in. The witches begin the film with the command 'Throw in' (words they never say in Shakespeare); they then list the unsavoury ingredients of their hell-broth. Welles might be reciting his own recipe for the film. Throw in Shakespearean tragedy, Caribbean sorcery, and medieval Celtic religion. Mix them up with the iconography of the American Western: the film was made on a disused set used for cowboy quickies at Republic studios, and the castle of the Macbeths had previously done duty as a coal mine. Lady Macbeth sleeps beneath animal pelts like a pioneer wife, while the wood choppers who heave to and cut down Birnam forest for camouflage might be Paul Bunyan and his fellow loggers clearing the American wilderness. The contents are disparate – like the filleted snakes, Jewish livers, Turkish noses and dragon's scales stirred by the witches – but they somehow gell or congeal.

Welles makes the camera, at the start of the film, submerge itself in this viscous gruel, which sluggishly quakes and curdles before our eyes like a hot version of the snowflakes inside the glass dome in *Citizen Kane*. This is Welles's creative source – the stewing imagination, about to boil over. The witches are the generative force in his film. What they generate, like Kane breathing 'Rosebud', is the hero – or a totemic substitute for him: a wooden mask in Harlem, and in the film a demon doll, moulded when the sludge in the pot thickens. Welles often likened acting to sculpture: the actor plastically refashions himself into the shape required by the role. Designing the make-up for Kane, Maurice Siederman encased Welles in jelly, then coated him with plaster, made a mould of his body and shaped it to match the modifications that go with ageing; he even sculpted rubber for the plutocrat's belly. The Harlem witches carved a facsimile of Macbeth's head, though in his film, the proper analogy is pottery: the character is pounded and pummelled into shape by those dabbling hands. The film exhibits the creative process, and suggests that there may be something infernal about it.

Welles plays Macbeth as a drunkard. He staggers through the castle with a sloppy goblet, slurring his speech. This decision has often been mocked, but it takes his self-characterisation further. Here the poet or artist admits his own need to be entranced before he can create. Opium freed Coleridge's imagination to engender Kubla Khan, whose private paradise leads in turn to Kane's Xanadu; liquor lubricates Macbeth's surrender to imagination. Despite what the even drunker porter says when he opens the gate, it eliminates the barrier between desire and performance. The pig-tailed holy father – invented by Welles, supplied with lines purloined from other characters or with speeches from the church liturgy, and played by Alan Napier – ought to hold unreason at bay, but his pious interventions are ineffectual. His warning to Lady Macduff of Macbeth's impending attack comes too late. If Macbeth takes direction from the witches, the priest takes dictation from Macbeth: he is the scribe who copies down Macbeth's letter to his wife. Christianity (as Welles put it in his summary of the action) cannot withstand the assault of chaos and magic.

When his film was criticised, Welles apologetically said it was no more than 'a violent sketched charcoal drawing of a great play'. *Macbeth*, filmed in that ersatz coal mine, is indeed charcoal-toned, and its sketchiness is equally deliberate: a mode of smudged, scratchy automatic writing. Similar sketches violently muddy the margins of the texts Welles illustrated for *Everybody's Shakespeare*, where they emerge from that cave of making he carried round inside his own head. The face of his Shylock is gnarled and inky, enveloped in a dark cloud. Caricature, which he practises here, is a black art: a devilish alchemy, which assumes that our human substance is unfixed and can be revised at will. The chiaroscura of Welles's sketches hints at the obfuscating powers of The Shadow, the omniscient detective who possessed, as he boasted, 'the hypnotic power to cloud men's minds so they cannot see him'. The Shadow remained out of sight; the suspects he tracked were palpable, leaving sinful stains – like the blood on the hands of the Macbeths – that enabled him to see the evil in their hearts. Welles, the man inside the radio, was just an immaterial voice. All the rest of us have bodies which incriminate us. In one of Welles's illustrations for *Julius Caesar*, the insomniac Caesar's black shadow escapes from his body and blots the wall. Quarrelling, the heads of Brutus and Cassius emerge from the same darkness, one full face and the other in profile: two versions of Welles, who played both parts? The scariest figure is one which casts no shadow, and is therefore as invisible as The Shadow himself. Feste the clown in *Twelfth Night* – sketched by Welles in the scene where he torments Malvolio, who is locked in a dark room – is a blank space, wearing a white sheet that scarcely imprints itself on the page.

To be everybody is to inhabit every body, or every kind of body. Welles made it easier for himself by distinguishing between two physical types, which correspond to alternative Shakespearean genres. In tragedy, the mind wears out the body, or obliterates it: the camera slips into the consciousness of Welles's Macbeth, leaving the physical remnant of him to lurch lopsidedly through an inept fight with Macduff. In comedy, the body contentedly absorbs and quietens the troublesome mind. Sir Toby Belch in *Twelfth Night*, sketched by Welles in his edition of the play, already has the swollen physique of Falstaff or of the middle-aged Welles, like an uninhibited baby in an all-over tunic. On his way through the ages of man, Welles advanced from one genre to the next. In 1949, MacLíammóir, to whom he offered the role of Iago in his film, said he had put on too much weight to play it. Welles, as MacLíammóir remembered in his diary, replied that 'so had he, and we'd be Chubby Tragedians together', camouflaged in bales of cheese-cloth. He had enough appreciation of paradox to know that chubbiness did not mean immunity to tragic pain. Hence his suggestion that Falstaff was Hamlet with a bigger belly, still conserving the prince's melancholy.

With a Shakespearean sagacity of his own, Welles hinted that comedy was not a decline from tragedy but a more serious and emotionally honest form. Tragedy, not comedy, became the softer option. In 1937 the composer Virgil Thomson, eager to score *The Duchess of Malfi* for Welles, ingratiated himself by inviting Welles to a feast at Sardi's before a performance of *Julius Caesar*. Welles ate rapaciously and at the end of the meal gave Thomson the commission for the score. 'The dinner did it,' he said, then squeezed into the canvas corset he wore when playing Brutus. 'And it's lucky I'm playing tragedy tonight, which needs no timing. Comedy would be difficult.' He made a similar discrimination in 1968 on the set of Michael Winner's film *I'll Never Forget What's 'Is Name*, in which he played a Mephistophelean advertising executive. He brought along his usual selection of noses, and Winner watched nervously as he sorted through them. But he never tried any of them on. Winner, relieved, asked him why not. 'Because it's a comedy,' said Welles. 'I don't wear them in comedy.' The genres had once more switched places. The comic body must exhibit its imperfection, whereas the tragic body – intent on preserving its dignity – is permitted some cosmetic help. The actor is not, like the rest of us, condemned to singularity. He can try bodies on for size, and discard them if they don't fit.

Welles brooded about the morality of the actor's succession of optional identities. Eugène Ionesco admitted in 1958 that when he was a young man, 'a theatrical performance had no magic for me'. Plays seemed absurd, or reprehensible and shameful. Ionesco could not understand why actors wanted to shed their own skins. In his play *Rhinoceros*, directed by Welles in London in 1960, he pressed the treason further: here people (except for the hero Berenger, played by Olivier) renounce their species. At the end of his life, Welles fancifully rewrote the beginning and imagined himself quitting the theatre. Late in the screenplay about his production of *The Cradle Will Rock*, he asks a Mercury Theatre colleague if he believes in seven-year cycles. For someone who lived as fast as Welles, the seven ages of man could be compressed into as many years: 'Seven years ago I stumbled into this profession . . . So if it's time for me to stumble out, I think I could manage that quite easily.' He got his first job in Dublin in 1931; he makes this remark in 1938, when the government had apparently curtailed his career by withdrawing funds from the Federal Theatre Project. Welles shrugs, aware that there are worlds elsewhere – other lives, new bodies to try on. What if he had then run for political office? He envied the freedom of Dinesen's Pellegrina, the opera singer who loses her voice and ventures into the arduous daylight world outside the theatre. Pellegrina's speech about becoming other people – delivered by Kodar in the film Welles began to make from Dinesen's stories – appealed to him because the singer rejoices in her release from the burden of genius. In *The Big Brass Ring*, Menaker muses about sneaking down a rabbit hole, like Alice on her way to wonderland, and becoming someone else. 'In a perfect world,' he believes, 'all of us should be allowed some short vacations from our own identities.'

Like Shakespeare in Coleridge's phrase, Welles was 'myriad-minded'. But his own virtuosity increasingly depressed or puzzled him. As a young man, he pretended to be other people. As a celebrity, he was forced to pretend to be himself, performing a self-parody on television talk shows or in Las Vegas nightclubs. In *The Big Brass Ring*, he ironically wondered whether this plethora of apparent selves may be the consequence of absence and emptiness, not superfluity. Menaker recalls Richard Nixon in his bugged office at the White House: he recorded his existence on tape, 'hoping a playback would eventually inform him who he was . . . He told us often what he *wasn't*, but he never really got it figured out.' Did Welles?

Welles puffing out his home-made inferno in *The Long, Hot Summer*.

CHAPTER 4

Faust

Welles's first role on Broadway defined himself when young, and established a prototype for his subsequent performances. In 1937 he appeared in his own production of Marlowe's *Doctor Faustus*, playing the magician who purchases divine power by bargaining with the devil. Kane, Kindler and Mr Clay enter into similar arrangements, as does Macbeth, who – in Welles's interpretation – is manipulated by diabolical agents. Van Stratten in the novel remarks when he concludes his business deal with Arkadin 'That was how I came to sell my soul.' Welles even blamed Kafka's persecuted hero in *The Trial* for craving a forbidden knowledge. In 1958, interviewed by André Bazin and some *Cahiers* colleagues, he summarised his career by conceding that 'all the characters I've played . . . are versions of Faust'. Offstage, his own character was equally Faustian. In *The Cradle Will Rock*, he had John Houseman call the lies he told in Dublin in 1931 'a pact with Hell', and in 1982 he unrepentantly assured a BBC interviewer 'I would have sold my soul to play the Godfather'. By this stage neither the devil nor Francis Coppola was interested in negotiating with him.

With an ingenuity and an ironic self-castigation that were typical of him, he assured Bazin 'I'm against every Faust'. Welles rebuked Renaissance humanism by declaring that a great man, if he is to be anything more than an egomaniac, must acknowledge something greater than himself. That superior value, he said, 'might be the Law, or God, or Art'. Quinlan warps the law, K questions its edicts, and in doing so they repeat Faustus's mockery of God. Welles himself, more humbly, worshipped art. He went on to suggest in the 1958 interview that there were 'two great human types in the world', of which Faust was one. Though he had played Faustian types all his life, he belonged personally to 'the other camp'. He did not identify that type with any particular character. Perhaps the anti-Faust was Quixote, or his close colleague Falstaff. Welles's progress through the decades took him, painfully and repentantly, from one type to the other – from infidel to chivalrous defender of faith, from tragic self-seeking to comic self-effacement.

The purgation was never as complete as Welles might have wished. Criticising the conceit of Faust, he accused the cinema's widescreen format of complicity in a metaphysical plot to alter the status of our species. He railed against the anamorphic lens like a churchman confiscating Galileo's telescope. 'Man is made in God's image,' he argued, and 'to enlarge that image is not to glorify but to deform it . . . One doesn't joke with God.' (This solemn disapproval did not debar him from going on in 1958 to narrate *South Seas Adventure*, a glossy Pacific travelogue made in Cinerama.) And immediately after assuring Bazin, a devout Catholic, that he deplored the arrogance of Faust the disbeliever, he indulged in a spasm of what he called 'Nietzschean morality', coveting Faust's immunity from timid, squeamish, humane laws. 'Sentimental bourgeois morality disgusts me,' he said. It might have been Harry Lime talking, with his lip contemptuously wrinkled.

Film was a by-product of the science that challenged God's creative monopoly, like the prodding chimneys and combustion engines that puncture and blacken the sky in *The Magnificent Ambersons*. 'We live', as Welles told Bazin, 'in a world that has been made by Faust.' He inherited this idea from the cloudily mythopoeic history of Oswald Spengler, who blamed the philosophical corruption of the West since the Renaissance on the spirit of Faust with his lust for intellectual dominion. Spengler published the two volumes of *The Decline of the West* in 1918 and 1922; Welles, playing Marlowe's hero just before and after the Second World War – in 1937 in New York, then again in 1950 on a tour through derelict Germany – acted out Spengler's thesis by showing Faust's collusion in this moral calamity.

Hallie Flanagan, who as director of the Federal Theatre Project subsidised Welles's Broadway *Faustus*, praised the production for its attunement to 'our own age'. Rather than retelling the story of 'a man being snatched away by the devil', she thought that Welles had emphasised the modern determination 'to lay hold on reality', to bare its physical secrets. The year after Welles's production, Gertrude Stein continued the updating in her play *Doctor Faustus Lights the Lights*. Stein's Faustus invents electricity and, consequently, switches God off. Irradiating the sky around the clock, his man-made light outshines the sun and obliterates the moon; eventually Faustus finds the glare to be boring, and descends to hell in quest of darkness. The necromantic wonders of Welles's *Faustus* were all technically engineered, made possible by thousand-watt lamps, flash boxes, eruptions of lycopodium flame, and a subterranean battery of what he called, in his script for *The Cradle Will Rock*, 'devilish engines'. He repeated these luminous explosions at the operatic première in *Citizen Kane*, where Susan's screeched high notes coincide with the popping of flash bulbs, while the tuneless demise of her voice is illustrated with a shot of a light filament flaring and then going out. And after the shoot-out in *The Lady from Shanghai*, O'Hara's wounded, bleeding hand flicks a switch to expose the splintered mess of the mirrored room. 'Give my love to the sunrise,' gasps Elsa as she dies, restoring the primacy of the light made by God, not Thomas Edison.

In Stein's version of the Faust myth, diabolism is replaced by science. Welles's interpretation was not so easily atheistic. Flanagan might have disparaged the notion of a diabolical pact, but as Houseman insisted in his memoirs, 'Orson really believed in the devil.' In the Harlem *Macbeth*, he turned Hecate, who presides over the revels of the witches, into a male devil, and issued him with a bullwhip which he used to lash Macbeth onto towards perdition. As Faustus, reeling every evening through a succession of unnatural scenic wonders, Welles let his own insatiably ambitious nature catapult him towards a doom he saw as inevitable. Modifying Houseman's words, it could also be said that he believed he was the devil. In *Bright Lucifer*, he cast himself as the archangel born of light but banished to burning darkness. Even George in *The Magnificent Ambersons*, the role Welles played on the radio, is said by Eugene (in a line of dialogue at the ball, sliced from the final print by the RKO editors) to possess 'the pride of Satan'. In 1958, Welles identified Harry Lime as one more manifestation of 'Lucifer, the fallen angel'. Dinesen's Pellegrina, his female alter ego, barters her soul in exchange for that divine voice, and is nicknamed Lucifera; in *The Dreamers* Welles played Pellegrina's Jewish companion, a magician known as 'the old Wizard of Amsterdam'. With catty perspicacity, MacLíammóir likened Welles to an African witch doctor when they began to rehearse *Othello*: the reason was that he waved his arms about as if casting a spell. Welles adjusted his personal history to match the myth, and claimed that his maternal grandmother was a witch who ritually slaughtered pigeons on a domestic altar.

Flanagan saw Welles's Faust as a physicist not an alchemist. For Welles, however, there was no strict division between magic and science; his Faustian genius juggled both. The stagecraft of the production showed off his skills as a conjurer, with a flying pig, a troupe of lascivious puppets as the Seven Deadly Sins, thunder beneath the floor and forked lightning gashing the air. He had already trafficked with these infernal forces in his Harlem *Macbeth*, and his film of the play is even more overtly satanic. The holy father, a character Welles invented, conducts a non-Shakespearean exorcism, rousing his congregation to renounce Satan and all his works. Malcolm and Macduff on their avenging ride to Dunsinane wear helmets topped by Celtic crosses. But Macbeth, shunning the crucifix, favours the devil's headgear. His square crown has horns at its four corners, and he swigs from a drinking horn on the throne. He skewers the priest with his spear at the end of the film and kills him: Macbeth – in Welles's primitivist interpretation – aspires to be both king and priest, ruling with the aid of fetishes.

Whether or not Welles thought of himself as damned, he understood that the theatre is a place where strange, deranging energies can be enticed into play. Here, rather than in the woods, is the home ground of panic. Jean Cocteau was overwhelmed by the 'barbaric frenzies' of the Harlem *Macbeth*, and later commentators on Welles repeatedly insist on the delirious nature of his films, with their swirling camera movements, toppling angles and overlapping dialogue, all applied to scenes of giddy, contagiously uncontrolled revelry. Henri Agel, using Cocteau's word, called the characteristic Wellesian effect frenetic. Welles loved to choreograph mayhem, as at Arkadin's parties in Spain or Munich or when K in *The Trial* is chased by a posse of little girls who shriek and cackle like trainee witches. Peter Brook, paraphrasing Antonin Artaud, dreamed in 1968 of 'a theatre working like the plague, by intoxication, by infection, by analogy, by magic'. Artaud called this the Theatre of Cruelty. Brook preferred to think of it as the Holy Theatre, sanctified by its rioting madness. More profanely, it might be called the Damned Theatre – licensed to create havoc, torment the nerves, stun the ears with drumming and daze the eyes with pyrotechnics, all of which that 1936 *Macbeth* apparently managed to do. Interestingly, Brook exemplified his theory by referring to the magical practices Welles put on stage in Harlem: 'In Haitian voodoo, all you need to begin a ceremony is a pole and people. You begin to beat the drum and far away in Africa the gods hear the call.' Devils, as *Faustus* made plain, hear it too, which is why Mephistophilis arrives so promptly. Hallie Flanagan praised Welles's *Faustus* for the 'satanic forces' it unleashed, and went on to commend his farce *Horse Eats Hat* for its 'inspired lunacy'.

During these years, Welles had a glancing relationship with Brecht, to whom Blitzstein dedicated *The Cradle Will Rock*. In 1945 Welles planned to direct Brecht's *Galileo*, though he dropped out to mount *Around the World*, his musical version of Verne's novel. Despite their cordiality, the two had opposed views of theatre. Though the conjuring tricks in Welles's *Faustus* deceived the eye, Brecht specified that scene changes in his epic drama must happen in full view because 'this is not magic but / Work, my friends.' Instead of Wellesian frenzy, he inculcated rational alertness. In his 1948 *Short Organum*, he criticised audience members who 'look at the stage as if in a trance – an expression which comes from the Middle Ages, the days of witches and priests', regressing from 'children of the scientific era' into 'a cowed, credulous, hypnotised mass'. Hypnotism, however, was exactly what Welles intended. Brecht warned in 1930 against stupefying the spectator: 'Witchcraft . . . must . . . be fought against. Whatever . . . is likely to produce sordid intoxication, or creates fog, has got to be given up.' For Welles, the theatre's proper business was sorcery, and his film of *Macbeth*, in which he spends much of the time sordidly intoxicated, depends on machines that puff out obfuscating fog. This may have been why Welles so often said he disliked *Rhinoceros*, even though he agreed to direct it. Ionesco explained that his fable about the herd mentality, in which men gang up to join another species, was an attack on 'collective hysteria and the epidemics . . . passed off as ideologies'. How could Welles approve? His own theatre stirred up this contagious ecstasy, rather than counselling against it. In different ways, his *Macbeth* and *Faustus* productions both toyed with the black arts. The blackness of *Macbeth* was a matter of race: Mary McCarthy praised Welles for administering a blood transfusion to 'our white culture'. His fellow magician Jim Steinmeyer called *Faustus* an 'all-black art show', but he was referring to technique rather than skin colour (though Jack Carter, who played Macbeth in Harlem, was re-engaged as Mephistophilis). Drapes of black velvet obliterated the stage; dancers clad in the same fabric remained unseen as they hoisted the dishes at the Pope's banquet high into the air, making it look as if the pig, the beef and the gooey pudding were flying of their own accord. In the theatre, this trickery is known as 'black magic'.

Marlowe's Mephistophilis defrauds Faustus. Quizzed about heaven and hell, he shrugs and cannot give answers. Perhaps he was the first faker in Welles's career. In fact, the alliance between Faustus and Mephistophilis is a collusion of charlatans. Despite the satanic magic of his production, the play forced Welles to consider the possibility that his own powers depended on imposture. There are many Fausts in the

Renaissance tradition: like all myths, this one is a confluence of different versions. Doctor Johannes Faust, who died about 1540, advertised himself as a necromancer. Necromancy summons the dead from their graves for consultations: that is why Macbeth backs away from the ghost of Banquo, who has unearthed himself without being asked to do so. Welles played a black magician who raises the dead in *Necromancy*, also known as *The Witching*, a horror film made in 1972. But contemporary humanists overlooked Faust's occult boasts, and laughed at him as a paltry juggler. Only later did clerical reformers like Luther insist that he was in league with the devil. In 1587, the *Faustbuch* crudely cobbled together stories told about ancient magi and modern wizards and attributed them all to Faust. Marlowe's play, first performed somewhere between 1588 and 1592, had not yet sorted out these contradictions. His Faustus begins as the scornful enemy of God; then he reverts to playing practical jokes, which suggests that he was never more than a mountebank. The contradiction did not bother Welles, because the alternative views of the character were two sides of his own nature – grandiose yet tawdry, a creative genius with a talent for self-destruction.

Welles returned to the role of Faust in 1950, the year after he appeared in *The Third Man* and *Black Magic*. His sense of the character was now richer and more contradictory, because he incorporated all that had happened to him in the previous decade. His Hollywood contract, which gratified his most vainglorious wishes, turned out to be a Faustian bargain. He was outsmarted by the cynical and devious studio executives, who almost destroyed *Citizen Kane* in deference to Hearst, recut *The Magnificent Ambersons* in his absence, and cancelled his South American film, *It's All True*. By 1950 he had decamped to Europe, where he was reduced to financing his own projects. He had begun *Othello*, but soon ran out of money. By redeploying the actors in two stage shows, he hoped to keep his cast together and raise funds to continue filming.

First, in Paris, he presented *The Beautiful and the Damned*, which comprised two of his own plays. Suzanne Cloutier, his Desdemona, represented beauty in a rancorous satire, *The Unthinking Lobster*. Hollywood is making tawdry religious films about miracle-workers like Bernadette. The star of one such vehicle is fired for looking insufficiently spiritual; the typist who replaces her actually possesses saintly powers, and cures the ailments of some deformed extras. As a result, Hollywood – which had always been concerned with the manufacture of divinities – becomes an official site of pilgrimage. Penitents crawl on their knees through the studio gates in quest of indulgences, souvenir shops do a brisk trade in amulets, but otherwise the film industry is stalled. Eventually an archangel swoops down to negotiate a deal with the executives in the front office. The emissary promises an end to miracles, so long as Hollywood makes no more religious films: heaven is sickened by the treacly, commercialised piety of the earthlings, while the earthly bosses are relieved to be left in charge of their own profane realm.

Welles incarnated damnation by playing Faust in the second play of the evening, *Time Runs*, with Hilton Edwards (Roderigo in the *Othello* film) as Mephistophilis. He pasted together a multi-faceted account of the satanic over-reacher from Marlowe, Milton's *Paradise Lost* and Dante's *Divine Comedy*, commissioning songs from Duke Ellington and hiring Eartha Kitt, his Helen of Troy, to sing them. The title for this second part came from the last gabbling soliloquy of Marlowe's Faustus as his final hour speeds by:

> The stars move still, time runs, the clock will strike,
> The devil will come, and Faustus must be damn'd.

The pace of time terrified Welles, who by 1950 felt he had squandered his youth and forfeited its promise. A clock remorselessly ticks through the twenty-five minutes of *The Fountain of Youth* and through the first three minutes of *Touch of Evil*, both made in 1958. In one case the timer is counting down to decay, while in the other it leads to an explosion.

The Beautiful and the Damned proved unprofitable, so Welles instantly had half-a-dozen brilliant, unworkable new ideas. He dropped *The Unthinking Lobster* but preserved *Time Runs* and added to it a shortened version of the first act of Wilde's *The Importance of Being Earnest*, a set of songs by Eartha Kitt, the final scene from the third part of Shakespeare's *Henry VI*, and a magic act of his own; he called this compendium *An Evening with Orson Welles* and performed it during the summer of 1950 in Frankfurt, Hamburg, Munich, Düsseldorf, Berlin and Brussels, after which he used the cash to resume work on *Othello*. He and MacLíammóir had three scenes together in the course of the evening. They played Faustus and Mephistophilis, analogues for their Othello and Iago. Then they returned as Wilde's flirtatious dandies Algernon and Jack (who are both beautiful and damned). Finally, Welles as Gloucester, the future Richard III, killed MacLíammóir's effete Henry VI. Lying uncomfortably dead on the stage, MacLíammóir planned his diary entry for the day; his chronicle of the tour was published in 1961.

Audiences in the ruined cities of Germany were puzzled, then irritated by the show. Muddled advertising led them to expect that Welles would be playing Goethe's Faust, not Marlowe's Faustus. There was a crucial difference. Goethe's hero is concerned for the betterment of the world, and he has none of the squalid lust and moral cowardice Marlowe found in the character. Germany itself had grown comfortably accustomed to seeing its own experience between 1933 and 1945 as a Faustian adventure; Thomas Mann's novel *Doktor Faustus*, which treated the Nazi experiment as a grandiosely self-destructive quest, was published the year before Welles's tour. Germans who wanted to sentimentalise or ennoble the country's downfall were affronted by Marlowe's character, whose sole ambition is to play tricks and enjoy himself – a man who wastes time, and collapses in gibbering, unredeemed terror when his time runs out. Welles, who claimed to hate the Faustian part of himself, refused to countenance the idea that a diabolical genius could lead a man or a country astray. To disabuse the Germans of their infatuation with a Faust who was sublimely errant, the digest of the myth that he took on tour mixed up tragedy, comedy of manners, jazz (which the Nazis had condemned on racial grounds) and some consciously deceitful magic tricks. Returning to *Othello*, he told MacLíammóir not to play a Mephistophelean Iago. That, he said, was 'démodé'; rather than romantically pondering the mystery of evil, he preferred to think that Iago had a banal, rankling grudge, motivated by sexual impotence and envy.

His attempt to re-educate the conquered Germans and to shed his own Faustian mystique was a failure. His fans insisted on seeing the villain as a hero. If he wouldn't allow them to admire him as Goethe's Faust, they were determined to acclaim him as Harry Lime, who for them was sanctified, despite his crimes, by his aura of celebrity. In Hamburg Welles was besieged by women shrieking 'der Dritte Mann! der Dritte Mann!' He told them that he found it 'nauseating to his soul' to be identified with Harry, which scared them off. But in self-defence he employed methods resembling those of the Faustian heroes he played. He glared at the women, MacLíammóir noted, like a voodoo mask, and threatened, if they went on calling him the Third Man, to put them to death. Harry, murderously charming, would have behaved in exactly the same way.

Welles could not divest himself of the character, who was recognised by the Germans as a modern Faust. The year after *Time Runs*, he played Harry in a series of radio broadcasts, using the money to pay for the editing of *Othello*. He wrote some episodes himself; in one of these, *A Ticket to Tangiers*, he begins by admitting – what choice did he have? – that 'I am Harry Lime' and takes it for granted, with a long-suffering sigh, that his listeners will all 'have seen the movie *The Third Man*'. He explains away his death in the sewer, but in this ghostly afterlife he is still haunted by the jaunty tune played by Anton Karas on the zither. He is even required to whistle it to identify himself (which Lime in the film never has to do). Lured to Tangiers by a drug-smuggling air hostess called Patsy, Harry sniffily condemns heroin as 'nasty and habit-forming', and reminds her that its sale is controlled by international law – a far cry from the Viennese Harry with his watered-down penicillin. He dupes the gangsters by selling them seven packets of confectioner's sugar, and keeps the prayer rug the consignment was wrapped in. He punningly tells the treacherous Patsy, 'There isn't any heroin in this story, only a hero'; he might be O'Hara in *The Lady from Shanghai* all over again, scornfully rejecting a heroine who is as addictive and deranging as heroin. Patsy sneers 'So *this* is the notorious Harry Lime?' But here Welles's irony intervened. How could he make the satanic Harry so angelic? Harry's reply raises the charges of fraudulence and self-counterfeiting Welles so often made against himself. Many people, he points out, know how to whistle that Karas tune. 'Maybe I'm not Harry Lime,' he says, 'not the original but a facsimile.' Welles lets Harry off the hook, but only by placing himself on it, conceding that – as the imitator of all his successive fictional selves – he no longer knows who he is.

This is why, at once fondly remembering and disparaging his youthful bravado, Welles returned to that 1937 *Faustus* in his script for *The Cradle Will Rock*. He did so in order to demolish its illusions. In the script, he examines the basement beneath the stage, analyses the positioning of spotlights and the use of mirrors; though the production relied on blackness, he specifies that the sequence with the floating pig was to be filmed in daylight and 'without camera tricks'. The old magician allows us to see through his impostures, and thereby renounces his power over us. He had obviously read the memoir in which Houseman identified him with Faustus. Now he bestowed a subtler, more painfully intimate insight on the fictional Houseman, who – given an air of cool, incontrovertible authority by the stage directions in the script – says 'I should explain something about Orson. He is Mephistophilis to his own Faust.' The script directs that there should be an 'interested murmur' among the backstage listeners when Houseman makes this comment. The myth now explains how a man could be his worst enemy, and nurturing inside him the devil who caused his downfall.

Magic, the lowly craft of Marlowe's Faust, remained part of Welles's stock in trade. In *Casino Royale*, playing Le Chiffre, he amuses himself by causing a courtesan to hover above the gaming table. This, he says, is 'an illusion taught to me by an ancient vegetarian in the mountain fastnesses of Tibet'.

In 1945, Irving Penn photographed Welles, calling the result *Portrait with Symbols*. With a raffish bow tie and boyishly tousled hair, he gives the camera a sideways look, as shifty as a naughty child warily awaiting forgiveness. A cigar in his hand, he rests one foot on a table where Penn laid out the gadgetry of his various arts, along with other props that mutely comment on his character. Beside him hangs a print of a gryphon in flight attached to its prey, with jagged Gothic cliffs in the background. The beast might be Welles's familiar, a reminder of Faust's diabolical helper. A gramophone horn, growing out of an antique still camera, recalls his radio days; a train on circular tracks alludes to his description of a movie set. More puzzlingly, a horn lies propped on its back, its mouthpiece almost plugged into the end of Welles's cigar. The conjunction comments on the supplementary art of publicity: Welles was an expert at blowing his own trumpet. But the cigar suggests how self-wasting the effort of puffery must be. A magician's accoutrements are strewn about – a top hat, a hoop, a raven that is either stuffed or very well-trained. Here, too, is the evidence of Welles's Falstaffian appetites, a glass of beer and a carafe of red wine. Another pair of symbols functions as a memento mori: a distended red balloon and a stick of dynamite. The balloon jokes about Welles's inflation. The Irish critic Mary Manning, meeting him in New York in 1940, called him 'a big gas-filled balloon'. The stick of dynamite warns of the same fate as the balloon. The photograph prophesies that Welles will either burst or blow himself up. Was the magician entirely in control of his own tricks? And what value did those tricks have?

'Magic' in André Gide's novel *The Counterfeiters* is a schoolboy code word for clandestine practices that are deemed to be vicious. The suicidal Boris has indulged in them, and falls neurotically ill as a result of his guilt. The secret 'magic', with its facile and self-defrauding ecstasy, is masturbation. Welles too thought of his aptitude for magic as a shameful, immature weakness. He once conceded that magic bores women and only appeals to men. Could this be because it is self-soliciting, making happiness materialise too easily? Women have no use for its illusory benefits, which the grown-ups in Gide's novel call 'imaginary goods'; they expect men to grapple with reality rather than resorting to fantasy.

In *The Golden Bough*, a study of myth published in 1890, James G. Frazer concluded that the evolution of human intelligence entwined 'the black thread of magic, the red thread of religion, and the white thread of science'. Those 'conflicting tendencies' accounted for 'the state of modern thought'. Knotted and tangled, they also accounted for Welles's mixed motives. Pico della Mirandola thought that the arts of the human magician dazingly replicated the way in which nature had brought forth man. Magic – at least what the Renaissance called white magic – was for him 'a marriage of heaven and earth'; black magic, as practised by Faustus, coupled earth and hell. But by the time Marlowe wrote his play, magic was in retreat. The exorcism was performed by Francis Bacon, whose pronouncements on the subject directly address some of Welles's lifelong concerns.

In 1594, during the Gray's Inn Revels, Bacon advised an imaginary prince to exchange the magi for the wiser counsel of natural philosophers, or scientists. In 1605, in his treatise *Of the Advancement of Learning*, dedicated to King James I, he aimed to construct 'a small Globe of the Intellectual World', which was his alternative to the Globe in which Shakespeare performed his magic; 'it is not good', Bacon averred, 'to stay too long in the theatre.' He saw science as whitened, purified magic, and decried witchcraft as a 'declination from religion'. He hoped that King James would ground and rationalise 'the Secrets and Mysteries of Learning', leading his subjects through 'the entrance into the Kingdom of Man, founded on the sciences'. These may have been commendable aims, but Welles refuted them more than three centuries later, when the legacy of scientific reason seemed more questionable. Bacon predicted that, when 'Miracles and Wonders' were overruled by science, his prince would become a Trismegistus. This was the honorific name given to the Greek god Hermes, triply empowered as priest, king and philosopher, and awarded authority over religion, law and art. Welles knew that this potentate was merely a by-product of the slippery polynymy that begets all our myths. Hermes is Mercury the trickster, and a few months after that *Faustus* production Welles placed his theatre under the patronage of this intellectually disreputable god.

87

Another of Bacon's missions had an unexpected resonance for Welles. In the *Advancement*, he discusses 'the facility of credit' (by which he means credulity, not one of those tolerant long-term financial agreements that Welles tried in vain to set up with studios and private backers). He names three 'sciences . . . which have had better confederacy with the imagination of man than with his reason': astrology, natural magic and alchemy. These pseudo-sciences were liable to 'error and vanity; which the great professors themselves have sought to veil over and conceal by enigmatical writings' and 'other devices to save the credit of impostures'. Is the magician, when compared with the true scientist, no better than a liar and an intellectual pickpocket? Welles, whose mind was divided on the issue, answered Bacon's charge in two contradictory ways. With telling anachronism, he used the word 'credit' just as Bacon did. In *Touch of Evil*, when the charges Vargas makes against Quinlan seem to have been disproved, he turns to his sceptical ally Schwartz and asks 'Have I still any credit left with you?' It is an unidiomatic, beautifully ambiguous turn of phrase. Referring to his own believability, Vargas deliberately evokes the financial analogy: trust is like credit, and with friends we have a fund of it on which we can draw. Vargas wants to know how much is left in his account. Schwartz evasively answers 'Some.' Welles the moralist agrees with Bacon that credit must not be too facile. We are required to provide evidence for what we say, using scientific methods (as Vargas eventually does, with Schwartz's help); we are in debt to the truth, and must make regular payments. Welles may have respected the principle, but he flouted it in practice and justified his derelictions by citing the example of Bacon himself. Discussing Falstaff's chicanery as a recruiting officer, Welles paused during his interview with Marienstras to ask himself who, after Shakespeare, was the greatest man in Elizabethan England. He answered 'I'd say it was Francis Bacon.' He then pointed out that Bacon, condemned for corruption, had tumbled from the top of society to the bottom, from Chancellor to felon. If Bacon took bribes, why – Welles asked – shouldn't poor Falstaff do the same? And why also should Welles have been expected to settle with creditors or tax inspectors?

Bacon succeeded in casting out magic, and in his *Novum Organum* science brings philosophy down 'from heaven to earth'. But in the nineteenth century, when Goethe restored Faust's magic powers, an earth transformed by science and technology seemed indistinguishable from heaven. Welles was born into an America where life was newly eased by machines, and bodies were propelled through space by motor cars. The country could hardly accredit its astral good fortune: Faust's wishes had been granted, apparently without any of the need for any arrangement with the devil. In 1932, in his book *Wild Talents*, Charles Fort cleanly dissociated magic from the occult, and celebrated 'sorceries as public utilities'.

Melville teased this irreligious mentality in *The Confidence-Man*, where a conjurer on the Mississippi boat brags that his trick with coins proves that 'the age of magic and magicians is not over'. The hustler predicts that American affluence – helped along by diddles and swindles – will perform the great work that the Renaissance entrusted to alchemy, which set out to transfigure base reality and gild it. 'We golden boys, we moderns,' he says, can look forward to a literal golden age of unlimited financial credit, 'when the whole world shall have been genialised'. Melville's novel was published in 1857; in 1889 Mark Twain took up the subject of science and its competition with magic in *A Connecticut Yankee in King Arthur's Court*. Twain's satire treats American inventions as white magic, and teasingly refers to innovators like Alexander Graham Bell as gods, the creators of this paradise. The narrator Hank Morgan is dreamily repatriated from nineteenth-century America to sixth-century England, and sets about industrialising this backward realm. The results suggest that science might be malevolent magic, reponsible – like the obnoxious, lethal horseless carriages in *The Magnificent Ambersons* – for the disenchantment and desecration of an older, less efficient but more lovably idealistic world.

Welles grew up in 'Mark Twain country', as he told Bogdanovich when describing holidays in the rural retreat of Grand Detour in Illinois. He adapted *Huckleberry Finn* for radio, and perhaps he also made use of *A Connecticut Yankee*: the anachronistic plot of his own *Don Quixote* film – which projects Quixote and Sancho forward from sixteenth-century to twentieth-century Spain – reverses the time-travel in Twain's novel, but makes the same abrasive contrast between different ages. At Twain's Camelot, the knight-errant (a figure dear to Welles, and a self-image in his later years of quixotic wandering) is a travelling salesman. Morgan's magical bequests to King Arthur include some of the contraptions that disfigure the landscape in Welles's films. He introduces the telegraph and telephone, laying ground wires because poles would attract too much attention. Such poles, however, span the grimy, lowered sky when George trudges home at the end of *The Magnificent Ambersons*. 'I hate a country without a derrick,' remarks the Yankee, who would have admired the creaking derricks that drill for oil along the ravaged Californian coast in *Touch of Evil*. And when Morgan hears newspaper headlines being shouted in the street, he feels he has witnessed a 'mighty birth', a prophetic annunciation of Kane and his empire of loud, dirty print: 'One greater than kings had arrived – the newsboy.' After overthrowing chivalry, Morgan congratulates himself that 'the march of civilization was begun'. As Spengler would have understood, this is Faust talking.

Modern science confronts antique sorcery in Twain's novel. Morgan outwits Merlin by deploying a dynamite bomb, whose black magic instantaneously abolishes the world, reducing 'the chivalry of England' to 'homogenous protoplasm, with alloys of iron and buttons'. Welles staged the same showdown between medieval and modern worlds at the battle of Shrewsbury in *Chimes at Midnight*. On other occasions, his characters actually use dynamite to speed the pace of change. Dynamite is the murder weapon in *Touch of Evil*, stolen from supplies used to blast a highway through a hill, and K's killers in *The Trial* blow him up rather than stabbing him, as they do in Kafka's novel. Such miracles or wonders, as Twain (like Bacon) sarcastically calls them, are the preserve of science. All that Merlin can manage is pretence. Morgan pities him because 'he did everything by incantations; he never used his intellect'. He also 'believed in his own magic; and no magician can thrive who is handicapped with a superstition like that'. Welles did not share this superstition, but he was equally sceptical about the magical powers of science. Sooner a magician who understands that he is dealing with illusions than a scientist fanatically convinced that he knows the truth. Welles mistrusted Merlin's contemporary heirs. Experts, he argues in *F for Fake*, are now our oracles, speaking with 'the absolute authority of the computer'; his script for *The Trial* describes a computer operator (played by Katina Paxinou, whose role was eventually cut) as 'the priestess serving a powerful, millenary mystery' – a witch doctor in a white lab coat. In 1955, justifying his *War of the Worlds* hoax, he complained that Americans had too much faith in radio, 'this new magic box'. The broadcast, he said, 'was an assault on the credibility of that machine'.

L. Frank Baum's stories about the Wizard of Oz, published between 1904 and 1919, used magic to explain and lament the abrupt disappearance of the genteel, pastoral, unmechanised America in which Welles grew up. The wizard of course is a fraud, like Twain's Merlin and like the Welles of *F for Fake*. He complains that 'all these people make me do things that everybody knows can't be done'. This is what makes him so pathetic, especially when he is played by Frank Morgan, first seen touring Kansas as Professor Marvel, in the 1939 film. *The Wizard of Oz* assesses the social changes that Welles lived through by reviving the distinction between black and white magic. The Wicked Witch of the West, with her skywriting and her air force of gnomes, represents a science that is determined to uproot people and dispense with ancient verities. She is the evil genius of what Americans had come to call Popular Mechanics. Her whiter opponents, the Good Witch and the Wizard himself, are powerless to resist. And Dorothy cannot object, since she longs to set out on the road that leads to Oz – which happens to resemble Manhattan, the destination of all ambitious dreamers from the hinterland. The film fudges the choice by allowing her to enjoy the polychrome delights of Oz before going back to her staid monochrome home in Kansas. Welles, however, never returned to Grand Detour.

Between 1939 and 1958, T. H. White published his own Arthurian chronicle, *The Once and Future King*, using magic to analyse and deplore the scientific disasters of modern history; this became one of Welles's talismanic books, which he compulsively recommended to friends. White's Arthur is nicknamed the Wart, which rhymes with Art. He is the artist, apprenticed to Merlyn who practises magic but sternly refuses to use it to ease life, as if it were merely technology. He will not employ charms to trap birds. What he calls 'the Great Arts' forbid glib tricks. You must cut a statue out with a chisel, not conjure it up by abracadabra. Art requires work, whereas technology alleviates our labour. 'White magic, I hope?' Sir Ector asks Merlyn. 'Arthur's civilization', as White points out, 'was [not] weak in this famous science of ours.' He warns us not to be scornful of alchemy, since our scientific culture is getting nearer to it by splitting the atom. There is black magic here as well. Mordred, Arthur's bastard son who destroys Camelot, practises a devaluing alchemy in reverse. He fakes emotions that he does not feel: 'he was acting, and had ceased to be real'. He has learned this talent from his mother, whose presence in him makes him a necromancer: 'now that she was dead, he had become her grave'. As with Faustus and Mephistophilis, Welles could see Merlyn and Mordred as his good and evil angels; once more he was both hero and villain.

White jocularly mentions a medieval magician called Baptista Porta, who apparently 'invented the cinema – though he sensibly declined to develop it'. Thanks to his renunciation, Lancelot and Guinever can fall in love properly, rather than mimicking 'the ignoble spasms of the cinematograph'. Welles's personal genealogy of the medium also traced it back to a magus. Film, he hoped, was an art in which magic and science, at odds since the Renaissance, might at last make peace. Therefore, in a diagram illustrating the family tree of cinema, he placed himself in a tradition deriving from Georges Méliès. A professional magician, Méliès recorded the illusions of his 'théâtre de féerie' on film between 1897 and 1908. He had studied with Robert-Houdin, to whom Welles pays ceremonious tribute at the beginning of *F for Fake*. Robert-Houdin designed mechanical conjuring equipment which made bodies appear to float, and worked out a signalling system for magicians who specialised in thought transference, used by Welles when he roped in accomplices to help him perform tricks with cards or coins. By applying Robert-Houdin's deceptive science, Méliès claimed to have personally discovered 'all the so-called 'mysterious' processes of the cinematograph'. The first dissolve occurred between two scenes in his 1902 fantasy about a farcical rocket trip to the moon; he happened upon the spectral possibilities of double exposure when the film jammed in his camera.

Welles was right to claim Méliès as an ancestor, though he complicated his pedigree by placing D. W. Griffith and Eisenstein on the same branch of the tree. Was it really possible to be influenced by all three? Perhaps Griffith's dramatisation of social change in *The Birth of a Nation* prompted the chronicle of America's emergence from the nineteenth century in *Citizen Kane* and *The Magnificent Ambersons*; Eisenstein is present in the heroic barbarism of Welles's *Macbeth*, in his solemn, processional choreography of the Brazilian fisherman's funeral in *It's All True*, and in the brutal battle in *Chimes at Midnight*. But the dominant influence was always Méliès. *Citizen Kane*, with its baffling array of optical trickery, added to the store of gimmicks devised by Méliès, and a poster for one of his films appears outside the cinema in *The Magnificent Ambersons* – arguably too avant-garde for a town in Indiana. In his 1946 staging of *Around the World*, Welles returned this magic to the theatre, where Méliès began. A railway bridge collapsed, an oil well spouted, and an eagle swooped down to gather up Fogg like Ganymede. The show's initial producer Mike Todd filmed *Around the World in 80 Days* in 1956, pointedly excluding Welles from the project but borrowing his homage to Méliès. The film begins with an abbreviation of Méliès's *Voyage to the Moon*, followed by documentary footage of a rocket launch in the American desert. Welles reclaimed Méliès for himself in his *Don Quixote* project, which sends Quixote and Sancho to the moon.

Cocteau in 1946 praised Welles for extending the 'mischievous cunning' of Méliès to a realer world. 'A wave of the wand is too easy,' Cocteau said, and he admired the way that Welles, doing without surreal darkness, created magic 'in the half-light of the extraordinary house in which he places the Ambersons'. A dark house is the magician's lair, whether it is located in the Florida swamps like Xanadu, in a San Francisco amusement park like the funfair in *The Lady from Shanghai*, or inside the disused Gare d'Orsay, where Welles rigged up an entire labyrinthine city for *The Trial*. Truffaut, reviewing *Touch of Evil* in 1958, was reminded that 'Méliès and Feuillade were among the pioneers of cinema.' (Feuillade filmed the *Fantômas* serials in 1913–14, making the grey, grainy Paris streets look haunted.) Ignoring the affinities between *Touch of Evil* and film noir, Truffaut brilliantly acclaimed it as 'a magical film that brings to mind fairy tales such as Beauty and the Beast or Tom Thumb'. As Welles recognised in acknowledging Méliès, his films were exercises in trompe-l'oeil. Out of money as usual, he amazed the crew of *Othello* by improvising the hero's funeral at the harbour in Cyprus using only a few cheap ingredients he was able to lay his hands on. He erected some rickety platforms in the landlocked Roman countryside, and stood extras on the rostra to suggest the receding perspective of Renaissance paintings. Then he strung bed sheets on a line near a bowl of water. When the sun struck the water and bounced its reflections onto the sheets, the bowl became a miniature Mediterranean and the linen stood in for the flapping sails of the Venetian fleet. The budget of *Chimes at Midnight* did not allow for a crowd to witness Henry V's coronation, so Welles relied on a row of cardboard scarecrows, with scraps of fabric attached to them fluttering in a breeze. These were exercises in sorcery performed by a grown-up who willed himself back into credulous infancy. Welles defined magic as 'a return to childhood, playing with toys. It's pure play.' Old, dying men in *Citizen Kane*, *Chimes at Midnight* and *The Immortal Story* revert to the nursery, clutching their toys – a globe of snow, a bottle, a conch – and reciting the spells that made them feel secure when they were children.

'I am not a magician,' Quixote indignantly declares in Welles's film. 'You are when you talk about Dulcinea,' replies Sancho Panza. Magicians are Quixote's avowed enemies, enchanters who deform and distort reality. But Quixote himself, as Sancho knows, has magically transformed a sluttish village girl whose breath smells of onions into a courtly paragon. Though Quixote refuses the compliment, Welles himself must have envied Mark Twain's Merlin. 'Great magic,' Welles once said with a sigh, 'you know, there's a moment when you suspend disbelief.' All his life, he tried without success to make himself believe in his own magic.

Welles performed one of his earliest magic tricks on the radio, where his sleight of hand had to be believed because listeners could not see it. In his 1937 *Les misérables,* Jean Valjean inexplicably escapes from his pursuers in a closed-off street. This feat, invisibly performed by Welles the actor and breathlessly described by Welles the narrator, is as magical a disappearing act as that of Harry Lime, who vanishes from an empty square. Valjean scales an eighteen-foot wall without a rope or any other support but his own muscular control. During his term as a galley slave he has 'learned the dark sciences of the impossible', which include such techniques. On the other side of the wall is a convent garden. Valjean tells the bewildered gardener 'I fell from the sky', but the old man prefers to think 'You have fallen from heaven': God must have picked him up to have a look at him, then set him down again – though in the wrong place. Later, smuggled out of his hiding place in the convent inside a coffin, Valjean manages another miracle. He dies (or pretends to), is buried and then resurrected. The magician in *Journey into Fear* is less fortunate. Billing himself as 'le roi des arts diaboliques', he beds down with his ancestors in a coffin. He confidently expects to rise again, but is shot before he can do so.

Welles's South American compilation included a Mexican episode, filmed by his deputy Norman Foster. It contains a scene of harmless white magic, in which a peasant boy brings his pet bull Bonito to church to be blessed – along with a festooned rabble of mules, oxen, sheep, chickens and dogs – by the local priest. Goats were slaughtered and skinned for the voodoo drums in the Harlem *Macbeth*. Tragedy requires such sacrifices, but here comedy doles out a smiling salvation, even for animals which supposedly lack souls. Welles delegated the sentimental benediction to Foster; meanwhile, in Rio, he acquainted himself with a more savage, bloodthirsty magic by watching the ritual slaughter of roosters at African rites in the slums. After the studio cancelled *It's All True*, he enjoyed describing the curse placed on the project by a witch doctor who, balked at his consultant's fee, pierced the script with a steel needle which had a thread of red wool spooled through it. When he told the story on television, he deferentially referred to the disgruntled sorcerer simply as 'the doctor', according him the same status as Marlowe's Faustus. Then in 1954, for his role in *Trouble in the Glen*, he adopted a more scornful view of such practices. In this comedy directed by Herbert Wilcox, Welles plays an Argentinian moneybags who inherits a Scottish castle. He sneers at the folklore of his tenants, but despite his disbelief, a white, healing magic prevails, bestowing grace like the village priest in *It's All True*. The father of a little girl bedridden by polio assures her that she will be cured by magic. The 'magic ways' he invokes include physiotherapy, and among the 'magic words' he recites is gammaglobulin.

Welles intermittently interrupted his other activities to devote himself to magic. In 1943, his *Mercury Wonder Show*, occupying a tent on Cahuenga Boulevard in Los Angeles, entertained troops on their way to or from battle stations in the Pacific. Marlene Dietrich allowed Welles to saw her in half; his grizzled, undersized chauffeur George 'Shorty' Chirello – later cast as Macbeth's valet in the 1948 film – fetched and carried, while Agnes Moorehead played the calliope. In what was billed as the 'Grand Finale Voodoo!', Joseph Cotten, renamed Jo-Jo the Great, reprised his 'interesting experiences among the witch doctors in dark Africa'. Having read minds, plucked rabbits from hats and 'defied the laws of science in feats of legerdemain', Welles said to his audience 'We trust you like to be fooled, and we hope we fooled you.' An excerpt from his act appears in *Follow the Boys*, a compendium of skits for servicemen assembled in 1944. He introduces himself with an undiabolical reprise of the black magic he used in *Faustus*: a cigar glides through the air, spontaneously plugs itself into his mouth, then flies away.

Volunteering to perform in *Follow the Boys*, Welles calls himself 'an amateur magician'. The atmosphere is relaxed, but here too he tensely balances the innocent playfulness of magic and its possible malevolence. Dietrich treats her own sectioning as a joke. Costumed as an oriental temple girl, she puffs lazily on a cigarette and shrieks with glee as the saw bites into her: 'It tickles!' When the operation is complete, her lower half wanders off independently. Welles asks anyone who sees Miss Dietrich's missing legs to direct them back to the show tent, because they're wearing her last pair of nylons. He then tries hypnosis to convince her that she is whole again, and tells her to gaze into the yolks of his eyes. She stares at him with her usual impassivity, and it is he who blinks, blacks out and keels over – an inefficient sorcerer, outwitted by his apprentice.

Yet, despite this good-humoured self-mockery, the performance hints at shadier, more psychologically sinister purposes. In *Follow the Boys* Welles does not seal Dietrich invisibly in a casket; she stands upright for surgery, with a box around her midriff. He calls this tub her 'wooden rompers'. It ought to function as a chastity belt, but with the saw's ticklish help she breaches it. The upper and lower halves of the female body, goddess and beast, do not belong together. The blade sets free her ulterior, and her legs stroll away to fraternise. Dietrich signed on for the show because – as she purrs when questioned by Welles – she would go anywhere for the company of soldiers, sailors and marines. Lacking legs, she is given a little pedestal to support what remains of her. Now her treacherous nether parts have been lopped off, she can pretend to be a classical bust. Suzanne Cloutier, the last of the Desdemonas Welles used in his *Othello* film, said that he 'always put women on a pedestal. He thought of them as goddesses, and then, when they proved unworthy . . .' The ellipsis hinted at untold rages and revenges.

In 1947 Welles contributed a foreword to *Magic as a Hobby*, a collection of tricks – including one of Welles's own – by Bruce Elliott. Establishing its role in Welles's story, the book has an epigraph from Marlowe's *Faustus*. The lines chosen are a choral lament for the hero's intellectual betrayal and spiritual corruption:

> Nothing so sweet as magic is to him,
> Which he prefers before his chiefest bliss.

Welles's foreword is characteristically generous and graceful, and also ironic in its attitude to magic. He begins by deploring the book he has volunteered to puff (and in doing so he manages a sly allusion to an untrustworthy Shakespearean rhetorician: 'I come not to bury magic,' he says, half-quoting Antony). He worries because Elliott's work gives away the magician's jealously guarded lore and shows, with the aid of diagrams, how tricks can be performed. In 'magic's golden age', Welles insists, practitioners 'never permitted disenchantment'; having acknowledged magic's connection with alchemy, he concludes that we now live in 'the least interesting and least secretive of all the ages of magic'. The art has 'fallen into decadence', and his commentary on its decline might be a recollection of that outing to the squalid Turkish nightclub in *Journey into Fear*: 'Wizards, deposed from the appropriate gilt and glamour of the playhouse, work their wonders . . . in the frowzy hubbub of the cabaret, competing with bad whiskey for control of their beholders' minds.' This warning is meant to inculcate a 'high respect' or reverence for a profession that once had supernatural ambitions. 'The reader', he says, 'proceeds at magic's risk', but if his intentions are honourable he will find that 'here . . . – in spite of years of syndicated exposés – are miracles.' And if not, Welles calculates the consequences with the aid of another reference to Shakespeare: 'something is rotten in the state of the Union'. Our indifference to magic shows that we have outgrown the capacity for astonishment and delight; if we cannot consent to be fooled, then we are incapable of faith.

Having announced that 'a real magician's task . . . is to abolish the solution', Welles proceeded, with his usual double-mindedness, to break that rule by allowing Elliott to explicate one of the tricks in his personal repertory. The demystification does no harm, because the routine hints at a greater Wellesian mystery. The trick Elliott describes begins with a folding coin, which Welles borrows from someone in the audience and then causes to vanish. He then produces a grapefruit, and says that the vanished coin is now inside it. He cuts it open and finds that the grapefruit actually contains an orange. He takes his penknife to the orange, which turns out to have swallowed an egg. Cracking the egg, he roots around inside the glutinous mess and discovers the missing coin: 'Climax!' The routine, according to Elliott, is fussy to prepare, since you have to hollow out the grapefruit and the orange, but easy to execute. He reminds amateurs to be sure the egg is fresh.

Knowing how it is done does not decrease our respect for Welles the 'wonder-worker', as Elliott calls him, because the routine is a rehearsal of the ultimate, insoluble Wellesian mystery – one of his continuing preoccupations, from Kane's smashing of his globe to Quinlan's inadvertent cracking of an egg. How can you account for the origins of your own inborn imagination? How is genius generated? The grapefruit, orange and egg are worlds within worlds. Each time we penetrate one container we find another. The last of these is the most fertile and also the most fragile. Does creative enquiry require an act of violent intrusion and irreparable destruction, like the splitting of the atom or a war of the worlds? Magic here playfully enacts a metaphysical parable. At the same time, since the magus is a mountebank, it involves a practical joke. Welles, when rounding up finance for his films, regularly made other people's money vanish. They seldom got it back, and might not even have minded if their coins had been returned with egg stains on them.

In 1947, as well as writing this small essay on magic, Welles played a latter-day Faust in *Black Magic*. Gregory Ratoff supposedly directed the film, though Welles is alleged to have put a spell on him and taken over when he fell asleep. The black magician here is Cagliostro, a hypnotist who used his mind-controlling mumbo-jumbo to gain power at a succession of courts in late eighteenth-century Europe. In a prologue to the film, the elder Alexandre Dumas wonders 'Was he a charlatan?' This was the question always being asked about Welles, who also asked it of himself. Dumas fils dismisses Cagliostro as a faker, but his father, now fictionalising his career, is not so sure. 'I wrote them,' he says, enumerating his previous books. 'This man's writing me!' Welles knew what this state of possession felt like. He too was taken over, pre-empted and predestined, by the characters he played – Faust, Kurtz, Ahab, Lime, Lear, Falstaff. Dumas père muses on the alternatives, as if pondering Welles: he is unable to decide whether his hero is a fool, a mountebank, or a devil.

Welles's Cagliostro begins by performing stunts at a Viennese carnival, like Welles busking in the circus tent on Cahuenga Boulevard. There he wore a silken gown topped by a fez; in *Black Magic* he first sports a flashier astrological robe inlaid with stars and a witch's peaked hat, though he trades up to the fez when his career takes him to the French court. With the myth-maker's synthetic glibness, he stitches on to his costume (as Dumas notes) 'mystic symbols, and insignia stolen from secret fraternal societies' like the Freemasons. In Vienna, Cagliostro has not yet perfected his satanic act. He smirks and winks, overdoing the barbarous accent that is one of his arcane credentials. After making a woman vanish and transforming himself into a circus clown, he settles down to tout the elixir of life, 'bottled by me in the fountains of youth'. That, of course, was the potion whose efficacy Welles derided a decade later when he made his *Fountain of Youth* for television. He surprises himself when he saves the life of a hag who has drunk lamp fluid. In a shot that looks inimitably Wellesian, his face is surrounded by shadow as his gleaming eyes stare into the camera: film, invading our brains by way of the eyes, also has a hypnotic power over our reason. Cagliostro's skills are accredited by a Viennese doctor, who turns out to be Franz Anton Mesmer, the specialist in animal magnetism. Again there is a reminiscence of the *Wonder Show*, when Welles as carnival barker promised customers they would see 'original experiments in animal magnetism'. When Cagliostro reaches France, Marie Antoinette laughs at him as a 'witch doctor'. But for Welles, witch doctors were doctors too, and in an article in the *New York Times* he insisted that magicians who practised faith healing could be 'more successful in less time than the legitimate man of medicine'. As well as curing, they could kill. Abdul, the witch doctor in the cast of the Harlem *Macbeth*, reportedly drummed to death a critic who wrote a bad notice of the show: another one of the Welles stories that, like his hypnotising of Ratoff, ought to be true even if it is not. Adopting the shaman's techniques, Cagliostro heals a crowd of palsied, paralysed invalids, who throw away their crutches and, only too nimbly, begin a minuet: they are courtiers, shamming to trap him. He responds to this practical joke by forcing one of the dancers to his knees and crippling him. A faker or a veritable evil genius?

'Power! power! power!' raves Cagliostro during his trial. Dumas, narrating the film, says that 'the magnificent charlatan' exploited 'hysterical faith and emotional instability . . . to sell himself as a god'. The comment could be applied to other Welles characters. Kurtz in *Heart of Darkness* is worshipped by a populace of excited natives. Arkadin, according to the British diplomat's summary, also takes advantage of 'dissolution and crisis'. So does Kane with his warmongering headlines, and so did Welles at Halloween in 1938. Technology, augmenting his voice and beaming it across the continent in the *War of the Worlds* broadcast, took care of the deifying and the selling for him. Modern man, as Freud declared, is raised to the status of a divinity by the machines or technical media he uses. 'In your madness,' Mesmer tells Cagliostro, 'you thought you could rule the world.' That was the delusion of the tycoons and demagogues Welles played, like McGafferty or Donovan; the comment serves as a terrified self-reproof. Cagliostro rejoices in his capacity to manipulate the mob: 'They're all mine, to play God with . . . Why else have I his power? . . . The Lord God came to the world once before as a man. Perhaps this time he will remould that world to his liking.' Cagliostro has advanced from Marlowe's Faustus, who only wants to enjoy himself and play childish games, to the messianic zeal of Goethe's Faust, who outdoes God by remoulding his world when he reclaims land from the sea.

Welles always customised the dialogue in his films, and this moment of deranged hubris sounds like something he might have allowed himself to say during the late 1930s, when – thanks to his Martian hoax, and the power it gave him at RKO – it seemed that he could get away with anything. By 1947, this identification of himself with Christ had become a symptom of mania. Cagliostro here paraphrases the ideology of Welles's Kindler in *The Stranger*, made the year before – except that the Nazi repudiates the meek, forgiving gospel of Christ, and wants to mould a harsher, less insipidly humane world. The fantasy, for all Welles's fearful retraction, persisted. Renaissance humanism, whose reckless ambition Faust embodies, raised man to parity with the classical gods. Why shouldn't a man presume to announce that he was the incarnate son of God? Throughout his career Welles had designs on Christianity. When first in Hollywood, he wanted to film the life of Christ in the deserts of the American south-west; eventually, playing a parody of himself, he presided over the death of Christ in Pier Paolo Pasolini's contribution to *RoGoPaG*, an anthology of satirical squibs by Rossellini, Godard, Pasolini and Gregoretti. Here Welles's efforts to direct a film about the crucifixion in the Roman slums are sabotaged by incompetent technicians and unruly actors. Mary Magdalene strips to titillate the crew, and the stand-in for Christ – whose crown of thorns is stored in a pasta carton – climbs down from the cross to gorge himself on ricotta cheese at the lunch buffet, after which he dies of indigestion. Between takes, Welles gives an ill-tempered interview in which he excoriates the illiteracy and ignorance of the Italian public. The interviewer backs away, making a sign to protect himself from the evil eye: the director is the devil. Pasolini's desecrations made Welles uncomfortable, but he went along with them. Under cover of a persona, he could say seditious, incendiary things he secretly meant, while leaving Pasolini – who was put on trial for blasphemy and given a suspended prison sentence – to take responsibility. When the director intones a poem by Pasolini, Welles makes it a personal statement. He calls himself a force out of the past, a monster incubated in ruined churches and born from the innards of a dead woman, 'more modern than any modern' because he has come to perform in 'the first acts of Afterhistory'. This is Christ's second coming. He arrives not to save the world, but to gloat over its destruction. In 1962, the year of Pasolini's *La ricotta*, Cocteau declared that two qualities made Welles a great poet, his violence and his grace. Cocteau gave priority to the violence – an uprising of free-thinking intellect and inflamed imagination, like the rebellion of Faust. Another French admirer (or worshipper) risked describing him in Christian terms, celebrating him as both creator and destroyer. Henri Agel, composing a cosmic rhapsody about Welles in 1959, said that his films were 'the birth of a new planet, suspended between Genesis and Apocalypse'.

The War of the Worlds was Welles's first experiment at inducing apocalypse. Ten years later, at Acapulco in *The Lady from Shanghai*, Grisby (Glenn Anders) – here playing Mephistophilis to Welles's naive O'Hara – looks forward to the planet's incineration, made possible by our Faustian science. For Welles, the dangerous appeal of magic lay in its flirtation with the destructive energies unleashed by dynamite or atomic fission. It, too, was a science of disembodiment. In Welles's *Doctor Faustus*, Hallie Flanagan was astounded to see 'properties disappearing in a clap of thunder'. In 1972, older and therefore less elated by the prospect of extinction, Welles inserted a touching personal essay on the subject into Brian de Palma's absurdist farce *Get To Know Your Rabbit*. Here he plays a shabby magus giving lessons to Tom Smothers, a corporate drop-out. His voice suddenly turns soft, grave, grief-stricken, as he drills Smothers: 'When you remove the silken foulade from the bowling ball, you must do it tenderly, for in a sense it is a farewell. True, you will in a moment whip off the scarf revealing the pitcher of milk, but there must be implicit in your performance a lingering sense of nostalgia for the bowling ball.' Magic atomises things without an explosion. With luck, it can also make them rematerialise after the noiseless big bang. It is a beautiful idea, though Welles as usual has trouble putting it into practice. Despite two puffs of smoke, he fails to vaporise. He and Smothers next seal themselves in a gilded sack and try to disappear, but their bodies, amorphously grappling, remain only too, too solid. At least Welles succeeds in conjuring up a glass of booze for himself: 'Hoopla!' Finally, after one more rejection – he asks Smothers if he'd like to be the son Welles himself never had, and his apprentice says no – he wraps himself in his black cape, puffs out more smoke, and manages to make himself vanish.

He returned to the idea of apocalypse in 1981, when he narrated *The Man Who Saw the Future*, a dramatised documentary about Nostradamus. Sitting in a mocked-up study, he wears the floppy cravat that had become part of his magician's costume. Along with the inevitable cigar, his other prop is a walking stick, or cane. His initial question about the so-called prophet repeats the discussion of Cagliostro at the start of *Black Magic*, which by 1981 was even more relevant to Welles's own case: 'Was he a quack? a charlatan?' He averts his eyes as he says the line. Mesmer in *Black Magic* calls Cagliostro 'a carnival faker'; Welles applied the jibe to himself in 1973 in *F for Fake*.

The clairvoyance of Nostradamus took Welles back to his own beginnings. We can best understand prophecy as a kind of science fiction.

Nostradamus allegedly foresaw a global war in the 1990s. The film illustrates this with some cut-rate special effects showing a missile attack on New York, as if updating the Martian broadcast. *The Man Who Saw the Future* includes an interview with the psychic Jeanne Dixon, who predicted the assassination of President Kennedy a decade before the event. She explains that the astral information came to her 'like when you turn on the radio or television and pick up a certain channel'; she herself, to use New Age jargon, channelled the advance warning. Welles flirts with the same analogy when he describes how Nostradamus attributed his visions to 'a subtle spirit of fire'. He took dictation, Welles goes on, from 'a voice coming from limbo'. This might have been Welles's own voice, emerging from limbo on the radio – especially because he adds that the vocal evidence was 'fragmented', like the cut-up, overlapping, gabbled dialogue in Welles's plays and films. Radio was a technical medium, but it also functioned like the medium at a séance, transmitting messages from the ether.

Welles is personally implicated in another sequence, which deals with Nostradamus's anticipation of the Napoleonic wars. Waterloo is restaged with some excerpts from Bondarchuk's epic about the battle, in which Welles played the abdicating French king. The fictional recreation is presented as if it were documentary footage, filmed in colour with an anamorphic lens long before the invention of photography. Though he was happy to fool the public at the *Wonder Show*, Welles now seems uneasy about such deceptive montages, which erase the difference between fact and fiction, the verifiable past and the conjectural future. Nostradamus, he says, thought that his gift of foresight came from God, who could 'make all time – past, present and future – become one time'. As Welles demonstrated in putting together *F for Fake*, a clever editor could do exactly the same, merging flash-backs and flash-forwards, muddling our certainty about where and when things happened or whether they happened at all. Sartre commented acutely on the 'false disorder' created by the patchwork, unconsecutive narrative of *Citizen Kane*. MacLíammóir, while filming *Othello*, fretted about his concentration on single lines or phrases rather than entire scenes. Welles told him that there were 'movie reasons' for fracturing the text and altering the camera set-up every few seconds. There might have been personal reasons as well. That scrambled incoherence corresponds to the self-fragmentation of Welles.

These techniques are Faustian, devilish not divine. This is why Bazin thought montage irreverent, even atheistic: it broke up the natural,

God-given order of the world and (to use Cagliostro's word) remoulded it to suit an artist's liking. 'In Nostradamus's day', Welles notes, 'it was believed that only witches and warlocks, or those who served the devil, could see through time.' Though Welles played the prophet Tiresias in a 1967 film of *Oedipus Rex*, his own visionary impatience for the future had now given way to regret for the irretrievable past. Near the end of his life, he wanted to see through time in the opposite direction. For this, he had no need of the devil's assistance. *Bright Lucifer* and the 1937 *Faustus* were premonitions. Seen in retrospect, the story they told about over-reachers and their plummeting fall summarised Welles's life, and made its outcome a foregone conclusion.

Apocalypse again: Welles performs an encore of his 'panic broadcast' for television in *The Rowan and Martin Laugh-In*.

CHAPTER 5

Mercury

Welles began his New York career with a series of Federal Theatre productions. The Harlem *Macbeth*, *Horse Eats Hat*, *Doctor Faustus* and *The Cradle Will Rock* were all made possible by the Works Progress Administration, which extended Roosevelt's New Deal to the arts. The relationship ended in June 1937, when guards policing budget cuts locked Welles and his company out of the theatre the day before the first preview of Blitzstein's proletarian opera. Welles demagogically rallied an audience of supporters and conducted them up Broadway to a vacant theatre. A union directive barred the performers from using the stage but, as so often, Welles turned an obstacle to advantage. The actors declaimed their lines and sang Blitzstein's incitements to strike from the floor of the theatre, like civilians spontaneously roused to self-assertion and political engagement. The opera turned into a seemingly informal political demonstration, a radical carnival. Welles took *The Cradle Will Rock* on the road to a funfair in Bethlehem, Pennsylvania, then to other industrial cities that might have been prototypes for Steeltown, USA, where Blitzstein's diatribe about the class war is set.

Later in the summer, Welles and Houseman decided to form a theatre company of their own. They published a manifesto in *The New York Times*, got themselves registered as a corporation by the state government, and began their first season with *Caesar*, followed by *The Cradle Will Rock*. The opera was now reduced to an oratorio, and used the same set as *Caesar*. Their new venture had to be given a saleable identity. Houseman claims that, while discussing the matter, they glanced at the cover of an out-of-date magazine, lying ready to light the fire in Welles's house at Sneden's Landing. It was called *The American Mercury*. They spontaneously borrowed its name, and also inherited something of its style. Its founders, who until 1924 had collaborated on the magazine *Smart Set*, were the satirist H. L. Mencken and the theatre critic George Jean Nathan. They ensured that the *Mercury* was mercurial – famous for its contrariness and unpredictability.

The brand, once established, proved invincible. By January 1938 the Mercury Theatre had four productions in repertory at three playhouses on West 41st Street, which was temporarily renamed Mercury Street. *The Mercury Theatre on the Air* began broadcasts with *Dracula* in July 1938. The acting editions Welles prepared with Roger Hill were reissued as *The Mercury Shakespeare*. He took his Mercury Players with him to Hollywood in 1939, and in the trailer for *Citizen Kane* introduced them to an audience which, as he assumed, already knew their voices from the radio. When the studio would not back his plan to film the life of Christ, Welles tried to recycle his script, directly adapted from the Gospels, as *The Mercury Bible*. He could not find a publisher. *The Mercury Wonder Show*, however, relaunched the brand under canvas.

If the choice of name was fortuitous, it was the happiest of accidents. Welles – who had affinities with Pan and Proteus, not to mention the toppled archangel Lucifer – now acquired another dubious divine mentor. Mercury, otherwise known as Hermes, the son of Zeus and Maia, was even more of an infant prodigy than Welles had been. He grew to the size of a four year old within minutes of his birth, abandoned his cradle and set off to perform great works. The first of these was a theft: he stole some white cows belonging to Apollo, and gutted them to make a musical instrument. Reprimanded by Apollo, he pleaded that he had been born only yesterday, and as a minor could not be put on trial. He persuaded Apollo to accept the stringed instrument in exchange for the slaughtered cattle. This ploy made him the god of the deal, and Zeus gave him sovereignty over all commercial transactions. (Welles did not share his expertise in this area.) Zeus worried about his son's mendacity, but made the best of it by licensing him to skim over the clouds and deliver messages for the Olympians. He agreed not to tell barefaced lies, but reserved the right to alter the truth, or conceal it.

This made him an ideal sponsor for Welles. 'I had at times been a crook, and a confidence man,' says van Stratten in the *Arkadin* novel, 'I had fooled people, lived on them.' He sees no reason to apologise, because such graft is what makes the world go round. During the twentieth century, the ancient tradition of myth was annexed by advertisers, who made miraculous claims for their products and hired deities or demigods to back these up. Lux, the word that marked God's creation of light when he made the world in Genesis, lent its shining allure to a detergent, and the winged goddess Nike sold running shoes. Once Welles gained mythical status, advertisers tempted him to make similar recommendations from on high. He began with Campbell's Soup, which took over sponsorship of his radio plays late in 1938. Houseman was aghast when his trombonal tones became 'the voice of Chocolate Pudding'. By the end of his life he was best known as the spokesman for mass-produced Californian wine. 'Paul Masson', he used to fruitily aver, 'sells no wine before its time.' Advertisers calculated that consumers would not mind Welles's hyperbolic recommendations, which could be explained away as a consequence of his mythomania. Even if no one believed the bogus sales pitch, the product still profited from its association with the man who, long ago, made *Citizen Kane*. Welles's attitude to this demeaning work became increasingly mercurial. Why shouldn't he admit, as Mercury did, his own quick-witted, silver-tongued untruthfulness? In television ads for lager during the early 1980s, he is heard off-screen while the agitated needle of a polygraph responds to his fibs. He says that Carlsberg will put hairs on your chest and make you more attractive to women, immediately qualifying these overstatements as 'somewhat unbelievable'. 'However,' he concludes, 'if we said we believed Carlsberg was the best lager in the world, it'd be true.' Then, after a tiny pause for remorseful reflection, he adds a disclaimer: the single word 'Probably.'

As Mercury's myth developed, he was honoured for inventing the alphabet, grammar, musical scales, and the weights and measures we use when buying and selling. Not even Welles was quite so profusely creative. Renaissance humanists dignified Mercury, deflecting attention from his skill at barter and his gift of the gab to praise him as a metaphysician, the guardian of lore that came to be called hermetic, sacred to the figure Bacon called Trismegistus. Welles combined these two faces. Adroit, evasive, he excelled at talking his way out of trouble. But he also fancied himself as a mystagogue, mediating – like the loftier Mercury of the humanists – between earth and heaven. 'The camera', Welles said, 'is much more than a recording apparatus. It is a medium via which messages reach us from another world.'

The roguish, mutable Mercury lent his name to one of Welles's first Shakespearean characters. John Barrymore, who played Mercutio in George Cukor's 1936 film of *Romeo and Juliet*, called him 'a mercurial sort of fellow – his name suggests it'. The slipperiness of Mercury meant that the magical science of the Renaissance identified him with a chemical substance: the alchemists believed that quicksilver, a metal that was unaccountably liquid, owed its properties to the influence of the planet Mercury. When Richard Fleischer, who directed Welles in *Compulsion* and *Crack in the Mirror*, said 'He is mercurial', he was referring to this ungraspable enigma. Though 'you think you've got a hold on him,' Fleischer said, 'you don't'. The alchemists believed that mercury's behaviour demonstrated that it was possible to transmute matter. Welles seemed to be aware of these connections between his chosen god and the mysteries of chemistry. At the station in *The Magnificent Ambersons*, Jack (Ray Collins) says a wistful goodbye to his nephew George and reflects on the dissolution of the spendthrift family's assets: 'Life and money both behave like – loose quicksilver in a nest o' cracks . . . When they're gone you can't tell where, or what the devil you did with 'em!' The metaphor was taken over from Booth Tarkington's novel, but it acquired extra resonance now that Welles had adopted Mercury as his patron. In this case, quicksilver disproves the alchemical fantasy about restoring the age of gold: reality refutes transcendental romance.

Cocteau – the boldest of modern mythographers, who always dressed as Mercury when attending costume balls – redefined the classical gods for the twentieth century. He called them 'monstres sacrés'. Sometimes the monsters were sanctified by their blithe carnality, like Dietrich or Hayworth. Failing that, they were raised to Olympus by their extravagant misbehaviour, like Hearst and Kane, Onassis and Arkadin, Callas and Pellegrina, Welles and such intemperate alter egos as Kim Menakar in *The Big Brass Ring* or Jake Hannaford in *The Other Side of the Wind* or Max Buda in *The V.I.Ps*. Although Cocteau knew that celebrities were our modern gods, he also glimpsed their classical predecessors everywhere. In 1936 he repeated Phileas Fogg's global itinerary, publishing his notes on the tour as *Round the World Again in 80 Days*; en route, he often caught sight of Mercury. He mistook an aeroplane above the Acropolis for 'the god of commerce' on his errands, and admired the oriental coolies who imitated Mercury's streamlined hat and sandals. On the boat from Hong Kong to Japan he met Chaplin, and reflected on his chemical self-multiplication: he had somehow split up 'his innumerable self' and sent it 'like mercury ad infinitum . . . flying to every corner of the globe'. San Francisco seemed feverish, because elevators shot up inside its skyscrapers 'like the mercury in a clinical thermometer'. Cocteau also had a Wellesian reaction to Coit Tower, the phallic stump on top of Telegraph Hill. He called the setting a 'sacred hill', and wondered if the female sightseers at the landmark were 'praying to the great god Pan'.

In New York, his last stop before returning to Paris, Cocteau finally encountered Welles. Virgil Thomson took him to see the Harlem

Macbeth, and though Cocteau's report on the occasion does not mention Welles or Mercury by name, he makes clear that the alchemical miracle had occurred. He referred to the production's 'black fires', and was thrilled to see 'the confusion of the final scene . . . transmuted into a gorgeous ballet of catastrophe and death'. It was not quite the transmutation the alchemists had hoped for when they set out to restore the golden age. Rather, in a bright green jungle, the production created a black world of unleashed instinct and murderous joy. Instead of the feast gatecrashed by Banquo's ghost, Welles laid on a costume ball, a dance of death with an orchestra of thundering drums. The revels were triumphantly pagan. The curriculum vitae of the Macbeth, Jack Carter, included a conviction for murder, Mafia affiliations, and a tendency to absent himself for alcoholic binges; white critics from midtown ogled his tights which, as one of them said, did 'justice to his anatomy'. Cocteau appreciatively sniffed 'those pungent fumes from the . . . midden', as if he had been peering over the edge of the pit. Occupying an Olympian hill, Harlem at this time liked to refer to itself as New York's heaven. Welles, as usual combining the roles of god and devil, had organised a Walpurgisnacht.

Mercury began as Welles's theatrical mascot. When the company started its broadcasts, the winged emissary returned to the air, where he belonged.

Technology soon becomes banal, as we take its blessings for granted. Welles never lost his wary respect for the media he employed. Like magic, his chosen media offered him power, which, as the classical gods well knew, is most enjoyable when abused. Narrating *The War of the Worlds*, he quotes H. G. Wells's opening comment about the 'intellects vast, cool and unsympathetic' that look down on puny earthlings from above, 'minds that are to our minds as ours are to the beasts in the jungle'. Those intellects belong to the Martians, but the description also applied to the young Welles, exempted from ordinary human feeling by the possession of genius. The aerial perspective suited him, even when it was as close to the ground as Lime's view of those moving dots from the Prater wheel, and radio conferred on him this princedom of the air. The Raja in *The Green Goddess* sadistically jokes that no 'god from the machine' has flown in – as such deities were prone to do in Greek tragedy – to interfere with the execution of his hostages. But a more up-to-date ethereal influence does intercede: the victims send out a call for help on the Raja's wireless. The science that made such magic possible was recent. James Clerk Maxwell imagined the possibility of propagating electromagnetic waves in 1864. Heinrich Hertz actually conjured them up in a laboratory, and by 1894 Marconi devised a way of transmitting them. During the imbroglio over Marie Antoinette's necklace in *Black Magic*, Welles's Cagliostro strolls in, despite having been banished, and remarks with a smirk that the queen has sent for him. She angrily denies it. He replies: 'Majesty, waves of thought travel faster than any messenger. I believe you need my help.' He lightly invokes and supersedes Mercury; those thought waves ultimately came to travel by radio, which could transmit images as well. RKO Radio Pictures, the studio that enticed Welles to Hollywood, summed up the miracle in the logo introducing all of its films. A radio mast planted on top of the world emitted lightning bolts, while a propeller plane buzzed along the equator, putting a girdle, like Shakespeare's Puck, around the earth.

As always with a new technology, enthusiasts claimed that radio would better the human lot. When the *Titanic* sank in 1912, lives were saved because the ship sent out distress signals by radio. A week later, *The New York Times* rhapsodised about radio as an angelic go-between, or a ladder enabling men to scramble up towards God: 'people grasp the thin air and use it as a thing more potent for human aid than any strand of wire or cable that was ever spun or woven'. Radio was wireless, but no less sturdy for that, and it wove a safety net from thin air. The newspaper reminded New Yorkers that 'over the housetops and even through the walls of buildings and in the very air one breathes are written words of electricity'. In 1932 Brecht predicted that radio, like 'a vast network of pipes', would create a forum for true social communication. Welles lent his voice to this optimistic choir when he took part in Blitzstein's *Airborne Symphony*, commissioned by the US Army to boost morale in 1943 but not performed until 1946. He narrated the cantata at its first performance, while rehearsing *Around the World*, and he recorded it, with Leonard Bernstein conducting, twenty years later. Welles plays the Monitor, a Brechtian announcer who summarises the spiritual adventure of manned flight and extols its military value. He begins by saying that we live in 'The Age of the Air'; the chorus muses on his words, and yearns 'To be Airborne, / To be Airborne.'

Cocteau, before travelling up to Harlem for *Macbeth*, visited Radio City, but was unimpressed by its gimmickry. So what if he could see his voice 'recorded as a track of light'? No machine, he declared, could record his dreams, or 'elicit from the Unknown the worlds, so near yet so remote, that throng it!' Welles proved him wrong, and two years later used the radio to bring those remote worlds into proximity, goading them to make war on New York. Welles's radio performances altered the benevolent assurances of that *Times* article. The air could transmit fear as well as comfort, and if the walls of buildings were permeable by sounds then so, perhaps, was the human mind or heart, on whose guilty secrets Welles eavesdropped in his role as The Shadow. The invisible detective, solving cases by telepathy, explained his infallibility by likening himself to a radioactive force in the air; he was, he said, 'the oldest wireless in the world'. Welles recognised that radio had a ghostly, ghoulish quality: Mercury was the god who ushered men into the afterlife.

In his introduction to *The War of the Worlds*, Welles solemnly advised that mankind was being studied 'across an immense ethereal gulf' by extra-terrestrial scrutineers and predators. That gulf is the empty space traversed by radio. Idly rotating the dial, the programme samples the messages written on the air, including a weather report that, through crackling ether, announces a 'slight atmospheric disturbance' over the north-eastern United States. The set is performing its mystical function, bringing hermetic news from the beyond. Marshall McLuhan called radio a 'tribal drum', arguing that it attuned and synchronised the central nervous systems of the people who listened, creating a state of trance. In their way, the Haitian drummers imported by Welles for *Macbeth* were radio transmitters, and they tapped out alarms, rumours of disturbance, ghastly portents. Welles himself did the drumming in *The War of the Worlds*, and electrified the tribe of Americans who listened in.

It was he who suggested that Howard Koch should turn Wells's story into a broadcast, relayed in real time. The novel is written in the past historic tense, which means that the war is over and the human race has survived: how else could the narrative have been written? Radio, however, caught incidents on the hop, before any outcome was clear. The broadcast used the present tense, which is why listeners who tuned in after the programme began thought it was really happening. The gabbled emergency reports and scrambled interviews with eyewit-nesses are regularly interrupted, first by the sedative resumption of normal programming as the network switches back to a droning dance band in a New York hotel, and then – as reporters eliminated by the Martian advance let their microphones drop – by passages of dead air. Between 1935 and 1939, Welles regularly performed in a radio programme called *The March of Time*, which dramatised the week's news. The sponsor was Time, Inc., so the view of contemporary history the series inculcated was relentlessly progressive, with all problems promptly resolved by the end of the transmission. This adoption of the march tempo – predictable, concerted, consoling – told a lie. Forced to be truthful in *The War of the Worlds*, radio revealed that time was not a march but a race, flurried, breathless, with no goal in sight. News broadcasts lacked the judicious detachment needed for history; they were better at the hasty, day-to-day surmises of journalism. The historian is expected to arrive at a conclusion. The journalist just has to keep talking, and can never be sure where the onrush of events is leading.

Sometimes those events need a little help from the observer. Mercury's understanding with Zeus allowed him considerable liberty when passing on messages. In *The War of the Worlds*, Welles and his various surrogates in the field hint that they are inventing the end of the world. Radio absolves them from the need to produce proofs of the calamity, since they are giving eyewitness accounts of sights we cannot see. A newsman at the New Jersey farm where the space vehicle bumped down to earth is asked for a 'word picture' of the invisible scene. But when the first Martian crawls out of the ship, he can only say 'Ladies and gentlemen, it's indescribable.' Later he calls the creature 'a monster – or whatever it is': listeners had to do their own visualising, which made them responsible for what they thought they saw. The reporter then retreats, conveniently apologising: 'I'll have to stop the description until I can take a new position.' When the broadcast resumes, he vows 'I'll give you every detail as long as I can talk and as long as I can see.' The promise is not kept. All he can say about the second creature to emerge from the crater is that it's 'a small beam of light against a mirror'. Then he is seared by a heat ray, his body – as another unreliable looker-on puts it – 'distorted beyond all recognition'. The professional describer can neither describe nor, in his present atomised state, be described. A Princeton professor, played by Welles, steps in to analyse the sorcery of the invaders, and says that the death ray was projected by 'a polished parabolic mirror of unknown composition'. It might be Cagliostro or the orotund Great Orson talking.

The killing ray is a form of radiation, which makes it a demonstration of radio's power. After the reporter's demise, a broadcasting executive comes on the air to say, in pious tones, that the network's facilities have been handed over to the state militia because 'radio has a responsibility to serve in the public interest at all times' – except, presumably, when it is inciting that public to a collective nervous breakdown. The Martians disrupt communications by tearing down power lines and uprooting railways so as 'to disorganise human society'; the broadcast, using its communicative medium to disseminate a terrifying fiction, did the same. In the process, it turned that medium inside out. A message from a state trooper concludes with more silent air when he is eliminated. Such tricks go against the imperative of the garrulous new medium, which guaranteed that the air waves would always be alive. 'Is there anyone on the air?' croaks a solitary voice. 'Is there anyone?' Welles had a dangerous attraction to such moments of formal nullification, when you can see (or hear) right through the illusion. The empty air in *The War of the Worlds* becomes a glimpse of empty space in *Citizen Kane*. When Susan stalks out of Xanadu, Welles superimposed on her exit a close-up of a screeching white cockatoo. She leaves without a final showdown; the bird's shrill cry voices her protest. The image is a palimpsest of three separate layers, since Welles also back-projected an ocean onto a screen, to supply a view beyond the terrace. But the layers do not quite merge, and because of a printing hitch in the laboratory the cockatoo's eye is transparent, a hole you can look straight through. In his cheeky conclusion to the broadcast, Welles boasted that 'We annihilated the world before your very ears', teasing his audience with a reminder of its gullibility. He added that he and his colleagues had 'utterly destroyed the CBS', the network which had engaged the Mercury Theatre. The world and CBS luckily materialised again, like a rabbit reappearing from a hat or a sectioned lady who grows back together. 'Both institutions', said Welles, 'are still open for business.' The brash, impudent young superman found it easy to demolish reality. Soon enough, the businesslike, institutionalised world decided to destroy him.

In 1947, the cinema delivered its judgement on the morality of Welles's radio career in a film noir called *The Unsuspected*, directed by Michael Curtiz. It concerns the suave host of a radio programme about true crimes, who commits murders of his own while using the delayed airing of his broadcasts to provide an alibi. Welles was offered the role, but refused it; Claude Rains played it instead, though the script makes pointed references to Welles. Rains in his first broadcast describes the unease of an anonymous murderer, and says that the man's guilt 'follows him like a shadow' – or like The Shadow? The film then illustrates the magically long arm of technology. The camera moves from Rains's microphone in the studio to a loudspeaker on the wall, travels down the dark tunnel behind the mouthpiece and surfaces again beside a train charging through the night. It then re-emerges from a radio in the train carriage, studies reflections in the window before passing through it, crossing a street and craning into a cheap room at the Peekskill Hotel where Rains's voice is speaking through another radio. A guilty man lies quaking on the bed, while a neon sign that says KILL pulses outside his window. A quick round-up shows other listeners in other places, all equally perturbed by Rains's monologue. Radio functions as a collective unconsciousness.

Only a god could presume to possess such shamingly intimate knowledge of our nocturnal thoughts. Later in the film, Rains's wise-cracking female producer hands him a telegram that has just been delivered to his home north of Manhattan (perhaps near Sneden's Landing, where Welles lived during his radio days). 'Mercury on a bicycle', she says, 'just brought this.'

Brecht welcomed radio as a public address system. A master of ceremonies for society, it led the public rejoicing in *Der Lindberghflug*, the cantata by Brecht and Kurt Weill about Lindbergh's Atlantic flight, first performed in 1929; a year later, in their opera *Aufstieg and Fall der Stadt Mahagonny*, it sought to protect public safety by announcing the approach of a hurricane. Less benignly, the microphone amplified the voices and egos of the demagogues who seized power during the 1930s. In 1934, T. H. White – whose Arthurian epic made him one of Welles's favourite writers – imagined a communist production of *Henry V*, in which the king would carry round a microphone and relay his bellicose harangues through it. White decided that any character who made 'a particularly bogus speech' would be granted temporary use of the microphone, and imagined that 'sharp tussles' for access to it might break out between the combatants.

Welles did not use radio to make such stentorian appeals, even though as an orator at political rallies he exhorted the masses to vote for Roosevelt or support American entry into the war against Hitler. For him, radio was a more psychologically insidious medium. The voice alone, resonating from inside a body that remained unseen, was a spirit whispering in the listener's ear. His confidential, seductive manner at the microphone caused problems in 1937 when he narrated *The Spanish*

Earth, a partisan documentary about the Spanish civil war, for which Hemingway had written a taciturn script. When he heard Welles's delivery, Hemingway called it 'faggoty', and said it reminded him of 'a cocksucker swallowing'. He re-recorded the voice-over himself in a yarning, gruffly manly drawl. Welles certainly sounds uneasy with a language that Hemingway intended to be 'dry and hard', like the soil of Spain. His finely tuned modulations are wasted on statements such as 'It is good bread – stamped with the union label.' Being a non-combatant like Falstaff, he could not plausibly assert, as Hemingway's script required in a scene showing troops crouched miserably in a trench, that 'This is the true face of men going into battle.' A further reason for his lack of sympathy emerges when the film shows 'the loudspeaker of the People's Army' being hauled from the barracks on the back of a truck and parked in the fields near the front lines. Here, projecting its uproar over a range of two kilometres, it blares out marches, anthems and a harangue by the agitator known as La Pasionara. It resembles a singing tank; its black oblong mouth is a cinema screen without imagery. Welles must have flinched from the blatancy of such propagandist amplification.

He developed his own style of commentary in another project during the busy year of 1937, when he played the Announcer in Archibald MacLeish's radio play *The Fall of the City*. Here, after being introduced by a Studio Director, Welles poetically evokes events in the plaza of a city at once classical and modern, where a crowd exchanges rumours, quarrels over the contrasting appeals of priests and generals, and finally succumbs to a conqueror, a metallic giant who is – as the Announcer whispers – merely a bundle of armour. MacLeish declared that 'the Announcer is the most useful dramatic personage since the Greek Chorus'. But the Greek Chorus was an ensemble, representing the consensus of a community, whereas the Announcer is a solitary, powerless individual, aghast at the irrationality of a crowd which lacks the gravity and judicial conscience of the assembled citizens in Sophocles or Aeschlyus. By the 1930s, the choir had become a mob, expressing itself in inarticulate muttering or hysterical shouts. The Announcer passes on one of its rabid cries: 'Down with liberal learned minds!'

MacLeish modelled *The Fall of the City* on the dispute in the market-place in *Julius Caesar*. Welles's *Caesar* took up the hint six months later, and presented Shakespeare's play as an adjudication of the contemporary ideological crisis. On stage and then in his Mercury recording of *Julius Caesar*, Welles played both sides in the argument – the principled Brutus and the rabble-rousing Antony. But in *The Fall of the City* he is banished to the sidelines, announcing rather than orating, allowed only to describe the volatile temper of the city folk, who believe the last person to have harangued them. Their life is collective, faceless, and for that reason they dream of a despot who possesses the strong-minded individuality they lack. As the conqueror advances, they screech 'He's one man: we are but thousands!' This, unlike the Greek polis or the forum in republican Rome, is a mass society, eagerly subservient to what Nazi theorists called the Führerprinzip.

'The age is his!' cry the people, greeting their saviour. 'It's his century!' MacLeish acknowledged that radio could not supply the 'live and vigorous audience' needed for radical drama, but hoped that it would shape its millions of disparate listeners into 'a living audience which the poet and his actors can feel'. This was the fond illusion of a liberal: the society convened by radio is made up of air. Though MacLeish wanted the medium to provide a political education, his preface to *The Fall of the City* hints at its power to misinform, to whip up spurious excitements. He contrasts the suggestibility of the ear with the literalism of the eye. 'The ear is already half a poet. It believes at once: creates and believes. It is the eye which is the realist.' That willingness makes the listeners to a radio play accept the artifice of blank verse; it also makes the crowd in this particular play worship the conqueror. As the Announcer puts it near the end, 'The people invent their oppressors: they wish to believe in them.' Welles proved the point at Halloween the following year, when he became one of those oppressors, whose victories were won by hallucinations.

Radio was used by Hitler to bully a society into submission. 'The city has fallen! The city has fallen!' shrieks MacLeish's crowd, glad to be deprived of its freedom. Choral unanimity is death to the self-reliance of the individual: this might be the noise made by the chanting pack at a Nazi rally. The Announcer, signing off, lowers his voice, and repeats in a flat, dispirited, unexclamatory tone, 'The city has fallen . . .' Though Welles did his share of ranting when things went wrong in the studio, radio taught him to value such sotto voce effects. *Citizen Kane* is, among other things, about the new mass media – radio, the newsreel, the tabloid newspaper – and it bemoans their output of visual and typographic noise. The unseated editor of the *Inquirer*, Mr Carter, maintains a strict regime of silence in the newsroom, announced by a capitalised placard on the wall and enforced by churchy shushing. This is disrupted by Kane and his obstreperous roaring boys, with their eager, polyphonic babble. During the party, the newsroom is overtaken by noisemakers: a brass band, shrilling chorines, and kazoos played by Kane's employees. He wants the typefaces of the revamped paper to be large and therefore loud, and demands a three-column headline for inflationary reasons: 'If the headline is big enough, it *makes* the news big enough.' Brecht recommended 'the foundation of a paper like the *Völkischer Beobachter*', which was the official Nazi rag, as a properly instructive subject for epic theatre. Welles dealt with just such an episode when Kane overhauls the *Inquirer*, but his purpose was not a staged analysis of capitalism. He emphasises instead what Brecht called 'the individual's lust for power', ignoring 'the exceedingly complicated machinery within which the struggle for power nowadays takes place'.

Kane gloats as the newsboys shout a summary of the front page through the city streets at dawn. But is this megaphonic din merely self-deception? The film shows voices reverberating in empty echo chambers. Kane the political candidate addresses an auditorium filled with a painted crowd, Susan the opera singer caterwauls for the benefit of an unseen audience, and at the end the journalists test the acoustics of the hall at Xanadu by shouting at each other across it. Ironically, RKO marketed *Citizen Kane* – without success – by using the deafening tactics the film itself derides. The first posters tried to orchestrate a hubbub of popular acclaim with exclamatory banner headlines and strident typefaces: 'Everybody's Talking About It! *It's Terrific!*'

Welles's remorse the morning after the Martian broadcast may have been affected, but the experience startled him into a recognition of technology's perils and delusions. You can increase the size of the inky capital letters you use, or rotate a knob and boost the volume of a single voice. The result is not necessarily an augmentation of power. MacLeish's conqueror in *The Fall of the City* may be just a voicebox, a booming nullity. In *The Lady from Shanghai*, Banister – recruiting O'Hara for the crew of his yacht – flatters him as a tough guy. Goldie, O'Hara's friend, denies that there is any such thing. A tough guy is an ordinary fellow given a competitive edge by a gun or a knife. He nods towards the juke box in the saloon, which is dispensing the film's theme song, and asks 'What makes him sing better'n me? Something in here,' he says, gesturing to his throat. 'That's his edge. What makes it loud? A microphone.' This is Welles's brisk demystification of himself. The more noise a man makes, the more hollowly reverberant he is.

Arkadin's global control, which enables him to manipulate governments in countries where he has financial interests and to kill by remote control, dwindles at the end of the film. He can no longer command obedience; he is just a man who shouts and is not listened to. In the Munich airport he offers bribes to obtain a seat on a fully booked flight. Welles intercedes on the soundtrack to obstruct him (or, since he is also Arkadin, to censure his own egomania). A Teutonic voice – recognisably Welles's, guttural and yet blade-sharp – barks a militaristic summons: 'Announcing the departure of Flight 16 for Barcelona and Madrid!' The voice is accompanied by a close-up of a loudspeaker, which equates man and machine. Arkadin flies his own plane to Barcelona, and buzzes the airport there like an angry divinity who uses the radio to bully his subjects on the ground. Railing through the microphone, he tells his daughter not to listen to the charges against him. She stares up at the grille in the roof of the airport control tower from which his voice blusters, and devoutly says 'Yes, father.' Then she turns away, while the loudspeaker goes on drily crackling. Arkadin has already jumped from his plane; the static is an electric death rattle.

Enumerating his accomplishments, Welles told Bogdanovich that he 'invented the use of narration in radio' and carried it over into his films. Whereas Hitchcock insisted that film should be purely visual, dispensing with words whenever it could, Welles thought that 'words are terribly important in talking pictures'. Sound precedes sight in *The Magnificent Ambersons*. Over a black screen, Welles's voice utters Tarkington's account of the dynasty's inception; first he speaks this defunct world into being, and only then are we permitted to see it, as an image glimmers into view, stiffly framed but jerky like a souvenir of early cinema or one of our own first memories, puzzlingly removed from context – a gabled, shingled house, and a streetcar halting outside it. The word begets the image, as when Kane whispers 'Rosebud'. The ear, as in MacLeish's radio play, gives directions to the eye.

Yet whenever he enunciated a principle, Welles flouted it; as a man of ideas, he enjoyed debates, even if they were disagreements with himself. The contradiction here derived from the indiscriminateness of the microphone, which recorded not only words but noises, like the battery of special effects in *The War of the Worlds*: hissings and hummings from the spaceship, the clanking of extra-terrestrial metal, the coughing of pilots flying through suffocating smoke, and the thud of bodies hitting the floor. In one scene in *The Magnificent Ambersons*, Welles allowed a mechanical clangour of special effects to concuss speech. When George and Jack quarrel in the bathroom, their dispute has to compete with the spluttering, chugging, moaning eructations of the pipes that have filled the tub. For the tour of Eugene's automobile factory, Bernard Herrmann composed a toccata, scrapped when RKO commissioned a new score. The piece was a minute's worth of percussive taps and thumps on metal and thunderous drums, paying homage to Soviet industrial anthems like Mosolov's *Zavod*, which is set in an iron foundry, or Prokofiev's *Le pas d'acier*, a ballet about a steel mill. Modernity has knocked at the door, and temperate, harmonised music must give way to noise. The verbose Welles also allowed himself to enjoy characters who lacked the power of speech. Richard Bennett, persuaded out of retirement by Welles, could not remember lines. As the ship's captain in *Journey into Fear*, he therefore expresses himself by slurping soup or bellowing with careless, contemptuous laughter. As Silence in *Chimes at Midnight*, Walter Chiari loses the words Shakespeare wrote for him. Welles afflicted him with a stammer, so he either fluffs his lines or ineffectually whistles and puffs as he tries to utter a problematic consonant. 'D-d-d', he stutters, shaking his head in vexation. 'Dead', concludes his companion Shallow. Inarticulacy has its own inane poetry.

Welles disparaged his reputation as a technical innovator, telling Bogdanovich that he had often been given credit for things he did not invent, and confessed that 'I'm not actually a pro-innovation man.' Each new invention brings with it the possibility of novel misdemeanours. In *Citizen Kane*, Welles teasingly alludes to his Martian prank: Kane, interviewed in 1935, warns a reporter 'Don't believe everything you hear on the radio.' 'I hate this machine!' says Vargas at the end of *Touch of Evil* as he secretly tapes Quinlan's admission that he framed Sanchez and the other suspects. Technical mishaps make audible Vargas's shame at this electronic snooping. The recorder wheezes and whistles as he trails Vargas through the oil field. Quinlan hears his own voice bouncing back to him, ricocheting from some obstacle in this waste place like an incoherent relay from the beyond: 'An echo', he comments. When he realises that his own sergeant is wearing the wire, he upbraids Menzies as 'this walking microphone that used to work for me'. In *The Trial* too, a mute electronic appliance gives evidence against K. The police who come to arrest him seize on a moment of stammering confusion when – in a subliminal, self-referring pun – he calls his phonograph a 'pornograph'. This whimsy was Welles's idea. Kafka's K owns no such equipment, so it can tell no tales about him.

Welles once claimed, not very believably, that he preferred to do without his dependence on technical media which, like Mercury, tampered with the messages they carried. 'Like most performers,' he said, 'I naturally prefer a live audience to that lie-detector full of celluloid.' It is an interestingly oblique accusation of the camera, and of himself. The camera, examining faces in close-up, catches all the tics and twinges that betray the actor's dishonesty or insincerity. Radio at least saved Welles from being impugned by his own appearance. His feelings on the matter peep through an uncomradely comment he made on Everett Sloane, the Mercury Theatre colleague who appeared with him in *Citizen Kane*, *Journey into Fear*, *The Lady from Shanghai* and *Prince of Foxes*. Welles described Sloane as primarily a radio actor, who never learned how to move properly for the camera. That, he said, is why he chose to prop Sloane up on those spiderlegged crutches in *The Lady from Shanghai*. It was an odd appraisal, because the actor who had most difficulty in making the transition between media was Welles himself. With his lopsided gait and flapping arms, he looks comically flustered as he escapes from the murder scene in *The Stranger*. He stumbles through a sword fight in *Macbeth*, belying the hero's martial reputation. Clumsiest of all is the punch-up with the policeman when he breaks out of custody after the trial in *The Lady from Shanghai*. Welles's awkwardness admits what a strain it was to risk himself in front of the camera. Once, evading its gaze altogether, he even proposed giving a radio performance in a film. When he was approached to play Ben Yussef in Anthony Mann's *El Cid*, he noticed that the character was a Muslim and, therefore, wore a veil throughout the action. Why shouldn't a double do all the scenes, leaving Welles to add his voice to the soundtrack later? The producer unsurprisingly engaged someone else.

Welles may have said that he preferred a live audience, but unmediated contact with another human being made him nervous, as the *Cahiers* critic Bill Krohn – one of the most sympathetic and perceptive commentators on his work – found in 1982 when trying to arrange an interview. Though they were both in Los Angeles, Welles wriggled out of meeting Krohn and insisted on postponing the conversation until after he had flown to New York. Krohn then spent $300 on a telephone call from coast to coast. To delay, be difficult, and cause expense to others are among celebrity's royal prerogatives, but Welles had a more plaintive reason. 'If I can't see your face,' he explained to Krohn, 'I won't tell so many lies to entertain you.' It was a paradox, or an outright reversal of the truth. The voice can lie, as Welles's multiple roles on radio or on the soundtracks of his films so deviously demonstrated. It is harder, even if you are an actor, to hide behind the face. Did Welles really want to spare Krohn by ensuring that he was out of hypnotic range, or was he defending his own invisibility? Either way, the fussy, frustrating proviso worked to his moral advantage: he was Mercury with a conscience.

Welles as Harry Lime's shadow in *The Third Man*.

CHAPTER 6

Kurtz

A week after *The War of the Worlds*, Welles presented his radio adaptation of Joseph Conrad's fable about imperial profiteering, *Heart of Darkness*, first published in 1902. He cast himself as Kurtz, the Belgian colonist in the Congo driven mad by his realisation that Europeans are as savage as the Africans they exploit and despoil. He also delivered a scene-setting narration, though he allowed Ray Collins to play the story's actual narrator Marlow, who travels up a snaking river to meet Kurtz, listens to his demented monologues, reports on his death, and returns to tell decorous lies about him in civilised Europe. When he moved to Hollywood in 1939, Welles's first choice of subject for a film was *Heart of Darkness*. He wrote the script, designed and cast it. He intended to treat it as a stream of consciousness for the camera, with a dual role for himself. As Marlow he would look through the lens; as Kurtz he would be looked at. Eventually he decided to stick to the directorial role of Marlow, who would stay behind the camera and be glimpsed only as a reflection in mirrors or on the surface of the water. Before he could find a surrogate to play Kurtz, RKO cancelled the project.

Welles was not deterred, and made his version of *Heart of Darkness* by stealth, distributing it through other films – *Citizen Kane*, *The Lady from Shanghai*, *The Third Man*. More than forty years later, he even jauntily smuggled it into his script for *The Big Brass Ring*. When Blake Pellarin interrupts his political campaign and absconds to Morocco, a friend reassures his wife: 'It's not the Congo, darling . . . You make it sound like Blake is off to the Heart of Darkness.' Pellarin and Menaker do indeed travel into a wilderness of liberated instinct, and then – in a comic revision of Conrad's stark fable – return safely home. By the end of Welles's life, Conrad's story had grown into a pervasive, abiding modern myth. The process began in 1925 when T. S. Eliot used a native boy's contemptuous announcement 'Mistah Kurtz – he dead' as the epigraph for his poem 'The Hollow Men'; he elliptically suggested that post-war men were hollowed-out by what they had experienced, and lived on in an undead state. Kurtz – an overlord whose methods (called 'unsound' in *Apocalypse Now*, Coppola's adaptation of the story) are Faustian – speaks of an unspecific 'horror' as he dies. As the twentieth century continued, his confession became an allusion to whatever political horror was currently being perpetrated. Welles had already contributed to this interpretative afterlife: Howard Koch's script for the *War of the Worlds* broadcast tersely quotes from *Heart of Darkness*. Among Kurtz's incoherent memos to himself in the story, Marlow discovers the command 'Exterminate all the brutes!' The phrase raises the possibility of genocide, conducting the annihilation of inferior races scientifically (and it is turned against Kurtz himself in *Apocalypse Now* when the intelligence officers tell Willard, Coppola's Marlow, that Kurtz must be 'terminated – with extreme prejudice'). Near the end of the broadcast, Welles as Professor Pierson describes his journey across wrecked New Jersey. He corresponds to Marlow, except that he travels not up a river into the jungle but through the Holland Tunnel beneath the Hudson River into Manhattan. Conrad's plot has been reversed: this time the brutes have done the exterminating. *The War of the Worlds* even includes the cannibalism that, as Conrad hints, is Kurtz's personal horror. The Martians feed on humans, who to them are 'edible ants'. Pierson meets a militia man who thinks that we are well rid of 'cities, nations, civilizations, progress', but has a plan for resisting the Martians. 'We're not going to be exterminated,' he says, using Kurtz's word.

He raves about turning the heat ray on Martians and men alike: 'We'd bring everybody down to their knees. You and me and a few more of us – we'd own the world.' The script calls him only a Stranger, an identity he passes on to the undercover Nazi in Welles's *The Stranger*, who shares his dream of a military uprising. Pierson, not wanting to live in this fascistic world of virile steel, shakes his head and walks off. By the time Welles began to plan his cinematic *Heart of Darkness,* the European war was underway, and he allowed Kurtz, who tells Marlow that his barbarism follows 'the method of my government', to enlist Hitler as a colleague: 'There's a man now in Europe trying to do what I've done in the jungle.' Kindler in *The Stranger* is said to have devised the Nazi policy of genocide, and when asked how he would solve the problem of Germany, he applies Kurtz's methods and recommends 'annihilation, down to the last babe in arms'. Arkadin achieves the same result by dispensing alcohol. Guests at his parties are required to down three large vodkas before they are admitted. In the novel, Raina, explaining the custom, paraphrases Kurtz's memo: 'It's his way of eliminating the weaklings.' She agrees that it's a harsh initiatic test, but knows her father is 'a bit of a savage'. Van Stratten places this Russian ogre in Conrad's jungle when describing his voice which is 'inhumanly soft', like the muttered chant of 'savage priests . . . when carrying out some bloody rite'.

Interpretation for Welles was a matter of elective affinity. Discovering his personal obsessions in the stories he adapted, he felt a sense of collusion with the writer. This entitled him to rewrite those texts and make them more intimately his own; the book or play enabled him, using subterfuge, to explore alternative selves. But what of himself did he find in *Heart of Darkness*?

While Marlow is sailing up the river towards Kurtz in Conrad's story, he tries to imagine this man whose reputation – for good or ill – seems so much larger than any individual could ever be. He conceives of Kurtz in advance 'as a voice', as if he were Welles whispering sedition on the radio. 'A voice,' he repeats. 'He was very little more than a voice.' When he hears that voice, it sounds portentously 'like a hail through a speaking-trumpet': Kurtz's ego is magnified by a mechanical amplifier. Someone remembers his eloquence, and says, 'He electrified large meetings', just as Welles did when barnstorming for liberal causes. Kurtz later booms a vocal command to fend off a 'sorcerer' or 'witch-man' who menaces Marlow. Here was another potential role for Welles, since Marlow calls the horned shaman 'that Shadow – this wandering and tormented thing'. Kurtz has undergone a 'devilish initiation' with his black mistress; Welles acquired a taste for exotic, equatorial sexual partners at this time, when he began an affair with Dolores Del Rio, the Mexican actress who dances the role of a cat woman (complete with whiskers) in the cabaret episode of *Journey into Fear*. She was followed by a troupe of Brazilian samba dancers, and – back in Hollywood – by Lena Horne. While in North Africa in 1949, playing a warlord in Henry Hathaway's *The Black Rose*, he dallied with a Berber woman. His choice of Eartha Kitt as the demon who impersonates Helen of Troy in *Time Runs* was not accidental. The manager of an intermediate station on the river strikes Conrad's Marlow as a 'papier-mâché Mephistopheles'. Welles intended to bring his own Mephistophilis from Marlowe's play along for the ride: he cast Jack Carter as the boat's helmsman.

Kurtz is destroyed by wildness. The jungle works on him as Mephistophilis did on Faustus, enticing his 'unlawful soul beyond the bounds of permitted aspirations'. Once again, as in his reading of

Shakespeare's seven ages, Welles's source proved prophetic. His Brazilian mission in 1942 placed him in a position dangerously similar to Kurtz's. Nelson Rockefeller told him he had a 'patriotic duty' to make a film shoring up support for US policy in South America, just as Kurtz's sponsors had despatched him to Africa with the high-minded aim of civilising infidels (though the actual purpose was to stockpile ivory). Welles behaved in Brazil like a reckless, jumped-up tyrant, and one instance of his petulant folly was foreseen by Conrad. Marlow scornfully comments in the story that Kurtz 'desired to have kings meet him at railway stations on his return from some ghastly Nowhere'. Welles, flying back from Rio, suffered from a similar conceit, and whenever his plane touched down he threw a tantrum if he was not greeted by US consular officials of sufficiently exalted rank. His government sponsors had accorded him the honorary status of Brigadier General, a pretence that impressed Brazilian officials. When he returned to the United States, he tried to go on playing the role, and had to be humiliatingly reminded that he was still a civilian.

Conrad's Marlow sceptically investigates the mystique of Kurtz, and questions whether it is any more than hearsay. He is supposed to be a 'universal genius', like Welles – though Welles defensively insisted that the term was only applied to him pejoratively, and pointed out that RKO's letterhead, when the studio was trying to forget about its deal with him, promised 'Showmanship, Not Genius'. Marlow wonders what Kurtz's profession was – painter? musician? journalist? demagogic orator? There were so many of him. All Marlow himself will grudgingly admit is that he was 'a remarkable man'.

Marlow performs an act of exorcism by insisting that Kurtz was 'no idol of mine'. The plenitude of Welles's warring selves meant that, having divided himself between the two men, he could not make this denial. Repeating his adaptation of *Heart of Darkness* on the radio in 1945, he now played both roles. Marlow vouched for his liberal creed, as Brutus had done, while Kurtz, a backwoods Caesar, represented the absolutism of his actual methods. Welles got his way by guile – as when he began to film *Citizen Kane* without the studio's approval, by pretending that he was only making tests – or with the aid of intimidating rages. His profligacy advertised his freedom. Society tolerates such antics in artists, but the same behaviour looks malevolent when you remove it from the charmed frivolity of the theatre or the movie studio. 'I'm the first absolute dictator', Kurtz tells Marlow in Welles's script. It was a remark

Welles often paraphrased when describing his contract with RKO. No one before, he told *Cahiers* in 1964, had ever enjoyed such 'absolute power' inside the Hollywood system. He added, with a twinge of remorse, 'I had too much power.' Despite these misgivings, in his 1982 BBC interview he proclaimed himself 'absolute producer' of *Kane*. He even attempted to increase his personal dominion by proposing that Mankiewicz, with whom he wrote the script, should not take a credit on screen. Kane's friend Leland says that he 'was disappointed in the world, so he built one of his own – an absolute monarchy'. In retrospect, Welles saw RKO as his private Xanadu. 'I brought all my Mercury actors with me,' he said in the same BBC interview, 'so I had a little world of my own.' The dictators with whom Kane schmoozes in the obituary newsreel also saw themselves as artists, exercising a monopolistic power like Welles's. They designed the state, and treated the people who lived in it as costumed extras in a crowd scene. Like Kane, they had a special fondness for statues, which fix the human body into an upright posture of obedience.

Welles continued telling stories about aesthetes with fascist ambitions, since they were implicit autobiographies. *Donovan's Brain*, broadcast in 1944, offered a variant. Dr Patrick Corey, given to arcane surgical experimentation, salvages the brain of the rich megalomaniac Donovan, who is killed in a rail crash. The brain goes on transmitting commands in a neural Morse code, and makes the doctor do its bidding. Corey is Frankenstein, psychologically invaded by his monster. He realises that Donovan was financing a putsch and aspired to 'domination of the world', seeing himself as 'the absolute ruler of all mankind'. Welles played both roles, using different vocal registers – light and nervously febrile for Corey, croaky and guttural for Donovan. In the dreaming mind of the disinterested intellectual, an 'evil fantasy' instigated by Donovan forces itself into view: Corey imagines a 'young giant bestriding the earth'. This, as it happens, was exactly how the first posters chose to represent *Citizen Kane*. The marketing campaign used an image of Welles with his legs spread like the colossus to whom Shakespeare's conspirators compare Caesar. His fists belligerently clenched, Kane towered over hordes of diminutive subjects. In some European markets, the translated title of *Citizen Kane* underlined the image: in Portugal, the film was called *O Mundo A Seus Pés*, meaning The World at His Feet. Corey sees Donovan's scheme as a 'vast cosmic ballet presided over by the colossal figure of a young man', with the peoples of the world – assembled by the Nazi choreographers of the Nuremberg rallies, or by Busby Berkeley in his drilled dance routines – paying homage.

In art, Welles's encyclopaedic talents made him, if you like, a universal genius. In politics, one man's insistence on omniscient control – enforced by cameras, microphones and other instruments of surveillance, as well as by the magical power to make doubters vanish – creates a totalitarian regime.

Despite his reputation as a spendthrift, when it came to ideas Welles let nothing go to waste. As soon as the studio called off *Heart of Darkness*, he proposed another adaptation which told the same story. His new source was *The Smiler with the Knife*, a political thriller by Nicholas Blake (the pseudonym of the poet C. Day Lewis). The story was the one he always told: a quest – like Marlow's for Kurtz, or the journalist Thompson's for Kane, or van Stratten's for Arkadin. But whereas Marlow, Thompson and van Stratten know who their quarry is, the investigator in *The Smiler with the Knife* seeks a man who lives incognito. Absconded somewhere inside a secret political party, he is planning a military insurrection in pre-war England. He embodies the fascist notion of 'the Superior Person', which remained dear to Welles despite its doctrinal embarrassments: in 1958 he said that *Touch of Evil* was 'about a superior being', because Vargas is 'a superior man'. 'Only a great man could have done it,' says an acolyte in *The Smiler with the Knife* when discussing the unknown leader's strategy. The undercover investigator is puzzled by the idea of an 'anonymous genius'. Doesn't genius, like that of Kurtz or Welles, involve brazen self-declaration?

The studio again used its veto, but Welles held onto the idea of a 'future dictator' camouflaged by anonymity, and made his version of the novel six years later, calling it *The Stranger*. The detective in *The Smiler with the Knife* is a woman, Georgia Strangeways, and Welles – against the studio's better judgement – wanted to give the role of Georgia Strangeways to Lucille Ball. He remembered this when planning *The Stranger*, where his first choice for the government sleuth was Agnes Moorehead. Welles – who had a wary, fearful respect for the grounded good sense and intuitive understanding that are female prerogatives – knew that the person likeliest to demystify a great man was a woman. Macbeth is henpecked, and Desdemona treats Othello as a big baby. Once more a meddlesome producer prevailed, and the part was rewritten for Edward G. Robinson.

The plot of *The Smiler with the Knife* turns up two candidates for Führer in waiting, both of whom are intriguingly Wellesian. The first to come under suspicion is a modern scientific magus, a Faust whose cabbalistic specialty is bacteriology. His colleagues dismiss Professor Hargreaves Steele as '"a charlatan" or "a bit of a mountebank"'. He adores 'putting on a show. It was as though, entering the laboratory, he assumed the weird cloak of an ancient alchemist.' But rather than magicking base metals into gold, he incubates cholera, tuberculosis and bubonic plague, with which he infects those who betray the cause. Georgia, when she attends a fascist conclave, compares this cult and its mouldy rites to a broken-down vaudeville act. The ceremony's atmosphere reminds her of the 'crankiness, make-believe and rather seedy mysticism which is apt to overcome a religion . . . in its decadence'. She could be describing Cagliostro with his misappropriated masonic symbols. But the parody also coincides with the truth, since the Third Reich was both a brutally efficient bureaucratic system and an insanely idealised anachronistic romance. The judge in *The Stranger* seems to recall Georgia's account when he considers rumours of a Nazi resurgence in Germany after the war: 'men drilling by night, underground meeting-places and pagan rituals'. As Kurtz is buried, Conrad's Marlow ponders 'the unearthly hate of the mysteries [he] had penetrated'. By 1940, those mysteries were the foundation of a political doctrine, and the 'extreme party' Kurtz's cousin vaguely says he might have led had acquired a name.

In the novel, Georgia identifies Lord Chilton Canteloe as the presumptive despot because 'he was a self-deceiver on the heroic scale, and of that stuff dictators are made'. He deceives himself because he 'could never doubt . . . the truth of his own words'. The insight served as a remonstrance to Welles: self-disbelief and the confession of fraudulence were a means of moral and political insurance. Nevertheless, the changes he made to the novel brought Canteloe closer to himself. Canteloe is an experimental aviator. Welles, when he Americanised the setting, identified him with Howard Hughes, who had circumnavigated the earth by air in 1938, and struggled – like a propulsive superman – to get his lumbering Spruce Goose to fly. Grounded in later life, Hughes became a misanthropic recluse, letting his hair and his fingernails grow, living in hermetically sealed hotel rooms and eating from sterilised plates. In *F for Fake*, Welles looks up at his eyrie on the top floor of a Las Vegas hotel, as if peering through the fence at Xanadu at his unseen double. By this stage he had become, as he told Keith Baxter, 'the Howard Hughes of the cinema'.

The Hughes of *The Smiler with the Knife* was not yet this embittered wild man. As a pilot, he is a technological autocrat, accustomed to supremacy. Welles knew all about this unholy conviction of pre-eminence, however sincerely he disapproved of it. He therefore saw the dictator emerging from his own profession: the script predicts that the American Führer will 'look like a movie star and everybody'll love him'. Welles thought that there were controls built into American politics, and accepted the check on his own ambitions. He decided not to run for the Senate in 1944, because that could only have been a rehearsal for an eventual bid to become chief executive. Kane marries a President's niece, and wants to make her a President's wife. Welles dared not hope for the same outcome: he was convinced that a divorced actor could never be elected President. He smirked sorrowfully when Reagan proved him wrong. But he was right about Hughes, who after the war consolidated his aerial empire by founding TWA and buying up RKO. America's homegrown versions of Kurtz no longer needed to rely on extermination. Tycoons like Hughes or Hearst wielded power outside politics, because they owned the media of communication.

When *The Smiler with the Knife* fell through, Welles transposed Conrad's fable from Africa to Latin America, and between 1940 and 1942 again tried to film it, this time using a novel by Arthur Calder-Marshall, *The Way to Santiago,* as his pretext. He prepared a script, which was given the off-hand, generic title *Mexican Melodrama*; the result once more was *Heart of Darkness* by other means – a journey through the jungle in quest of a fascist who is plotting to overthrow Mexico's revolutionary government and install a totalitarian regime modelled on and bankrolled by the Third Reich. Welles improved Calder-Marshall's plot and made it more personal (though with the usual sly disclaimers). The novel sends a journalist – who complains that he is 'just a news-agency man, a damned loudspeaker' – to a jungle outpost where oil is secretly traded for German arms; the fascist mastermind Lionel Transit, who feels 'it was god-like to take a life', stays behind in Mexico City. Marlow is not travelling to meet Kurtz. He has known him all along, without suspecting his political machinations. As if taking the hint about the loudspeaker, Welles places a radio station in the jungle, and has his Kurtz, who is given the chiming alliterative name of Kellar, broadcast treacherous propaganda from there, calling himself Mr England. Welles was to play a man with amnesia who is mistaken for Kellar; he makes the journey to discover the quisling's real identity, and is captured and tortured by Kellar. Managing to escape, he takes over the radio station, and transmits a warning about the coup. He claims on air that he is holding a time bomb which will blow up the munitions stored by the fascists; it ticks inexorably through his oration, as in *The Fountain of Youth*, and then noisily detonates. Has Welles gallantly laid down his life for the cause? Not really: the film was to end, like the *War of the Worlds* broadcast, by admitting its own fraudulence, with Welles revealed after the blast cheerfully holding an alarm clock up to the microphone.

Since Welles is Kellar's double, he has another chance to play Kurtz, though he soon safely reverts to the role of Marlow. Still, the final twist he gives to Calder-Marshall's plot complicates matters. *Heart of Darkness* ends with a lie, when Marlow deceives the Intended. *Mexican Melodrama* was to end with a hoax, as Welles deceives an entire nation. He must have appreciated an ironic epilogue to the failed coup in Calder-Marshall's novel. General Torres, the future military dictator whose waddles give him the look of 'a Disney toad', escapes to Los Angeles, and Transit jeers that Hearst will probably invite him for weekends at San Simeon.

Heart of Darkness influenced the subject of *Citizen Kane*, its setting and, above all, its form. Xanadu, by the time Welles began to film *Kane* in mid-1940, contained reminiscences of the imaginary landscapes he had travelled through on his way there – Calder-Marshall's 'hot country', and above all Conrad's Congo. Swampy and fetid, Kane's estate might be the malarial outpost over which Kurtz presides. Leland tells Kane, as if he were Kurtz, to 'sail away to a desert island and lord it over the monkeys'; he has done exactly that, which justified Welles's use of sets for Skull Island left over from RKO's *Son of Kong*. Chimpanzees survey Kane's rank garden from inside their cages, and alligators snap and squabble in a pit. Leathern-winged predators flap through the undergrowth during the torch-lit picnic. Perhaps these resemblances are coincidental, but the analogy with *Heart of Darkness* is clear enough in the construction of Welles's narrative. Like Conrad's story, the film is a series of partial, subjective, chronologically jumbled reports on a character who never testifies directly. The enigma of both Kurtz and Kane is summed up in their dying utterances. When Kurtz breathily cries out 'The horror! The horror!', Marlow asks 'Did he live his entire life again in every detail of desire, temptation, and surrender during that supreme moment of complete knowledge?' The same question is asked throughout the film by the reporters who try to interpret Kane's one-word testimonial, 'Rosebud'. The investigator Thompson, played by William Alland, registers a doubt when questioned about it: 'I don't think any word can explain a man's life.' This agnostic aside enables Welles to puncture his own illusion. At least a reliable narrator heard Kurtz say 'The horror', but how do the journalists know about Kane's dying utterance, since there was no witness in the room? Raymond the butler, played by Paul Stewart, says he overheard that last gasp; we know he was not there. Already the myth has started to accrete, and people are writing themselves into it. Raymond weakens his reliability as narrator and interpreter when he remarks that Kane 'said all kinds of things that didn't mean anything'. So is meaning attributed after the event, with no chance of certainty? That is Conrad's suggestion when, as in *Lord Jim*, he collates the contradictory testimonies of bystanders, each of whom sees only a particle of the elusive truth.

The Lady from Shanghai, on which Welles began work in 1946, also grew out of that unrealised, unforgotten *Heart of Darkness*. Welles's script changed the initial setting of Conrad's story: instead of beginning with a meeting of old mariners in the Pool of London, it would have started in New York harbour. This is where *The Lady from Shanghai* starts, with an establishing shot of the Brooklyn Bridge, and O'Hara develops into a Conradian character: a meditative mariner, compromised by landed entanglements. The most telling overlap between the two projects is in the name given to Kurtz's anonymous fiancée, to whom Marlow tells emollient lies about his end. Conrad honorifically identifies her as the Intended, the generic woman who waits at home and weeps. But Welles decided she should be called Elsa, and she bequeathed that name to the lady from Shanghai.

There is a difference. The Elsa in the later film, a gelid blonde played by Rita Hayworth, is most definitely not 'out of it', as Conrad says women should be – remote from the fray, protected from political involvement. Conrad's Kurtz begs Marlow to remember him to the Intended. Marlow – upholding the hypocritical fiction of social morality – spares her 'the horror' and vows that his last words were of her. Welles did not favour such genteel clemency. In *The Stranger*, Mary (Loretta Young), who has trustingly married Kindler, is shown a film documenting the industrial system he devised for murdering Jews. The script's choice of words makes it clear that this Intended is not to be shielded from the truth. 'Why do you want me to look at these horrors?' she demands. In adapting *Heart of Darkness*, Welles came up with an ingenious variant of Conrad's evasive, merciful conclusion. Kurtz in the film was to bestow Elsa on Marlow as a parting gift, and the producers were ready to promote *Heart of Darkness* as a torrid tropical romance, improbably emphasising Welles's tanned muscularity. This triangle is sickeningly complicated in *The Lady from Shanghai*, where the crippled, impotent Bannister acquiesces in Elsa's seduction of O'Hara, even using her as bait.

Welles filmed a truncated sequence from *Heart of Darkness* when the yacht in *The Lady from Shanghai* cruises down the Mexican coast on its way from New York to San Francisco. On the journey up the African river, Welles's Marlow was to deposit Elsa at the Third Station while he travelled on alone to encounter Kurtz. In the later film, Elsa refuses to be left behind, and – rakishly affecting a naval cap – even charts the yacht's course. Off the Mexican coast, she insists on a pause for a picnic, and a fleet of row boats edges up a jungly river, with an alligator maliciously yawning in the scum-crusted water. The Conradian outing is all the more suggestive because the picnic is held on a beach. Why did they have to explore that dangerous stream? Why not simply anchor in the bay? Welles was literally taking the characters out of their way in order to make this allusion to *Heart of Darkness*. Such reminiscential detours had become a habit. The ship in *Journey into Fear* travels across the Aegean, but its itinerary is as regressive as Marlow's voyage through the Congo; the threatened hero of Eric Ambler's novel (on which Welles and Joseph Cotten based their script) learns during the voyage that 'civilisation was a word and . . . [he] still lived in the jungle'. The old Nazi played by Konstantin Shayne in *The Stranger* escapes from a prison in Germany and makes his way to New England, but with a stopover in South America. Welles filmed an extended sequence that showed Meinike skulking in alleys in fetid equatorial cities; the studio threw it away. It may not have been relevant to the plot, but it allowed another of Kurtz's avatars to bring the jungle with him to the Connecticut woods.

Welles played Kurtz once again in *The Third Man*, benefiting from Graham Greene's obsession with the Conrad story. Greene acknowledged his debt by giving Kurtz's name to one of Harry Lime's cronies, a vulpine baron who cradles a sycophantic dachshund; two parents in his novel *It's A Battlefield* repay the same debt by naming their son Conrad, in memory of a lodger who used to be a merchant seaman. Greene's Baron Kurtz, played by Ernst Deutsch, acts as a post-mortem spokesman for

Harry Lime, and in reporting his last words to the ingenuous Holly Martins he paraphrases the lie told by Marlow at the end of *Heart of Darkness*. Marlow assures the Intended that 'The last word he pronounced was – your name.' Martins, played by Joseph Cotten, is now the Intended, whose shock and grief the Baron tries to soothe by saying that, as Lime lay dying in the street, 'Even at the end his thoughts were of you.' Martins asks 'What did he say?' Kurtz squirms and admits 'I can't remember the exact words.' Later Martins assumes Marlow's role, and is challenged by Anna (Alida Valli), Lime's true Intended, to tell the same sentimental lie. At the station buffet, when Martins is trying to coax her back on to the train, she guesses that he has seen Lime. 'Did he say anything about me?' she asks. 'Tell me.' Holly, not wanting to reveal that Lime betrayed her to the Russians, replies 'Oh, the usual things.' This time the Intended is not so trusting, and Anna demands 'Why are you lying?' Despite the euphemisms of his loyal friends, Lime is a Kurtz whose supercilious amorality saves him from being horrified by his own crimes.

The most unsettling identification between Welles and Kurtz comes in a creepily vivid description of him in MacLíammóir's memoir *All for Hecuba*. The passage, recalling Welles's theatrical apprenticeship in Dublin, does not mention *Heart of Darkness*, but the primitivism of the story pervades it. Roaring with mockery after his recital of all those precocious, fantastical triumphs, Welles releases what MacLíammóir calls 'a frenzy of laughter': once again that word, recurrent in commentaries on the man and his work, hints at delirium and derangement. His teeth flash, his eyes retract into slits, his brow furrows and 'a big pale tongue', adder-like, darts out of hiding. MacLíammóir, stunned by the explosion, only slowly 'emerged from the jungle whence he had dragged me'. Tynan concurred when describing Welles's laughter in a profile written five years later in 1951. As the chortling fit began, Tynan said that Welles's shoulders rose like milk on the boil, and he fumed 'like an awakened volcano'. In 1961, in another profile, he tried out another alarmingly sublime image, and called Welles's laughter as 'irresistible as Niagara'.

Watching Welles act during that first Dublin season, MacLíammóir might have been analysing the methods by which Kurtz established his rule in a wilderness beyond the boundary of civilisation. 'The demon of showmanship' made Welles behave in a 'dark and brutal way', teasing and tyrannising audiences he despised, performing with 'impromptu savagery' and once more 'trumpeting his jungle laughter', like an obstreperous elephant. At curtain calls, the same laugh, 'like fire in the jungle', rampaged through lips that resembled 'dark tropical plants'. In a later passage, MacLíammóir remembers being met by Welles on a Manhattan pier when he and Edwards arrived for their summer season at Todd School in 1934. Their host swelled and towered, like a primitive plant whose growth had been freakishly accelerated; though the geometrical, mechanistic city of New York reared behind him, MacLíammóir saw Welles as a 'jungle that yawned and laughed'.

In his account of that summer, MacLíammóir edges nearer to the unholy riot of Welles's energy, and finds in it an expression of the national character. At Todd, Welles played Svengali the hypnotist in Gerald du Maurier's *Trilby*, but misjudged the emotional temper of the piece. Since he knew nothing 'of love, of intimacy', he turned the character into a 'lowering barbarian' – thus making him, in MacLíammóir's view, a self-portrait. Welles, suddenly comprehensible now that MacLíammóir had seen him on native ground, embodied the barbarism and titanism of his young, brawling country. Looking back, MacLíammóir wisely concluded that Welles 'had not yet found his true métier, which was a preoccupation with restless grandeur and intoxication, a view of life wholly American, welling up from the soil of that huge territory which had given him birth' – welling up, it could be added, like the geyser of oil that spurted out of the rich American ground in his production of *Around the World*. Welles used the same image to describe his talent, and the indulgence it won him at RKO. 'A certain amount of outrage always goes with hitting a gusher,' he told Bogdanovich. 'Here was the unique gusher of all time.'

There is rapture in these romantic metaphors, and also a sense of what Kurtz called horror. Whenever Welles lazily yawned or convulsively laughed, MacLíammóir felt he was looking into the heart – or at least the mouth – of a dangerous, engulfing darkness.

The stories Welles told or acted out are fables of power – of its acquisition, its heady misuse, and its loss. Bright Lucifer is cast out of heaven, Arkadin abruptly deplanes without a parachute. Mr Clay, in *The Immortal Story*, challenges the limits of human life by attempting to meddle with the future. He wants, as his clerk says, 'to demonstrate his omnipotence – to do the thing which cannot be done'. Welles overreached like all these characters, and had performed in enough tragedies to know the penalty for such exorbitant desires.

Thanks to adoring adults who sent reports of his childish achieve-ments to the newspapers, Welles had greatness thrust upon him. The unconditional love of his mother and his guardian Dr Maurice Bernstein (whose surname Welles gave to one of Kane's cronies) persuaded him of his invincibility. In Conrad's *Heart of Darkness*, others prattle about the supremacy of Kurtz, leaving Marlow free to wonder what he has done to deserve such veneration. Welles's script goads Kurtz himself to make the claim, and to do so four times over (though still without vouchsafing any details). 'I'm a great man, Marlow,' he says, 'really great – greater than the great men before me.' He sounds like a giddy adolescent perusing a fanciful wish list, rather than Conrad's disillusioned hollow man. Megalomania is pardonable in the young, but the Welles who wrote this blabbing, unguarded speech never entirely outgrew his belief that greatness was a vocation, an end that justified whatever profligate or violent means you used along the way. He once made the offhand, revealing remark that Macbeth 'is detestable until he becomes king; after that he becomes a great man'. Did he mean that greatness licenses Macbeth's crimes? that it inheres in royalty? or that, when achieved, it has to be paid for with insomniac misery? Macbeth himself does not excuse his actions by bragging of his greatness, as Lear, Othello and Hamlet all do. On the contrary, he feels like an imposter, a fraud: the giant's cloak is worn by a dwarfish thief. Welles's own sozzled, reeling Macbeth confirms the point. Mentioning Macbeth on another occasion, he called him 'a great man, who knows good wine and has lost the taste for it'. An impromptu definition hides in the phrase. The great man has the power to gratify all his lusts, but cannot afford to take pleasure in doing so. This is why, having worked through Shakespeare's tragedies, Welles attached himself to Falstaff, who – in his view – represents not greatness but goodness and never loses any of his appetites.

Charles Laughton once said that he acted because he liked to imitate great men. Welles may have written those lines for Kurtz, but he later set himself to live down the boast or threat they contain. Rather than wanting to be great by association, he whittled away at the greatness others wished upon him, hoping to free himself from his own myth. He gently deflected the tributes of hero worshippers. Tynan – whose flushed tract on stardom, *He That Plays The King*, was published in 1950 with an avuncular foreword by Welles – regretted this demurral. At the end of his book he calls *Citizen Kane* 'a very great picture' but, after acclaiming the 'roaring-valiant fanfare' of Olivier's voice, he goes on to regret that

Welles, 'an actor of heroic pretensions', had made a film that 'introduces us to heroes . . . to cure us of hero-worship . . . We need, not cure, but reinfection.' Tynan called for a resurgence of heroic acting as a reproof to the shabby, straitened, unheroic times he lived in: as Welles said, 'I do not believe that a book like this . . . would, or could have been written before the war.' In 1943, aged sixteen, Tynan had written a hymn of praise to Welles in his school magazine, which began by announcing 'There is a man flourishing now and being mighty on the other side of the Atlantic.' It was, coincidentally, the same devout turn of phrase Kurtz uses in Welles's script when commending the heroism of Hitler: 'There's a man now in Europe . . .' Nevertheless, despite his avuncular discouragement of Tynan's idolatry, Welles was not pleased when his fan made a rapid recovery. In 1951 Tynan reviewed Welles's *Othello* on stage in London, and found it 'grand and gross' but not great. He nicknamed the performance Citizen Coon, and intended the first word – with its allusion to mean, democratic drabness – to be just as insulting as the second. Welles was infuriated. If he was to be brutally dragged down to ground, he preferred to do the work of desecration himself.

At the end of *Touch of Evil*, Schwartz, using the tempting, toxic adjective, calls Quinlan a great detective. Tanya adds that he was a lousy cop. Welles relied on such remorseful memos to himself, because all his life he retained a giddy infatuation with power, which he saw as a pre-condition of greatness. As an old man, he wondered whether he might not have reversed the course of American history during the 1950s. If he had run for the Senate in Wisconsin in 1946 and won, he would have kept McCarthy out of office and forestalled McCarthyism. He invited America to bewail its lost leader. It was a fantasy: it is hard to imagine Welles dealing and compromising, as an elected official has to do. But he indulged this dream of an alternative life by playing potentates of every kind, from the atavistic chieftain Burundai in an Italian extravaganza called *The Tartars* to Kurtz, the modern engineer of genocide. Welles pretended to be a pair of emperors, Haile Selasse and Hirohito, on *The March of Time*.

In 1966 he spent a day or two as Cardinal Wolsey in Fred Zinnemann's *A Man for All Seasons*. In his robes of office he looks like an overblown, pustular tomato, and when he browbeats Paul Scofield's Thomas More to support a royal divorce he utters the repeated word 'pressure' with a malevolent wheezing hiss, as air rushes out through a vent in his inflated body. Welles's weight was the crudest and most irresistible kind of power. Even the merchant Mr Clay behaves imperiously, like the most unhinged of Roman emperors. Virginie in *The Immortal Story*, played by Jeanne Moreau, likens him to Nero, who thought he 'owned all the world'. Welles even brought the same fantasy of dominion and absolute, irresponsible power to his role in *Man in the Shadow*, a Western he appeared in for Universal immediately before *Touch of Evil*. As a tyrannical rancher, he plays The Shadow again, and during the credit titles skulks in the gloom behind the chain-link fence that encloses his property. The sign, like the one at Xanadu, warns NO TRESPASSING; the name of the spread, evoking all the realms Welles had lorded it over and lost, is The Golden Empire. He boasts that the ranch is larger than five or six European countries (thus outdoing Hearst's San Simeon, which was merely half the size of Rhode Island). But his influence extends beyond the fortified perimeter. 'I can whip the whole county!' he yells. 'Like you were God,' snarls his rebellious daughter. Welles enjoys the same feudal authority over a private demesne in *Trouble in the Glen*. A tinker who went to war against Hitler grumbles 'I didn't fight one dictator to come home and bow my neck before another.' The film begins, like *Citizen Kane*, at the forbidding fence of a misty estate – except that the owner, a tawny-complexioned Welles, strolls on and invites us in. He gestures towards his distant castle, though it cannot be seen through the blue fog, much of which is exhaled by his cigar. Near the end, more embattled, he closes off the right of way and posts a NO TRESPASSING sign – just as in *Kane*, though now the lettering is in Gaelic.

Welles had a queasy fellow-feeling for the politicians who, during the 1930s, bullied whole countries into capitulation. He nudged his way into proximity with them, and claimed to have stumbled across Hitler in a Tyrolean beer-garden in the 1920s. Among his temporary residences in the 1950s was a villa at Fregene, built in the muscle-bound fascist style by one of Mussolini's henchmen. The newsreel in *Citizen Kane* shows the magnate fraternising with a scruffy Hitler lookalike, and includes documentary footage of Stalin, for whom Welles nurtured a certain tenderness.

He based the appearance of Colonel Haki, the Turkish police chief in *Journey into Fear*, on Stalin, with eyebrows like barbed wire and a fiercely interrogatory gaze. The resemblance is underlined by a poster of Stalin glaring from a wall when the ship docks at Batumi, in Russian territory. Characters in Eric Ambler's novel gossip about the Asiatic savagery of Haki, who enjoys tormenting captives; Haki himself scoffs at 'the so-called democratic forms of government', which impede his swift revenges. The script by Welles and Cotten cut such philosophising, and Welles plays Haki, allegedly a sexual satyr, as little more than a gruff, awkward flirt. The West, needing Stalin as an ally during the war against Hitler, preferred to think of him as Uncle Joe, bear-like and brutish but ultimately amiable. Welles also used Stalin as a physiognomic reference-point in *Mr Arkadin* and, as before, did his best to exonerate him. He said that Arkadin resembled what Stalin might have been if he had left Russia before becoming a communist; they were both Slavic characters, combining ruthlessness with mawkish sentimentality. Arkadin negligently sentences inconvenient nobodies to death, but he dearly loves his daughter.

Welles's special pleading on Stalin's behalf brought him into collusion with Eisenstein, who in 1944–45 paid homage to Stalin's favourite Czar in *Ivan the Terrible*. While Eisenstein was on location in Kazakhstan, the producer Alexander Korda tried to entice him into collaborating with Welles on a film of *War and Peace*. Korda wanted Welles to act in it and Eisenstein to direct; they would have written the script together. Ivan wields power with the aid of bodyguards, spies and ruffians with axes; Kane owes his omnipresence to the media he manages. Compared with *Ivan*, however, *Kane* has the saving grace of irony. In the newsreel, assorted opponents describe Kane as both a fascist and a communist. Eisenstein's Soviet overseers allowed him no such ambiguity. Kane may joke about starting the Spanish-American war to boost circulation of his papers, but Ivan actually raises a permanent army and sends it into battle against the Crimean Khan. Eisenstein's film is about the ruthless consolidation of power, Welles's about its gradual erosion. Ivan frets over the succession, but Kane seems not to notice his only son's death in a car crash: he knows that nothing can be perpetuated. *Ivan the Terrible* is a militant epic, *Citizen Kane* an elegy.

As well as consorting with Hitler, Kane confers in the newsreel with a Winston Churchill imitator. Welles brashly instigated an acquaintance with Churchill at a hotel on the Lido in Venice. He was trying to raise money to continue filming *Othello*, and gambled on impressing a Russian backer by greeting Churchill in the restaurant. The bluff worked; Churchill returned his salute, and Welles got the Russian funds. Welles gratefully called him 'this great man – the greatest living fellow'. But Churchill was also a disgruntled lion in winter, a lost leader who no longer held office. Observing him, Welles began to appreciate the celebrity's irresponsibility, so unlike the politician's obligation to behave in whatever way society deems proper. He and Churchill were both invited to a costume ball, notorious for its ostentation. Welles, speeding off across the lagoon in fancy dress in his launch, saw Churchill lingering enviously on the dock. He didn't dare to accept the invitation, because he hoped to be returned to power in a forthcoming election, and could not afford to be photographed disporting himself in such louche company.

Welles had the chance to impersonate Churchill in 1967, when the National Theatre planned to stage Rolf Hochhuth's *Soldiers*, in which Churchill – blackmailed by the Russians in 1943 – consents to the murder of General Sikorski, the chivalrous leader of the Free Poles. Peter Brook suggested Welles for the role, reasoning that 'anyone who can play Lear can play Churchill'. Hochhuth might have written the part with Welles in mind. Though his decision send tens of thousands of men into motion, Churchill spends much of the play 'motionless as a Buddha', lolling in bed or wallowing in a bath; Welles, oppressively heavy, could not be expected to exert himself. When Churchill emerges barefoot from the bathroom, dripping as if a breaker had dashed itself on the beach, Hochhuth – virtually quoting the secretary when Arkadin says he wants to go waterskiing – likens him to 'Neptune rising from the waves'. Hochhuth expected the actor at this point to undertake a 'leap from comedy to myth'. Welles managed the transmutation when playing Falstaff, and hinted that he was ready to do so again: as he said, he already had the cigar – an inseparable prop for him as for Churchill. But the National Theatre gave in to political persuasion and rejected the play. Welles later agreed to play Churchill in a Russian film about the liberation of Europe, with Paul Scofield as Roosevelt; it was never made.

He had another chance to be a modern warlord in 1970, when he appeared as General Dreedle in *Catch-22*, directed by Mike Nichols. Elephantine in khaki, he has the bulldog mien of Churchill, and hands his cigar to a nubile female assistant before inspecting the troops. His jowls quiver with menace as he orders a subordinate to be marched off to the firing squad, and he blinks when reminded that he has no such executive power. In his second scene, he visits the Italian front to present a bombing crew with medals for hitting the wrong target. As his plane taxis to a halt, he puffs into view, preceded by the usual fuming cigar, and the soundtrack blares out the fanfare from Strauss's *Also sprach Zarathustra*: Welles found it hard to cast off the role of superman, even though this Zarathustra could no longer dance on the peaks of mountains and vault over crevasses.

Aristotle thought of tragedy as the preserve of great men – emperors, generals, or Welles's twentieth-century plutocrats – and said that comedy dealt with mean, lowly, ridiculous creatures, morally and socially inferior. Welles merged the genres because he found both human categories within himself. His Falstaff in *Chimes at Midnight*, when sent out as a recruiting officer, takes bribes from unwilling conscripts, and protects himself from blame by his usual evasive irony. Welles's Dreedle, however, is forced to preside over a bloody farce, and has to reward racketeers, cowards and incompetents for their heroism. Alan Arkin, playing Yossarian, strips naked on parade, which means that his medal can't be pinned on. 'What the hell do I care?' says Welles, having reached a point of jesting despair which is midway between tragedy and comedy. His question colloquially compresses a speech by another besieged, demoralised general, Macbeth, who also contemplates the idiocy of history. No wonder Welles had longed to make his own film of Joseph Heller's novel, before the studio assigned the project to Nichols.

Borrowing the title of Tynan's book, Welles liked to define himself as a 'king-actor', the kind of performer whose physique and commanding voice made him an inevitable choice for royal roles. Who else could play the 'certain great and powerful king' referred to in the epigraph that introduces *Mr Arkadin*? But in the same epigraph, Welles sketched a second, antagonistic role for himself. The great and powerful king asks a poet to grant him a favour, which is to accept a gift. The poet agrees, though he makes a condition: the king can bestow on him 'anything, sir, but your secret'. Once you know the king's secret – as Falstaff or Poins know Hal's in *Chimes at Midnight* – you can destroy him; and he, knowing that, will take steps to destroy you first. Welles was both the great man and the great man's intimately seditious enemy. Inside him, Kurtz and Marlow fought it out, each vowing to exterminate the other. He who plays the king must also enact what Richard II calls the 'death of kings'.

Brutus kills Caesar because he plays the king and wants to accept the crown offered to him. That early role established Welles's rectitude – as a citizen of the American republic, as a liberal critic of authoritarian rule. But he could also play Caesar or Cesare Borgia (who was a would-be

Caesar), Kane or a Khan (and not only the Khan called Kubla: as a child he was said to resemble Genghis Khan, and was capable of murderous fury if left unfed). Ione, McGafferty's mistress in MacLeish's *Panic,* calls him Caesar and refers to herself as the empire he can pillage or ravish at will. Real-life McGaffertys were not shy about deploying the same analogies. In 1976, J. Paul Getty, who housed his art collection in a Malibu villa modelled on a pleasure palace at Herculaneum, said 'I feel no qualms . . . about likening the Getty Oil Company to an Empire – and myself to a Caesar.' The domineering hero is no longer a king or a general, as Aristotle expected. In *Panic* he is a financier, whose downfall derives from no moral flaw: it is the logical consequence of an infirm economic system. No knife is necessary, and MacLeish's play does not even reveal how he kills himself. His fall is the devaluation of a share in the market, rather than a stockbroker's plunge from a Wall Street window ledge. Declared unbankable when workers, depositors, investors and politicians revoke their trust, he simply implodes.

For a while, McGafferty keeps himself afloat by scrambling to raise cash: 'A hundred million does it', he says. His methods are those Welles later adopted. He issues paper, making promises which (like Welles's contractual undertakings) will never be kept. The result for McGafferty is a collapse of confidence, though that did not deter Welles. Françoise Sagan admired the 'royal disdain' with which he treated producers and accountants. Rather than pleading for hand-outs, he behaved as if he were requisitioning booty or levying taxes, and defied the backers to expect anything definite from him in return. Bill Krohn's experience when attempting to arrange that interview convinced him that Welles possessed a personality that was 'authentically royal'. He insisted on exercising his divine right to be difficult, in order to warn lesser mortals that they were his subjects, not fellow citizens. You could not make contractual deals with him, because this implied reciprocity and there-fore equality. He granted favours from on high, as a generous whim, like the king in *Mr Arkadin*, and there was no way to make him beholden to you. Krohn only secured his telephone interview by deferentially presenting Welles with a morsel of food. You do not offer kings money. Even if down on their luck, like Welles, they must go on pre-tending to have everything. But you are allowed to feed them. Krohn arranged to have a loaf of pumpernickel bread sent from a Manhattan bakery to Welles's hotel; constrained by the ethic of noblesse oblige, Welles consented to receive his telephone call. As always when flattered by admirers, Welles was ready with a caustic self-parody. Recording *The Merchant of Venice* in 1938, he played both Shylock and Portia's suitor the Prince of Morocco, who in his performance is an affectedly histrionic mimic of Othello. Welles tartly describes the man in a spoken stage direction: 'a somewhat windy, somewhat self-important and very regal person'.

Welles reminded Krohn of Louis XIV, with his solar munificence. He did play Louis XVIII in Bondarchuk's *Waterloo*, but made the part into a comment on his own diminished autocracy. Napoleon denounces the 'fat king', burns him in a portly effigy, then evicts him from his palace. In the first of his two brief scenes, Welles sits impassively while flustered courtiers bring the news of the upstart's escape from Elba, too sluggish to respond. Only his lips petulantly twitch, as if he would rather be eating. As a king he is just a solemn, ceremonious totem, not the force of heroic will represented by Napoleon – or by the youthful Welles when he set out on his own Napoleonic adventure of conquest. In those leaner days he might have played the self-made emperor: Korda, trying to recruit Welles for that unmade film of *War and Peace*, offered him a choice between the roles of Napoleon and the bookish idealist Pierre, who tries to assassinate the invader as Moscow burns. (Welles, pledged as always to symbolic acts of self-destruction, would probably have preferred to play both parts.) In his second scene in *Waterloo*, he walks unsteadily down a staircase, supported by a cane and observed by his grieving court, then steps into a sagging carriage which will carry him off into oblivion. The physical effort is obvious. Those long spindly legs, not much stronger than the self-referring cane, have to support his bulk; he struggles to maintain control, though his lips quiver.

He felt a sense of kinship with such characters, physically retrieving them from the limbo of elapsed time. In a spasm of italicised excitement, he told Bogdanovich that he was '*just three handshakes from Napoleon!*' As a boy he had shaken the hand (he said) of Sarah Bernhardt, who when young had met one of Napoleon's mistresses; adding a few more links to the chain of affinity and reminiscence, he thought that 'four or five very old men could join hands and take you right back to Shakespeare', since 'history is so short'. This is why the middle-aged Welles treated the doddery Shallow in *Chimes at Midnight* so tenderly, and why the young Welles aged himself with the help of prostheses. Old men are historians, and the ancestry of the world is inscribed in their bodies.

Those handshakes reached out across a century and quickened the dead. But Welles realised that this warm manual contact was illusory. History cannot be so easily abridged, and there is no arguing with the oblivion that democratically equalises great men and nonentities. Therefore he took a grim pleasure in attempting to efface Napoleon from history when he accepted a walk-on in a biographical film about the emperor. In Sacha Guitry's *Napoleon*, made in 1954, Welles plays the bigoted gaoler Hudson-Lowe, in charge of funeral arrangements for his single illustrious prisoner on St Helena. With an adamantine rampart of grey hair and eyebrows as thick as hedges, he denies honorific titles to Napoleon, tears up sketches for flattering memorials, and at last curtly agrees to a blank tombstone. The historian tries to save lives by writing them. Time all the same erases all trace of us, like the fire that melts away the name written on Kane's sled.

In 1975, making amends for the cruelty of youth, Welles wrote a foreword to the memoirs of Marion Davies, whom he had traduced as the mewling soprano in *Citizen Kane*. He must have sympathised with the title of the book, which looked back to long-ago revels at San Simeon. It was called *The Times We Had*, which echoes Shallow's recollection of juvenile capers in the prologue to *Chimes at Midnight*: 'Jesus, the days that we have seen!' Having posthumously apologised to Davies, who died before her book was published, Welles went on to reappraise Hearst. His foreword returns to the old issue of Hearst's similarity to Kane, but also deals with a subtler and more unsettling similarity between Hearst and himself. He quotes Hearst's cable to Frederic Remington, whom he despatched to Cuba to sketch hostilities between the rival empires of Spain and America. When Remington reported that there was nothing to draw, Hearst commanded 'You make the pictures, I'll make the war.' The exchange got into *Kane* almost verbatim, though it is prose poems the reporter is asked to transmit: Welles could hardly let anyone else make pictures. Quoting the cable, Welles disingenuously calls it 'the only purely Hearstian element in *Citizen Kane*'. In fact, this aspect of Kane's managerial dealings is probably carried over from *The Cradle Will Rock*, in which the boss of Steeltown, Mr Mister, visits the local newspaper office to bludgeon Editor Daily. 'News', he tells the quaking hack, 'can be made to order.' Editor Daily is enlisted for Mr Mister's Liberty Committee, which wants to deny liberty to union members – the source, conceivably, for that soon-perjured Declaration of Principles drawn up by Kane, in which he promises to 'tell all the news honestly'. Leland also paraphrases Larry Foreman in *The Cradle Will Rock* when he warns Kane about unionised labour, which means that the worker will expect benefits 'as his right, and not your gift'.

In the foreword, Welles then makes a more reliably confessional remark on Hearst's message to Remington: this, he says, is 'the true voice of power', and power is supposedly the prerogative of great men (who, according to Aristotle, have a sinecure on tragedy). Welles contrasts Hearst with the buccaneering tycoon Onassis, who was 'neither a great man nor a great force in the world; he was – quite simply and purely – a celebrity'. This new category of supernatural beings had been created by the Hearst press, which 'practically invented' the gossip column; it was Hearst's scavenger of Hollywood tittle-tattle, Louella Parsons, who alerted him to the slander in *Citizen Kane*. In 1940, after the break-up of their partnership, Houseman noted with astonishment that 'Orson has become a public figure only less frequently and massively projected into the news than Franklin D. Roosevelt, N. Chamberlain and A. Hitler.' Having so skilfully aped the voice of power on the radio by mimicking all those politicians, it was hard for him to realise that he was not, like them, a force in the world. Once, speaking at the Cinémathèque française, Welles indignantly denied that he was a movie star, and insisted on calling himself an actor. Stars, he explained, were more than actors: their status made them comparable with the President of the United States. In saying this, he conceded that the chief executive was also a man who merely played at being king. What other kind of power was there? Thanks to the media managed by Hearst or Kane, politicians and performers had been equated, since both belonged to a floating consortium of show people.

The theologian Xenophanes clucked his tongue over Greek myth because 'Homer and Hesiod say that the gods do all manner of things which man would consider disgraceful – adultery, stealing, deceiving each other.' Celebrities are also profane deities, whose vices we enviously license. They have no power to make war; they can only make scandalous extra-marital love. A great man bereft of power can enjoy a shoddy second career as a celebrity. This shaming fate overtook Churchill, who joined Onassis's circus: he went along on the Mediterranean cruise in 1959 when Onassis seduced Maria Callas. The same ignominy befell both Onassis and Welles in Terence Rattigan's script for *The V.I.P.s*. The V.I.P.s are celebrities, gods grounded by bad weather at London airport.

Welles plays a harried, impecunious film director, while Burton helpfully introduces himself as a 'near-mythical tycoon called Paul Andros', based on Onassis. They air their private tribulations in public, as celebrities are required to do. Welles schemes to abscond from the tax authorities while scavenging funds for a new film, Burton quarrels with Elizabeth Taylor and boozily makes peace.

Such people are temporary gods, tolerated so long as their misbehaviour amuses us; they exist to make spectacles of themselves. By Welles's reckoning, Hearst belonged to their company because he was 'not a great man'. In saying this, Welles seemed to be accusing himself of not attaining greatness – or of having attained it and let it slip away. He prevaricates intriguingly in *Citizen Kane* by allowing Leland to say that Kane had a 'private sort of greatness', which he kept to himself. Aristotle would have been puzzled by the idea, since for him greatness belonged to the public man; great-heartedness, expressed in private in Kane's yearning for Rosebud, would not count. By 1975, there was another definition of greatness abroad in the world, which ignored public achievements and paid attention instead to the fabrications of publicity. A person's celebrity consisted of an image or aura, a hazy nimbus with a fluctuating market value – as Welles discovered when making deals with the companies whose products he sponsored. As a celebrity, he was famous for the wrong things: for his unruliness and unreliability, his cigars and his size. He used the invidious word to introduce himself in his script for *Touch of Evil*. Ray Collins asks Heston if he knows 'our local police celebrity'. Heston says he'd like to, and Joseph Cotten, on duty here (though uncredited) as a drunken coroner, snarls 'That's what you think.' Then Welles – bloated and slobbering, seen from a low angle so that he spills into the camera's field of vision – is decanted from his car. The shot neatly, hurtfully identifies celebrity with infamy.

During the 1980s Welles tried to finance a film of *King Lear*, and taped a proposal which he played to likely backers. He now saw the octogenarian Lear as a superannuated leader, like Churchill, General de Gaulle, Chairman Mao or himself, and blamed him for voluntarily renouncing the throne. His comments on Lear's retirement disclose his own dejection and his bitter craving for vindication: 'The strong old man, the leader of the tribe – the city, the church, the state, the political party, or corporation – demands love as a tyrant demands tribute; and, bereft of power, he must, like Lear, plead for it like a beggar.' Is the human family really analogous to a political party or a corporation, where love, or at least unquestioning adhesion, is compulsory? Are our personal relationships governed by the laws of power politics? It might be Arkadin talking: he too, before killing himself, begs his daughter to go on loving him. This is one of Welles's grimmest statements, justifiably bleak because its appeal, as always, went unheeded. The proud absolutist who called himself a 'king-actor' ended by playing deposed monarchs.

The Khan and his 'miracle of rare device'.

CHAPTER 7

Kubla Cain

Welles bluffed when he said that the belligerent telegram was the only explicit reference to Hearst in *Citizen Kane*, but at the same time he tantalisingly hinted at the truth. Hearst was a cover, as Kurtz, Faust and all those Shakespearean characters had been. The film is Welles's fractured, refracted self-portrait. *Citizen Kane* resembles a Gothic ghost story when it explores Xanadu, a Brechtian epic when it summarises Kane's political career, a screwball comedy when it shows the roué combining business with pleasure at the newspaper office. But above all it is a film about Welles making a film, and about our watching it. Describing it in the trailer or in his radio conversation with H. G. Wells, he called it a new kind of movie. Its novelty lay in its exposure of its maker, his methods and his self-aggrandising, self-accusing myths.

Welles as Kane admits his inexperience: 'I don't know how to run a newspaper – I just try everything I can think of.' That is the structural principle of *Citizen Kane*, a variety show of ingenious contrivances. Welles liked the confession so much that he repeated it in *Journey into Fear*, the thriller in which he somehow found time to appear while directing *The Magnificent Ambersons*. 'What's to become of me?' simpers Ruth Warrick: once the genteel Mrs Kane, she now plays Joseph Cotten's wife, placed in the care of Welles's lecherous Colonel Haki. Welles smirks 'We'll think of something.' He always did. He had already made good Kane's most hubristic boast, 'I'll provide the war', by organising a Martian invasion of New Jersey. Emergencies excited him, because they required him to improvise. The shrill agitation onstage at the opera before the curtain rises is a snapshot, like Houseman's comment on the wrestling match 'with Chaos and Time' before a radio broadcast, of the conditions in which Welles customarily worked. When Kane wiggles his ears or makes shadowgraphs to divert Susan, she says 'Gee, you know an awful lot of tricks. You're not a professional magician, are you?' Her question allows Welles to congratulate himself on the compendium of trick shots in *Kane*. The journalists who investigate Kane's life supposedly want to write about him, so the film waves a wand to explain the presence of cameras as well as notebooks. Thompson, interviewing the dipsomaniac Susan, reminds her 'We run a picture magazine.' 'Yes,' she yawns, 'I know.' An order is given to photograph everything at Xanadu, which could just as well be RKO. The hall with its pyramids of packing cases is the hangar where the studio stores props; the staircase belongs among an assortment of useless staircases on the backlot, jokingly noticed by Vincente Minnelli in his own film about film-making, *The Bad and the Beautiful*.

In the last scene, the reporters shake their heads over Kane's architectural scavenging. How could he have glued together a Scottish castle, a Burmese temple and three Spanish ceilings, all waiting to be incorporated into Xanadu? A French Gothic cathedral is somewhere in the eclectic mixture, since the newsreel's clips of Xanadu under construction use footage of sets being built for RKO's *Hunchback of Notre Dame*; so is that Scottish castle, as Welles recycled scenery left over from John Ford's *Mary of Scotland*. The India of the Raj undergoes annexation: other hand-me-downs, according to Charles Higham, came from *Gunga Din*. Welles tried everything he could think of, and in his coltish eagerness did all those different things at once. With its erratic array of different genres, the film learned the lesson of simultaneity from the layout of Kane's newspapers. On those pages, divergent stories jostle in the same space, rather than being sorted into a temporal sequence as traditional narrative ordained. Incoherence – in the muddle of Freudian consciousness or the convergence of separate, relative events in Einstein's physics, or in the cubistic clutter on the café tables of Picasso and Braque – was a modernist virtue. For Welles it was also a psychological convenience. There were so many Welleses, and in *Citizen Kane* he set them loose to fight it out.

When the critic Donald Ritchie wandered in to see *Citizen Kane* as an adolescent in rural Ohio in 1941, he was convinced that a dozy projectionist had muddled up the cans of film. First came 'some old guy dying in a castle'; then the man in the booth seemed to have mistakenly started the newsreel. Ritchie's bemusement paid a proper tribute to the film's mystifying method. By temporally scrambling the narrative – beginning at the end and then going round in inconclusive circles as separate characters make failed attempts to explain Kane – Welles suggests that we do not live our lives in correct chronological order. The child is the father of the man: Wordsworth's romantic aphorism is proved true by our single glimpse of Kane's childhood. Perhaps, by the time we reach adulthood, life – except for the routine of breathing, or the getting and spending with which we pass the time – is all over. But with luck, like the magician in T. H. White's *The Once and Future King*, we 'youthen' instead of age-ing. As young men, Kane and Welles were alike: energetic jokers, who treated the newspaper business, politics and the movies as arenas for play. Kane's games are made possible by unlimited money, Welles's by boundless talent. In middle age, they parted company. Kane, devoted to accumulation, builds his own reclusive museum, where he paces to and fro taking inventory. Welles, whose property was his ideas, stayed agile, invigorated by disappointments because they challenged him to recover, to think his way out of trouble. The more his body anchored him to earth, the sprightlier his mind became. Like Falstaff fleeing from the bat-tle, he spent much of his subsequent life on the run; but at least he was still moving. At the end lay recovered paradise, a second childhood. At the beginning of *Chimes at Midnight,* Falstaff seems to have squeezed into Kane's globe, which contains a wintry landscape with no power to chill. Safe inside that bubble, he capers through snow as if it were spring-time foliage, and lives his juvenile escapades all over again.

Jorge Luis Borges called *Citizen Kane* a labyrinth without a centre. The film encourages such bafflement, making us suspect nihilism and self-annihilation. The NO TRESPASSING sign, seen at the beginning and end, deters interpreters. The glass ball that breaks on the floor con-tains only evanescent snowflakes, or incommunicable memories: since we cannot know ourselves, why should we imagine that we can know another human being? Borges cleverly described *Kane* as Kafkaesque; Welles himself might have been paraphrasing Borges' review of the film when he had the narrator of *The Trial* – in another embargo on inter-pretative trespassing, later cut – announce that 'A true mystery is unfath-omable, and there is nothing hidden inside it.' Yet if there were really nothing hidden, why would he have gone to such trouble to hide it – or to hide himself? His labyrinth does have a centre, even if he warns us against penetrating it.

In Egypt, Herodotus visited a labyrinth whose underground passages, off limits to him, contained the tombs of kings. *Citizen Kane* is cryptic, because it invades a succession of crypts. The screening room where the reporters watch the newsreel is a gloomy limbo, occupied by shades. Thompson reads Thatcher's memoir in a funereal library, guarded by his stone ghost, and visits the dying Leland in a hospital overshadowed by the span of the George Washington Bridge. At Xanadu, Kane pharaoni-cally rules over a court of dead statues; the place was meant to contain a private chapel where, in a scene written but not filmed, he would have buried his son. Perhaps there is a further crypt that we never see: the cleft in a Colorado mountain from which all Kane's riches were dug.

In Crete a labyrinth was home to the Minotaur. This labyrinth was designed by Daedalus, whose name meant 'cunningly wrought'. Daedalus was not a man at all; he served as a mythic embodiment of the artist or artificer, the technician of guile. *Citizen Kane* is wrought with Daedalan cunning, made up of puzzles and riddles. Like a myth, it conflates or superimposes different stories. Hearst's story merges with that of Kubla Khan, from whom Kane borrows the name of his private kingdom; their story is also Welles's. The overlaid stories are joined by puns, which function like lap dissolves in cinematic editing. *Citizen Kane* alliteratively evokes Coleridge's poem 'Kubla Khan', quoted in the newsreel, which introduces Kane as 'America's Kubla Khan'. Coleridge's source was a book of legendary travelling that describes the domain of the Khan Kubla, the dynasty who was Genghis Khan's successor. A khan, as in the Tartary of *Ivan the Terrible*, is a Mongol sovereign. In 1949, Welles played just such a figure in Henry Hathaway's *The Black Rose*: a general called Bayan, with slit Asiatic eyes, bristling pelts, and a spike sticking out of his helmeted head. Gradually the title was demoted to an honorary gesture of respect in Muslim countries, like Don in Spanish. In *Moby Dick*, Melville describes Captain Ahab – another of Welles's diabolical, obsessive self-images – as 'a Khan of the plank, and a king of the sea, and a great lord of Leviathans'. Welles took this honorary rank and passed it off as Kane's surname, but his resonant slogan contained a contradiction. A khan is a lord, who owes his authority to arms, and cannot be a citizen. The two clashing words, which splice together the different identities of Marlow and Kurtz, force us to confront the disparity in Welles between political liberal and artistic autocrat, democrat and great man.

Because khan is a title not a name, it raises the question of what the hero's real surname might be. Another pun proposes an answer: could he be Citizen Cain? Bernard Herrmann made the associative leap when, in 1942, he arranged excerpts from his scores for *Citizen Kane* and *The Magnificent Ambersons* in a suite which he entitled *Welles Raises Kane*. Herrmann emphasised hilarity and mayhem, not diabolism: yoking together a helterskelter can-can from *Citizen Kane* with a wistful waltz from *The Magnificent Ambersons*, he called his compilation a 'musical frolic', and said that it characterised Welles – like Kane when he hires a troop of bordello girls for an office party, or Eugene Morgan when he tipsily serenades Isabel and topples over on to the bass fiddle – as 'the last of the Victorian gay blades'. But Welles had other reasons for associating the hero with the son of Adam and Eve, who committed the first murder when he killed his brother Abel. In Byron's play *Cain*, written in 1821, Lucifer – adopted by Welles as a self-image in his own adolescent drama – tempts Adam's first-born son by appealing to his 'immortal part' and pitying him as 'poor clay'. He encourages Cain to repudiate a God who 'makes but to destroy'. John Steinbeck's novel *East of Eden*, published in 1952, relocates the unfallen garden to California, where the farmer Adam names his twin sons Aaron and Caleb, not wanting to tempt fate by calling them Abel and Cain. A bearded patriarch from a nearby ranch, the Jehovah of Steinbeck's story, agrees with the choice: 'Cain is maybe the best-known name in the whole world and . . . only one man has ever borne it.' That is precisely the kind of singularity Welles claimed for the hero who was his self-image. In the novel *Mr Arkadin*, the owner of the flea circus – dubbed by Welles himself in the film – leaves another clue to this identification. 'It's twenty thousand years since Cain,' he says, 'and murder's a business that's still mainly in the hands of amateurs.'

Welles shared the arrogant autonomy of one of D. H. Lawrence's heroes, who 'never felt identified with the great humanity. He belonged to a race apart, like the race of Cain.' His crime was not wishful fratricide – though such a self-invented creature could hardly have liked the idea of a sibling, whose existence diminished his own uniqueness. His brother Richard was diagnosed as a schizophrenic in 1927, and banished to an institution; Welles seldom visited him, but sent money whenever he remembered. The mark of Cain is inherited by us all, so each of us is free to attribute it to a sin of our own choosing. The fathomable mystery in *Citizen Kane* is that of the deviant romantic imagination, which can dream its way back to paradise and at the same time recover uninhibited childhood, as Coleridge did when writing about Kubla Khan. That is why Kane, on a wet night in New York, makes what he calls a 'sentimental journey' to the warehouse on the West Side where the relics of his infancy are stored. The Welles who deplored Faust and his progeny worried that the romantic imagination was engaged in conjuring up artificial paradises, as flimsy and factitious as film sets. Kane, playing in the snow, is the 'marvellous boy' of Wordsworth's poems, romping in Eden. But his happiness is abruptly curtailed, and he is sent away to be corrupted by society. By the end, the film is concerned with a romantic hero of another kind: the Cain of Byron, whose crime – mercenary in Kane's case, mental in Welles's – confirms our expulsion from Eden. So the humble citizen is in fact a khan, while Kane has discreetly re-spelled his family name to disguise his derivation from Cain.

Welles saw himself as a Byronic hero, beautiful because damned. Elsa in Sherwood King's novel *If I Die Before I Wake* says to the sailor whom she beguiles 'You have a romantic mind, for a chauffeur.' Welles, stepping into the role when he adapted the book in *The Lady from Shanghai*, awarded the character a properly romantic lineage. The Bannisters and Grisby kept the names King gave them, but the chauffeur was given a new identity: Laurence Planter from North Dakota became Michael O'Hara from Ireland, where Welles spent a footloose summer in 1931. In the novel, Planter corrects Elsa by telling her that he is a sailor, who has been around the world on tramp steamers, not in the navy. His romanticism makes him a wanderer, who spends his life in open-ended questing and questioning.

The Renaissance, extolled by Harry Lime in the speech Welles wrote for himself in *The Third Man*, discovered human individuality, and began to question our subservience to religious morality. Romanticism freed the individual from all remaining restraints, and turned the artist into a Promethean creator. Welles was excited by this lurid apostasy. In 1940, while working on *Citizen Kane*, he imagined how a romanticised Shakespeare would look on film: '*Macbeth* and its gloomy moors might be grand. A perfect cross between *Wuthering Heights* and *The Bride of Frankenstein*.' This explains the electrical storm during which Macbeth summons the witches in the film Welles eventually made. The hero contends with the turbulent elements like Emily Brontë's characters in *Wuthering Heights*, and the lightning bolts that crackle across the black screen and obliterate a Celtic cross demonstrate the power of electricity, used to animate dead matter in Mary Shelley's *Frankenstein*. On location for *Othello*, MacLíammóir described Welles in a threatening mood as 'a thunder-cloud in indigo overalls': the image is a choice specimen of romantic irony, at once sublime and ridiculous.

Coleridge published 'Kubla Khan' at the behest of Byron, a doomed amoral fantasist who might have seen himself in the poem. Welles stepped into the persona, remarking in 1958 that he was 'cut out to follow in the footsteps of the Byronic adventurer' and describing Arkadin as 'a corsair', like one of Byron's protagonists. He played Charlotte Brontë's version of the Byronic hero in the 1943 film version of *Jane Eyre*; he had already dramatised the novel for radio in 1938. His Rochester whirls out of the fog to the accompaniment of a raging musical cavalcade by Bernard Herrmann, or strides through a blizzard, his cape billowing in the blasts of wind; his house is as draughtily vast as Xanadu.

This was romanticism interpreted by America, where all it takes to realise your vision – to 'build that dome in air, / That sunny dome, those caves of ice!' – is a comfortable financial surplus. When Rochester in Robert Stevenson's film returns with his snooty fiancée, Jane (played by Joan Fontaine) overhears one of their friends remark 'Well, he is very romantic, and he's enormously rich.' It is an important proviso. The American romantic is a spendthrift capitalist, like Fitzgerald's Gatsby. Kane, an 'emperor of newsprint', rules by means of the communications industry, not conquest. He flourishes in an economy that promises to instantly gratify all our wishes. A greedy consumer, he gobbles a meal in his office; when Leland asks if he's still eating, he replies 'I'm still hungry.' Food is fuel, like the forests chopped down to make paper pulp for his presses. Welles's characters often have ravenous romantic appetites: George Minafer wolfs strawberry shortcake, Quinlan munches candy bars. But Kane's true delight, like Gatsby's, is in sumptuary, luxurious expenditure. When the Metropolitan Opera rejects the twittering Susan, he builds a theatre for her in Chicago, then presumably abandons it after the fiasco of *Salammbô*. In a speech deleted from *The Magnificent Ambersons* by RKO's editors, Uncle Jack brags to guests at the ball about the sixty thousand dollars spent on the house's walnut balustrades: 'Spent money like water! Always did! Still do! Like water!' Instead of the Khan's 'sacred river / Five miles meandering with a mazy motion', Kane has, as the newsreel says, 'the wealth of the earth's third richest gold mine', dispensed – for fifty years at least – in 'an unending stream' of fluid money.

Kane is able to exceed the imaginative decrees of the Khan, because American technology performs miracles for him. In the poem the Khan's commands are architectural, but Kane issues topographical orders, like a plutocratic God creating the world all over again. The newsreel reports that at Xanadu (as at San Simeon) 'a private mountain was commissioned', and we see the earth-moving equipment revising the profile of the land to pile up the summit on which the castle sits. God ignites and enlightens the world in saying 'Let there be light.' For Kane, such a feat is easy and automatic, as it was for Welles who calls for a spotlight in the trailer advertising *Citizen Kane*. The first issue of the *Inquirer* goes on sale at dawn, with the gas jets on the office wall still flaring. Kane vows to make the paper 'as essential to New York as the gas in that light is'; having said so, he promptly demonstrates his power by shutting the jet off.

Welles loved to play the demiurge, even if his creative fiat proved to be destructive. Othello quenches the candle before suffocating Desdemona, and doubly darkens the world: 'Put out the light, and then put out the light.' After the gunfight in the hall of mirrors at the end of *The Lady from Shanghai*, O'Hara switches on the electric light to expose the disintegration of this brittle, illusory world, reduced to splintered glass and blood. He then walks outside into the cleansing dawn. The same quarrel between dark and light goes on inconclusively at the motel in *Touch of Evil*. Dennis Weaver plays the freakish, gibbering caretaker, who calls himself 'the night man' and is due to vanish at sunrise. He resembles Macbeth's drunken porter, incapable of protecting the premises against nocturnal hauntings. Weaver's character is a Pierrot Lunaire, a figment of lunar, misleading light, like film itself. There is no dutiful changing of the guard when morning comes: his replacement, 'the day man', does not turn up, so the nightmare continues.

When Welles began to read Karen Blixen, he was touched to discover an epigraph from 'Kubla Khan' in her novel *The Angelic Avengers*, published under her pseudonym Isak Dinesen in 1946. The avenging female angels are two romantic girls from the 1840s who, infatuated by Byron, reel through a plot which combines devil-worship, white slavery and Caribbean voodoo. Coleridge is quoted (or rather misquoted) when Lucan first sees the country house where her friend Zosine lives: 'In Xanadu', she recalls, 'did Kubla Khan a mighty pleasure-dome decree.' Coleridge's dome was stately, but might is the issue for Lucan. She sees the house as a tribute to romantic wishful thinking. 'It is equally wonderful', she reflects, 'that people can have the imagination to invent all these things and that they have the power to turn them into realities.' Kubla Khan in Coleridge's poem possesses this romantic imagination at its most impious and authoritative. He is the 'demon lover' for whom the woman in the 'deep romantic chasm' wails, and he listens with excitement not alarm to 'voices prophesying war'. His pleasure-dome is his private sensorium. His violent energy is, to use William Blake's phrase, eternal delight; what others call satanic vices are for him merely liberated instincts. Coleridge's poem has remained synonymous with romantic conduct at its most passionately flagrant, and romantic language at its most Orphic and irrational. In the episode of *Around the World with Orson Welles* filmed on the Left Bank in Paris, a bard in a St Germain des Prés cabaret chants surreal absurdities in a made-up language consisting of nondescript Arabic sounds, then surprises himself by concluding with an alliterative flourish, 'Kubla Kubla Kubla Khan'. Coleridge's title might be the primal babble of the unconsciousness.

The young Welles naturally saw himself as Kubla Khan, and even found tenuous ways of connecting the peculiarities of the poem's composition with his own life. Coleridge claimed to have written 'Kubla Khan' after an opium dream. He fell asleep while reading the travel book about the Khan's estate, and in his delirium 'all the images rose up before him as *things*'. When he awoke he found that the poem had dictated itself, but while writing it down he was interrupted by 'a person on business from Porlock'; this, he hoped, would explain and apologise for what he pretended was the poem's incoherent state. Drugs released the romantic imagination from the control of reason. Welles may not have experimented with such potions (though he did rely on benzedrine to keep himself revved up during his New York days). Instead he transferred Coleridge's addiction to his father, who – as he informed a press conference in Boston in 1977 – used to smoke opium. Since the occasion was the opening of *F for Fake*, anyone who believed him did so at their own risk. Welles had his equivalent to the person from Porlock, the intruder who inadvertently curtails the poem. This was Herman Mankiewicz, with whom he wrote the script of *Citizen Kane*. At the time he begrudged Mankiewicz a screen credit. Much later, Welles used him as a scapegoat, alleging that Mankiewicz had carried the project off in a contrary direction. 'Everything concerning Rosebud', Welles said, 'belongs to him.' When not claiming total ownership of *Citizen Kane*, he evasively disowned the most personal part of it. The shiftiness is worthy of Coleridge, and it has the same motive: it denies responsibility for a dream that gives away too much about the artist's desires and ambitions.

The Khan's Xanadu, a 'miracle of rare device', amazes Coleridge and also scares him, because it couples two inconsistent elements that cannot coexist in the physical world: the 'sunny pleasure-dome' has 'caves of ice'. The images propose a paradox about the relation between nature and art, God's creativity and the poet's (or the film-maker's). Symbols here materialise, in Coleridge's words, 'as *things*', and they do so as well in *Citizen Kane*, which uses them to suggest both the divine fury and the wasteful folly of Welles's imagination. As with the gas jet, Welles shows how the miracle can be instantaneously accomplished, thanks to the rare devisings of technology. The dissolve that introduces Susan at the El Rancho cabaret in Atlantic City shows fire in the sky and humanity huddling for shelter as if in a cave, with only a thin membrane of glass – like the brittle, transparent shell enclosing the landscape of Kane's childhood – in between. The camera begins on the roof, with a neon sign crackling in the sodden gloom, then moves in to peer through a skylight. A lightning bolt covers the transition from outer to inner; now the camera, as if it had passed through the waterproof barrier, cranes down from the air towards the woman slumped at her table. El Rancho is at once a pleasure-dome, lit by a man-made sun not the stormy electricity of nature, and also a cave of chilly remorse, Susan's miserable refuge.

Sun in Coleridge's poem is vital, germinating life and therefore making pleasure possible. Ice is deathly, a rigid mortification which anaesthetises nature. Romanticism tried to balance the two. Imagination was the principle of heat: its 'lava flow', as Byron said, produced a poem, though Shelley called the mind in creation a 'fading coal', from which the original scorching radiance bleeds away as the rational consciousness takes over. Imagination is torrential, but like the streamy wealth of Kane or the Ambersons it can run away or run out. Coleridge, who left poems like 'Kubla Khan' unfinished rather than tampering with their wanton spontaneity, worried about how to combine the impetuosity of feeling with the rigour of form. He therefore invoked what he called the 'shaping spirit of imagination': a structure, imposed by reason, is a container, moulding and shaping the fiery, fluid, molten substance of fantasy. Cold kills, but ice can also preserve. Helped by the damsel with the dulcimer, the poem's mystical muse, Coleridge believes that he might be able to repeat the Khan's miraculous conjuring act. But at the end of the poem he suddenly, guiltily desists. Shifting ahead into a subjunctive future tense and changing from the first to the third person, he acknowledges the transgressiveness of imagination and anathematises the poet, who is now no longer himself:

> . . . all should cry, Beware! Beware!
> His flashing eyes, his floating hair!
> Weave a circle round him thrice,
> And close your eyes with holy dread,
> For he on honey-dew hath fed,
> And drunk the milk of Paradise.

So the poem breaks off, unable to admit that it has done what it forbids the poet to do: capturing light or conserving heat, enclosing the sun in a receptacle of ice.

Citizen Kane uses all these images, but arranges them in an equation of its own to match Welles's different temperament and world view. It begins with ice and ends with fire. First comes the snowfall cyclonically aroused – in a cut between two close-ups – by the final breath that issues from Kane's lips; last is the furnace, that indiscriminate crematorium. The meaning of Coleridge's symbols has been switched back to front. Fire, in that funeral pyre of Kane's possessions, is the destructive element, not a germinal source. Ice, by cautiously lowering the temperature and forestalling decay, allows the perpetuation of pleasure.

Kane's childhood is a field whitened by snow, not the sunny, flowering scene that most of us probably recall when thinking back to our earliest, happiest years. Kane tells Susan that he was walking through the rain to the warehouse 'in search of my youth'. But his salad days, like Falstaff's, are white not green. Wordsworth defined poetry as 'emotion recollected in tranquillity'. The recollection happens behind glass, whether beneath the skylight of El Rancho or inside the globe Kane grips so tenaciously; tranquillity is another prescription for cooling the intensity of experience, enabling us to derive a gentler, sustaining warmth from our memories. For Welles, snow paradoxically rejuvenated the world. But its restoration of paradise reminded him at once that paradise was lost, thanks to some breach for which he blamed himself; snow, which ought to betoken innocence, instead enforces our guilt by tempting us to blacken it. The guests at a tea party in *The Stranger* combine to recall a quotation from Emerson which, when pieced together, explains the moralised landscape of Welles's films: 'Commit a crime and it seems as if a coat of snow fell on the ground, such as reveals in the woods the path of every partridge and fox . . . You cannot wipe out the foot-track.' Those incriminating inscriptions on whiteness, like the blood in *Macbeth*, do not obligingly melt away.

After the young Kane is forcibly taken away from home, his sled is seen slowly subsiding beneath a snowdrift. There the cold protects it, until it is consigned to the furnace. Shakespeare identified the dramatic genres with the two seasons whose alternation dramatises the battle between life and death in nature. Comedy is a song of spring, celebrating fertility. (Kane arranges a theatrical outing with Leland to see a play aptly called *The Spring Chicken*. He adds 'I'll get the girls. You get the tickets. A drama critic gets them free.' Does he mean the girls as well as the tickets?) Tragedy, by contrast, recites a winter's tale. After death causes the postponement of marriage in *Love's Labour's Lost*, Armado announces a showdown between Hiems and Ver, the owl and the cuckoo. The dispute is not resolved: 'The words of Mercury are harsh after the songs of Apollo,' Armado says at the end of the play. Apollo is the solar god, the sponsor of lyricism who endowed Orpheus with the gift of song; Mercury, who was Welles's patron, utters harsher truths. Welles reversed the relationship between the antagonistic seasons. Kane is happy in the Colorado blizzard, morose in the sticky heat of Florida. His comfortless mood at Xanadu is evident when he warms himself at a log fire which burns in a yawning grate – hardly probable in a coastal estate on the Gulf of Mexico, but emotionally apt.

The brothel girls who serenade Kane at the party in the *Inquirer* office call him a man who 'loves to smoke'. It's a succinct summary: Kane cannot be separated from his cigar, and the wand of fire came to serve as a metonym for Welles himself. The script jokes about the identification when Kane tries to bully Leland into going to Cuba as a war correspondent. 'Richard Harding Davis is doing all right,' he says. 'They just named a cigar after him.' Davis was a star reporter who covered every battlefront between the Greek-Turkish conflict and World War I. But Leland is not tempted by this form of immortality, and replies 'It's hardly what you'd call a cigar.' The man who smokes should have paused to ponder the comment. As it is, we see him reduced to a plume of smoke at the end of the film, when the chimney at Xanadu breathes out the residue of his junked possessions.

Before then, ice intervenes to arrest time or at least to slow it down, and to conserve a remembered happiness as a photograph does. At the farewell party in the newspaper office, the three volatile partners sit in front of tributes to themselves carved in ice. The heads of Bernstein and Leland are white, clear, translucent, like Platonic ideas; the cigar poking from Leland's mouth is frozen, unlightable and therefore not a symbol of the heat that drains from our bodies as we careen towards death, like Byron's lava or Shelley's coal. Kane, already less a man than a logo or a brand, is represented in ice by a gigantic K, as on the gate of Xanadu. Better this clean, abstract sign than the anthropomorphic dummies – Kane as a hollow man like Kurtz, stuffed with straw – that are burned by a protesting rabble during the newsreel. The carvings create a serene, poised, apparently eternal state of amity and understanding between the three men, who will never be friends again. Like the 'cold pastoral' sculpted on Keats's Grecian urn, where static lovers embrace forever and white trees will never need to lose their leaves, these are totems that magically fend off mortality.

Kane populates Xanadu with statues, which are icons of the body saved from death. But the chilly effigies in ice are not paralysed in perfection. The medium from which they are made is water not stone, and they have been put on display in the hot, smoky den of the office, where the revelry itself will kill them off. These ice men await their own stealthy, implacable breakdown, like Shakespeare's deposed Richard II who describes himself as 'a mockery king of snow'. All of the humorous commiseration Welles absorbed from Shakespeare, exactly balancing the tragedy and comedy of our lives, is invested in these transitory monuments, funerary ornaments designed for a party which they will not outlast. You can imagine the doleful moment when the first drip is heard and the ice begins to soften: it will be the sound that Virgil called 'the tears in things'. The same threnody is audible in a phrase intoned by the narrator of the newsreel at the beginning of *Citizen Kane*. He refers to the *Inquirer*, before Kane buys the paper and forcibly rejuvenates it, as a 'dying daily'. The alliteration recalls a truth that Welles never forgot. We die daily; each day, living journalistically, we edge closer to death.

Menaced by time, Welles retained his trust in the protective virtue of ice, as opposed to fire with its uncontrollable ferment. His feeling for cold weather, associated with his upbringing in the frozen mid-West, is one of the most poetically intimate undercurrents in his work. At times it suggests an oddly Nordic moral rigour: the south is where moral rot begins, in the equatorial heat of Kurtz's jungle or the Acapulco of *The Lady from Shanghai*. The New Englanders of *The Stranger* keep their distance from South America, through whose swampy cities Meinike passes on his way north, by quoting that parable of Emerson's in which snow symbolises unbesmirched nature, before it is fouled by human intrusion. Welles, as romantic as Emerson, insisted on filming the sleigh ride in *The Magnificent Ambersons* in an ice-making plant downtown, rather than on a studio set. Hauled indoors from the desert heat of the city, the actors suffered, and complained about the stink of refrigerated fish. But Welles wanted their breath to steam, as a precious, poignant sign of life. Even a stream running between banks of snow in the sequence visibly gives off vapour. Because we cannot feel the cold that pinches the characters, the episode looks pristine, playfully Edenic.

When the sleigh overturns, George and Lucy tumble on to a feather-bed of snow and are not hurt. And the scene sounds paradisial too, because of the four celestas Herrmann used in scoring it: a heaven of chiming, shimmering crystal.

Ice hardens around the ancient mariner's stalled ship in Coleridge's poem, and threatens to kill him with its rigor mortis. America's magical technology, on display in that factory which manufactured coolness in sweltering Los Angeles, gave Welles another understanding of the matter. When Isabel marries Wilbur in *The Magnificent Ambersons*, a town gossip expects unseasonal luxuries at the reception, and imagines 'raw oysters floating in scooped-out blocks of ice'. Refrigeration preserved life; Welles applied the same techniques to memory, or to the perishable human body. In 1953 he developed this notion of cold and its aesthetic chastity in *The Lady in Ice*, a ballet whose story he worked out for the choreographer Roland Petit. The ballerina is a prehistoric woman, sealed in an ice floe. It's a hygienic prohibition: sexually inaccessible, she is also immune to death. A male dancer falls in love with this gelid relic, and his hot tears thaw her. But not for long, since when she kisses him, he freezes. Like Pygmalion in reverse, he joins her in a statuesque eternity.

Recreating his beginnings in the screenplay for *The Cradle Will Rock*, he returned to the ice sculptures that appear so tellingly in *Citizen Kane*. Between his productions of *Faustus* and Blitzstein's opera, the young Orson gives a party, for which his wife Virginia commissions likenesses in ice of himself as Faustus and Jack Carter as Mephistophilis. In doing so, she reprieves them both from the infernal reckoning prescribed by the tragedy. But although he has escaped the flames, Orson regards the ice dolefully, and quotes Edwin Booth who 'said that an actor is a sculptor in snow'. The thawing image provokes him to recognise the impermanence of his own trade, and of all art. Then, recovering his confidence, he goes on to give a demonstration of white magic by conjuring up a snow woman, like the lady in the ballet. He speaks the lines Faustus addresses to the phantasmal Helen of Troy; the script says that Orson should deliver the invocation 'coolly' while he moves gently, 'almost feather-light', across the room. The body that materialises 'out of nowhere' and floats down towards him is just as ethereal, a spirit released from the debility of the flesh.

The manufacture of the carvings in *The Cradle Will Rock* entices Welles into a tortuously whimsical, slyly confidential subplot. Virginia gives the order to a vagabond Irish sculptor called Kevan Kildare, who hauls a glacier through the streets of New York in a horse-drawn wagon. His cart is dragged by a spavined mare called (in Welles's chosen spelling) Rosinante: this was Quixote's broken-down nag. Kildare himself is enticingly described. Virginia appraises 'a sexy young man, stretched out in the straw' that blankets the ice in the back of his cart; the script adds that he is 'startlingly beautiful' and 'something of an early Brando' in his lazily sensual manner. When not chiselling ice, he acts in summer stock. Drawling in his affected brogue about 'the crool meejum of ice', he entices Virginia into his cart and drives off with her. Orson gives chase, calling out as the cart trots into the distance 'I know who you are! . . . And *what*!'

Who and what indeed? Kevan Kildare's initials are the clue to his encrypted identity. He is Kubla Khan or Kane or Kurtz, which means he is the young Welles, cryogenically preserved as he lolls on a bed inside his travelling hearse of ice – still beautiful, still sexually alluring, a souvenir of Welles during that summer when he trailed around Ireland, no doubt visiting County Kildare, with his painting kit in a pony trap like Kildare's cart. Welles's fall from grace (according to his myth) came when he arrived in Dublin and lied his way into the theatre. He was hired by the Gate; he therefore deceptively makes Kildare look like a dishevelled refugee from the rival company in Dublin, noting that his 'wardrobe suggests the peasant heroes of the Abbey Theatre'. (The Abbey presented the vernacular, homespun tragedies of J. M. Synge and Sean O'Casey, whereas MacLíammóir and Edwards at the Gate specialised in a more outlandish avant-garde repertory.) Welles makes Orson's wife commit adultery with his own younger self, which spares his vulnerable ego and neatly circumvents the betrayal he always feared. The iceman for Welles did not mean death, as the figure did for Eugene O'Neill, whose play *The Iceman Cometh* was written in 1939 and staged in 1946; Welles's ice age, paradoxically, is youth, before what Hamlet calls 'the heyday in the blood' begins to boil.

Upstairs at the party, Orson looks into the mirror and rehearses his meeting with this second self, slimmer and immemorially young like Peter Pan. 'I don't think we've been introduced,' he says to his reflection. He studies himself for a moment, then adds 'My name is Welles. Your name is Kevan Kildare, you are an unemployed actor, and I regret to say, quite a good one.' Quoting *Snow White and the Seven Dwarfs*, he asks the mirror on the wall to tell him which is the fairest – unspoiled Orson in 1931 in Dublin, seasoned Orson in 1937 in New York, or (small hope) the moribund Welles who wrote the script in Los Angeles in 1984, a year before his death. His own youth stares back at him from the glass, and reproaches him for what he has become, or what he has not become. Orson, flinching, cheers himself up with a boast. 'What do I see? I see the best man in my profession under forty!' Then his bravado sags, and he repeats the refrain of his adult life, making others responsible for a downfall that began when the ice started to melt: 'They set up rigid standards for me before I could talk. Who the hell could live up to them?'

Immediately after this self-pitying monologue, the traduced Virginia tells Houseman that Orson never had a childhood. There is a motherly solicitude in her remark. Welles has assigned his first wife to a maternal role; he expects her to supervise his playtime, and demands that she suspend her expectations of his future achievements. If she looks for sexual solace elsewhere, he makes sure that it is with his own even younger self. When he filmed their play-acting in *The Hearts of Age*, he prematurely turned himself and Virginia into old folks; in *The Cradle Will Rock*, he wished them both back into infancy. Either way, they were dispensed from adult responsibilities. In actuality, Virginia was less acquiescent, and after their divorce in 1940 she dunned Welles for child support. As a child himself, he did not understand why he should be compelled to support another one. In his own view, he left fairy gold behind when he walked out: the currency of imagination. The lease to the Colorado mine, after all, was – as the newsreel points out – a bequest from Mrs Kane's 'defaulting lodger'. At the end of his own life, Welles was still unable to forgive Kane's mother for calling him in from his games, handing him a bag she had packed a week earlier, and sending him off to make his name in the world. In *The Cradle Will Rock* the permissive Virginia therefore replaces adamantine Agnes Moorehead, her mouth – as she stoically gives up her son – so grimly set, convinced that her own pain has a higher purpose.

Already in *Citizen Kane*, Welles's nostalgia prompted him to rewrite 'Kubla Khan', dousing its erotic fire. Coleridge's poem mentions hail when it describes the fragments of earth scattered by the fountain as it forces its way through the ground, but those cold particles are ignited by the images that follow: 'rebounding hail' turns to 'chaffy grain' flailed by the thresher, then to 'dancing rocks'. Welles reverses the process, controlling the chaotic flurry of flakes and encasing it in glass, restoring icy purity. There is no 'woman wailing for her demon lover' in *Citizen Kane*, no embodiment of the imagination's lust. Susan whimpers when Kane first meets her, but only because she has toothache. She caterwauls when singing opera, but hardly possesses the sensual fascination of Flaubert's courtesan Salammbô. Nor does the film contain any 'damsel with a dulcimer'. *Citizen Kane* is about a boy wailing for his lost mother; she is the source of honey-dew and paradisial milk, the begetter of his imaginative wealth. The 'dome of pleasure' might have been the brothel run by the svelte madam Georgie, who brings her girls to the office party. But the censors demanded the excision of a scene that was to show Kane taking his ease in her establishment, and – because he is not a sexual being – it is not missed. The Khan's palace of carnal delights, set in a park of 'fertile ground' that is 'girdled round' by walls and towers, contracts into that innocent crystal ball, which shatters at the moment when Kane, dying, regains lost time.

Fire and ice are equated at the end, when the sled is hurled into the incinerator. Flames sear the paint, which bubbles and peels, then eat at the inscription. The word Rosebud melts, as if unfreezing. Welles's definition of film as 'a ribbon of dreams' is typically romantic, because it refers to the bobbins of imagery that unreel in our heads as we sleep and can never be satisfactorily recalled when we awake, just as Coleridge, after talking to the person from Porlock, found that his vision had been erased, like the reflections 'on the surface of a stream into which a stone has been cast'. *Citizen Kane*, after trying everything it can think of, concludes by recognising the vanity of its own virtuosity. Film – which motorises still frames and gives them the semblance of motion, like Frankenstein electrically animating corpses – is as ephemeral as we are. Its dissolves anticipate dissolution, and it sculpts in ice.

Because *Citizen Kane* is about Welles's frantic, uncontrollable creativity, it cannot help glancing at myths of creation, which diminish or limit its own achievement. The Welles who made the film must have looked bumptious and overconfident; the film itself gives away his secret sense of his inadequacy. Once again, the moralist reproves the man of ideas.

The romantic poets knew that creation was the prerogative of gods, from whom they happily stole it. *Citizen Kane* is about a man's self-deification, but Kane is a god who can create nothing and instead chooses to own everything. The newsreel, remembering the recruitment of animals for his private zoo, likens him to Noah stocking the ark. Noah's motive was to save the species, to protect creation against an angry creator who wanted to exercise his own divine prerogative, which is the power of destruction. Kane, on the other hand, merely asserts his monopolistic right, and subjugates the ceatures he buys: an elephant is humiliatingly trussed by ropes and hoisted through the air. The zoo is Kane's panopticon, allowing him to supervise the existence of creatures who are denied privacy, made to perform for his amusement. But the monsters have their own view of their human captors. Kane's octopus, thrashing in a tank, looks ahead to the San Francisco aquarium in *The Lady from Shanghai*, where Rita Hayworth lures Welles into an embrace as rubber-limbed predators glide and cavort behind glass.

After Kane gathers together his zoo, he goes on to assemble his museum, indiscriminately buying up paintings, sculpture, fragments of architecture – 'enough for ten museums, the loot of the world' as the newsreel puts it. As the crated trophies continue to arrive, Bernstein tries to deter Kane by reminding him that Europe is full of pictures and statues he still has not bought. Kane's smiling reply reveals one aspect of Welles's hubris: 'They've been making statues for two thousand years, and I've only been buying for five.' This was a man who felt that he could take possession – intellectually, at least – of those two thousand years, not by despoiling Europe but by interpreting its art and literature from Homer to Shakespeare and on to Conrad and Kafka. Wasn't this expropriation by other means, as Welles constructed his personal museum without walls, turning all those texts into commentaries on himself? Didn't it represent an American revenge on Europe, with Welles as a one-man colonising force? In 1952, Michael Powell tried to interest him in playing the slippery Odysseus in the Circe episode; he asked Dylan Thomas to write a script, and would have included it in an anthology called *Powell's Tales*. But Welles, who felt he had a prior claim on Homer, would not agree to appear in just one episode. 'He wanted *The Odyssey*, and nothing but *The Odyssey*', Powell discovered; wanting everything, he got nothing. The same thing occurred with his plans to film various sections of the Bible. Though he chose to work in a collaborative medium, Welles was the most jealously self-sufficient of individuals. *Citizen Kane* glances at the solipsistic misery of a god whose domain is large but contains no room for other people. Susan finds Xanadu boring: 'forty-nine thousand acres of nothing but scenery and statues. I'm lonesome.'

Kane's craving for statuary is another detail that discloses more about Welles than about Hearst. Kane is stung into self-appraisal when Susan says that her hobby of solving jigsaw puzzles makes more sense. 'You may be right,' he replies. 'I sometimes wonder. But you get into the habit,' he sighs. Welles, who often likened acting to sculpting, here confronts his own limitations. Kane's statues are calcified attitudes. John Gielgud wisely remarked that Welles always knew what the characters he played should look like; he found it harder to get inside them, to make the statue sentient. Sculptures are always heartless, and often headless too. During the inventory of the jumble left behind at Xanadu, someone points out a Venus worth twenty-five thousand dollars. A hard-boiled reporter snarls 'That's a lotta money to pay for a dame without a head.' Kane's glass ball, by contrast, is a transparent view of his head and the fluid, messy, unresolved feelings it contains. Welles could counterfeit emotion efficiently enough, but suspected that this very expertise derived from his own inhumanity: feeling, for him, was behaviour, which he studied in others and then duplicated. Only once did he surprise himself. This was in the scene when Kane demolishes Susan's bedroom, toppling shelves and trampling furniture, sparing only the globe of snow. He whirled through the single take, and gashed his hand in the process. Leaving the wrecked set, he said to himself, astonished, 'I *really* felt it!' For once he had experienced the self-estrangement of the creator, who (like Coleridge in 'Kubla Khan') discovers capacities he did not know he possessed, as if his consciousness has been visited by a god; and he experienced it in a scene which is about wanton destruction not creativity, since Kane's body has become a battering ram.

Shakespeare releases a statue from its frozen immunity to feeling at the end of *The Winter's Tale*, when blood begins to flow in the carved likeness of Hermione. The dead woman returns to life to greet the daughter who is a facsimile of herself, a statue formed from flesh not stone. We watch the instant of creation, a homage to the achievement of Daedalus who (according to legend) was the first to open the eyes of statues and separate their legs, coaxing them out of their trance. Daedalus in turn was imitating the creative rebellion of Prometheus, who formed the first man from the mud of the river bed and animated the figure with a spark stolen from the hearth of Zeus. A 'modern Prometheus', as Mary Shelley called Frankenstein, has more sophisticated surgical techniques at his disposal, and can harness the electricity in lightning rather than stealing fire. But is he able to create life? It is not surprising that Welles brooded about *The Bride of Frankenstein* – James Whale's sequel to his original *Frankenstein* film, made in 1935 – while he was working on *Citizen Kane*. In a prologue, Whale has Byron ask Shelley if his bland, simpering wife could possibly have 'conceived a Frankenstein'. The story goes on to show her conceiving once more, dreaming up a spouse for the monster.

Consummation, however, does not occur. The bridegroom blows up the laboratory which is his nuptial chamber. There are moments in *Citizen Kane* when Welles – pulverising Susan's furniture, then stiffly stalking away down the mirrored corridor – seems to mimic the gait of Boris Karloff as Frankenstein's undead ogre, who knows how to move but not how to feel. Unable to make the transition to sentience, he is the work of an incomplete, anguished artist. His rigidity recalls MacLeish's explanation of his use of blank verse in *Panic*: he wanted, he said, to convey 'an hysteria of statues'.

Instead of creating life, Welles at the age of twenty-five made himself experience death. The newsreel treats Kane's mausoleum as if it were Welles's film: 'Like the pharaohs, Xanadu's landlord leaves many stones to mark his grave. Since the pyramids, Xanadu is the costliest monument a man has built to himself.' But there is a crucial difference between Xanadu and *Citizen Kane*. Welles venerated Chartres – a monument built to an immaterial idea, not to any single man – rather than Xanadu. He coldly mocked Kane's effort to fend off mortality with bricks and mortar. Our death is certain, and final. What difference does it make if a film or a book or even a child outlasts you for a while? For another episode of his television series, Welles travelled to the Basque country and enviously described the wise pastoral contentment of its sheep herders. Still he worried whether the Basques could be called genuinely civilised, since all they had to show for their centuries of history was those herds of sheep, and an unintelligible language without a literature. You only deserve to be proud of your past, he says, 'if you've built a pyramid, or have a library of books to show for it'. On another occasion, he condemned the pyramids on principle. Jake Hannaford, Welles's spokesman in *The Other Side of the Wind,* sneers at the 'God-damned pyramids' as 'so many used-up movie sets'. He extends the dismissal to Venice, which Welles used as a movie set in *Othello*. The comment offers another glimpse of Welles's self-critical scruples about art. The pyramids tried to withstand time, outfacing it as arrogantly as classical statues; Venice, subsiding into the lagoon, is a romantic city, whose beauty derives from our awareness of its imminent death. Film ought to stop time passing, because a photographed moment lasts forever. Actually, in Welles's thinking, it did the opposite – depleting reality, using it up, reducing it to a replica. There is even a Venetian dock with a beached gondola in the swampy grounds of Xanadu – an image repeated during the credits of Welles's *Othello*, though now there are discarded clothes strewn in the boat. And when the camera rolls its eyes upwards into the theatre's flies during the opening of Kane's opera house, the scenic flats it passes include a suspended panorama of Venice, with more painted poles for two-dimensional gondolas.

André Bazin mentioned the pyramids in his 1945 essay on the ontology of the photographic image, which argued that film satisfied mankind's ancient desire for 'objectivity in time' and 'the survival of the corporeal body'. He called this our 'mummy-complex', and noted that the funerary precautions of the Egyptians – their 'pyramids and labyrinthine corridors' – could not prevent 'ultimate pillage'. Film, according to some enthusiasts, averted decay. As Siegfried Kracauer proclaimed in 1960, it made possible 'the redemption of physical reality'. Welles denied himself this consolation. Through his career as an actor, his double or Doppelgänger was a source of revulsion not astonished delight; it usually represented his worst self, not his ideal self-image. He embalmed himself in make-up to play the ageing Kane, then watched the mummy moulder.

Welles judged Kane to be a better man than Hearst because of his self-destructiveness. That, in his understanding, was what moral greatness meant. When the film opened in San Francisco, he found himself in a lift with Hearst at the Mark Hopkins Hotel. He offered Hearst, who had spent a year defaming Welles and trying to destroy his film, tickets to the première. Hearst took no notice of the cheeky invitation. When telling the story, Welles always added that Kane would have accepted. His grandest act in the film is just as shaming as it would have been for Hearst to sit through a travesty of his life: he completes Leland's scathing review of Susan's operatic début. It is not very plausible behaviour for a newspaper proprietor who has just spent a fortune commissioning an opera and constructing a theatre in which to stage it, and who now ventures to ridicule his wife in one of his own papers. But such a gratuitous, self-demeaning gesture made sense to Welles. He may have done his best to monopolise credit for *Citizen Kane*, but the film he made was a critique of megalomania, a demonstration of its futility. Belying the capitalist's obsession with ownership and control, the pitilessly truthful Kane admits that his most cherished and expensive asset is worthless, and accomplishes his own ruin. As he doggedly types in the empty office, he composes a plot for the rest of Welles's life.

Welles addressing 'demagogical America'.

CHAPTER 8

American, Pan-American

Preparing for his role in *Get To Know Your Rabbit*, Welles asked Brian De Palma to choose what accent the magician should have, and offered a range of options: he placed his finger on a map of the United States and let it wander like a water diviner's rod, changing his accent every time it strayed across a border. Like Whitman, Welles contained multitudes – enough ideas, selves and variable voices to stock an entire continent. He set out, in the first three films he directed, to chronicle the history of his family, his region, his nation itself and then of the land mass, stretching from the top to the bottom of the world, which it dominated. In 1945, he proclaimed this personal agenda in his recording of John Donne's sermon about the tolling bell. His reading begins in a thready, expiring whisper, but he revives by the time he gets to the passage denying the insularity of the self. When Donne asserts that 'every man is a piece of the continent', Welles inserts a sudden, vaulting climax, a recognition – breaking through the sermon's meditation on mortality – of his own vital powers and the worlds he intended to conquer. The excited inflection of his voice announces that this man does not merely belong to the continent; he is prepared to take possession of it. Kane declares 'I am, have been, and will be only one thing – an American.' Welles refused to be merely one thing, but his identity comprehended and then transcended his country. The project initially called *American* and then for a while entitled *John Citizen, U.S.A.* led in 1942 to the Brazilian venture, which was briefly called *Pan America*. In between came *The Magnificent Ambersons*.

In *Citizen Kane* Welles dealt with an individual's private Eden, a white idyll shattered a minute after the film begins. In *The Magnificent Ambersons* he made a more leisurely, affectionate study of that lost world, though now his concern was the childhood of America itself: the genteel time before the arrival of the automobile. As a teenager, Welles's mood was already elegiac. In 1934, he wrote some florid advertising copy for the theatre festival at his old school. He likened Woodstock to 'a wax-flower under a bell of glass', set in a 'paisley and gingham county': his sentimental metaphors turned the place into a paradise, where the memory of his happiness was preserved like that unwilting flower. Booth Tarkington's novel was set in Indiana, so Welles could easily imagine it transposed to Wisconsin or rural Illinois, where he grew up. As usual, he wrote himself into the story. He liked to pretend that his feckless father had been Tarkington's model for Eugene Morgan, who invents and markets the Tin Lizzie; on the winter outing, he had the characters sing 'The Man Who Broke the Bank at Monte Carlo' as the car rattles home, in fond tribute to another of his gambling father's supposed achievements. In *The Fall of the City* or *Panic*, *The Cradle Will Rock* or *The War of the Worlds*, he had dramatised societies foundering, assailed by the economic, political and psychological stress of modern times. Now, as if in atonement, he recreated the cushioned stability of the nineteenth century. Of course he did so only to show it collapsing all over again, but on this occasion there was aching regret rather than radical fury in the act of destruction.

The small town where the Ambersons are briefly magnificent is constructed, like Xanadu, out of fire and ice, and is ornamented with statues and fountains. The images are the same, but the ideas they evoke have changed.

Kane's castle consists mostly of shadows. Welles ran out of money to build a set for the hall where Susan does her puzzles; he therefore turned down the lights in the studio and had Kane converse with her across a cavernous, cheerless empty space. In *The Magnificent Ambersons*, ocular deceit gives way to the realistic solidity of the bourgeois novel. These sets could be lived in: as George and Lucy (Tim Holt and Anne Baxter) drive through town, shops across the street, never seen directly, are reflected in the windows they pass. But the Amberson mansion, despite its vertiginous stairwell and dim catacombed privacies, still has an enchanted capacity to blend heat and cold, like Coleridge's pleasure-dome: it, too, is a recess of imagination. When Lucy arrives for the ball with her father (Joseph Cotten), a wintry gale blows them through the front door and agitates the chandelier, whose glass shards are tinkling icicles. Inside, the house with its Moorish arches and festoons of greenery is tropically warm, like a stuffy conservatory.

When they leave, they are expelled into the punishing cold again. Their breath frosts over, and they shiver beneath bundled furs in Eugene's open car. Though the house resists the winter climate indoors, the contradiction between fire and ice cannot be resolved by a poetic paradox, as it is inside Kane's glass globe. Dying, Major Amberson (Richard Bennett) soliloquises about the life-force within the sun as fire-light flickers on his creased face: a rehearsal for the scene at the brazier in *Chimes at Midnight* when Welles's Falstaff, having come in from the snow, warms himself with tenuous, terminal memories. The verbal image with which Welles chose to conclude *Chimes at Midnight* is significant. The last line of Shakespeare's he uses – before the narrator's final quotation from Holinshed's chronicle, which looks forward to the reign of Henry V – is Bardolph's downcast joke about his own flaring nose, which Falstaff had compared to hellfire. As Falstaff's coffin is dragged away, Bardolph says: 'The fuel is gone that maintained that fire.' The major speculates about 'the sun in the first place'. But whatever is flammable is unstable, entropic, liable to ignite. Film might be a reverent tribute to holy light, as D. W. Griffith thought, but its nitrates can strike sparks as easily as nitroglycerin. In 1958, a fire-prevention official noticed that some reels of unedited film Welles brought back from his Brazilian expedition in 1942 had begun to decompose; as a precaution, the cans were drowned in the Pacific, which effectively destroyed *It's All True*. The sun gives off heat, but slowly expires as it does so. This is the conundrum the Major tries to comprehend. The kitchen of the house contains a starker reminder that the heat we rely on to stay alive is not guaranteed for all eternity. Fanny (Agnes Moorehead), depressed and now impoverished, sits propped against the boiler. George warns that she'll burn herself. 'It's not hot, it's cold, the plumbers disconnected it,' Moorehead shrieks in heart-rending desperation. 'I wouldn't mind if they hadn't, I wouldn't mind if it burned me!' Pain might rekindle her vitality.

The war between heat and cold is the principle that underlies this society. Romanticism derived its mythology from the industrial revolution, whose engines – 'burning bright' like Blake's tiger 'in the forests of the night' – consumed fire and converted it into steam and thus into speed or energy. Industrial smithies were dangerous because torrid, like Blake's 'dark satanic mills'. Eugene takes the Amberson women to visit the factory where he manufactures a car and a quarter a day. The first shot of this scene shows a blacksmith hammering; shrapnel singes the air, and the women giggle in nervous excitement. The industrial cauldron required a cooling device to prevent its mechanisms from overheating. The two extremes conduct their dispute when Eugene risks his temperamental car in the snow. It chugs along in fits and starts, pushed by George who chokes on its exhaust; its fumes blacken the white landscape.

The Ambersons are wrong to think that their magnificence will continue forever, because nothing can be permanent in a society based on this engineered collision of fire and ice. Welles's narration contrasts the horse-drawn street car, which kept to no schedule and waited for laggard passengers, with the conveyances that replaced it. They project us through space more quickly, but deprive us of time: 'the faster we're carried, the less time we have to spare'. Our propulsiveness aims unerringly at doom. (Perhaps this is why Cocteau was reminded of *The Magnificent Ambersons* when he saw Welles's film of *Macbeth*: the thane and his wife, swathed in bristling animal skins, looked to him like 'motorists at the turn of the century' – drivers whose vehicles are their own sleepless bodies and distraught minds.) But there is a suicidal romantic heroism in this volatile, combustible life. Fanny is stupefied when told that Eugene's cars are to have 'wheels all made of rubber, and blown up with air: I should think they'd explode!' The song about the man who broke the bank at Monte Carlo laughingly describes the industrial regime of inflation and deflation, overextension and collapse. George even more intrepidly quits the legal profession to take a more lucrative job in what he calls the 'dangerous trades'. Higher pay goes to 'people that handle touchy chemicals, high explosives, men in the dynamite factories'.

Lucy in Tarkington's novel admiringly calls her father a 'mechanical genius'. But whenever Welles employed machines, they had a tendency to go berserk. In 1939 he designed a turntable for *Five Kings*, using it to change sets and also to illustrate the circular repetitions of history; it started to run backwards, and bombarded the audience with any scenery that was not nailed down. Unqualified to play an engineer, he gave the role of Eugene to Cotten. If *The Magnificent Ambersons* is read as Welles's own Freudian family romance, then his part was that of George, his mother's pet, the pampered princeling who refuses to accept Eugene as his stepfather. When Welles and Cotten acted together – in *Citizen Kane*, *Journey into Fear* and *The Third Man* – Cotten played Welles's principled better self or better half. His honeyed Virginia drawl, which he kept in most of these performances no matter what the provenance of his characters was meant to be, vouched for his old-fashioned grace. Welles, castigating himself as usual, brought back one of Cotten's previous characters to witness George's comeuppance. The page of the newspaper which reports on George's injuries in a car accident contains a theatre review by Jedediah Leland, Kane's severe conscience who has obviously found employment elsewhere after being sacked from the *Inquirer*.

The Amberson mansion, like Xanadu, has an honour guard of statues. At the beginning, a classical figure preens on the front path, balanced by a second pedestal with an antlered stag (like Kane's chained bear). The next scene notices a wooden Indian on sentry duty outside the town's cigar store. But this society has little patience with stasis, and no belief in gods and their idealised marble physiques. In the barber's shop, Jack (Ray Collins) mentions the engagement of Isabel (Dolores Costello), and concedes that her mousy fiancé Wilbur 'may not be any Apollo, as it were'. Immediately after this, gossips in the dressmaker's shop flutter around a tailor's dummy, which is a modern statue of another kind: a see-through woman of wire with no head (like Kane's expensive Venus). She is cut off below the hips, so that under her swelling bustle she has spokes of wire, not legs.

Statues are the materialisation of communal value or belief. Characters in *The Magnificent Ambersons* are moulded into shape by public opinion, and made to metamorphose when the consensus changes. Hence the introductory sequence about male fashions, with Eugene squeezing into shoes that pinch him, lengthening his overcoat, and trying on baggy pants. Kane's sculptures are here replaced by the human body, which sculpts itself by wearing clothes rather than by Platonically undressing; and the fashion model, as the scene with Cotten in the changing room reveals, is a victim of industrial dynamism. In a brief memoir written in 1982, Welles defined his father by associating him with a fashion already defunct in the period of *The Magnificent Ambersons*. He wore black spats – a precaution adopted by nineteenth-century gentlemen to conceal the spatterings of horse dung on their shoes – and maintained the habit while everyone else, updating to the automobile era, took a chance with lighter colours. Tarkington's sartorial metaphors, illustrated in the essay on costume at the start of the film, emphasise the way that fashion tries to motorise the body, urging it into the future and thereby wearing it out. Tight shoes resemble 'the prows of racing shells', and an ephemeral variety of hat resembles the cooling chimney that releases heat and smoke from a domestic furnace: this is 'that rigid tall silk thing known to impudence as a stove pipe'. Major Amberson sports one of these in the film, and loses it to a gust of wind.

Friends advised Welles against driving himself as carelessly and dangerously as one of the automobiles that overtake the city in *The Magnificent Ambersons*. Didn't he realise that he was expending himself, using up mental fuel that could not easily be replaced? Thornton Wilder told him 'You must stop wasting your energy, Orson. Have capsule conversations.' Welles ignored the industrial tragedy of heat loss and dripping ice, even though he placed its outcome on display in his films. He told Tynan that he refused to consider energy 'a priceless juice that has to be kept in a secret bottle'. Disregarding Wilder's advice, he went on talking, and his ideas floated away on the air. In 1947, Aldous Huxley, introducing a translation of the *Bhagavad-Gita*, blamed the steam engine for spiritually corrupting the West. The efficiency of machines made men think that society could also be automatically improved and perfected, so 'attention . . . came to be paid, not to Eternity, but to the Utopian future'. Welles's internal combustion engines do not usher in Utopia. Despairing of the future, *The Magnificent Ambersons* chooses to commemorate the past. Hence its beautiful equivalent to Kane's glazed snowstorm. At the end of the wintry automobile ride, Welles uses a quaintly antiquated cinematic synonym for closure: an iris, which contracts the scene as if readying it for storage as an immaterial memory. The screen gradually blackens, and the image is compressed into a circle in the corner. Inside that telescope, the retreating car might be a toy, like the miniature cabin cramped inside Kane's microcosmic glass ball. At least the visual field, having diminished to a ball, does not smash like the globe Kane drops. It simply goes on decreasing until it obliterates itself. A dissolve merges it with funeral wreaths on the door of the mansion after Wilbur's death. Eugene and Lucy go into the house again, and the doors close behind them with an audible click. This, more tactfully, corresponds to the crash of glass on the paved floor in Kane's bedroom: the sound signifies that the happy memory has been switched off.

On the return from the trial run in the snow, RKO cut a telling comment by Eugene about the smoky horizon. 'As it grows bigger [the town] seems to get ashamed of itself,' he says in the script, 'so it makes that big cloud and hides in it.' He is bemoaning the loss of a dual innocence, social and sexual: he alludes to Adam and Eve recoiling after the fall and hiding their nakedness from God. Tarkington's novel describes the censorious dusting and scrubbing of the town's housewives, who – as grime implacably settles over them and shortens their lives – have to renounce 'the happiness of ever seeing anything white'. That image makes Welles's expanse of downy snow, an eiderdown for prelapsarian romping, all the more precious in retrospect. In the novel, Lucy admires a house that is neoclassically white. George passes it again later in the book, and sees that the town's greasy, smutty air has smirched it: the owners have now 'painted it a despairing chocolate'. Perhaps Richard Welles's black spats were not so otiose after all.

In noticing pollution, Eugene anticipates George's last walk home at the end of the film, when he traipses through a brawling, blackened city he no longer recognises. It is a crucial episode, because the corresponding passage in Tarkington hints at the presence of Kubla Khan's threshing fountain: 'The streets were thunderous; a vast energy heaved under the universal coating of dinginess.' That energy is no longer an elemental upsurgence from nature, as in Coleridge's poem. It represents the belligerence of industry, churning and mashing the earth. Welles's spoken commentary in the film takes up Tarkington's hint of a geyser: 'The town . . . was heaving up in the middle, . . . and as it heaved and spread it befouled itself and darkened its sky.'

This sequence documenting George's walk was photographed by Welles himself on the streets of downtown Los Angeles, which made possible a leap into the un-Utopian future. Telephone wires cross-hatch the sky, and the girders of skyscrapers block it off. Clapboard lodging houses straggle up Bunker Hill, making room for the city's population of transients. Metal fire-escapes – exiguous versions of the Amberson staircase with its stately landings – zigzag down the façades: these buildings expect an emergency. A factory appears, a tin shed indefinitely elongated. A derrick looks ahead to the rigs that gouge for oil on the coast in *Touch of Evil*. The studio sheared the long walk to forty seconds, but what remains is almost unbearably moving. The camera's view is subjective. We no longer see George; instead we stare up, intimidated, at the looming city as he trudges through it. At the beginning of the twentieth century, he foresees the world we now all live in. Ahead lies his accident, when he is knocked over by a car at one of these brawling intersections: Brecht suggested in 1938 that such an incident was the 'basic model for epic theatre', with eyewitnesses quarrelling about what actually happened and the driver of the car blaming the trampled pedestrian and refusing to pay damages – a small demonstration of the individual's devalued, expendable status in our society. The music during George's walk has the trudging pace of a funeral march, and every few seconds there is a weary fade-out as if the camera, rather than treasuring an image in its iris as it does at the end of the ride through the snow, had slowly blinked, wanting to erase these smudged, gritty sights. The final black-out compresses the album of grim snapshots into the head of George, as he kneels in his mother's bedroom in the empty house. What he says, over and over, is 'Forgive me.' He is asking the dead Isabel to forgive him for vetoeing her happiness, but Welles's montage, by connecting his remorse with that tour of the city, suggests another impolitic possibility: may America be forgiven for its assault on nature.

Like the American city, film has a self-obliterating kinesis. Tarkington describes some young people dressed up for a jaunt in a brassy red car as faddists of 'motorism'; film too only moves if motorised. Images are spooled through the projector at the rate of twenty-four per second, and each frame is gone before our laggard brain can notice that it is a still. The ribbon of dreams is in a rush to shred itself, to wipe itself out. 'This is our last walk together,' says George to Lucy near the end of the film, 'the last time we'll ever see each other.' The walk takes them past the Bijou, a cinema showing a Western with Tim Holt's father Jack, a forgotten silent star. Pausing to regret the loss of livery stables and streetcars, Tarkington calls these consignments to oblivion 'vanishings'. Their fate is the same as the flickerings of cinematic images: a St Vitus' dance of imperilled phenomena, an epilepsy of atoms. This notion of vanishings surely touched Welles, whose magic decreed such disappearances and, in the solemnity of its incantations, honoured the objects that passed away.

The jittery tempo of cinematic perception matched the temporariness of America itself. The magnificence of the Ambersons lasts for only as long as it takes to squander the Major's money. How could privileges be perpetuated in what Melville called 'demagogical America', which had 'no chartered aristocracy'? The hero of *Pierre* terminates his own family line by killing his cousin after he himself is disinherited. 'In our cities,' Melville comments, 'families rise and burst like bubbles in a vat.' Henry James, in his 1879 essay on Hawthorne, enumerated the deficiencies of America, which lacked the means to cultivate dynasts: 'no Oxford, nor Eton, nor Harrow; . . . no Epsom nor Ascot!' Steinbeck thought that Californian farmers were greedy for land because they remembered 'feudal Europe where great families became and remained great because they owned things'. Ownership, however, as the case of Kane demonstrates, is no more than a leasehold, soon due to reach its term. Despite the inequities of a so-called democracy, Melville's Pierre rejoices to discover that 'Death is this Democrat', who can be relied on to treat all men alike.

The Magnificent Ambersons accepts that outcome, even though its vanishings include all the scenes cut from the film – George lording it over his boys' club, Eugene and Lucy putting his car to bed after the ball, a nocturnal conference of the family on the Amberson porch, Fanny's stoically cheery afterlife in a raucous boarding-house – and destroyed late in 1942 by order of a new studio boss. In 1971, switching between television channels in a Beverly Hills hotel, Welles happened upon the film, or what remained of it. He sat through a few scenes, harumphing at the excisions, then quietly began to cry. Bogdanovich changed the channel. Much later, he found the courage to mention the incident, and tactfully tried to sympathise with Welles's distress about the mutilation of his work. Welles said he had missed the point. The cuts merely angered him; the reason for his sorrow was 'because it's the past – it's over'. His tears recognised a loss of happiness and hope that is common to us all. It was history, not himself, he mourned for.

After Tarkington's novel, Welles next planned a film which would have been an anthology of short stories, pan-American in its range. To begin with, there were to be four components, all based on fact. Though his first title was *Pan America*, he registered the project in July 1941 under the title *It's All True*.

One episode was set near the Arctic, in Hudson Bay: the source was *The Captain's Chair*, an account of survival in the frozen north by the documentary film-maker Robert Flaherty. The captain in Flaherty's story, who cajoles and lashes his ship through ice floes, might have been one of Welles's great characters. Like Kurtz, he is a trader who wants to 'open up the north', extracting ore from beneath the snow; on his cabin shelves Flaherty notices a copy of *Purchas his Pilgrimage*, the compilation of fantastic voyages in which Coleridge found the story of Kubla Khan and Xanadu. Travelling across the frozen tundra by sledge, Flaherty himself watches as Coleridge's mysterious metaphors are proved true when the Eskimos construct an igloo, a cave of ice lit from within by the fire of a blubber lamp. He admires 'this miracle in snow', and wonders at 'the symmetry of the dome'. Two other episodes in Welles's anthology covered aspects of ethnic experience in the United States: a love affair between Italian immigrants in San Francisco, and a biography of Louis Armstrong with a score by Duke Ellington. Then there was a southern excursion, also derived from a story by Flaherty: the story of a Mexican boy and his pet bull Bonito, which he reprieves from death in the arena.

It's All True was meant to be a synopsis of the continent, extending from the white waste of Labrador to the scorching, arid Mexican desert. As a natural transgressor, Welles was fascinated by borders, and the film should have allowed him to cross the official dividing lines between society and wildness, both at the top and bottom of the continent. Before Flaherty sets out on a canoeing expedition, he pauses on the frontier in Northern Ontario: 'I . . . remained in civilization until June,' he says, after which he launches himself into uncharted terrain.

Within a year, Welles's personal, whimsical itinerary had been politicised. After the United States joined the war at the end of 1941, its allies below the equator had to be charmed into remaining loyal. RKO no doubt thought it was being a good neighbour when it released *The Magnificent Ambersons* – after cutting forty minutes and adding some fuzzy, flattering close-ups and a perfunctory happy ending – on a double bill with a farce called *Mexican Spitfire Sees a Ghost*. While Welles was still working at the studio, the Office of the Co-ordinator of Inter-American Affairs asked him to make what he called 'a polyglot movie' designed 'for Americans in all the Americas'. Accepting the government's proposal, he reduced *It's All True* to three stories. The Mexican episode stayed, though he commissioned Norman Foster to direct it after finishing work on *Journey into Fear*. Early in 1942, Welles himself went to Brazil to research the other two strands of *It's All True*; he broke his journey in Miami, where he made a scrambled attempt to edit *The Magnificent Ambersons*. Remembering his pseudo-diplomatic responsibility, he broadcast from Rio de Janeiro on Pan-American Day, and joined in celebrating the birthday of the Brazilian dictator Getúlio Vargas. In his new scheme for the film, the jazz of Armstrong and Ellington was replaced by samba, as he recorded the convergence of dancing crowds during carnival in Rio. He also set out to film a re-enactment of the voyage of four jangadeiros, poor fishermen from Fortaleza in northern Brazil who, a few months before, had sailed to Rio to petition Vargas for an improvement to their slavish working conditions. They spent sixty-one days on a raft of six logs without chart or compass. *Time*, reporting on their trip, called it 'a Homeric voyage'.

Having abandoned his earlier plans, Welles admitted that *It's All True* was now a 'scriptless documentary'. Fiction can be plotted in advance; reality has a way of taking you by surprise. At first he treated this inconvenience with reckless disdain. When he arrived in Rio, a reporter asked him what the film would be about. 'Ask me again in six months,' he replied. Then he became aware of how difficult it would be to find a coherent narrative in the oceanic agitation of the samba schools. In May, while the arrival of the jangadeiros in Rio was being re-enacted on film, an unscripted accident sabotaged that story. A scene of marine carnage that might have come from *Moby Dick* reared out of the water: an octopus battling a shark. In their excitement, the jangadeiros upset their raft and fell overboard. Their leader Jacaré was a poor swimmer, and the shark gulped him down, along with the octopus. Soon afterwards, *It's All True* was cancelled. RKO sent an overseer to Rio to confiscate the colour cameras Welles was using and to discharge his crew. The Mercury employees left behind in Hollywood were expelled from the lot. The space they occupied had been requisitioned for the production team of a Tarzan film.

In retrospect, thanks to the fragments of Mexican and Brazilian footage assembled by Bill Krohn and others in 1993, it's possible to see how the documentary would have extended and completed Welles's investigation of American values and revised his notion of himself as an allegorical American. *Citizen Kane*, beginning in the present, places on show the joyless mercenary mania of capitalism and its final pointlessness. *The Magnificent Ambersons* returns to the country's provincial heartland before it was irrevocably invaded by what Eisenstein, in an essay written in 1944, called 'Super-Dynamic America' with its 'tempestuous tempi, dizzying action, breathtaking chases'. *It's All True* moves back even further, to an offshore frontier like that which was once the hardy nursery of American virtues.

The past was over for Americans when the frontier closed, which is why Welles, attempting to revive the American dream of a fresh start in a land with no history, had to look north to Flaherty's icy tundra or south to the tropics. According to the national myth, America's fall began when the garden made way for the city. Huck Finn, unwilling to be civilised by Aunt Sally, turns tail: 'I reckon I got to light out for the Territory ahead of the rest.' The very existence of the 'Midland town' where *The Magnificent Ambersons* is set makes official this decline from the unspoiled outdoors to an imprisoning sociability. Tarkington unregretfully recalls the lawlessness of the wild West when he likens a motorist who startles surreys drawn by 'honest old horses' to 'a cowboy shooting up a peaceful camp'. In his spoken prologue to the film, Welles as narrator pays more explicit homage to 'those "early settlers" who . . . opened the wilderness with wagons and axes and guns', stored food for the winter, traded goods to stay alive, and practised thrift as a religion. After the pioneers came the comfortable bourgeoisie, Welles's own people, who no longer needed to battle against nature. Even when they prospered, Welles notes that the first settlers refused to spend their surplus on '"art"'. That aside makes the mansion of the Ambersons look as frivolously wasteful as Xanadu. But at the same time it retrospectively challenges our view of Kane as a grasping materialist. Shouldn't he be seen as a benefactor, whose wholesale purchase of statues introduced the notion of art to utilitarian America? The remark also prepares for the arrival of Welles himself, a self-consciously extravagant artist who defied the rule Henry James propounded when writing about Hawthorne, that 'it is a considerable discomfort in the United States not to be "in business". The young man who attempts to launch himself in a career that does not belong to the so-called practical order . . . has but a limited place in the social system.' Profligacy and imaginative delinquency, Welles's personal foibles, challenge this unremittingly commercial culture. Welles's few sentences about the blinkered early settlers, cut by the studio, established the film's place in his personal history of America.

That history had to start in the West. The Western provided America with its epic, the moral fable of the nation's founding. Welles said that he learned the techniques of film-making by studying John Ford's *Stagecoach* (which is where he spotted Tim Holt, who has a small part as a lieutenant at a frontier outpost), and throughout his career he made his own displaced, sceptical versions of Ford's Westerns. Ford's abiding subject was the consolidation of community and the closure of the frontier. In *The Searchers*, a pioneer wife whose son has been killed predicts that this will be a fine country some day, though their bones will have to be planted in the ground before that can happen. Hence the importance of burial rites for Ford. Ethan (John Wayne) digs his niece's grave with his own hands, and wraps her in his army greatcoat; he desecrates the corpse of an Indian warrior to keep him out of heaven. Cemeteries create civilisations. Such founding rituals are absent from Welles's films. Arkadin leaves no body to bury, and Lime's coffin contains the wrong body. Discussing *The Trial* in 1965, Welles said that the stories he told were actually 'based not so much on a pursuit as a search'. But the search in Ford is for home, kinship, the sense of belonging, while the search in Welles is for knowledge, which alienates the individual from his fellows and from himself. There is no future for anyone to ride off into. In a scene deleted from *The Trial*, the scientist shows K an IBM card that spells out the crime he is most likely to commit: it is suicide.

Welles edged up on the Western obliquely. He took a sly pride in referring to *Man in the Shadow* as a horseless Western, since it is set in the new West where characters run their errands in pick-up trucks and no livestock is visible. *Trouble in the Glen* is a Celtic Western, a Scottish equivalent to Ford's *The Quiet Man*; the writers were the same, and Victor McLaglen appears in both films. Welles, the laird on an iron-fenced estate, is menaced by rebellious tinkers, who steal his cattle: they are the Indians, raiding the settler's stockade. His factor goes to Glasgow to recruit a private army: they are the bandit gang. And the situation is saved by a former paratrooper whose nickname is Sir Lancelot: he is the cavalryman, or – as Welles would have put it – the chevalier. With his enthusiasm for the romance of chivalry, Welles shared Ford's faith in the cavalry's nobility. Playing Rochester in *Jane Eyre*, Welles is indignant when the mousy governess frightens his horse, which throws him. Men on horseback are meant to rescue imperilled women, not to be unseated by them. 'Next time you see a man on a horse,' he says sternly, 'do not run out into the middle of the road until he has passed.' The Wellesian chevalier, however, did not need to be a rider. He called O'Hara in *The Lady from the Shanghai* 'chivalrous' because of his deluded idealism. O'Hara is a sailor not a horseman, but he does drive a horse-drawn carriage through Central Park at the beginning of the film and, like Kildare or the Ambersons, he has to suffer the competition of horseless carriages: 'Get that nag outta here!' yells a taxi driver.

The moral code mattered more to Welles than the mode of transport, which is why he instantly understood that the trip made by the jangadeiros on their flimsy raft was the ideal subject for a Western, despite its southern setting. This episode of *It's All True*, he said, was to be a 'Western of the sea'. The idea was brilliant, though not entirely new. In *The Captain's Chair*, Flaherty hears the grizzled sea-dogs in a Newfoundland port talking 'of ships as a cowboy talks of horses'. John Ford in 1940 had made his own maritime Western in *The Long Voyage Home*, based on four of Eugene O'Neill's one-act plays about wanderings at sea; the director of photography was Gregg Toland, who immediately afterwards offered his services to Welles for *Citizen Kane*.

In style, Welles's recreation of the voyage down the Brazilian coast evokes the proletarian epics of Eisenstein. The subject was the common man's concerted struggle against feudalism: the jangadeiros had to hand over half their catches to lazy, land-locked bosses. The fishermen are equalised by their white hats, the women by their black dresses. Individual emotions are disallowed. A bride is stoical when her husband drowns, because his loss depletes the entire community rather than only afflicting her; and it serves to prompt political action, as the destitute villagers confer and decide to take their grievance to Rio. But the earnest Soviet emphasis on industrial servitude is qualified by an American admiration for self-reliance. As if recalling the travails of settlers on the Western frontier, Welles documents the routines of labour – except that the Brazilian peasants have no guns, and must ingeniously charm nature into supplying them with the means of life. They weave baskets to hold fish, or saw and plane timbers for rafts. Two newlyweds quickly fabricate their house, which does not need to be a log cabin, fortified against the weather and the assault of savages: a rope is strung between palms to hold up a roof of fronds, with walls woven together from creepers.

Transferring the Western to the sea (which happens also in another of Welles's sacred American texts, *Moby Dick*) adds a newly tragic ending. Ford's Westerns end on a domesticated frontier which no longer needs military protection. O'Neill's sea plays, adapted by Ford in *The Long Voyage Home*, take a different view. The sea is the element of existential homelessness. Yank in one of them yearns for his farm, but a discontented permanent exile called Luke refuses to put down roots and be a 'damned dirt puncher'. For Welles too, there was no hope of anchorage on land: O'Hara in *The Lady from Shanghai* leaves Elsa to die and walks off towards the Pacific.

Ford softens this comfortless outcome at the end of *The Long Voyage Home*. Ole Olson (John Wayne again), on his way back to rural Sweden and his long-suffering mother, is drugged in the East End of London and hustled aboard a ship departing for Valparaiso. Welles, as it happened, later used this Chilean port for an impulsive abduction of his own. Entertaining Françoise Sagan one afternoon in his Paris hotel, he proposed carrying her off to Valparaiso. They were to leave in an hour. She felt 'a moment of terror' at the idea of a life so ungrounded and bewilderingly free, then compliantly left to collect her passport. But the phone rang just in time, reminding Welles that he was due in London, so they never got to Valparaiso. Nor does Ole in Ford's film: his mates rescue him, though one of them is knocked out and left behind as a replacement. This unconscious recruit does not get far, as the German navy torpedoes the ship in the English Channel. A final title announces that 'The Long Voyage never ends', no longer mentioning the possibility of home. Still, we know that the bucolic Ole got there, because the soundtrack plangently intones the mother's song from Grieg's *Peer Gynt*. The jangadeiros were not so lucky. Their trip was futile, their sacrifice vain. Vargas exploited their popularity, but did nothing to better their lot. This expedition could not end as northern Westerns usually did, with colonisation: clearing land and eliminating natives to make way for farms and then cities, extending iron rails from one ocean to another. After the incident with the shark, Welles inscribed on his script a memorial dedication to Jacaré, calling him 'an American hero'. But he left the story unfinished, because the wilderness of water remained unconquerable.

Like Hearst sending Remington to Cuba, Welles travelled to Brazil at the behest of Nelson Rockefeller, who – apart from his keenness to flush out Nazis – wanted to protect the interests of his own commercial empire below the Panama Canal. The United States began its exorbitant adventure of global domination during these war years, and Welles at first seemed keen to participate. In a broadcast immediately after the Japanese raid on Pearl Harbor in December 1941, he attested to his own 'energetic and unashamed patriotism' and said he was sure that his listeners would be satisfied by nothing less than 'complete victory' over the enemy.

As brashly confident as America, the young Welles universalised himself. When not making war on the world, he imagined himself travelling around it – or at least sent his voice or face to do the colonising work for him, carried by electrical impulses from the RKO mast planted on the North Pole. The hope persisted long after his corporate sponsors lost interest in engaging him as a missionary. He consoled MacLíammóir and Edwards when delays interrupted *Othello* by planning a theatrical world tour. They were to take six plays to Bombay, Buenos Aires, Shanghai and Sydney, travelling light because they would do without scenery and rely on the 'accompaniment of Philharmonic orchestras picked up in the cities visited'. They never left home. But Welles's characters found time and funds for such journeys. In the script of *American*, Kane reminds Susan, 'You always said that you wanted to go round the world', and they spend a year dilettantishly doing so on his yacht. In *The*

Magnificent Ambersons, George abruptly informs Lucy that he and his mother 'are starting on a trip around the world tomorrow' and have no plans for coming back, to which, pertly dissimulating, she replies 'My, that does sound like a long trip!' Sherwood King's novel *If I Die Before I Wake* is set on Long Island; Welles in *The Lady from Shanghai* opened it out, sending the characters on a voyage from New York to San Francisco. They travel by way of the Panama Canal – gained for America, as Bernstein argues in *Citizen Kane*, by the war with Spain which Kane takes responsibility for dreaming up. O'Hara and Elsa span the continent, but are divided by it. He, an Irishman, belongs to the Atlantic, she to the Pacific: she was born on 'the China coast'. Their journey, rather than following a colonial or conquistadorial route, is as regressive as Kurtz's. The Panama canal is a dividing line, like the waist of the human body, between the upper tier of reason and the nether zone of instinct. Even in San Francisco, the plot depends on shuttling across the bay from the city to Sausalito, as if these were the two opposed coasts or halves of the continent, still unbridgeable: the hills stacked with towers and the green, lush, unconquered earth.

In 1946, Welles circumnavigated the earth in three incident-laden, accident-prone hours when he staged *Around the World*, combining silent film, circus acts with a live elephant, conjuring tricks, and extravagant musical numbers scored by Cole Porter. Jules Verne's novel pays tribute to what he calls 'the colonising genius of the English'; Welles reclaimed the prerogative of world conquest for America. Though Verne's hero is an Englishman, the record-breaker on whom he based Phileas Fogg was a Bostonian, George Francis Tain, and Welles's show began its own disastrous tour in Boston. The subjugation of terrain did not quite proceed as planned, and its topography suggested the disoriented muddle of modern tourism rather than Fogg's steady advance across the continents. 'Is this London?' asked an actress in one scene, as stagehands lowered a drop representing the Rocky Mountains. Brecht praised the production, whose mechanics coincided with his own motorised dramaturgy. He thought that Aristotelian plays were static, showing 'the world as it is', whereas 'the learning-play is essentially dynamic; its task is to show the world as it changes'. But the rotating, revolutionary world, in Welles's staging, came close to spinning off its axis.

Interviewed by *Cahiers* in 1982, he insisted on his own similarity to Verne's punctual, punctilious hero, whose life is as exactly equilibrated and synchronised as a chronometer. 'I am just like Phileas Fogg, never late,' he said. 'I really am Phileas Fogg, no-one has ever seen me arrive late.' He eyed his timid questioners for a moment, then roared with laughter at the success of his imposture. He had come to be unrepentantly proud of his lateness, his indebtedness, his mazy incapacity to keep to an undeviating course; his vices proved his humanity, by contrast with the regularity and predictability of Fogg, who is described by Verne as 'method idealized'. W. H. Auden admired Fogg's maniacally exact time-keeping, which made him a human specimen of a new kind, attuned to the remorseless scheduling of industrial society. He could not have existed in the classical era, when men thought of time revolving in a repetitious circle rather than extending in a straight line from present to future: 'it was never said in praise of any Caesar', Auden commented, 'that he made whatever was the Roman equivalent of trains run on time'. Auden assigned Fogg to the genus of The Punctual Man, and added – more plausibly than Welles – that this was 'the type to which I personally belong'. For Welles, a 'phlegmatic gentleman' like Fogg could only be an ogre. The man is a machine, who conserves his vital forces by suppressing emotion and ignoring the importunity of experience. Travelling around the world with his eyes averted, he leaves his servant to look at it for him.

Verne's Fogg is more genuinely romantic (or, even better, quixotic) than Welles and Auden were prepared to concede. The book begins by noticing his resemblance to Byron – but he is a Byron who has escaped from the thermodynamic tragedy of romanticism, which requires the self-depleting expenditure of energy: unflappably tranquil, he looks as if he will 'live for a thousand years without growing old'. He undertakes his trip in response to a wager, spends money on a whim, and even burns the wooden innards of his iron-hulled ship when he needs to increase his speed across the Atlantic. Welles liked the self-destructive notion of disassembling the boat you travel on. In *American*, Kane and his first wife were to spend their honeymoon on a land-locked Wisconsin lake; his yacht was taken to pieces, driven overland through the forests, then put back together again so the newlyweds could go for a sail.

At the end of the 1930s, Welles had devised for himself an itinerary as punitive as Fogg's. When he first accepted the contract to make films at RKO, he planned to fly back to New York from Los Angeles each week to do his radio broadcasts. He was prepared for aeronautical mishaps: on one occasion he dashed into the New York studio at the last moment, wildly claiming that he had personally flown a plane from Chicago through an electrical storm after the vomiting crew deserted the controls. Unlike Fogg, Welles did not remain imperturbable. The likelihood of disaster elated him, which is why he fancied himself dodging lightning bolts and bouncing on downdraughts in that flimsy aircraft. Fogg was an organiser, budgeting time in order to speed himself through space. Welles's sublime fury revenged itself on such administrative schemes by wrecking them. When a New York critic jeered that *Around the World* contained everything but the kitchen sink, Welles, not wanting to leave anything out, strolled on stage at the next performance dragging a kitchen sink behind him.

He mimicked Phileas Fogg in the television series *Around the World with Orson Welles*. But the programmes he made for Granada in 1955 meandered across the countryside – he explained in one of them that he disliked flying and preferred to tootle along by train – and idled into regions, like the Basque country, that Phileas Fogg would not have considered worth the detour. He declined to exemplify the colonising genius of the Americans, and used the programmes to criticise the modernity of the new imperial power. The mother of a transplanted American boy tells him that her son gets a better education in a Basque mountain village than he would back home, which prompts Welles to philosophise about the conflict between civilised values and the brisk, brainless worship of technical innovation.

One after another, his characters outgrew the national dogma of irresistible progress. At the Amberson ball, Jack is convinced that 'old times . . . are starting all over again'. Eugene corrects him: his horseless carriages have caused an irrevocable breach with the plodding past. 'There aren't any old times,' he says. 'When times are gone, they're not old, they're dead!' This was what Welles meant when he turned away from the televised *Magnificent Ambersons* – though Eugene is elated by obsolescence, whereas Welles, feeling himself to be obsolete, quietly grieved over the days he had seen. Eugene adds a salute to the propulsive future, with which Welles would not have sympathised: 'There aren't any times but new times', he says. But by the end of the film, when he imagines that the dead Isabel has coaxed him into a reconciliation with George, he too has lost faith in the future and taken refuge in an imagined past. The house he builds with the proceeds from his factory is the Amberson mansion all over again, though its style is Georgian not Romanesque.

The dying Major Amberson – one of Welles's wise gerontocrats, a successor to the wrinkled sages who outlive Kane and convene to tell his story – comes to realise, as Welles's narration says, that 'all his buying and building and trading and banking' were 'trifling and waste'. Jack's voice is heard anxiously asking him when he deeded the house to Isabel; he can't remember, and can't imagine why anyone would care. 'Time', he decides, 'means nothing.' This phrase, the solemn conclusion of the Major's reverie, was cut by the studio, though Welles himself took it to heart. It justified his unpunctuality and all his other offences against the American creed of businesslike behaviour. It also led him, after setbacks forced him to reconsider his own existence, to a different, dissident view of the world. Instead of the onward and upward trajectory of history, he chose to trust myth, with its cruel cyclical justice, its rises and falls and its eternal returns which reassure us that, although everything is mutable, nothing changes.

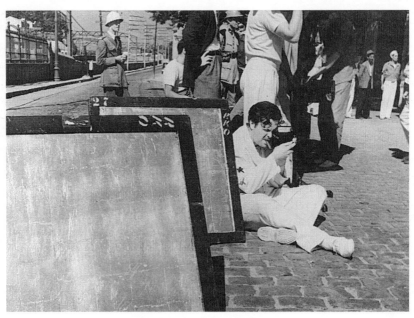

Welles improvising in Brazil.

CHAPTER 9

Lord of Misrule

In a letter to Bogdanovich, the ageing Welles referred to his Brazilian sojourn as 'the tragedy of South America' and 'the one key disaster in my story'. Alternatively, he sometimes said that RKO 'destroyed *Ambersons*, and the picture itself destroyed me'. When he left Hollywood in February 1942, he was – as he remarked in the letter, consciously adopting Dietrich's turn of phrase at the end of *Touch of Evil* – acknowledged to be 'some kind of artist'. When he returned in August, he was branded as 'some kind of lunatic', a capricious waster of company money.

Although Welles fancied that his experience was tragic, there is another way of interpreting those months in Brazil: they were a comedy, a hectic farce containing much wrecked household equipment and, when Jacaré tumbled overboard, a single, unforeseen death. Professionally, the experience may have destroyed Welles, but it also recreated him. Returning north, he thanked the country for providing him with 'the greatest and most enduring experience of my life'. The polite hyperbole might incidentally have been true.

He once told a friend that he was grateful not to have been born an Amazonian Indian. Even so, he liked to imagine that he came from a kind of wilderness. 'I belong to a wild nation,' he menacingly declared to Bazin and his colleagues in 1958. He warned the civilised French that he contained within himself 'the barbarity of America'. On his trip to South America, he came into contact with the barbaric rites that were the ancient, long-forgotten sources of both tragedy and comedy. Tragedy originates in a public sacrifice: hence the bullfight in the Mexican episode of *It's All True*. By contrast with this rigidly proper staging of death, comedy is about unpredictability and licence, the prerogatives of life itself. At the end of a Greek tragedy, satyrs sporting what Welles called 'leather phalluses' invaded the amphitheatre and obscenely rallied humanity to preserve itself. In 1938, when he directed *The Shoemaker's Holiday*, Thomas Dekker's comedy of Elizabethan low life, Welles equipped the actors with gloriously protuberant codpieces: the first time these accessories – a downward transposition of his false noses – had been seen on Broadway. He recognised the same bawdy, riotous impulse in the pelvic gyrations of the samba dancers during carnival in Rio de Janeiro.

Welles enjoyed the jolting transition between comedy and tragedy. The *War of the Worlds* broadcast began with a dance, accompanied by bands in the ballrooms of two New York hotels, but then – as the music was interrupted by emergency bulletins – broke down into a flurried, demented stampede. The Shakespearean cycle of ages and seasons, with its deaths and rebirths, preoccupied him: he once introduced a Christmas letter to MacLíammóir and Edwards by remarking that '1949 prepares to die of old age'. Carnival occurs at the next crucial moment of transition. It is a farewell to flesh, a last bout of merriment before Lenten abstinence takes over. Its ribaldry acknowledges death, but outfaces it and confidently prepares for the year's resurrection.

The opposition of the genres presented Welles with a choice between two ways of life, and two conceptions of himself. The bull represents the individual confronting death, while the comic crowd, spared this extremity by its huddled anonymity, enjoys the spectacle. Welles's cult of 'proud solitude', as Françoise Sagan called it, goaded him to play the tragic victim, raging in the arena. But the outcome of such combat is a foregone conclusion; Welles was too good a Shakespearean not to be tempted by the alternative – a comic life that permits you to eat, drink and make merry indefinitely, so long as you keep your head low and pass yourself off as just another human animal, merging with the mob. The bull named Bonito in *It's All True* was to be saved from death in the ring and allowed to go on living as a domestic pet. Why does tragedy derive such exhilaration from agony? Comedy, dealing with the body's enjoyments not its excruciation, has a superior wisdom.

During the Rio carnival, Welles tried to cast off his doomed singleness and lose himself in this collective life. His spent his youth pretending to be old, dying men: he played the nonagenarian Captain Shotover (in Shaw's *Heartbreak House*) when he was twenty-three. Now he rejuvenated himself, and took part in a celebration which, he hoped, would allow him to survive. Tragic heroes restore order to the world by destroying themselves. Welles the comedian fomented chaos instead, and rejoiced when it spun out of control. MacLíammóir – in another of his awed, alarmed metaphors – likened him to a vortex. Carnival, though it defeated his attempts to film it, suited his technique, with its careening camera movements and gabbled simultaneous dialogue. Even Faust the philosopher, in Goethe's version of the myth, attends a witches' Sabbath and takes part in a Walpurgisnacht of wild cavorting, just as Faustus in Welles's production sabotaged a papal banquet with a display of bad manners, magically causing drinks to splash in the faces of the guests and food to fly through the air. Whereas tragic characters sit apart and brood on the iniquities of life, comedy shows men on the run, coping with change and gamily outwitting chance. A character in *Horse Eats Hat* made a getaway on roller skates, while a chandelier turned into a spaceship and carried off the shrieking heroine.

Welles proclaimed this comic faith in his screenplay for *The Cradle Will Rock*, where he tells Blitzstein 'I'm *lucky*!' He makes the remark, as a note directs, 'with a strange kind of intensity', and amplifies it with reckless zeal: 'I'm riding a red-hot streak of wins. I'm lucky! . . . I'm on that red-hot lucky streak.' He and Blitzstein are swimming in a rock pool at the time: comedy is all about staying afloat. A water moccasin lunges at Welles but misses, which he takes to be proof of his immunity to disaster. He says he inherited this gambler's creed from his father, who taught him to trust in fortune and roll with the dice. Of course it is also a fatalistic creed, ironically disproved by a Welles whose luck, when he wrote the screenplay in 1984, had long since run out.

The young Welles saw himself as a conqueror, invested with absolute executive power like Kurtz. During the carnival, he found himself playing a new role, similar to that of Rei Momo, the lewd monarch elected to preside over the revels and encourage the dancers. At times of festivity, medieval and Renaissance courts also replaced the king with a fool, installed as the lord of misrule. Clowns like Feste in *Twelfth Night* were permitted, for as long as the party lasted, to express a festive disrespect for their betters. Buffoonery, like the antics of the satyrs in the amphitheatre, disregarded privilege and trounced sanctity. Twelfth Night comes at the end of the festival, and marks the moment at which the fool has to surrender his mocking sovereignty and resume life as a subordinate. Carnival likewise gives way to Lent and its devout preparation for Easter.

Welles, ever the extremist, refused to accept these necessary limits. After Rio de Janeiro, he lived and worked as if carnival could last for the whole year, or throughout an entire life.

The night before he went to South America, Welles completed his role in *Journey into Fear*. This underrated film was his induction into the philosophy of folly. He and Cotten wrote the script, adapting a novel by Eric Ambler; Norman Foster directed, paying homage to Welles – or perhaps accepting direction from him – whenever he used one of those steep vertical camera angles that suggest (as Marlene Dietrich said when summing up Welles's style) a frog's view of the world. Ambler's novel is a tense fable about one man's discovery of his own tenuous mortality. Welles and Cotten, however, changed the book into a muddled, occasionally deadly farce, a revelation of the moral and physical feebleness that all of us, as hapless comic creatures, share. As the victim Howard Graham, Cotten is a blundering incompetent. He fusses about the topcoat he leaves at the hotel; given a gun to defend himself with, he loses it. 'You must think me a fool,' he says to the dancer Josette. When he demands to be put ashore, the Italian steward derides him as 'loco'. 'Have you gone crazy?' chides his wife at the end, ordering him in out of the rain.

On his tramp steamer, Ambler's hero journeys across the Mediterranean in dread, aware that he is being ferried over the Styx. The boat in the film, a rowdy, promiscuous ark, is a lighter-headed, more buoyant vessel: a ship of fools, like that described by Sebastian Brant in the satire he wrote in 1564. Welles exempted himself from having to travel on this humbling craft, where all men are herded into equality. In his script, he had the police chief Colonel Haki – who calls the ship 'a floating slum' – fly from Istanbul to Batumi. But all the same Welles relished the idea of a leaky ark, a travelling asylum for hapless mankind. In 1976, in Stuart Rosenberg's film *Voyage of the Damned*, he played a Cuban industrialist who trades entry permits for a shipload of Jews expelled from the Third Reich just before the declaration of war. He does his negotiating at a gambling table in a casino. When the price of human lives is suddenly inflated, he gestures towards his customary fuming prop and, as if appearing in an advertisement for himself or for a tobacco company, says 'In Havana, the only thing one can be certain of is . . . a cigar.' He leaves the damned souls to bob inconclusively in the harbour, before their ship is ordered back to Germany. The idea was borrowed from Stanley Kramer's 1965 film *Ship of Fools*, based on Katharine Anne Porter's novel about a cargo of deluded emigrés on their way home from Mexico to Nazi Germany. The ship's doctor in Porter's novel is dismayed by the 'stupid comedy' of the errant, ailing mortals he treats, but comes to recognise the moral value of 'the merrier arts'. 'God bless the comedians', he reflects, for 'are we not all sinners?'

Embarkation on the ship of fools requires us to abandon the notion of hierarchy, since we are bedded down together, companionably united by our vices. Any attachment to the illusion of what *The Smiler with a Knife* calls 'the Superior Person' must be given up. So must any snobbery about the superiority of humans to animals. In *Journey into Fear*, cows, sheep, pigs and goats jostle on the lower deck of the ship. The Constantinople cabaret, where the magician gets himself killed while performing a trick, prepares for this promiscuous merger of the species. Josette (Dolores Del Rio) is a feline woman, costumed in a skimpy leopard skin with a whiskered skull cap and furry ears; the squashed snout of the beast hovers just above her forehead, ready to usurp her identity. The magician plucks a chicken out of Graham's inside pocket, and its flustered feathers thicken the smoky air. Eating his supper before he is lured out to the cabaret, Graham pulls faces, poking his finger in his mouth and distending his cheek. He has toothache, he says. These elastic distortions recall Aristotle's disapproval of comedy, which he considered to be an affront to human dignity: it disfigured the face, and reduced man to parity with lowlier beings. Welles gleefully insists on this demotion. Hence the importance of meals in *Journey into Fear*. These occasions place our appetites on show, expose the flaws in the table manners which we hope will conceal our shame, and remind us – as when Cotten complains about his dental twinge – that we are digging our graves with our teeth. The ship's captain (Richard Bennett) noisily slurps his food, while the killer Banat (Jack Moss, looking like Akim Tamiroff) guzzles a sweet in the street and discards the wrapper, messily crumbles a biscuit in his soup, or gorges on spaghetti and lets the sauce dribble down his chin.

Banat, repellent but somehow endearing, is a Shakespearean figure, like Uncle Joe Grandi in *Touch of Evil* or Jacob Zouk in *Mr Arkadin*. In his foul hotel room, he makes dandified preparations for an execution, raking through his lank hair with a greasy comb which he then wipes off on his bed sheets. Meanwhile he listens to a cracked gramophone record which stammers through a maudlin French cabaret song. This reptilian killer is capable of feeling pleasure, perhaps of falling in love. He fits the definition of 'the grotesque body' by the Russian critic Mikhail Bakhtin, who saw such warped, bloated monsters at large in societies given over to the revelling instincts of carnival. 'The grotesque body', for Bakhtin, is 'a body in the act of becoming', like Victor Hugo's bell-ringing gargoyle, Quasimodo. Such bodies arrive in the world 'half made-up', as Richard III remarks about his own deformity; they thus undermine tragedy's conviction that man is a finished product, 'the beauty of the world, the paragon of animals!' as Hamlet says. Strapped into his soiled raincoat, with a dumpy hat pulled down over his low brow, Banat is amorphous or amoeboid. In Ambler's novel, the threatened hero recovers his nerve and saves himself by shooting Banat in the face. In the film, the character's death touchingly demonstrates how physical defects drag us all down. He fails to kill the unarmed Cotten as they clamber round a high ledge in the rain because the downpour blurs the view through his thick spectacles, and he repeatedly has to interrupt his shooting to wipe them. His gun runs out of bullets, and his glasses too let him down. He slips, and tumbles into the gulf.

Medieval moralists valued what Erasmus called 'the praise of folly'. Welles, climbing down from the superman's lofty altitude, came to admire a creed which did not permit men to take themselves seriously or to claim kinship with the angels, as Hamlet the Renaissance humanist does. In Ambler's novel, the wife of the freethinking socialist Mathis describes the death of a fellow-passenger's husband, mistakenly shot as a looter after an earthquake because he collects water in a dented silver jug. 'Is that not a terrible tragedy?' she demands. But she defers to the will of 'the good God' who has ordained it. The tragedy, however, persuades Mathis that God is 'a comedian', who treats men like a waiter exterminating vermin with a fly-swatter. The script cuts this conversation, but instead invents a character who corresponds to the amused, malicious deity. This is the ship's captain, played by Bennett. There is no such figure in Ambler, whose hero appeals only to the purser. But Cotten throws himself on the captain's mercy and begs to be protected from the assassin. The captain responds by laughing at him. Though he can allegedly speak Greek, Italian, Russian and Turkish, the only words he utters (since Bennett could not memorise lines) are 'Boom boom!', followed by gales of cackling hilarity as he aims an invisible gun at his mortified passenger. On duty at the ship's wheel, he pensively sucks a lolly on a stick, then reaches inside his jacket, uses the sweet to scratch his armpit, contentedly withdraws it, and returns it to his mouth. An absent god pilots a drunken boat, whose freight consists of fools.

Adhering to his story that South America was an ill-fated detour, Welles took to claiming that he knew nothing about the Rio carnival before he arrived there, and added that he did not even enjoy Mardi Gras in New Orleans. 'I *hate* carnivals,' he told his loyally credulous biographer Barbara Leaming. At the time, he saw matters differently. In 1945 he wrote about the Brazilian festivity in the *New York Post*, and described it as a forfeited Eden. 'Carnival', he argued, 'isn't a religious observance, but it is fundamentally the celebration of religious people.' The religion in question is pagan, confronting the Lenten censorship of Christianity. Welles gave the celebration a vaguely Marxist gloss by adding that 'Wherever the money-changers have taken over, Carnival is no more. Wherever work is so hard that a holiday means a rest instead of a good time, Carnival is only a word for a tent show' – a self-reference to the one he staged on Cahuenga Boulevard in 1943. He continued to regret the loss of such festivities. At Chartres in *F for Fake*, he bemoans the technocratic atheism of our times, which ensures that in modern society 'there are no celebrations'.

Although Welles insisted that his expedition to Brazil was a political command not a personal choice, he seems to have been anticipating it for some time. In the prologue to his 1938 recording of *Twelfth Night*, he envisioned Illyria – the non-existent, abnormal country where the play is set – lying in 'improbable latitudes'. Welles the narrator advises the heroine Viola, who might be an Elizabethan voyager setting out to discover new worlds, that she is 'not on the map'. He compares her, as someone adjacent to geographical reality, to Alice in Wonderland or Dorothy transplanted from Kansas to Oz. The play may coincide with Christmas, or at least with the end of the Christmas holiday, but Welles changes the season because comedy is the song of a perpetual spring. The plot's complications, he says, are 'matters for a May morning'. He defines Illyria as 'a comedy climate where anything can happen'. The permissive subtitle of the play, after all, is *What You Will*. Welles's own comedy climate was Brazil, where anything could and did happen.

To acclimatise himself when he arrived there, he reconceived his own conception, and told his hosts that he considered himself to be almost Brazilian since his parents begot him while on holiday in the country. Although his bowels took a while to adjust, the rest of him was soon at home. He had his own interpretation of the 'goodwill' Rockefeller sent him to disseminate. In order to hitch a ride on a plane to the Amazon, he impersonated a leprosy doctor. In Rio, his ambassadorial chores included sexual encounters with a series of quick conquests (though on one occasion he had to dodge bullets from a furious husband). When Dolores Del Rio heard of his philandering, she broke off their engagement. Educating himself in native lore, Welles learned to play the tambourine, and sang a duet with the fruit-festooned Carmen Miranda. He attended voodoo ceremonies in the shanty towns on the cliffs above Rio, and encouraged the priests of macumba or candomblé to make themselves new vestments of white linen for their appearance in his film. There were escapades in higher society, when he and a Mexican diplomat trashed a Copacabana apartment. They excused themselves by saying that they were conducting a political purge: some of the kitchen crockery was Japanese, and they avenged Pearl Harbor by hurling it into the street.

In Rio, samba dancers were organised into so-called schools, and witch doctors sacrificed cockerels in so-called churches, but together they confounded all institutional attempts to discipline the energy vented by gyrating hips or the raving of demon-possessed mystics. Carnival flouted the caution of money-changers, and also relaxed the upright apparatus of military control. President Vargas imposed what opponents of his rule called 'fascism with sugar', but Welles did his best to disarm Brazil's military regime: he persuaded the air force to hand over most of its anti-aircraft searchlights so that he could film the battalions of dancers in the streets. He also set out to reconstruct an idyllic playground that the government had recently bulldozed. This was Praça Onze, where the dancers used to congregate after making their way down from the slums. As Bakhtin said, the basic requirement of carnival is a square, a promiscuous place where revels can occur, the antithesis of the hushed, hierarchical interior of the church. Dictators dislike such open spaces, in which crowds defy regimentation: hence the massacres outside the Winter Palace in St Petersburg in 1905 or in Tiananmen Square in 1989. Praça Onze was expunged when Vargas imposed a new street plan with Avenida Central as its axis, to make surveillance easier and to speed troop movements. Welles ordered Praça Onze to be rebuilt in the studio.

He blamed Brazil for leading him astray, or perhaps corrupting him. The Brazilians, however, hoped that he would corrupt them. In 1929, a modernist agitator called Oswaldo de Andrade published a *Manifesto Antropófago* in a São Paulo paper: anthropophagy is cannibalism, which Othello casually mentions having witnessed on his travels, and de Andrade made the practice the rallying cry for a Brazilian version of surrealism. He argued for a return to savagery, a greedy ingestion of physical experience appropriate to the country which, he said, had 'discovered happiness'. He challenged Brazil to discard the guilt-ridden Christianity spread by Portuguese missionaries. 'We were never catechised,' de Andrade declared. 'What we really invented was Carnival.' To unleash the cannibal instinct, he claimed, would create a love feast, as people gorged on their fellow men (and women). The samba probably derives from a belly-bumping Angolan fertility rite called semba. Aware of these origins, de Andrade called for a 'reaction against the dressed man', and hailed a potential saviour or redeemer: 'American movies will inform us.' The riotous Welles delivered the required information.

The surrealist Benjamin Péret thought that Brazilian voodoo presaged 'the downfall of all decomposing Gods and Christs', and hailed a new dispensation: 'Long live mankind, free and simple!' For de Andrade, this redeemed humanity did not need to produce great men, the monsters of overachievement who so fascinated Welles. 'No Caesar,' he specified. 'No Napoleon.' Recreating the voyage of the jangadeiros, Welles ennobled a group of humble workers. Their faces are grizzled, weathered: endurance is inscribed on them. He dug trenches in the ground so that his camera could gaze up at them as they valiantly battled the elements. When they make a landfall to pray, they choose a scaffolded church that does not yet have a roof. They take their hats off to the Christianity imported by the colonists, but their true religion is pantheistic. Their arrival in Rio, startling the supine hedonists on the beach at Copacabana, should have been the signal for revolution, with a parade through the streets like one of Eisenstein's proletarian jubilees.

Jacaré's death curtailed the party, but the intervention of the shark allowed Welles to write a new ending for the story, inadvertently concurring with de Andrade's declaration that 'cannibalism alone unites us' by creating 'a participatory consciousness'. As O'Hara in *The Lady from Shanghai*, he retells a version of the incident, situated off 'the hump of Brazil', though now the sharks feed on each other rather than gobbling up a man; and, at the end of the film, he sets himself to experience – perhaps in expiation – this gruesome death. In the crazy house, O'Hara slides down a chute and is decanted into the mouth of a papier-mâché dragon. Its eyes flash, and its serrated jaws snap shut on him. But its teeth do not chew him up. He descends unscathed into its intestines, staggers to his feet, and somehow escapes from its body, like Jonah regurgitated by the whale (which is the fable Welles's Father Mapple takes for his sermon in Huston's *Moby Dick*). The association between the dragon and the shark is even closer because Jacaré was a nickname, meaning alligator. Welles, taking advantage of the physiological comedy he discovered in Brazil, re-enacted Jacaré's tragedy, but comically allowed himself to survive it. Workers' rights, which is what the jangadeiros came to petition Vargas about, would have been an anticlimax. De Andrade boasted that 'the Carib Revolution' was 'greater than the French Revolution' because, unhampered by political principles, it sponsored a gormandising sensuality: 'The Golden Age heralded by America. The Golden Age. And all the *girls*.' European revolutions summoned crowds to maraud in the streets. In Brazil, the revolutionary mob came out to dance.

In *Strike*, made in 1924, Eisenstein treated an uprising in a factory as a carnival of ribald bodily mirth. Union agitators confer while squatting in a row of doorless lavatory stalls, with an informer eavesdropping at a urinal: men are equalised by these cosy, communal physical necessities. On an outing in the woods, the strikers continue making plans while a wheezing accordion covers their whispers. When hostilities start, two bruisers have a Chaplinesque fist fight on a seesawing plank. Taken captive, the managers are bundled into sacks, driven off in handcarts and rolled down a hill into a muddy river. The revolution should be a rollicking comedy. Blocked by an alliance between capitalists and soldiers, it concludes as a tragedy, with a reference to the ritualised slaughter of the corrida. While troops gun down the protesters, a butcher kills and sections a cow, which irrigates the ground with its blood. In *¡Que Viva Mexico!* – made between 1930 and 1932, and left incomplete, like Welles's Brazilian project – Eisenstein filmed a bullfight in Merida, then advanced from this tragedy to a resurgent comedy. On Mexico's Day of the Dead, he organised what he called 'a Carnival pageant'. Children eat skulls made of spun sugar (which might be a demonstration of de Andrade's laughing, nutritous cannibalism). Ghouls remove their skeletal masks to reveal the smiling, optimistic faces of 'the new growing Mexico', unafraid of death or any other prohibition. Welles had his own equivalent to this mischievous uprising of 'los muertos'. North of the border, the Day of the Dead is called Halloween, which is when he described extra-terrestrials rather than spooks laying siege to Manhattan. In 1938, Welles staged Georg Büchner's revolutionary tragedy *Danton's Death* while working on *The War of the Worlds*. His set for the play made visible the spectral plaything he describes at the end of the radio broadcast: Danton and his political opponents orated in front of a wall of piled-up Halloween masks – a palisade of leering skulls.

Like Eisenstein's strike, the union drive dramatised by Blitzstein in *The Cradle Will Rock* is a raucous festivity. In the opera, music overrules ideological speechifying, and Larry Foreman the radical tactician acts as a conductor, ordering groups of labourers to gang together and (as he puts it) 'strike up the band'. Factory workers arrive with bugles, fifes and drums, and Larry himself, in his final diatribe about the thunder and lightning of political retribution, 'joins in with the song and music'. Welles – who in 1937 led the audience and performers of the opera on a protest march up Broadway, accompanied by a tinny piano on the back of a truck – remembered the New York of those days as a festive community, like Eisenstein's Mexico. People, he claimed, were so nice to each other that a tough town turned into a friendly village. The screenplay for his film about *The Cradle Will Rock* includes a female philanthropist who showers hobos with stones that have money attached: exactly the kind of reversal encouraged by carnival.

To destroy an old world and create a new one had always been Welles's aim, and Brazil showed him how this might be done. Blitzstein's music did not manage to rock the cradle and toss the pampered, idle rich from their perches. The samba dancers in their successive, insistent waves made a more concerted assault on propriety. Vargas, afraid of carnival and its uproarious misrule, attempted to control it by banning the lambada, a dance whose coital rhythms offended him, and until the 1960s the government forbade floats mocking politicians or priests. The subversion went on unabated. During the 1962 carnival, the poet Elizabeth Bishop rejoiced to see 'a hundred male Negroes, in blue and white and silver Louis XV costumes seeded with tiny white light bulbs, and wearing white curled wigs and plumed hats, dancing down the middle of the main street at four a.m.'. The spectacle sounds not unlike the tropical revels of Welles's Harlem *Macbeth*, in which blacks mockingly sported the regalia of the European ancien régime and waltzed in a jungle clearing. Welles choreographed the carnival long before he ever saw it.

He rehearsed the riot in his Mercury Shakespeare productions. In Shakespeare's comedies, social order arms itself against the liberties of carnival, like Vargas outlawing those pelvic thrusts. In his recording of *The Merchant of Venice*, Welles the narrator comments on the din of the carnival merrymakers outside 'the sober house of the Jew'. As Shylock, Welles insulates his house against the ribaldry in the streets; as Malvolio in his recording of *Twelfth Night*, he censures the drunken disturbance below stairs. Here again he plays his own antithesis, and gives voice to an indwelling psychological enemy. In the prologue he wrote for *Twelfth Night*, Shakespeare explains to Burbage that Malvolio is a puritan, pledged to suppress carnal delight. 'I've put him into a comedy,' says Shakespeare, 'because I fear him.' In the epilogue, Welles also plays the intolerant preacher William Prynne, who attacked the immorality of the theatre in a diatribe published in 1632. Shylock shares this austere self-control. In Welles's edition of the text, his initial demand for a pound of flesh is presented as a harmless quibble, though a parenthetical note catches him 'repressing his laughter'. In his performance of the role, Welles – speaking in a sullen monotone – does not allow himself the jest, so there is no need to censor it. His recording of *Julius Caesar* also emphasises the seditious uses of festivity. The play, according to his narration, begins on 'a festive, sunshiny day' – an unofficial tradesmens' holiday, commemorated by the licentious language of the citizens, with raunchy screeches heard in the distance. As Antony, Welles is a sinister lord of misrule, who after inciting the populace to violence adds 'Mischief, though art afoot, / Take thou what course thou wilt.' In the next scene, a drunken mob casually kills the wrong Cinna.

At the end of his study of Rabelais, Bakhtin contends that 'All the acts of the drama of world history were performed before a chorus of the laughing people.' This was the critic's coded protest against the Soviet police state he lived in, a yearning recollection of those early days when revolution was a popular comedy, as joyously undisciplined as carnival. Bakhtin mentions Pushkin's Shakespearean history play *Boris Godunov*, in which a holy fool teases the murderous Czar and the pretender Dimitri imagines a crowd deriding him; he might also have been thinking of the factory workers and their retributive pranks in Eisenstein's *Strike*. Welles, true to the anarchism of his Halloween broadcast in 1938, continued to believe that revolution could be a laughing matter. In *Journey into Fear*, Frank Readick as the Frenchman Mathis explains that he first pretended to be a socialist to antagonise his snobbish wife, played by Agnes Moorehead. Then, to his own surprise, he found that the ironic pretence had become the truth: 'I, a capitalist by instinct, became a socialist by conviction.' He sympathised with the striking workers at his factory, and got the sack. The joke was on him, though the nihilist must be prepared for such reversals, like a king gallantly smiling on his way to execution.

Unable to complete his account of a ridiculous revolution when film-ing the carnival in Rio, Welles saved it for a later project. He let loose the impish, infectious spirit of misrule in the San Francisco courtroom at the end of *The Lady from Shanghai*. Welles's O'Hara, improbably enough, is a left-wing combatant. He claims to have fought in the Spanish civil war, and says he killed one of Franco's spies in Murcia in 1939; Glenn Anders as the sweaty, snorting Grisby brags of having served on a pro-Franco committee. But when the revolution breaks out, it provokes laughter rather than inciting violence. During the trial, a startling lunge into comedy overturns the solemnity of law and order. Interrogation develops into a shouting match between the lawyers, while a dozy judge sniggers. The grotesque compulsions of the body confound the mind's judicial impartiality: a juror interrupts the proceedings by convulsively sneezing, and a prurient looker-on sucks her chewing gum dry, then sticks it to the bottom of her seat.

O'Hara attempts suicide by swilling down Bannister's flask of pain-killers, but as a comic hero he is not permitted the mercy of death (just as he is later reprieved from the bowels of the dragon). Dragged back to the judge's chamber, he adds this to Welles's list of rooms playfully trashed. He pushes a guard against the glass bookcase, shattering its panes. Then he pulls the bookcase itself down on the reeling cop. When it misses, he kicks the man, who falls backwards and knocks over an umbrella stand and a water cooler. After this, he tries to brain him with the bust of a jurist. This misses its aim, and smashes a window. Throughout the scrambled fight, an unheeded telephone shrills. The judge returns to take stock of the damage, and grieves over his upset chess board, on which – like Susan in *Citizen Kane* sedatively composing a facsimile of the real world as she pores over her jigsaw puzzles – he had arranged kings, queens, knights and pawns in a slow-moving, stratified tournament.

O'Hara proceeds to disrupt another stately, slow-motion ritual when he interrupts the performance of the Chinese opera. Finally he is hustled, unconscious, into a temple of mysteries, the place where all the deranging energies of carnival are uncaged: the crazy house at the funfair. He stumbles through its nightmares, and lurches into a room which Bakhtin might have been describing when, in a 1929 essay on Dostoevsky, he summed up the parodic mayhem of carnival as 'an entire system of crooked mirrors, elongating, diminishing, distorting in various directions and to various degrees'. He finds the exit and, still immune to death, walks off through an uproarious silent chorus of placards, which stand in for Bakhtin's laughing people. LAFF says one of them, even though the entertainment it advertises is a ghost ride: a spectre's uninvited appear-ance at a feast, as in *Macbeth*, is the most unsettling of jokes. Other signs announce FUN! or FUN FOR ALL or AMUSEMENTS.

The name of this profane, lawless, topsy-turvy precinct appears on a turreted gateway as Welles leaves. It is called PLAYLAND: an actual San Francisco funfair, long since torn down, that was located between Golden Gate Park and Seal Rocks. Like the theatres, brothels and bullpits on the wrong side of the river in Elizabethan London, the land of play is situated outside the officious, rectilinear city, on the border between culture and nature, land and sea. The Pacific comes right up to its gate, and its erasing waters gradually and kindly wipe away human guilt and folly, as Lady Macbeth hoped to do by washing her hands. Carnival too overwhelms the individual: he goes under, though what he suffers is comic immersion, not tragic extinction.

According to Bakhtin, carnival is pervaded by 'the banquet spirit'. So are Welles's films. Kane has his office parties and his picnics under canvas, with convoys of limousines and a jazz band to play for the campers. Arkadin specialises in masked balls and Christmas blowouts. At the motel in *Touch of Evil*, the bike-riding thugs throw what the night porter calls 'a wild party – you know the kind'. Joseph Cotten, reappearing as the medical examiner, deftly defines it as a 'mixed party': a sexual free-for-all, which also mixed drink and drugs. In *Chimes at Midnight*, Falstaff dances with wassailing whores, barking dogs, and yelping children who bang on the inn's benches. Early in the saturnalian 1960s, Welles could afford to make party's wildness more explicit. Hal and Poins (Tony Beckley) clamber onto the pallet that serves Falstaff and Doll (Jeanne Moreau) as a bed, and wrestle amorously with them as an excuse for tussling with one another. 'I shall stand the push of your one thing,' says Poins to Hal with a smirk. At the banquet, indiscriminate coupling and tripling are encouraged.

With or without the sexual innuendo, such paroxysms of play became central to Welles's working life. A method underlay them, which Bill Krohn explains by associating Welles's habits with the tribal practice called 'potlatch' by Chinook natives. This apparently self-destructive ritual was first analysed by the anthropologist Marcel Mauss in the 1920s; Johan Huizinga made it central to his sociological study of 'the play element in culture' in *Homo Ludens*, published in 1938. Potlatch, in Huizinga's account, is a 'great solemn feast' laid on by the natives of British Columbia who, when entertaining, destroyed canoes, blankets and cooking utensils just to show they could do without them. The feast-givers' only expectation was that the guests would reciprocate, and immolate their own goods. The same aristocratic nonchalance impels the Thane of Cawdor in *Macbeth* to die as if discarding 'the dearest thing he owed / As 'twere a careless trifle.' Welles conducted his career as if it were a sustained potlatch. He enjoyed being regaled or bribed with food. When obliged to respond and play the giver, he frittered away his own dearest gift, which was his genius. He detested self-preservation, the capitalist's strict retention of assets. A villain, for Welles, was a man obsessed with making a profit, like Shylock dreaming of money bags or Iago who (as he told MacLíammóir) was 'a businessman dealing in destruction with neatness, method'. Kane is admirable when spending money and expending himself, detestable when he begins to concentrate on accumulation. Leland disqualifies him as a feast-giver when he remarks that Kane 'never gave himself away. He never gave anything away. He just left you a tip.'

The plot of *Mr Arkadin* elaborates Welles's personal economic system, demonstrating how value can be magicked out of nothing and then, with equal ease, negated. Bracco, dying in Naples, gasps two names. His legacy 'isn't money', he tells van Stratten, 'but it's worth millions . . . It will make you rich.' Arkadin offers van Stratten an even more unfairly favourable deal when he hires him to research his past: 'I am going to make you a present of something you can sell – and then I'm going to pay you for it.' The commodity in question is his secret. The Amsterdam pawnbroker played by Michael Redgrave is wilier in his setting of prices. The telescope he makes van Stratten buy is more expensive without its case than with it: a sign that all valuations are fictitious. Concluding the deal, he says 'I believe in giving value', though he has just doubled the price of the telescope again. Whatever the value he places on it, it is literally worthless, since it lacks a lens. Baroness Nagel, played by Suzanne Flon, tries a different, more open-handed and Wellesian approach when Arkadin wants to purchase information. She is reluctant to betray a confidence, so he proposes a wager. They agree on terms, then she changes her mind: 'I hate to sell information. Here, take it as a gift.' Her generosity proves fatal, since Arkadin can now eliminate her. But van Stratten has already purchased the same secret, which prompts Arkadin to reflect that 'A fool is a man who pays twice for the same thing.' The Baroness's donation leads to Sophie, played by Katina Paxinou, who also disobeys the usual selfish financial rules. She misses her chance to blackmail Arkadin: 'Money – money I don't need,' she sighs, and shrugs off the debt of two-hundred thousand Swiss francs he still owes her. 'I had my money's worth twenty years ago,' she says, and blissfully closes her eyes: her erotic memories are worth that much. Stranded at the Munich airport, Arkadin displays the subjectivity and relativity of value when he offers to pay fifty million marks, in dollars, for a seat on the last plane to Spain before Christmas; the bid is laughed at. A fool is a man who gives so much over the odds. A fool is also a man who gives himself away.

Welles's festive economy outraged Hollywood's prudent executives. He expected them to lavish funds on him; in return he would, perhaps, make them a film – though not because he was contracted to do so, rather in a spirit of noblesse oblige. He mocked the financial enablers, and expected them to laugh with him as Lear does (or is supposed to do) when ridiculed by his fool. Clowns live dangerously, because they assume that the great man they upbraid will have a capacity for self-criticism, or a secret self-hatred. At Cannes in 1958, Welles rounded on the producer Darryl F. Zanuck, who a few years earlier had given him seventy-five thousand dollars to save the film of *Othello* (and even added an extra 420 dollars to pay for the taxi which Welles had hired to bring him from Rome to Nice to do his begging: though penniless, he insisted on travelling in comfort). Now Welles needed a fresh infusion of money from Zanuck for another film. But, at their dinner together, he attacked Zanuck and his fellow moguls as 'cheap crooks'. Zanuck stalked out, taking his chequebook with him.

When not playing the clown, Welles behaved like an unconstitutional monarch, who levies taxes and tithes for his own sumptuary purposes or simply demands that his entourage of faithful courtiers attend him. George Chirello was officially retained as Welles's chauffeur. But Welles also borrowed money from him to pay wages to the company of *Around the World*, and expected him to work all night as an apprentice decorator repainting the set for the crazy house in *The Lady from Shanghai*. Chirello was cast as Macbeth's retainer in Welles's film of the play, and given some of Seyton's lines to mumble. Doing duty as a valet, he collects shaggy cloaks and hauls them away; when Macbeth's doom seems certain, he hangs himself rather than seeking employment elsewhere. Late in life, Welles found that he needed the actor Peter Jason for an afternoon's filming in a downtown Los Angeles theatre. He telephoned Jason, who was making a television programme: a paid job, from which he could not absent himself. Welles sweet-talked the director into letting Jason go. In payment for the loan, all the director asked was that Jason should bring him back one of Welles's cigars, as a souvenir and a symbolic recompense. 'Never!' grunted Welles when Jason relayed the request. It was like asking a king to part with his orb and sceptre. Monarchs carry no cash: how can they spend the coin of the realm, which only has value because they certify it with their imprinted faces? Welles's currency was curios, mementoes, relics of his presence. Finally, of course, he handed over not one but two cigars. According to the etiquette of potlatch, the director should have smoked them. Jason assumes, however, that he kept them under glass on his mantelpiece.

Needing to find an alternative to the studios, with their tedious emphasis on cost-efficiency, reliability and the mass-production of lookalike artefacts, Welles restored the economy that preceded industrialism: a feudal system in which there was no need for money because business dealings were regulated by barter. In 1950, he and MacLíammóir visited a Russian war cemetery in Berlin, where Welles – once investigated by the FBI as a seditious leftist – denounced communism. Hilton Edwards, recalling Welles's half-hearted efforts to please the studios, commented that he had spent his life 'in a frantic endeavour to become a Capitalist'. This prompted MacLíammóir to add, very perceptively, that Welles was 'profoundly Feudal'. When he accepted an award from the American Film Institute in 1975, Welles admitted that he was an anachronism, and likened himself to a corner grocery store that had somehow endured into 'this age of supermarkets'. In fact he was closer to the subsistence farmer who supplies the grocer, labouring with the aid of an extended family whose members are rewarded with goods (like the cigar he grumpily conceded to Jason's director) rather than salaries.

Welles, playing the king, took such sacrifices for granted. Yet as always he awarded himself a dual role: he played both the ruler and the reveller or agent of misrule, who derides royal pomp. Like a Shakespearean fool, he lived by his wits, thinking quickly to save himself from disaster. Jason defined this aspect of his precarious economy when he said that Welles had a way of 'capitalising on mistakes: there'd be an accident, and he'd go with the accident'. His *Othello* film had more than its share of accidents, with recurrent interruptions as he looked for new Desdemonas or scurried off to earn money or beg it from Zanuck and others. But with a gambler's trust in luck, he treated the accidents as opportunities or obscure divinations. In Morocco, he happened on a cistern constructed by the Portuguese, and used it for the chase after the brawl between Cassio and Roderigo. The shallowly flooded labyrinth looks like a submerged Venice, and the resemblance unifies the film's two disparate settings. Film is fixed, immutable, but Welles pined for the exhilarating uncertainty of the theatre, where anything can happen. Hence his tolerance for undirectable performers, like Roderigo's yapping lap dog or the chickens and donkeys that squabble and stumble through narrow alleys beneath the fortress. When some costumes did not arrive on time (they hadn't been paid for), he decided to film the murder of Roderigo in a Turkish bath, where the characters needed to wear nothing but towels. The setting exactly matched the humid sexual miasma of the play.

Having moved his company to North Africa, he permitted the location and its unruly climate to dictate what happened in the film. Inconveniences that would have irritated or dismayed another director became, for Welles, fortuitous visual commentaries on the verbal text. Flies crawl over Cassio's face as he watches Iago being strung up for punishment in his cage. The sight suggests the pettily vexatious origins of Iago's own plotting: he announces that, though Othello 'in fertile climate dwell', he will 'plague him with flies'. There are authentically rough seas for Othello's arrival at Cyprus – actually Mogador on the Atlantic coast – and wind whips the dandified plumes on Roderigo's hat and punishes Iago's wispy hair as they stand on the ramparts. The white, angry breakers lashing the rocks below vouch for the reality of the images Othello uses when, metaphorically describing his compulsion to revenge, he speaks about the Black Sea's current thrusting its way through the Hellespont into the Mediterranean. Goats graze and caper on the beach below the battlements, and are startled when cannons announce the Venetian fleet. Could this be why Othello salutes the arriving ambassadors as 'goats and monkeys'?

Iago gulls Othello, proving him pathetically gullible: Emilia calls him 'O gull! O dolt! / As ignorant as dirt!' Seagulls accordingly wheel and screech above Othello as he looks up into a vacant, blazing sky during his epileptic collapse. There is an obscure affinity between the noun referring to the bird and the verb referring to a man who resembles the bird, though the logic of the connection is unclear. Is the duped man an unfledged bird, or does his gulling evoke the bird's habit of scoffing down the food it hunts? Either way, the location enabled Welles to yoke together verbal and visual meanings in an impromptu pun. Along the battlements, the heads of gaping onlookers stare down at the prone hero, like birds preparing to dive for a kill. The banquet spirit still prevails, and misrule has levelled the upright embodiment of the state. But Othello is demoralised – rather than laughably humbled – by the recognition of his common folly, and the feast belongs to those beaked predators, screaming as they scavenge for raw, live flesh.

Despite his professed distaste for Mardi Gras, Welles was a connoisseur of carnivals. In December 1956, seated at a café table in St Tropez, he prepared a hand-written, hand-illustrated album as a gift for his second daughter Rebecca. The little book, entitled *Les Bravades*, documents the town's annual commemoration of its patron saint, whose relics are carried through the streets by a boisterous army of acolytes known as bravadeurs. Their parade is supposed to be a defiant reply to criticism of such image-worship. Actually, like the union drive in *The Cradle Will Rock*, it serves as an excuse to make a din with drums, flutes and explosive blunderbusses. Welles painted the noise of all those fusillades: a pointillistic fog of nitrous fumes, with futuristic spirals whirling in the blue murk. 'I've seen a lot of "fetes" "fiestas" and festivals, every sort and variety of saints' day high-jinks all over the world,' he assured Rebecca in his dodgily-typed commentary, and reeled off an itinerary like that with which he had regaled MacLíammóir and Edwards in Dublin: 'I've been to such events in Sicily and China, in southern Spain and Italy and on the alti-plano of Bolivia.' In all those jaunts, he insisted, he had seen nothing to equal the exultant bravado of St Tropez.

The celebration epitomised the emotional temper of carnival, because, as Welles told Rebecca, it is 'serious and gay at the same time'. It also mixed sanctity and profanity. Two years before, across the border in Spain, Welles had filmed a torchlit procession of wailing penitents in the village beneath Arkadin's castle. That was a rite of self-mortification; now in St Tropez the same religion smiled on this ecstatic, unashamed clamour. But the divine comedy was always liable to lurch into tragedy. Two years later, Welles remembered the festival in St Tropez when he planned the opening of *Touch of Evil*, set in an irreligious town whose lewd, loud business is pleasure. Music blares from cantinas, drunks reel on the sidewalks, a peddler pushes a food cart, and a flock of goats interrupts traffic. A car nudges its way through the throng, like one of the floats bearing an image of the saint in St Tropez. The rite concludes, as expected, in an eruption – but this time, instead of the blanks harmlessly discharged by the French musketeers, a bomb in the car goes off and atomises a local dignitary.

For his television film of *The Merchant of Venice* in 1969, Welles filmed the aquatic carnival on the Grand Canal; elsewhere in the city, he made the festivity look as spectral as Halloween. As Shylock, he totters across squares where the revellers hold calcified poses, their faces blanked out by white masks. Antonio (Charles Gray) confronts him from behind one of these cold visors. This carnival is a kingdom of shades, not the bacchic abandon of Rio. In a story by Isak Dinesen about the 1925 opera carnival in Copenhagen, an ironic harlequin protests against 'the fundamental falsity of the traditional idea of covering up the body and leaving the face bare, when it ought to be exactly the other way round'. Masks, the harlequin proposes, offer 'that release from self towards which all religions strive . . . Your centre of gravity is moved from the ego to the object; through the true humility of self-denial you arrive at an all-comprehending unity with life, and only thus can great works of art be accomplished.' The time, he concludes, has surely come for mankind 'to obtain freedom by giving up faces'. A girl in Dinesen's story gratefully retires behind her mask, sighing 'I am tired of being three-dimensional.' As an actor, Welles knew all about such psychological camouflage, and he also understood the dual purpose of the mask. It permits you to enjoy yourself incognito, as Arkadin does at his party. But it is also a retreat from three-dimensionality, from the contradictoriness of life and from the ruddy solidity of incarnation. Erasing individual features, it turns you into a spirit, which is why the carnival in Welles's *Merchant of Venice* looks so joyless. The ultimate farewell to flesh occurs when you die.

O'Hara in *The Lady from Shanghai* arrives at a last revelation after he lurches and tumbles through the crazy house, and Harry Lime in *The Third Man* chooses to reveal himself at the Prater, an open-air funfair just beyond the city limits. Both Playland and the Prater, significantly, are stranded out of season: Welles knew that the springtime ebullience of comedy was bound to sicken into the winter's tale of tragedy. The cycle repeats itself, like the earth's annual circuit around the sun or like an individual life with its ascent and decline, its first and second childhoods. The wheel Harry rides on, just as much as the cuckoo clock he sneers at, symbolises this circularity. You wind the cuckoo up, and it chirps and cackles until its mechanism runs down; then you resuscitate it. The gyrations of the carnival dancers in Rio, looked at in this way, suddenly seem sad, pointless, self-deceiving. Behind Harry, as he strides across the icy, empty Prater, is the RODELBAHN, a railway that goes round in circles like the ghost train in *The Lady from Shanghai*. From mid-air, he looks down at a carousel. But as he steps off the wheel, we notice that its movement is strained, effortful, not animated by a giddy life-force. Vienna has no fuel to spare for merry-go-rounds; a little girl is pushing it, making its freight of toy cars and unfrisky horses circulate very slowly for the benefit of another mounted child.

After San Francisco's demented Playland and Vienna's derelict Prater, Welles finally filmed an authentically joyous carnival in his 1955 television programme about the feast of Pentecost in the Basque country. A Catherine wheel fizzes in the night sky, and men crouched inside a pantomime bull stuffed with firecrackers race through the streets. The infuriated snorts of the 'toro del fuego' are detonations; as it expires, it spits fire not blood. At Pentecost, the holy ghost made itself manifest in tongues of flame. The Basques turn those vocal flares into exclamatory fireworks. Welles, standing aside prudently as the bull erupts, says 'Miraculously enough – I don't know why – nobody ever seems to get hurt.' In *Les Bravades*, he sketched a sailor brandishing a sword with a fried fish impaled on it: the weapon, disabled, is used as a cooking implement. Comedy once more averts tragedy.

The prophetic babble of Pentecost allowed all tribes and races to mingle and converse. Among the Basques, that serves as a justification for breaching the border between Spain and France. Crowds jostle past the DOUANE sign, cheekily carrying prohibited flasks of wine or bulging paniers; they wade streams on piggyback like illegal immigrants fording the Rio Grande. The arbitrary line drawn through the fields is disregarded during this holiday, and Welles's remarks on the disappearance of guards enthusiastically endorse the politics of carnival: 'Yes, the fences and frontiers are really down. People are free for this one day to move without passports, carrying whatever they want in any direction that pleases them. It's like a big party, and I can't think of a better reason for celebrating.' It gave him a keen private pleasure to see the border trampled into the ground, because comedy leaps over such officious barriers or wriggles beneath them. Welles, impelled to see how far he could go before encountering resistance or refusal, viewed boundaries as temptations to trespass. The jurisdiction of Vienna in *The Third Man* is divided between the four occupying powers, who set up polyglot interdictions everywhere; Harry Lime slithers across frontiers without a passport because he travels a carnal torrent of effluent beneath the streets. Welles remembered the sectioning of Vienna when he made the film about the Basques, and likened their border, sealed after the Spanish civil war, to 'a miniature Iron Curtain'.

Touch of Evil takes place on the so-called Tortilla Curtain, the border where Mexico and the United States suspiciously eye each other. Whit Masterson's novel *Badge of Evil* was set in San Diego; transplanting it to a porous, precarious town he called Los Robles, Welles revived and modified his original plan for *It's All True*. Now, rather than sponsoring pan-American concord, he emphasised conflict between the continent's upper and lower halves. In Los Robles, Vargas and his wife Susan go north in search of an innocent chocolate soda, while others go south in quest of spicier delights. Soldiers employed by the US Customs and Immigration Service patrol the border, but Vargas, furious not festive, crashes through it in his car on his way to rescue his abducted wife, knocking the obstructive wooden arm aside.

Misrule defies social rules, and also ignores the rules of art. No border has ever been more strictly policed than that between tragedy and comedy. The genres were cordoned off from each other by Aristotle's claim that tragic characters are our betters, whose fall provokes awe and pity, while comic characters are our inferiors, whose embarrassments we can ridicule without compunction. Shakespeare refused to accept this division: *Othello* is a tragedy about the comic predicament of cuckoldry, and *The Merchant of Venice* is a comedy about a man who is tragically persecuted. Welles, excited by this festive merger of forms, went so far as to argue that Shakespeare never wrote tragedy. He preferred to call *Othello* or *King Lear* melodramas, because the tragedy in them derives from comic muddle and misunderstanding. Comedy is just as likely to be stopped short by the announcement of a tragedy, as when death cancels the marriages at the end of *Love's Labour's Lost*. A marriage and a funeral overlap in *The Stranger*: Kindler deserts his new bride at their wedding reception and sneaks off to bury the Nazi colleague he has throttled in the woods. In *Othello* too, Welles reordered the action of the play so that the funeral procession of Othello and Desdemona immediately precedes their marriage. Arkadin, as the host of the party at the Spanish castle, repeatedly halts the merriment. Reciting the fable about the scorpion, he brings the news of death to a circle of frivolous women, who giggle as if he had told them a joke. Confronting his daughter and her lover in a bedroom, he prohibits the relationship between them, even though the purpose of carnival is to license copulation. In Welles's *Don Quixote*, Sancho is mystified by the cowled Easter procession in Seville, and wonders if the fiesta is a wedding or a burial. 'It amounts to the same in the end,' remarks Quixote.

In *The Merchant of Venice*, Portia proposes instant marriage to Bassanio, but adds that their wedding night must wait until Antonio is rescued. Comic consummation is adjourned so that a tragic problem can be resolved. Welles employed the same tantalising deferment in *Touch of Evil*. While Portia purportedly checks into a nearby monastery, Susan is deposited at a motel for safekeeping. Here, itchily awaiting her preoccupied husband, she spends her wedding night with the gang of leather-jacketed ruffians, who weaken her resistance with reefers. Welles, prevented by Universal from cutting the film himself, reminded the editors engaged by the studio that the story was about 'a honeymoon couple, desperately in love' who are 'abruptly separated by a violent incident'. Vargas reaches out to clasp Susan and says 'I haven't kissed you in at least an hour.' The bomb intervenes. Discreetly euphemistic, he tells her that 'We'll have to postpone that soda, I'm afraid.' In his memo, Welles emphasised the contrast between the husband's 'masculine idealism' or 'urgent professional concern' and the smoochy wife's insistence on making love, and concluded that the relationship demonstrated 'woman's classic failure to fully appreciate . . . that sense of abstract duty so peculiar to the male'. He could not help believing that every man was a Quixote, intent on an intellectual mission, while every woman was a down-to-earth Dulcinea. Men have a responsibility to the law, or to some personal code of honour. Women, less exigent (in Welles's view), are concerned only with love, like Doll Tearsheet in *Chimes at Midnight* trying to keep Falstaff out of the fray or Desdemona nagging Othello to pardon Cassio.

As *Touch of Evil* begins, a bomb hurls the car into the air like a meteorite. At the end, a similar eruption occurs in the eyes of the strangled Grandi, as if the last thing he saw was a frozen frame of that explosion: his eyes have swollen, preparing to pop out of their sockets, and the veins are jagged, like forked lightning made of blood. His plump body hangs over Susan as she sprawls on the bed. Death appears to have interrupted their love making, transferring the climax to his distended eyes and to the stiff tongue that pokes at her through his lips, its erectness prolonged by rigor mortis. She escapes onto the fire-escape of the cheap hotel and calls for help; a gang of construction workers and soldiers wave back, treating her cries as a sexual invitation. She screams, but the sound merges with the boozy hilarity of the street outside. In the contagious frenzy of carnival, it is difficult to tell shrieking terror from unhinged glee. Tragedy and comedy merge in a laughing apocalypse.

A city convulsed by panic like New York in the *War of the Worlds* broadcast, or given over to shrill merriment like Rio or Los Robles: this kind of outdoor rumpus room was Welles's preferred location. George Minafer whips his pony cart through the drowsy town. A drunken brawl upsets military discipline at the fortress in *Othello*. In *The Lady from Shanghai* or *The Trial*, courts lay on entertainments for barracking mobs. In unruly psychological zones like these, Welles felt at home. Carnival allowed him to forget his exorbitant ambitions, and surrender to the soliciting of those lambada dancers. Faust, who insists on making the world perfect (and, if that fails, prefers to destroy it), gives way to Falstaff, who merely wants to eat, drink, make love, and go back to sleep.

Welles in the crazy house, his personal museum of modern art.

CHAPTER 10

Mr Poet

Kane tells the banker Thatcher that it is his ambition to become 'everything you hate'. Falstaff outwits the law by cajoling a judge to lend him a thousand pounds that will never be repaid. 'Lawyers, bankers!' scoffs George at the ball in *The Magnificent Ambersons*. 'What do they get out of life, I want to know?' He tells Lucy he intends to be a yachtsman, and whirls her away in a dance. Refusing to accept the authority of financial regulators and legal quibblers, Welles defined himself as an artist – self-willed, impractical, expensive, answering only to the dictates of his own imagination. In 1946 he advertised this new identity in *The Lady from Shanghai*. For the plot's purposes, O'Hara needs to be nothing more than a simple sailor, duped by the landed cynics who employ him. Welles, however, made him a writer. His grizzled crony Goldie mocks his lyrical inflections, and says he 'talks fancy'; the maid Bessie nicknames him 'Mr Poet'.

While he waits in the New York hiring office to pick up a day job, O'Hara busily types a novel. As if not entirely convinced by O'Hara's qualifications for this line of work, Welles made the shrewd lawyer Bannister question them. Bannister says that O'Hara has been 'travelling around the world too much to find out anything about it'. Welles directed the jibe at himself: he persuaded Columbia to finance *The Lady from Shanghai* because he needed the advance to pay debts accrued by his production of *Around the World*. Elsa, Bannister's wife, also tells O'Hara that he has 'no knowledge of world'. He replies: 'Lately I've been rounding out my education.' But his naïveté makes him incapable of reading the characters of people and deducing their motives, which ought to be what a novelist is educated to do. When he wants to quit, Bannister accuses him of having 'no sense of adventure'. How can you write a novel unless you have an aptitude for plots, or a capacity to devise them? Everyone in *The Lady from Shanghai* is a plotter except the blundering O'Hara.

As a poet, he is somewhat more plausible, though his sense of the vocation is old-fashioned. He is a poet of the romantic kind, irradiating reality with his visionary idealism. The romantics worshipped imagination as a generative force like that of God. A poet requires a muse, a private deity who will come when called, the symbol of the imagination's spiritual aspirations and its fleshly desires. Faustus begs Mephistophilis to conjure up Helen of Troy for him. O'Hara, less choosy, decides to worship the woman he meets in Central Park. After rescuing Elsa from her assailants, he renames her Princess Rosalie, associating her with the inspiring ladies of courtly romance. She accepts him as her 'foolish knight errant'. Aware of his moral error, O'Hara says 'Once I had seen her – once I had seen her – I was not in my right mind for quite some time.'

By personifying the imagination as a woman, the romantics placed it beyond rational control. The muse became a cruel, destructive mistress, like Keats's 'belle dame sans merci' or Baudelaire's Venus attached to her prey, or like Flaubert's lustful Salammbô, the subject of the opera Kane commissions for Susan. In 1948, the year *The Lady from Shanghai* was released, Robert Graves published *The White Goddess: A Historical Grammar of Poetic Myth,* in which he insisted that 'the function of poetry is religious invocation of the Muse', whose presence excites a 'mixed exaltation and horror'. The book became the basis of Welles's admiration for Graves, whom he described as 'the greatest living poet' and nominated in 1967 – ahead of Chou En-lai and Pope John XXIII – as the contemporary he would most like to meet. He had not read *The White Goddess* when he wrote *The Lady from Shanghai.* But he was familiar with Graves's subject, thanks to William Archer's *The Green Goddess,* which he directed and acted in during 1939. In Archer's melodrama, a plane crash-lands in the Himalayan temple honouring a bloodthirsty female deity whose idol 'of forbidding aspect' is 'coloured dark green'. Her altar – like that of Hecate in the Harlem *Macbeth* – is littered with the freshly-severed heads of goats, and she waves six arms at the intruders. 'She could give you a jolly good hug,' says one of the passengers. 'You wouldn't want another,' remarks his friend.

When in due course Welles read Graves's mythopoeic fantasia, it became indispensable to him, and he enthusiastically pressed it on friends and colleagues. *The White Goddess* helped him to understand his own life: its analysis of myth suggested that his downfall was an inevitable part of a cycle, like the year with its Shakespearean circuit of seasons. According to Graves, 'the White Goddess of Life-in-Death and Death-in-Life' lives for ever, as inexhaustibly fertile as the earth. He who serves her may expire but she will revive him, as surely as winter quickens into spring. Graves explains carnival as a religious observance, not (like Bakhtin) a political rebellion. The Romans had their Saturnalia, and likewise during 'the old English Yule, all social restraints were temporarily abandoned', enabling Saturn – as Graves puts it – to sneak back as 'Lord of Misrule' and leader of the revels. The popular cult of Mary the virgin, metamorphosed into Robin Hood's Maid Marian, provided the god with a woodland bride, a 'Lady of Misrule'. Graves, like Welles in his reveries about Falstaff, pines for the rural rites of an imaginary Merry England, with its maypoles, ageless oaks, cakes, ale and covens of witches.

Though he sympathised with these aspects of *The White Goddess*, Welles could not accept a crucial article of Graves's gynocratic faith. Graves demanded that the artist prove his devotion to the goddess by volunteering to be her victim. Adding a postscript to his book in 1960, he decreed that 'every Muse-poet must, in a sense, die for the Goddess whom he adores'. Welles was not ready to make this infatuated sacrifice. In 1967, Tynan asked him to choose a model of male conduct towards women. Welles replied, 'Robert Graves. In other words, total adoration.' But he immediately added 'Mine is less total than it ought to be.' Welles's women are killers, whether a man adoringly consents to die for them or not. In his script for *The Trial*, he invented a character who does not appear in Kafka's novel. This is the scientist who services the computer in K's office, described as 'the archetype of a priestess serving a power- ful, millenary mystery'. The role was played by Katina Paxinou, though her scene was cut before the film's release. K superstitiously calls the computer 'the brain thing', and refers to it as 'she': the man thinks of his creativity as a female force and is therefore afraid of it, like the poet in 'Kubla Khan' when he backs away from the damsel with the dulcimer. K's uncle asks him if the pronoun he uses denotes affection. 'More than that,' says K. His uncle guesses 'Love, terror?' and goes on, as if flinching from Archer's green goddess, to warn 'If she's a woman, I'd be careful.' This female is an automaton, with a body of cold stainless steel. Another of the women who harass the twitchy, sexually ambiguous K of Anthony Perkins is a monster, a mutant belonging to some hybrid species. The Advocate's nurse (Romy Schneider) displays her webbed fingers as she seduces K. 'Pretty little paw,' he says, fondling it.

Man, Graves argued, is never more than a demi-god, whereas woman is divine. A war between the sexes starts from this disparity. Graves thought that 'woman worships the infant, not the grown man'. Welles, the prodigious child, received this adoration from his own mother. Once grown, the man diminishes in the woman's eyes, so he must rely on egomania to make good the loss. According to Graves's theory, 'Man envies her and tells himself lies about his own completeness, and thereby makes himself miserable; because if he is divine she is not even a demi-goddess – she is a mere nymph and his love for her turns to scorn and hate.' The reversal resounds in a scrap of dialogue overheard at Acapulco in *The Lady from Shanghai*, as a preening gigolo tells his female client 'Of course you pay me.' At the end of the film, O'Hara leaves the grovelling Elsa to die on the floor. From now on, the poet will concentrate on being merely a sailor.

In 1950, fondly deriding the Victorian actor William Charles Macready, Welles called him 'a true-hearted, yearning artist' and said that despite his blustery style he was 'a poet all the same, the genuine article'. So was Welles. The poet, for him, was a quixotic being, always thinking better of the world than it deserved. He argued that O'Hara represented 'the cavalier point of view'; if Hamlet matures and fattens into Falstaff, then perhaps O'Hara – after leaving Elsa and returning to the sea – might age into the narrator of Isak Dinesen's 'The Old Chevalier', included in *Seven Gothic Tales*. (Welles planned to film this story in 1953, as part of a compilation called *Paris by Night*, and shortly before he died in 1985 he devised a one-man show for UCLA in which he intended to do some magic tricks, stage a truncated *Julius Caesar* – omitting Brutus, a sad memento of his youthful self – and read 'The Old Chevalier'.) When young, Dinesen's hero falls in love with 'a blonde, the fairest . . . that I have ever seen', and reveres her like a page doting on his lady. But he becomes convinced that his mistress is a witch, and likens her to the weird sisters in *Macbeth*. Reversing roles, she is the imperious Othello, and he is her abject Desdemona. To cure himself of his fixation, he makes love to a prostitute, though when he undresses her his idealism transforms her into 'the idea of Woman'. Welles was entranced by this scene, which reminded him, the delectable labour required to remove Dolores Del Rio's ethereally layered underclothes before he made love to her. Time, which O'Hara relies on when he says he will try to forget his lady from Shanghai, takes revenge on the mistress in Dinesen's story. The old chevalier sees her later at the opera, elderly and no longer lovely. Mortality is kinder to the prostitute. Death beautifies or perhaps beatifies her: the chevalier comes upon what he believes to be her skull, clear, clean and noble like a Platonic idea, its 'white polished bone . . . so pure'.

In his foreword to *The White Goddess*, Graves claimed that obedience to the behests of the muse or goddess might help to salvage a world ruined by 'experiments in philosophy, science and industry'. Today, as Graves said, we are ruled by 'the unholy triumvirate of Pluto god of wealth, Apollo god of science, and Mercury god of thieves'. Welles at least had attempted, with nervous irony, to give Mercury back some of the hermetic powers he had forfeited. But the sun-god, newly vindictive, now plots the destruction of our earth: Graves warns that 'Apollo wields the atomic bomb as if it were a thunderbolt.' After Hiroshima, President Truman boasted that the bomb was brighter than the sun, and more toxic. That impending calamity overshadows *The Lady from Shanghai* as the characters walk through the searing Acapulco sun. O'Hara accepts that the world, having started, will one day stop. Grisby hopes to escape from nuclear disaster by engineering his reincarnation with a new identity, which is why he pays O'Hara to kill him.

Graves reassigned responsibility for Orpheus's singing, which is the mythical source of poetry. 'It was the Moon-goddess, not the Sun-god,' he argues, who inspired Orpheus. 'Poetry', he adds later, 'began in the matriarchal age, and derives its magic from the moon, not the sun.' In his film of *Don Quixote*, Welles made the dotty hero virtually quote Graves when he addresses the moon as 'the temple of poetry'. Elsa in *The Lady from Shanghai* is a lunar woman, who shimmers out of the darkness in Central Park, riding in a carriage that seems to be lit by her aloof, chiddy radiance. The beach picnic she asks for is laid on by moonlight. At Acapulco, she remains invisible during the day, prompting Grisby to ask O'Hara where she is. She emerges after dark and, dressed in white, drifts along a cliff as if in transit across the scintillating nocturnal sky. Then she descends into the squalid, brawling town. But despite her moonlit sheen, she is a false goddess. In the new scientific dispensation, the moon – formerly one of the 'prime emblems of poetry', as Graves said – has been eclipsed, reduced to 'a burned-out satellite of the earth'. Another of Welles's favourite latter-day romantics, T. H. White, grumbled in 1957 about the impiety of aiming rockets at the moon, and said that the only reason scientists could give for exploring outer space was that 'it will help the motor industry'. After the American flag was planted on the lunar surface in 1969, Welles repeated this lament for the deconsecration of space. Speaking to a college audience, he said that he was 'awfully serious about the moon', and thought that 'Robert Graves was right: . . . the most blasphemous thing that has happened since

Alexander cut the Gordian Knot was when we landed on the moon'. Welles attributed the same notion to Don Quixote. In his film, Quixote has a nervous breakdown, dismayed by the failure of his quest. Sancho tries to rally him by describing television reports of a mission to the moon, but Quixote replies 'The moon is dead.' He later recovers his faith and makes his own trip to the moon, where he hopes there will still be room there for knight errantry. That journey is an act of poetic speculation, not a colonising sortie.

Welles declared that he wished 'to use the motion picture camera as an instrument of poetry'. But poetry, like chivalry, had no place in a society 'geared' (as Graves said) 'to the industrial machine' rather than 'ruled by the old agricultural cycle'. For Graves, the visionary mania of Don Quixote signified the poet's intransigent 'failure to come to terms with the modern world'. In *The Lady from Shanghai*, Elsa corrupts her knightly devotee O'Hara by advising compromise with a bad world. 'Get along with it, deal with it, make terms,' she advises. She wonders if she'll have to 'take in washing to support him': an unlikely occupation for Rita Hayworth who, after divorcing Welles, eloped with Aly Khan in 1949. Graves, however, followed Quixote's example, and wrote his book in a 'remote unmechanized' village in the mountains of Majorca, where he lived as a 'romantic shepherd'. In 1964, Welles likewise took up residence in Spain, whose economic backwardness and political conservatism made it his refuge from modernity.

His earlier heroes had been men empowered by technology: Faust the scientist, the megaphonic orators in *Caesar* or *The Cradle Will Rock*, Kane with his mass media. Now, no longer fantasising about greatness like Kurtz, he became preoccupied with the nobility of a defeat brought on by his refusal to sacrifice his ideals. In Massenet's opera *Don Quichotte*, one of the knight's detractors calls him a madman; Dulcinée agrees that he is mad, but calls him 'un fou sublime'. Discussing O'Hara in 1961, Welles claimed that the naive sailor was a natural aristocrat, whose ethical system 'corresponds to very ancient European ideas'; he called him, in a telling conjunction, 'the poet and the victim'. Equating the poet with the victim, Welles had begun to elaborate a new myth for himself. He was not so much a failure as a martyr. He may have been a fool, but at least he was a holy one.

In the twentieth century, a romantic poet assumes an alarming responsibility. He must protect the ravaged earth and the dishonoured gods who once lived on or in it. Graves, declaring poetry immune to 'scientific analysis', said that it was 'rooted in magic', and protested that, for atheistic modern man, 'magic is disreputable'. Welles too was a magus, although – more ironically self-divided than Graves – he shared the popular suspicion about the trivial, deceptive nature of his own conjuring. He was also, unlike Graves, troubled by a political conscience. Graves had no qualms about praising 'spiritual regression' – a return to obscure, irrational, pre-scientific ways of thinking – as a way of making poetry 'magically potent'. In 1948 this was a provocation, since the Nazis, using spells and runes and atavistic German lore, had developed a mythopoeic politics that engendered social and psychological regression. More self-aware and self-critical, Welles said in 1950, during the Paris run of his anthological play about Faust, that he was alarmed by the success his film of *Macbeth* was then enjoying in Germany: 'I don't take it as a compliment . . . People are probably attracted by the medieval savagery of the subject.'

Repudiating scientific progress, the latter-day romantic poet concentrates instead on immortal stories of recurrence: nature's seasons, or those successive ages of fruition and decay that Welles found in Shakespeare. The wizard in *Journey into Fear* – whose cabaret turn is one of Welles's additions to Eric Ambler's plot – announces 'un ancien miracle divin'. 'That was a good trick,' says Joseph Cotten as he clambers out of the coffin with the nailed-down lid. Exhumed, amazed like Welles by his own serial lives, Cotten resembles one of the deities in the myths Graves investigates in *The White Goddess*: a god who is not so much undying as unkillable. As Haki, Welles's first line in the film – a fuller and more eloquent version of the speech Ambler wrote for the character – expounds the mystery. After a glowering silence, he gets up, crosses the room, shuts off the twittering of the Morse code, and shouts for attention. 'The spring will be here,' he bellows, 'and the Russian winter will be over.' The Russian fleet is immobilised by winter, its ships confined to port and unable to engage the Nazis. Cotten, a trader in armaments, is due to supply the Russians with new guns and torpedos. If he were to be killed, spring would not bring rebirth.

This earthy cult, with its sacrificial rites and its sappy chthonic miracles, is hinted at throughout *Journey into Fear*. Death, towards which the hero thinks he is helplessly journeying, is not to be feared; the victim turns out to be a resilient comic character, who recuperates from his own mortality. Except for his opening salvo about the seasons, Welles, writing the script with Cotten, confined the myth to the film's subtext. In Ambler's novel, however, it is explicated at length by the Nazi spy Haller (called Moeller in the film). He poses as an archaeologist, a scholar who has taken up the Teutonic worship of those bloodthirsty pagan gods disestablished by Christianity. The Nazis despised the mercy and meekness of the new, redemptive religion; they preferred what Oswald Spengler, quoted by Haller, called the 'dark almightiness'. Allegedly returning from a field trip, Haller recites lectures he has learned by heart from a Spenglerian tract called *The Sumerian Pantheon*. Welles retained the book, and allowed Moeller to hide his gun behind it. He also bore the book's theory in mind, and saved it up for examination in two later films. When Cotten emerges from the coffin, he might be demonstrating the first of Haller's theses, which is later restated by Graves in *The White Goddess*. 'The weeping for Tammuz', says Haller in the novel, 'was always a focal point of the prehistoric religions – the cult of the dying and risen god. Tammuz, Osiris and Adonis are the same Sumerian deity personified by three different races.' Now that deity, with the dew of American innocence glistening on him, is called Howard Graham and personified by Cotten.

In the novel, the boat makes a stop at Athens, an incident for which the film has no time. This port of call gives Haller an occasion to summarise Spengler's historical myth, which described the transition from classical calm and poise to the strife and stress of romanticism. He remembers his youthful visits to the Parthenon, and bewails Western man's loss of the world view implicit in the building's regularity: 'The god of superlative shape has been replaced by the god of superlative force . . . The destiny idea symbolised by the Doric columns is incomprehensible to the children of Faust.' Welles – himself a child of Faust, increasingly shapeless but undeniably forceful – surely took the speech to heart. Haller breaks off because he notices the embarkation of the hired killer Banat, whose freedom from humane qualms represents one aspect of the Faustian legacy. Haki, in another speech Welles cut, has his own thesis about Banat. 'They are perverts,' he says of such mercenary assassins, 'with an idée fixe about the father whom they identify not as a virile god but with their own impotence. When they kill, they are thus killing their own weakness.' Welles, the man of ideas, added this one to his collection, and it explains several of his characters. He made MacLíammóir's Iago enviously impotent, and Bannister in *The Lady from Shanghai* – homosexual in Sherwood King's novel – is embittered by the same affliction: Everett Sloane winces with self-disgust whenever love making is mentioned. Welles perhaps proved the truth of Haki's supposition by sentencing his own father to death in the stories he told about him. But he covered his tracks by presenting himself always as the most priapic of gods. Haki is a lecher, Kane and Arkadin have their harems, and even Othello is seen, on arrival in Cyprus, consummating his marriage to Desdemona. There is a touching, pardonable vanity in this. Welles never managed to be a convincing lover, despite his promiscuity. His fertility was mental, not physical – all the more reason for him to be attracted by Graves's account of the poet's role as a magus, drawing on 'the powers of the gods'.

After 1942 Welles had no chance to direct another film until *The Stranger* in 1946. A few months later he made *The Lady from Shanghai*, then *Macbeth* in 1947. Another long hiatus ensued, at the end of which he financed *Othello* himself. He began to distinguish between commercial work and personal projects, relying on the former to subsidise the latter. Because *The Stranger* was done for hire, he always disparaged it as 'the worst of my films', insisting that 'there is nothing of me in that picture'. But how could Welles – who as usual directed it, acted in it, and wrote a good deal of the script – leave himself out?

The denial is as untrustworthy as the incognito of Franz Kindler, the Nazi engineer of extermination who escapes from justice and, calling himself Charles Rankin, teaches at a boys' school in a placid Connecticut town. He boasts to his former colleague Meinike of having destroyed every piece of paper in Germany and Poland that could have identified him. Welles himself was mimicking Kindler's subterfuge. Anxious to live down his reputation for being troublesome and exorbitant, he wanted to show the producer Sam Spiegel that he was a good citizen, able to turn out a saleably conventional product. James Agee grudgingly praised *The Stranger* for its lack of pretension, taking this as a sign that Welles had now realised that he 'never was and never will be a genius'. But Kindler's well-behaved cover slips, as so does Welles's. The poet had not, after all, consented to be prosaic in *The Stranger*. The mythology suppressed in *Journey into Fear* resurfaces here, enabling Welles to dramatise two of the religious wars which, as Graves argued, were the true subject of poetry: the conflict between Christianity and the bellicose tribal gods it replaced, and the necessary antagonism between the poet – who was, as Graves said, 'originally a priest and judge as well and whose person was sacrosanct' – and the timid, law-abiding society to which he pretends to belong. In a dinner-table tirade, Welles's Kindler announces that 'Mankind is waiting for the Messiah.' He adds, in a dangerously ironic revelation of his own agenda, that 'for the German, the Messiah is not the prince of peace – he's another Barbarossa, another Hitler'. Craving anonymity and integration, Kindler manages all the same to reclaim the primitive powers forfeited by Graves's poet. He takes over the local church as his headquarters, while mending the clock in its tower. Peering down from the steeple at the diminished figures searching for him in the woods, he likens himself to God, 'looking at little ants'.

In his speech about German rearmament, Kindler deviously mocks the complacency of the Americans to whom he delivers this arch warning. He speaks of 'subterranean meeting-places that you don't believe in', where the resurgent Nazis dig by night, listen to Wagner and pay homage to their warrior deities. Those bunkers might be the hiding places of myth, driven into retreat by modern rationality. Down there, Kindler adds, the German's 'dream-world comes alive'. The church is built of wood and painted white, an emblem of puritanical America. But the clock Kindler restores has been imported from Strasbourg, on the border between Germany and France, and it brings a Gothic demonology with it: a sword-bearing angel and a blackened, grimacing devil rotate on the tower when it strikes. Kindler, tinkering with its movements, plays Wellesian tricks with time. He first thrusts up-to-date America back into the primordial past: during a trial run, the clock's hands speed backwards, anticlockwise. His new wife Mary, played by Loretta Young, says she prefers the town as it used to be, 'even to the clock that doesn't run', and Mr Potter (Billy House) – who as town clerk and owner of an all-purpose convenience store represents the consensus of the community – complains about its disruption of the peace: 'If it's gonna strike all night, how's a body to get any sleep? Them chickens of yours will be on and off the roost every fifteen minutes.' The enlightened eighteenth century described God as a watchmaker, who designed the world as a morally punctilious mechanism which could be left to run at its own steady pace. When Kindler scrambles up that shaky, unsupported ladder into the clock tower, Welles once more tests man's capacity to transform himself into a god by escaping from mortal inhibitions. He was forever Lucifer, envious of the Messiah.

Gods who recover from their own deaths abound in *The Stranger*. The film begins with the escape from prison of Meinike, released so that he can lead investigators to Kindler. The door of his cell is left open: he interprets this as a miracle, allowing him to quit his tomb. After Kindler kills him, he almost has another involuntary resurrection when a curious dog – which Kindler subsequently poisons – begins to scratch at his rough grave. Meinike believes he has killed Wilson, the investigator who trails him (Edward G. Robinson), though he too, concussed by a suspended iron ring in the school gymnasium, struggles up from the floor after an interval of unconsciousness. Presiding over these characters are two other unseen renascent divinities, both referred to as 'the All-Highest'. Meinike first uses the phrase in South America, as a password which compels a photographer to fake an identity card for him. The photographer snaps to attention, thinking that Meinike means the Führer, who has perhaps escaped from his reported death in the ruins of Berlin. Actually, Meinike is invoking the Christian God, in whom, after his own reprieve, he now believes.

Though Welles disowned The Stranger, he was pleased when Bogdanovich reminded him of one extended, technically arduous scene: the showdown between Kindler and Meinike in the woods, filmed in a continuous shot. 'I had to be a young man for that,' he remembered. 'Jesus, that was a physically tough shot – it nearly killed both of us.' His oath is apt, because the scene is about the poetic and sacred mystery of dying and being born again. It takes place near a graveyard, which the laughing boys skirt as they run downhill: the opposite ages or seasons of life collide. The encounter begins by looking down from behind Kindler as he greets his runaway colleague. The tall Welles stretches out his arms as Konstantin Shayne, small and abashed, approaches. There is no doubt, at this point, about the identity of the All-Highest; the angle suggests that Welles is playing Christ the redeemer, about to gather up a poor sinner anxious for salvation.

Their first exchanges, ambiguously overlapping, deal with the mystery or myth of rebirth. Kindler reaches down as if to raise Meinike up, and says 'I thought –' . Meinike immediately completes the sentence: 'I had been hanged.' Welles's fragmentation of the dialogue enables his statement to stand alone: he has been hanged, and has now come back to tell the tale. (The film was to begin by showing another revenant. Welles filmed a sequence in which Mary sleepwalked through the cemetery in her nightgown, like a vampirish bride; it was eliminated by the producer.) Meinike goes on to explain: 'The others, but not I. A dead man could not stand face to face with you, Franz.' Kindler remarks that he is not much changed, despite his passage through the netherworld. Give him a uniform, and he'll be as before. But Meinike disagrees: 'I am a different man than before.' When Kindler agrees 'I too am different', he is referring only to a change of name, not of belief. In describing his alias, he mocks two creeds, spiritual and secular. Later that afternoon – he says with chuckling, Mephistophelean effrontery – he will stand before 'a minister of the gospel' and marry the daughter of a judge. His father-in-law, he sneers, is 'a famous liberal' who sits in the Supreme Court of the United States. A reversal occurs, altering the identity of the All-Highest. Meinike has not come in quest of absolution. Instead, he hopes to save this false redeemer by converting him to Christianity. Meinike believes that the investigator who pursued him was 'the Evil One', though Edward G. Robinson is an officious, assiduous, petit-bourgeois devil: 'he even smoked a pipe', marvels Meinike. He is unaware that the Evil One is Kindler, who a moment ago resembled a succouring saviour.

As the shot continues, Kindler guides Meinike sideways into the birches. The camera follows, keeping to its high angle. Strolling along, Kindler predicts 'We'll strike again.' Meinike then reveals that the All-Highest set him free, and sent him on this mission. Excited, Kindler asks who the All-Highest is; he too assumes that it's the undead Hitler. When Meinike answers 'God', he laughs contemptuously and says 'You, Konrad – religious?' The camera has now moved closer to them, and lower. They pause. Meinike describes his execution of the demon in the gym, as if an angel armed with a metal cudgel had swooped to earth on an errand: 'Striking from on high, down. God's will be done.' He then pulls out a Bible, holds it up, and completes the reversal of roles by imploring Kindler to confess his guilt. Meinike kneels, and drags Kindler down to pray with him, inverting the movement at the start of the shot – so long ago – when it looked as if Kindler was about to lift Meinike up into his soothing embrace. Reciting the prayer, Kindler clasps Meinike once more, but tightens his hands round his neck and falls on top of him.

This is one of Welles's primal scenes, which he constantly rewrote and restaged. Holly Martins pleads with Harry Lime on the Prater wheel, Starbuck in *Moby Dick – Rehearsed* attempts to restrain the hubris and blasphemy of Ahab, the clerk in *The Immortal Story* warns Mr Clay that he cannot revise the past or control the future. Welles needed, as in his commentary on the lies he told in Dublin, to provide himself with just such a tragic crux, an instant of decision when safety or even salvation would have been made available to him, if only he had consented to be law-abiding or God-fearing or at least regular in his habits (which is what he claimed to be doing in making *The Stranger*). Like Faustus in Marlowe's play, he listened attentively to the good angel's entreaties, then disregarded them. We expect the tragic hero to remain unrepentant, to persist in his mad quest, and Welles demanded nothing less of himself. In *The Stranger* it takes him precisely four minutes to reverse the relationship between heaven and earth. There can be no cuts, because we are being made to witness, without editorial intervention, a world turning upside down or falling apart. Borges, alarmed by the violence and arrogance of Welles's imagination, called *Citizen Kane* unintelligent but had to concede that it was 'a work of *genius* – in the most nocturnal and Germanic sense of that bad word'. His judgement is all the more acute because he was writing in 1941, in the middle of World War II; the devious virtuosity of this scene in *The Stranger* proves him right. No wonder Agee was so anxious to lay the aspersion of genius to rest, and so wrong to think that Welles had done so.

Kindler brings his contempt for Christianity to a New England where all the men have been baptised in honour of Old Testament patriarchs. The judge's first name is Adam, his son is Noah, and the all-knowing busybody Potter (according to the sign on his shop window, glimpsed back to front near the end of the film) is Solomon. Welles, contradicting his professed indifference to *The Stranger*, was proud of the character of Potter, and told Bogdanovich 'I invented him. He was mostly written on the set.' He also insisted on giving the role to Billy House, a sluggish, bulky, slyly malevolent burlesque comedian, and was gratified when Edward G. Robinson complained about having to play the straight man to this supposedly secondary character. Though the film ought to be about the investigator's pursuit of Kindler, its real dramatic energy lies in the polarity of Kindler and Potter, who resemble rival deities.

Kindler is the strange, savage god, at home – before he assumes control of the church – in a subterranean dream-world. Potter is the god worshipped locally: a Christian facilitator of commerce, whose church is his shop. Potter first boasts of knowing everybody in town and then says that, as town clerk, he runs the place. During the hunt for Kindler, he is deputised as a sheriff. His drugstore has a window overlooking the street and a counter from behind which he supervises his stock. The radio is always playing, providing – as Brecht thought it should – an aural guarantee of sociability. Installed beside the cash register, Potter behaves like an unmoved mover. If effort has to be expended, he harries his minion, the elderly Mr Peabody; otherwise, complacently uncaring, he runs a world whose principle is self-service. He believes he has foreseen all eventualities, and recites to customers a slogan which becomes a mantra:

> All your needs are on our shelves,
> Just look around and help yourselves.

His cheery benevolence masks a contempt, corresponding to Kindler's remark about the ants, for those who depend on him to supply the means of life. 'I assume no responsibility,' he declares when he agrees to look after Meinike's case. Wilson is ordered to pour his own coffee. When he asks if there is a limit to the cream, Potter grudgingly snarls that most people take it black. Affecting concern about Wilson's headache, he points to the location of the aspirin. Then, when Wilson glances sideways, Potter cheats at chequers and demands a forfeit. So much for Christian commiseration.

God, as Welles remarked after that Bible reading at the Gate in Dublin, gets to win most of the time. But not always: one customer beats Potter at this compulsory game, which he plays for his own amusement and profit. It is Kindler. Desperate to regain control, the glowering Potter offers his competitor a final round, double or nothing. Kindler whistles, as if he could not care less about the outcome. He is idling in the store to supply himself with an alibi for his wife's death, which he has meticulously planned; rising to leave, he sketches a series of winning moves on the board with his fingers without bothering to touch the chequers, then strolls away, too supercilious to collect the few cents he has won. Here, not in any struggle between Kindler and Wilson, is the film's sedentary, cerebral showdown. A militant maniac who fantasises about annihilation confronts a smug proprietor for whom the world consists of commodities. Which of the two is more terrifying?

Toying with personal confession, *The Stranger* mentions a particular evil genius by whom Welles was intrigued. The dainty, proper guests at the tea party gossip about serial killers and try to remember 'the name of that Frenchman'. They mean Landru, who beguiled, married and then killed a succession of women. Welles had begun planning a documentary film about him when he completed *Citizen Kane*; while working on *The Stranger*, he sold the idea to Charlie Chaplin, who in *Monsieur Verdoux* turned Landru into a dapper satirist, revenging himself on the hypocrisy of a society that awards medals to serial killers in wartime but takes to executing them as soon as peace is declared.

Welles's fascination with Landru suggests the ambivalence of his feelings towards Graves's goddess. Kindler does not expect absolution and moral rescue from Mary. Instead, scaling the broken, wobbling ladder to the church tower, she intends to exterminate him. 'Lift me up!' Mary demands. This is Gretchen's service to Faust in Goethe's play: his soul is salvaged when, after her own death, she pardons him for the wrong he has done her. That intercession is reversed here. Kindler, leaning down through the trapdoor, reaches for her arm, pulls her away from the ladder, and lets her sway above the pit. (Loretta Young gamely braved the drop, without the benefit of a safety net.) Dragged on to the landing, she tells Kindler she has come to kill him, and says she is happy to die too, so long as she takes him with her. Grabbing a gun, she wounds him; she also fires the shot that starts the clock's mechanism, and sends the angel to stick its sword through him. Loretta Young wears a filmy nightdress in this scene, with a fur coat over it to protect her during her walk through the snowy cemetery. Pallidly lunar, she is Graves's moon-goddess, indignantly destroying the man who has trifled with her. She takes on other identities in Welles's subsequent films, *Macbeth* and *The Lady from Shanghai*. Cybele and Ishtar, according to Graves, are alternative names for Hecate, who consumes the offerings of Shakespeare's witches; the murderous Elsa travels on a yacht called – in tribute to another deranging, devouring mythological female – the *Circe*, whose wheel she commandeers in one scene.

Graves challenged would-be poets to 'come to terms with the Goddess' in whatever way they chose. Welles could only come to terms with that matriarchal source by challenging her to a mortal struggle. The muse for him was a harpy, or at least a shrill wife, like Susan shrieking at Kane before she stalks out of Xanadu. When Kindler makes a first attempt to strangle Mary in their bedroom, she upbraids him, as if Desdemona were repulsing Othello. 'Kill me!' she cries. 'But when you kill me, don't put your hands on me! Here, use this.' She then hands him a poker. Kane slaps Susan's face to shut her up. When filming *Othello*, Welles struck Suzanne Cloutier in the quarrel scene, because he despaired of provoking a plausible reaction from her without using violence. Exasperated by Cloutier's affectations, he joked that the strangling of Desdemona had better be left until the end of the shoot, in case she did not survive for a retake.

In his *Macbeth*, the hero – as well as being manipulated by a wife who calls him unmanly when he repents his crimes – is the plaything of the witches. Graves saw the coven at their bubbling cauldron as Shakespeare's tribute to the Triple Goddess and her fertility dances. After lamenting the rise of a patriarchal Christian religion that disenfranchised the goddess and her cackling acolytes, Graves notes an exception: 'in the British witch-cult the male sorcerer was dominant – though in parts of Scotland Hecate, or the Queen of Elfin or Faerie, still ruled'. Welles's Harlem *Macbeth* maintained the character's maleness, and had a virile Hecate discipline his witches with a bullwhip. Graves confidently declares that the spirit of 'the Triple Hecate . . . takes possession of Lady Macbeth and inspires her to murder King Duncan'. Hecate, he says elsewhere, is 'the Death-goddess', and he links her with Maia, the mother of Welles's patron Mercury. The idea of murder, instilled by her, is a poetic inspiration. Lady Macbeth ensures that the crime is committed by using her sexual wiles, which is why Welles's film introduces Jeanette Nolan lolling and writhing on a bed of animal skins. Welles's interpretation, however, protested against this female monopoly. He saw himself as the male sorcerer, a practised wizard, expert at shape-changing and the dissemination of misrule.

What he valued most keenly was the witch's power as a seer. He wrote a pair of weird sisters into *Touch of Evil*. Tanya the fortune teller is one, and the other, even more sybilline, is the woman in the shop on whose telephone Vargas calls Susan at the motel. She is blind, with one eye pursed shut and the other open, revolving in its socket as she meditatively sucks her teeth. Dressed in a pinafore, she is somehow both childish and ancient. Norn-like, she listens to Vargas's connubial endearments; her presence embarrasses him into lowering his voice. She is a white witch, shaming him by her innocence. Despite her blindness, a sign above the cash register establishes her vigilance. It regulates the conduct of her customers by appealing to their consciences. 'If You are mean enough to Steal from the Blind,' it says, 'Help Yourself.' The snooping, prying Mr Potter in *The Stranger* has been replaced by a woman who sees through people without needing to use her eyes.

The goddess, according to Graves, does not only make herself manifest in poetry. She recurs in 'dreams, paranoiac visions and delusions'. Even Othello's black-out in Welles's film, subjectively recorded by the camera, might qualify as a revelatory vision: Graves interprets an epileptic fit as a 'spiritual orgasm', proof of acute poetic sensitivity. Can poems be distinguished from hallucinations? Welles's *Macbeth* suggests not. At the banquet, he shouts 'Look!' and points to the ghost. The shadow of his index finger, flickering in firelight, is imprinted on the bumpy rock face, which is indented with crevasses and secretive hollows like the cerebral cortex. The camera slowly tracks it, and the finger elongates into a pole before it arrives at the thing it is pointing to: a vision invisible to everyone but Macbeth. We might be present in the cave at Lascaux, witnessing the moment when primitive man – clad in pelts like Welles and his court of scowling ruffians – first depicted something that could not be seen, except by the mind's eye.

Wide-eyed, Macbeth then hurtles outside to consult the 'midnight hags', and as a Gothic thunderstorm cracks overhead, he cries 'I conjure you.' What follows is Welles's equivalent to the scene in the play when five witches, festally sacrificing to Hecate, summon up a show of future kings and predict that Macbeth is safe until Birnam wood moves and a man not of woman born comes to challenge him. In Welles's version, however, no witches are seen, and Macbeth himself does the conjuring. Orating, he spits into the wind; a lightning bolt projects the shadow of a Celtic cross onto the studio wall, as a token of his sacrilege. Macbeth is exhilarated, as Welles always was, by the prospect of apocalypse. He goads the storm to make 'nature's germens tumble all together / Even till destruction sicken.' Harnessing this wild energy, he brings about the usurpation lamented by Graves, who believed that 'the Thunder-god won the day' by venting his spite on the Triple Goddess and her attendants. A flare scythes through the sky, as though Macbeth had been concussed by lightning. Then the weather is pacified. In a long shot, Macbeth – no bigger than the embryonic manikin made by the witches – kneels in a pool of light, encircled by darkness. Voices mutter and shriek from the air, but they come from inside the necromancer's head.

Gradually the camera moves in for a close-up, a glimpse of Welles's imagination at work. After hearing the prophecies – which, if Macbeth is reciting them to himself, are no more than comforting illusions – he stares directly into the lens and asks 'What, is this so?' A cracked female voice replies 'Aye sir, all this is so.' The text of the play attributes the line to Hecate; unseen, she here addresses herself directly to Macbeth, rather than (as Graves argued) using his wife as her conduit. His face relaxes into a wide-eyed, childishly credulous smile. The muse has spoken, persuading him to believe in his own imaginative delusions.

Hollywood catered to Graves's romantic religion by manufacturing nubile divinities on its production line. In 1948, Ava Gardner played

Aphrodite, who quits the pedestal on which she statuesquely poses in a shop window, in *One Touch of Venus*; the previous year Rita Hayworth played Terpsichore, the celestial patron of dance, in *Down to Earth*. Welles and Hayworth were married in 1943, which should have demonstrated the intensity of his poetic infatuation with the goddess.

The union, for him at least, was a mythological merger, like Faust's conquest of Helen of Troy. In Marlowe's play, Helen is a succubus, whose kiss damns Faust. In *Time Runs*, Welles made the condemnation clear in the verses he wrote for Eartha Kitt, a sweater girl chosen to be Helen in a school play. 'Hungry little trouble,' she purred to Duke Ellington's score, 'damned in a bubble, yearning to be, be or be free, all that you see is about me.' But for Goethe, the classical sabbath – when the most beautiful woman of antiquity is joined to the most intelligent modern man – represented a reconciliation of body and mind, south and north, classical and romantic. The nuptials of Welles and Hayworth, like those of Arthur Miller and Marilyn Monroe, were literally made in heaven where such astral conjunctions are plotted; cohabitation on earth proved more difficult. Welles expected this relationship to lead both him and Hayworth aloft into purer and more humanitarian air. He announced that they would suspend their careers. He intended to travel, giving speeches in support of Roosevelt; her job would be to gaze up at him admiringly. The erstwhile goddess was unhappy to find herself dwindling into a trophy wife. 'I'm not Mrs Orson Welles,' she once snapped. 'I'm Rita Hayworth!' Scornfully unfaithful, Welles mistreated her, alleging that – neurotic, inclined to alcoholism – she deserved no better. Later, embellishing his personal myth, he came to think of her as Marlowe's destructive Helen, not Goethe's idealised muse. He identified Hayworth with the fatal Helen in his screenplay for *The Cradle Will Rock*, where – remembering the character in his production of *Faustus* – he emphasises her 'great fall of reddish blonde hair' reaching almost to the ground. He goes on to open Helen up, and shows that she is empty.

Welles celebrated their engagement by sawing Hayworth in half at his magic show. The Columbia boss Harry Cohn, worried about damage to physical goods that were under contract to him, demanded her withdrawal from the act, so Dietrich replaced her after the first night. In 1946, Welles performed another symbolic massacre. He had Hayworth's waterfall of auburn hair chopped off, and bleached it blonde in preparation for *The Lady from Shanghai*. It was a drastic decision, making her look like a photographic negative of herself. She had become the white goddess – unfeeling, implacable, spectral not carnal. At the end of *The Lady from Shanghai*, Welles escapes from the court where he is being tried for murder by joining the jury from another trial as it is ushered out; a female juror, who thinks that he is hearing the same case as her, delays him by gossiping about the defendant. 'That woman's too nice-looking to have stolen all that jewellery,' she says. Are the beautiful necessarily good? Welles expresses no opinion. On the yacht, a radio jingle advertising a product called Glossolusto – guaranteed to make your hair shine and to please your man – hints that beauty is a false façade, a commercial ploy. Even Hayworth's resplendent red hair came from a bottle, when the studio made her over. Enraged by Welles's desecration of its star, Columbia delayed the film so that glamorous close-ups of Hayworth could be inserted. By the time it was released in 1948, they were divorced.

Welles had himself photographed supervising Hayworth's severe new hair-cut. In the film, she retaliates by a symbolic emasculation. O'Hara, introducing himself, offers Elsa a cigarette, his last one. Though she claims not to smoke, she takes it anyway and – levelly fixing him with her gaze – wraps it in a handkerchief and puts it in her purse. A man entrusts his penis to a woman. She takes it into custody, causes it to vanish. Will it ever reappear, and if so, how much of it will be left? O'Hara finds the cigarette, still unsmoked, poking out of the handkerchief: she has dropped the purse when being dragged away by her attackers. But of course it is only a bait, calculated to lure him back. During the cruise, she asks him for a cigarette, which she holds upright, erectile not horizontal, between her fingers. She then tries to kiss him; he slaps her, and she plugs her unoccupied mouth with the cigarette instead. It trembles between her lips, and fulminates in his face.

The Lady from Shanghai casts the goddess as a demon. If the story is a chivalric romance, as O'Hara wants it to be, then Elsa turns out to be the equivalent of those oriental sorceresses like Armida who beguile and madden the crusader in Ariosto's *Orlando Furioso*. She has a menagerie of animal familiars – a cantankerous black dachshund, or the ibis and the alligator, the screeching tropical parrots and the wriggling snake in the swamp through which she is rowed to the picnic site. In other shapes, they might have been Circe's lovers. Elsewhere she is a marine Venus, born from the sea and diving back into it as Grisby watches her through his spyglass. In the San Francisco aquarium, the aquatic ogres in the tanks behind her – an octopus with lithe rubbery tentacles, sleek eels, a magnified fish with a gaping dentated mouth – stand for the play of her thoughts. The watery light ripples over her face when she embraces O'Hara, as if she were submerging him. She has the universality of a truly mythical character. When she pursues O'Hara into Chinatown, Hayworth's familiar face is suddenly estranged when she begins to speak Chinese: are we watching a copy of the film dubbed for export? Though Elsa tells O'Hara that her parents were 'Russian, White Russian', she served her sexual apprenticeship in Shanghai, where she also picked up the language. She explains her incorrigibility by quoting a Chinese proverb, which attests that 'Human nature is eternal. Therefore one who follows his nature keeps his original nature in the end.' This is her equiv- alent to the fable about the scorpion recited by Welles himself in *Mr Arkadin*. The insect obeys its nature by stinging a frog that ferries it across a stream, drowning both of them. The nature at issue here is not human, since that implies moral accountability, a capacity to learn and change. Gods for Welles resembled animals: they could not be expected to help themselves, and were impelled, as he was, by appetite or a doomed compulsion.

Before his relationship with Hayworth frayed, he made plans to work through the pantheon with her, casting her as a succession of such praying mantises (and, in every case, killing her all over again). The sisters of the lady from Shanghai whom they discussed included Prosper Mérimée's Carmen and Oscar Wilde's Salome. When further collaborations with Hayworth were vetoed, he said he favoured Paulette Goddard as Carmen and Vivien Leigh as Salome. Hayworth subsequently made both films without Welles, so the characters were timidly sanitised.

The Loves of Carmen, directed by Charles Vidor in 1948, borrowed Welles's notion of the character, seeing her as a hard-boiled moll like one of Raymond Chandler's hoydens, not an operatic siren. Hayworth hurls oranges at a bride whose whiteness she despises, and smashes a pitcher of nurturing milk. Like a goddess she is ubiquitous, and evades suitors by leaving word that she has crossed the border into Portugal or left for Gibraltar. When her Basque lover José grows tired of life as a bandit and yearns 'to live like other people', she sneers at his plan to migrate to a Mexican farm: like Elsa refusing to take in laundry, she says 'I wasn't born to grow cabbages.' José, mulishly played by Glenn Ford, is an O'Hara who does not manage to resist the temptress. A ruffian in the gang analyses him as a victim of his own idolatry: 'The only really wicked men I've ever known started as idealists. That's what depravity feeds on – illusions and idealism and love gone wrong.' The production code required Carmen and José to marry, like respectable suburbanites. A gipsy ceremony is arranged, after which Carmen sarcastically sends out an invitation to all the whores and outlaws of her acquaintance, announcing that Señor and Señora Lizzarrabengoa will be at home for the winter in the caves of Granada. As Welles knew, the poet should not set up housekeeping with his fantasy.

Hayworth went on to make *Salome* in 1953, with William Dieterle as director. Welles had planned an ingenious adaptation of Wilde's play, in which the conflict between Salome and John the Baptist – executed by Herod to repay his step-daughter for the dance of the seven veils – represents the war between pagan sensuality and Christian abstinence. Welles reserved a double role for himself. As Herod, Welles would have attempted to forestall Christianity by killing the evangelist who announced its coming; but he also intended to play Oscar Wilde, for whom decadence revived the worship of older, more lascivious gods. A note in Welles's script speculates that Salome was perhaps Herod's daughter, not his niece and step-daughter: a callous allusion to Hayworth's dancing duets with her incestuous father. With Welles out of the way, the project was chastened. Now Salome dances in the hope of saving the Baptist; this exonerates her, and rather than being abruptly executed as in Wilde's play, she escapes with a Roman soldier who happens to be a Christian convert. They are last seen attentively listening to the Sermon on the Mount, in a panorama as roseate as a stained-glass window at Forest Lawn cemetery. As the music swells, a legend glimmers in the sky: not 'The End' but 'This is The Beginning'.

Welles planned a very different epilogue, in which Pilate and his wife Procula survey the city from their terrace after the condemnation of Christ. Smoke clogs the air: Herod, repentant, has ordered Salome's body to be put to the torch, hoping to erase all trace of her infamy. Procula urges Pilate to come to bed, and says he must be exhausted, having presided over the trial of 'that Man'. He suspects that he may soon be recalled to Rome, chased away by the new revolutionary religion that will unsettle the empire, and tells Procula that the responsibility of governing is the heaviest burden in the world. 'Is that true?' she asks. Pilate, smiling ironically, repeats the phrase he used when disclaiming responsibility for Christ: 'After all, my dear, what is truth?' He does not demand a false certainty, like Macbeth in Welles's film when he asks Hecate to confirm that 'this is so'. Stranded between two dispensations, he is resigned to living in doubt. Procula replies 'More riddles!' and they laugh while the sky, as at Xanadu, is blackened by fumes from a funeral pyre.

As Kindler in *The Stranger*, Welles proclaimed the advent of another Messiah, who can only take over the world once Christ with his benevolent pacifism has been expunged. Though he never made his *Salome*, Welles got the chance, when he played the director in Pasolini's *RoGoPaG* in 1962, to organise that salutary deicide. 'Nail them to the crosses!' he barks as he prepares to film the crucifixion. 'Motori! Azione!' Kindler's alternative Messiah was a fascist, and Pasolini's was to have been a communist; Welles, however, had no interest in such doctrines of political deliverance. When an interviewer in the film asks what he thinks of death, he replies 'As a Marxist, I don't even consider it.' For Pasolini, that may have been sound dogma, but Welles spent most of his life considering death, and even made Salome share his wry, wise fatalism. In his script, the Baptist prophesies that the Lord will send a fire to destroy the ivory palaces of Jerusalem. Salome reacts like O'Hara at Acapulco when he outfaces the explosion forecast by Grisby. 'Everything has an end, prophet,' she says, and adds a joke that is not unworthy of Wilde: 'Even sermons come to an end.'

Much later, Welles tried to make amends to Hayworth's maligned gender. He found an analysis of his ailment in Isak Dinesen's 'The Old Chevalier', which ends with the besotted hero listening to Gluck's *Orfeo ed Euridice* at the Opéra in Paris: he has fallen in love with that white, polished, bodiless skull exhumed from the ground, like an Orfeo who prefers his Euridice dead and buried. Aware of his unworthiness, Welles adopted Karen Blixen as his muse, a daunting white goddess. He travelled to Copenhagen to meet her, then panicked and fled before the encounter. Oja Kodar – his last companion and a genuine helpmate, whom he cast as Pellegrina in his film of Dinesen's *The Dreamers* – was a less terrifying stand-in. Contented and adoring, he began his confessional documentary *F for Fake* with a sequence about Kodar, but found himself once more using the techniques he had vengefully applied to Hayworth in the crazy house.

The film starts with Kodar stopping traffic as she strides through Nice in a scanty, filmy dress. We see the heads of the male motorists who ogle her; all Welles shows of Kodar is her legs, her groin, her buttocks in close-up. She is, to borrow the scholastic distinction made by Dinesen's chevalier, Woman not a woman, so her head is sliced off by the camera.

Her torso sashays across a series of television screens, like Hayworth multiplied by the mirrors, while the men in stalled cars grab cameras to capture her as she wiggles by. Here Kodar is only too perturbingly visible. Welles therefore, in the scene that follows at Orly airport, makes her disappear. He does not cut her in half, as he did with Hayworth in his tent show. Instead, needing to squeeze her on to an overbooked flight, he stuffs her into an upright box and lowers a steel plate, apparently crushing and pulverising her. The compacting is supposed to be temporary, but Welles does not retrieve her from this magical killing-chamber. 'We'll leave Miss Kodar aside for the moment,' he says, and drives happily away. The poet still cannot forgive the goddess for compelling him to worship her. If she represents his creative power, she reminds him that it is a curse.

Welles as Cesare Borgia, with a Mona Lisa smirk.

Renaissance Man

In 1967, Tynan asked Welles whether it was still possible to be a Renaissance man, with an equal comprehension of the arts and sciences. Welles replied 'It's possible and it's also necessary', because our over-specialised culture requires synthesis: 'We have to get these scattered things together and make sense of them.' He then proved the point by claiming that he could explain the principles of nuclear fission. After all, he had often enough been compared to a bomb. Whether or not he understood atomic physics, Welles possessed the required array of talents. He embodied the spiritual effrontery of the Renaissance when playing Faustus, and among the projects he proposed to RKO were lives of Leonardo da Vinci and Machiavelli: he could see himself as either or both, embodying the godlike aspiration and the godless free-thinking of Renaissance man. In 1971 he played the dying sorcerer Cassavius in *Malpertius,* directed by Harry Kümel. Cassavius has populated a Flemish town with creatures as ideally beautiful as classical statues. They turn out to be Greek gods, spared Christianity's anathema and persuaded to return to life. He wants to interbreed them with contemporary earthlings to fabricate a master race. Welles, given credit for this miraculous revival, is here the Renaissance in person. Who else – Kümel asked himself when casting the film – could play a demiurge?

But whenever a defining label was applied to him, Welles preserved his freedom by rejecting it. In 1958 the *Cahiers* critic Jean Domarchi flattered him as 'a man of the sixteenth century', likening him to Shakespeare, Cervantes and Montaigne. Welles retaliated by saying that if he could choose to live in any period of the past, he would have selected the twelfth century. One evening in 1949, discussing plans to begin filming *Othello* in Venice, he treated MacLíammóir to a high-flown monologue, a cyclone of free-associating intellect. 'Entire Renaissance was dealt with and practically exploded by him,' MacLíammóir reported in his journal. Welles's reasoning, left unrecorded, has evaporated; all that's possible is to imagine what he said. But there are clues. During his first year of work on *Othello* – which remained intermittently in production until 1952 –

he took time off to raise money by appearing in other people's films. In *The Third Man*, the speech he wrote for Harry Lime ends with a cynical vindication of the Renaissance, when the Italy of the Borgias had 'warfare, terror, murder, bloodshed' but produced Michelangelo and Leonardo da Vinci; he then went on to play Cesare Borgia, one of the Renaissance men admired by Lime, in *Prince of Foxes*.

The views Welles attributed to Lime derive from Jacob Burckhardt, who published *The Civilisation of the Renaissance in Italy* in 1860. Burckhardt deplored the chicanery of the Milanese despot Ludovico Sforza and called Cesare Borgia a 'great criminal', but he could not deny the collusion between vice and culture. Both Sforza and Borgia employed Leonardo da Vinci, whose intellectual curiosity testified to a new faith in what Burckhardt called 'the highest individual development'. The individual, universalising himself, refused to be limited any longer to membership of one city or state. Dante said that the whole world was his home. Welles must have sympathised: his interest in the Renaissance coincided with his uprooted life after 1947 when, unable to work at home, he drifted between Rome, Paris, London and (much later) Madrid, until eventually in 1975 he returned to live in Los Angeles and Las Vegas. But Leonardo's versatility was self-defeating, just as Dante's cosmopolitanism was the consequence of exile. In neither case was the affinity comforting for Welles.

A tragic paradox is at the centre of Burckhart's book; Welles found the same contradiction in his own character. Burckhardt's Renaissance is about the discovery of man, and that liberated man's discovery of the world. He imagines a literal nascence of the individual, calling the fifteenth-century Italian 'the first-born among the sons of modern Europe'; awakened to his own idiosyncrasy, man now graduates through the stages of 'uomo singolare' and 'uomo unico'. Such an exploratory venture, Burckhardt supposes, was inconceivable earlier, because medieval man 'was conscious of himself only as a member of a race, people, party, family, or corporation – only through some general category'. Orsini in Shellabarger's novel *Prince of Foxes* measures the difference with convenient simplicity when some soldiers challenge him to fight over a point of honour: 'They were medieval; he had become a modern.' Welles shared that modernity. Acclaimed from his infancy for being singular and unique, he advertised the escape from what Burckhardt called general categories. And if Burckhardt's version of history is read in the context of the 1930s and 1940s, an individuality like Welles's is more than mere eccentricity. The political regimes of the period attempted to re-medievalise the world, incorporating the individual all over again in race, people, party. Welles obstinately and ostentatiously symbolised freedom, the right to be different. But when individuality, rejoicing in its own liberty of action, spurns moral and religious authority, the result is scandal, sacrilege, outrage. For Burckhardt, such wilful arrogance was both the 'fundamental vice' of Renaissance character and 'a condition of its greatness', and he believed that it propelled men like Sigismondo Malatesta, the tyrant of Rimini who attempted to murder his own son, 'into the hands of the powers of darkness'.

In 1958, Welles summed up the moral predicament identified by Burckhardt. 'In the Renaissance,' he said, 'man became the central theme in the tragedy of life.' He looked fondly on the myth of Christ's divinity, because 'in the highest tragic sense, it dramatises the idea that man is divine'. His story is tragic, as Welles's was, because the man in whom divinity is invested is at the same time a prey to demons. The dark powers in Welles's case were his physical appetites, his reckless mental energies, and the rages that ensued when anyone interfered with the gratification of his wishes.

Burckhardt's theory about idiosyncracy and its perils is acted out in Welles's *Othello*. The hero's first agonised bout of introspection occurs in his armoury, where – after Iago disarms him and hangs up his metal defences – he studies himself in a circular mirror on the wall. After railing at Desdemona and rejecting her handkerchief, he goes back to the mirror to check on his state of mind. As she rushes off, a second mirror is glimpsed, standing free in the centre of the room. Like an actor in his dressing room (which is what the armoury is), Othello constructs an identity by fashioning an image of himself. But mirrors are unreliable, as the crazy house in *The Lady from Shanghai* demonstrates; now, with Othello's armour off and his occupation gone, that image has started to splinter. Roderigo, lounging in the Turkish bath where he is murdered, gazes wistfully into a mirror whose glass is blurred by steam and scrawls Desdemona's name on its misty surface. Mirrors are consulted by men who do not know themselves and want to be told lies, since the person we see in the glass is a stranger. Desdemona, by contrast, seems not yet to have woken up to her individuality, and still happily defers to the general categories that in Burckhardt's view governed and restrained medieval humanity. Welles made her as pious as Desdemona in Verdi's operatic version of the play, where her mournful willow song leads to a seraphic Ave Maria. After her humiliation before the ambassadors, she retires to a chapel and fingers her rosary as incense smokes on an altar. The set for her bedroom was a ruined church at Viterbo. She has a statuette of the Virgin on the wall, with a candle below it which Othello snuffs out when he comes to kill her. The two funeral processions at the start of the film mark the difference between medieval orthodoxy and the narcissistic autonomy of Renaissance man. Desdemona is attended by cowled monks with crosses and mitres chanting Latin prayers, while Othello – who invented himself by looking in a mirror – is denied the benefit of clergy.

Welles's critique of the Renaissance was an act of self-criticism. It also counted as a gesture of filial rebellion, because he had been born during the Renaissance – at least the American version of it, the period of affluence and triumphally ornate expenditure that lasted from the end of the Civil War until American entry into the First World War. The dates correspond with the magnificence of the Ambersons: the Major gained his fortune in 1873, but by 1916 – when Tarkington begins the retrospective narrative of his novel, a year after Welles's arrival in the world – the money has all been spent. In calling the Ambersons magnificent, Tarkington teasingly aligned the twin Renaissances. In his first paragraph he says that 'Magnificent Lorenzo' – the Medici who befriended and supported Botticelli, Verrocchio and Pico della Mirandola – would have felt distinctly shabby if he could have seen New York when the magnates of the gilded age were rebuilding it. By the time Burckhardt's book was translated in 1878, it had become a manifesto for the confident, plutocratic America into which Welles's parents – his father the globetrotting inventor, his mother the concert pianist and suffragette – were born. 'We are children of the Renaissance,' said a New York reviewer in 1880. T. H. White, on an American lecture tour in the autumn of 1963, thought that the country's richly endowed colleges and libraries and museums proved that this Renaissance was still thriving, and when President Kennedy was assassinated he commented in his journal that 'People who live in Renaissances are apt to live with violence – think of Marlowe . . . We are among the Borgias again.'

Italy had its mercantile princes like the Medici and the Borgias, America its captains of industry like the Fricks, Guggenheims and Whitneys. In both societies, civilisation was the result of economic surplus; culture began as an exercise in conspicuous consumption. The New York architects Charles McKim and Stanford White – who designed the

Brooklyn Museum, the arch in Grand Army Plaza, the Pierpont Morgan Library and Columbia University – were nicknamed Bramante and Benvenuto Cellini. Early in the 1880s, the Vanderbilt clan constructed a competitive series of mansions on Fifth Avenue: emporia of gilt and ebony, red marble and iridescent glass, with mosaic pavements overlaid by Oriental rugs. In the vestibule of his residence, W. H. Vanderbilt installed a reproduction of Ghiberti's bronze doors from the Baptistery in Florence, known as The Gates of Paradise. They opened on to a heaven of riches. Xanadu and (more modestly) the Amberson mansion are both relics of this American Renaissance, with its gaudy, rapacious excess.

In a ten-volume inventory of W. H. Vanderbilt's pile, Earl Shinn rejoiced that 'wealth is consenting to act the Medicean part in America', venturing 'to create the arts'. To create the arts, or to loot them ready-made from another pauperised continent? At San Simeon, Hearst posed a bronze copy of Donatello's *David* above a fountain on the terrace. The marble doors to his assembly room had been sculpted by Sansovino, with inlaid crests commemorating Julius II, the Warrior Pope; a refectory ceiling came complete with carved saints. One of the bedrooms occupied by weekending socialites was called the Doge's Suite, because its ceiling had been imported from Venice, along with a ceramic *Virgin and Child* by Della Robbia above the fireplace. In *American*, Welles and Mankiewicz described Kane the robber baron, newly flush with funds, on a spending spree in Italy in 1890: he celebrates his twenty-fifth birthday in a Renaissance palazzo in Rome, surrounded by down-at-heel aristocrats anxious to unload their heirlooms. Stanford White justified the spoliation of Europe by his moneyed clients, citing a Darwinian theory of civilisation which also applied to Kurtz's gouging of ivory in the Congo. 'In the past', White said, 'dominant nations . . . always plundered works of art from their predecessors; . . . America was taking a leading place among nations and had, therefore, the right to obtain art wherever she could.' Was art then no more than imperial booty?

Welles knew that art, being a luxury not a necessity, relied on the patronage of men with money; the art he chose to practice was, as he lamented, forbiddingly expensive. But though he mocked the nouveau-riche acquisitiveness of Kane and the Ambersons, he was American enough to see himself as part of the maturing country's triumphal destiny. This is the implication of his comments on the Elizabethan Renaissance in *Everybody's Shakespeare*: the riches of the Americas, shipped home to

England, made Shakespeare possible, so why shouldn't America's home-grown wealth – dispensed by the government through the New Deal, or handed over in the form of blank cheques by Hollywood moguls – make Orson Welles possible? The country needed a homegrown genius. The Washington collector Duncan Phillips announced in 1914 'the coming of an American Renaissance' – an indigenous one this time, not dependent on foraging for European antiques but generated by 'our mingling of races, our material prosperity, . . . our eagerness of invention, our buoyancy of spirit' and the 'big thoughts and big emotions' stirred by contact with a wide-open land. Welles, a punctual Messiah, was born the following year.

Art had a duty to ravage American puritanism: James Huneker's novel *Painted Veils*, published in 1928, contrasts the Seven Deadly Virtues with the Seven Deadly Arts, the proponents of civilising vice. The young Welles, like one of Burckhardt's stylish malefactors, staged an infernal riot in Harlem, rehearsed revolution on Broadway, and played a fiendish practical joke on the entire country at Halloween. But America did not appreciate his assaults on its propriety, and was disinclined to subsidise his extravagances. Disillusioned, he began to understand how precarious and temporary the Renaissance was. Tarkington warns that 'magnificence, like the size of a fortune, is always comparative'. Welles billed himself as a magnifico in his Los Angeles magic show, where a banner announced a fire-swallowing act by ORSON THE MAGNIFICENT, but he did so ironically. Propagandists for the American Renaissance had looked forward to a future of unchecked ascent, of rebirths with no intervening deaths: the painter John La Farge said that the American Academy in Rome, founded on the Janiculum by McKim in 1894, announced that 'we too are rivals of all that has been done, and intend to rival all that shall be done, and we can then feel that the old cycle is closed and that a new one has begun'. Welles, coming later, saw such swaggering optimism in a longer, sadder perspective. When Bogdanovich bemoaned the end of the golden age of movies, he retorted that even the Renaissance lasted only sixty years. In *The Third Man*, he halved the term, contrasting five centuries of dull democracy in Switzerland with Italy's 'thirty years under the Borgias'. Power and glory were always short-lived: Welles's own instalment of magnificence lasted a scant five years, from 1937 to 1942.

In 1927, Percy Wyndham Lewis – a critic and satirical novelist who campaigned against the effete subjectivity of modernism in a periodical he called *Blast* – published a book on the Shakespearean hero, called *The Lion and the Fox*. He took the title from Machiavelli's fable about the necessary cunning of the ruler: the prince must imitate both, roaring like a lion to frighten wolves while guilefully evading traps like a fox. For Lewis, the contrast between the valiant beast and the shrewd one summed up a conflict in the culture of the Renaissance. Shakespeare, he argued, 'had one foot in the old world of chivalrous romance and the other in the new one of commerce and science'. Lewis detected the same divided allegiance in Cervantes and Rabelais, who also described a world in transition between sacred mystery and a brisk, brutal positivism. Welles shared these mixed motives, commuting as he did between Falstaff's Merry England or the Celtic kingdom of Arthur and the godless, emancipated society in which Faustus conjured up riches for himself. The Renaissance for him was a psychodrama, a combat between his contradictory selves.

He acted out the disparity defined by Lewis, appearing as both lion and fox. In *Othello*, he portrayed the imperious, bombastic lion of Venice: MacLíammóir's Iago plots against him on a balcony inside the Doge's Palace, pacing to and fro before a carving of St Mark with a winged lion. The lion was the emblem of Venice, associated with the prophet because it guarded the throne of God, just as Mark – whose remains Venetian merchants claimed to have brought back from Alexandria – protected the city. In Verdi's opera, Othello himself turns into that totemic beast: the chorus cries 'Evviva Otello! Gloria al Leone di Venezia!' and Iago, jeering at the prostrate, inglorious hero, says 'Ecco il Leone!' Welles, instinctively playing the king, possessed the qualities Lewis enumerated as 'requisites of the Shakespearean *lion*', who – whether he is called Othello or Lear or Antony or Coriolanus – is 'completely helpless, childlike, truthful and unfortunate', a left-over from the unsocialised infancy of mankind. Like Machiavelli's lion, Welles also knew how to growl at possible enemies or rivals, to warn them away from the territory he had staked out. During his season as Othello on stage in London in 1951, he suggested that Olivier might think of playing Iago. 'Why not Othello?' asked Olivier, bristling. Welles pointed out that Olivier was a light tenor, whereas for Othello you needed to be a bass-baritone. A lion could not have done a better job of vocal intimidation.

But just as his film of *Othello* got underway, Welles turned aside to play Machiavelli's scheming prince of foxes, Cesare Borgia. The projects overlapped: both were partly shot on location in Venice, and Welles carried off some of the rich Renaissance costumes made for Henry King's film to clothe his own less lavishly outfitted cast. *Prince of Foxes* had a crucial place in his imaginary autobiography, because it is about Cesare's partnership with the ruthless fixer Orsini (Tyrone Power). If Orson believed the family legend, or even if – as is more likely – he made it up, then he was dealing here with one of his own ancestors.

Having seized power in Ferrara, Welles's Borgia recruits Orsini as an undercover surrogate. Staring confidentially into the camera, he says he needs a henchman with an assassin's wrist and an incapacity for love. 'Have you the stomach for greatness?' he asks Orsini. This is the question that preoccupied Welles and so many of his heroes. As if he could gain power over the world by gobbling it up, Orsini replies 'The stomach, and the appetite.' Paraphrasing Burckhardt, he announces the advent of the Renaissance: 'A new world is being born. Sham and trickery are only weapons of policy.' He even uses the word 'ego' – for Burckhardt the source of that aesthetic evil by which the Renaissance was beguiled – during a skirmishing enconter with his lover Camilla in Rome. But Power's stardom demanded that Orsini should eventually be redeemed by love, so his Machiavelli acquired an even more Machiavellian alter ego of his own: a skulking hired killer, played by Everett Sloane (who was Welles's first choice for Iago). This exquisitely, inventively wicked intriguer also undergoes a change of heart in deference to the Hollywood production code and, when Cesare orders him to put out Orsini's eyes, he smuggles him to safety instead.

Tortured for disloyalty, Orsini resists the tyrant and tells Cesare 'There is no victory in power.' So soon after World War II, that was Hollywood's preferred verdict on despotism; Welles wrote an alternative version of history for Harry Lime to deliver as he surveys pulverised Vienna. Military and political victories are of no interest to this profiteer, a capitalist who hides in the Russian sector of the occupied city. What matters is commerce, practised as starkly and neutrally as if it were a science. Harry's eyrie is a cabin on the revolving wheel, just as Iago – hauled into the air for punishment at the start of Welles's film – looks down at a diminished, insignificant crowd from inside a cage in which he will slowly starve, die and putrefy. Welles took the idea for this incarceration from *Prince of Foxes*, where Cesare orders Orsini exposed in a cage on the tower, there to remain until his bones drop apart. In all three cases, the container gives spatial form to the affectless ego analysed by Burckhardt. The proud self hovers above the human world, emotionally disconnected and contemptuous. But its cubicle is a cell, and will turn into a transparent grave.

Lewis considered Machiavelli to be the 'master figure' of Elizabethan drama, and thought that the Borgias and Sforzas were 'more important to the Elizabethan dramatists than any of their own eminent countrymen'. Iago's duplicity derives from Machiavelli, and for Lewis his prosecution of his 'ruthless mechanical intrigue' makes him prematurely modern: his cynical banter could be spoken by 'any solicitor, stockbroker, politician or man-about-town in England today'. This explains why it is so startling and yet so right that Harry Lime should invoke the Borgias. Because *The Third Man* and *Prince of Foxes* were made within a few months of each other, the aristocratic politician and the trader in poisonous medicines look interchangeable, differentiated only by their costumes. Instead of Harry's muffling coat and hat, Cesare wears a rakish bonnet when out riding, and sports encrustations of medallions and jewels on his portly chest when dressed for dinner in a besieged city; he has also grown a scruffy goatee, apt for a satyr. Otherwise they are the same man.

Lewis guessed that 'the contemporary European must find it easier to get an imaginative foothold in Renaissance Italy than his father or grandfather would', because he too was living through a transitional time – not a change from 'the values of the feudal commune to the more generous and elastic conditions of the modern state', but the reverse of that development, sliding back from bourgeois individuality to the mass society mobilised by fascism. Welles showed this happening in *Caesar* or *The Fall of the City*. The transition between two ages described by Lewis takes place, with dizzy rapidity, in *Othello*. The play, he argues, is a battle between lion and fox: Othello with his exalted faith is corrupted by the bantering rationalist Iago, and the spectacle reveals Shakespeare – who topples so many medieval kings in his history plays – to be a 'pious and discreet executioner of feudal personages'. Because the wrenching social change happens both in the Renaissance and in the twentieth century, Lewis proposes up-to-date analogies for the orotund general and his prosaic non-commissioned officer. His example of a modern Iago is Charlie Chaplin. Tripping up 'the dignified boss', the cheeky tramp re-enacts the ancient battle between authority and anarchy, which nowadays, as in Blitzstein's Steeltown, is a stand-off between capital and labour. Lewis calls Iago 'the *small* destroyer' or 'the ideal *little man*', while Othello, a naval commander defending the maritime empire of

ORSON WELLES

Venice, is 'the ideal human galleon, twenty storeys high, with his head in the clouds, that the little can vanquish'.

This verbal metaphor turns into a visual image at the start of Welles's film. To accompany his spoken recitation of the credits, he assembles a rapid montage of galleons, anchored – or so he makes it seem – just off the Piazza San Marco. When he arrives at his own name in the cast list, mock-modestly placed after those of MacLíammóir and Suzanne Cloutier, the image he chooses directly translates Lewis's characterisation of Othello: the shadow of a galleon, its denuded forest of masts imprinted on the wall of the Doge's Palace, seen from a low angle as it rears into a cloudy nocturnal sky. Unable to afford the real thing, like the ship on which Orsini languidly cruises past Santa Maria della Salute in *Prince of Foxes*, Welles had to make do with models. But his use of miniatures serves to illustrate how illusory the difference between greatness and littleness actually is. Though the galleons of balsa wood pretend to be twenty storeys high, their masts tremble like twigs and their rope ladders shudder insecurely.

By filming the first scenes on location in Venice, Welles associated the hero's collapse with the city's decline during the Renaissance. Tynan – puzzled by the incidental shots of overshadowed canals and receding colonnades, with cats prowling across tiled roofs to hunt flustered pigeons – said that Welles had adapted Ruskin's *The Stones of Venice* rather than Shakespeare's tragedy. The wisecrack had a certain inadvertent accuracy. Ruskin's study described Venice as it slid into decadence, its artists surrendering their Christian souls as they concentrated on the decorative 'pursuit of pleasure'. He particularly loathed the leering gargoyles added to Venetian churches, which he called 'the perpetuation in stone of the ribaldries of drunkenness'. Cassio's disgrace presaged the fall of the city. Venice, in Ruskin's estimation, was ruined by hubris. The 'pride in knowledge' which he considered to be the flaw of the Renaissance mind was here abetted by 'Pride of State'. Showing Othello among the city's vainglorious, insecurely founded monuments, Welles made him the personification of that civic arrogance. Meanwhile, Iago skulks behind ornate columns: 'the perfect Renaissance,' according to Ruskin, was 'subtle in its vice'. 'All is to be Carpaccio', Welles decreed when designing the film. Iago's costume was modelled on the gondoliers in Carpaccio's paintings, and Roderigo's yapping terrier comes from the same source. But Carpaccio depicted a Venice becalmed in idleness, with courtesans occupying the time between clients by teasing an equally ennui-ridden dog.

248

Though Venice during the Renaissance was a strongbox of commodities, its vaults glutted with gold, jewels, cloth and spices from the East, Welles like Ruskin saw only the bereft aftermath of this commercial power, and mournfully emphasised what Henry James in 1870 called its 'sad elegance of ruin'. Hence the inverted reflection of the campanile during the credits: a defining image of collapse and dissolution. In his edition of *The Merchant of Venice*, Welles enviously described Henry Irving's 'immortal production' of the play in 1879, in which Jessica, eloping with Lorenzo, 'stepped into a gondola and glided away down the canal!' Othello and Desdemona do the same at the beginning of his film: he calls for her at the Ca'd'Oro, marries her in an empty church, then spirits her off on the water. But the atmosphere here is not festive. This moonlit, black and white Venice is deprived of its glittering sun and polychrome decoration. The Ca'd'Oro is grey not gilded, and the rest of the city looks dead, deserted, abandoned to those cats and the pigeons they prey on. Distant figures squabble in an empty square, oddly silent: two women drag a drunken man away from a well, while a dog frisks around them. Another couple grapple far off beneath an arch beside a narrow canal. Are they revenants, like Welles, who in his documentary *Filming 'Othello'* morosely revisits the city, travelling in a sluggish, overburdened gondola?

Beneath the city's thin pavements Henry James heard a 'steady, liquid lapse'; Welles makes that erosive lapping of water visible. The flashback from the funeral procession to the elopement happens underwater, as a reflection of the upside-down fortress in Cyprus blurs, ripples and is replaced by those reflected Venetian galleons. Speaking the credits, Welles announces that 'This is a motion picture' and adds, after a significant pause, 'based on a play by William Shakespeare.' The pause purposefully sunders play and film: the play is landed, solid, housed within the wooden O of Shakespeare's theatre, but the film takes place in and on water, and the impermanence of its images suggests a stream of fluid, elapsing consciousness. Even in the theatre, Welles's stages were thin membranes stretched over turbulence. A geyser was meant to erupt through the floorboards in *Around the World*, and in *Moby Dick – Rehearsed* the planks covered a pitching ocean. In the first scenes of his *Othello*, the text, like Venice itself, deliquesces. When Iago, spying on the departure of the newlyweds, first shows his face, it is immediately erased by a dissolve to water; Roderigo meanwhile complains about losing Desdemona, and threatens to drown himself. Burckhardt emphasised the craving for glory that impelled Renaissance artists: Dante 'strove for the poet's garland with all the power of his soul' and was rewarded with 'a fame which fell little short of deification', being serenaded by trumpeters and incense burners every Christmas Day. In *Othello*, Welles – siding with the sceptical fox not the self-immortalising lion – undermines this conceit. Film, in his perusal of those dank, crumbling canals, is written on water.

McGafferty, the tycoon played by Welles in MacLeish's *Panic*, has the arrogance of a latter-day lion. He disdains humanitarianism, which he calls a hatred of manhood, and rants about the Nietzschean supermen who, as Wyndham Lewis argued, were the descendants of Shakespeare's lions. In his invective against the mob he has pauperised, he voices the young Welles's conceit:

> Christ it's always one man makes a world: –
> One man called Magellan: called Lenin:
> Called Cromwell: Rothschild: Leonardo.

Welles outgrew this faith in the great man as a saviour, or perhaps was forced to renounce it. He continued to admire and to emulate Leonardo, though he did not overlook his involvement in the venal despotism of his time. Harry Lime's link between Leonardo and the Borgias is not casual: in 1502 he served as chief engineer in Cesare Borgia's army, inventing automata for the prosecution of war, and took part in a campaign for which Machiavelli was also enlisted. In Shellabarger's novel, the dilettante painter Orsini – Orson's fancied namesake – enjoys the praise and patronage of Leonardo. But Orsini, called a 'lord-of-all-trades', does not concentrate on his art, and therefore repeats his mentor's error. For Welles, Leonardo came to represent the tragedy of the Renaissance man – a polymath and a potential god, ruined by his own dissatisfied inventiveness. He made the analogy with his own predicament indirectly, using his father as a scapegoat. He attributed to Richard Welles one of Leonardo's most sublimely impractical projects, a design for a flying machine. His father, he told Tynan, 'tried very hard to invent the airplane'. Convinced that the Wright brothers were mistaken, he envisaged instead 'a steam-driven car with a kind of glider attached to it'. Icarus proved not to be airworthy.

Leonardo called the artist 'lord of all types of people and all things', mentally and manually capable of revising nature. Painters were not restricted to observing reality or mimicking it, but could create beauty or monstrosity as they pleased and 'be lord or god thereof'. This sounds like a manifesto for Welles's use of the camera, which – as Leonardo said of painting – brought 'subtle speculation to bear on the nature of all forms'. Leonardo has often been credited with a prematurely cinematic eye, which enabled him, as if isolating single frames in a strip of celluloid, to analyse the manouevres of a bird's wing as it flew. Technique in Welles was always, in Leonardo's sense of the word, philosophical or investigative. The distorting perspectives of *Citizen Kane* realign objects to suggest relationships of causality and complicity between them, as when Susan's bedroom is seen through the glass she has used in her suicide attempt. The dissolves to fog in *Macbeth* and to water in *Othello* probe the relationship between the verbal and the visual, and question whether the process of thinking can be imagined and therefore photographed. The sustained shots in *Touch of Evil* – during the car's trip to the border, or in the apartment of Sanchez during his interrogation – follow our forensic efforts to sort through the randomness and distraction of visual data. The montage in *F for Fake* demonstrates with wicked cunning the falsity of the narratives we construct in order to discover (or invent) meaning.

The analytical method is dangerous: Welles's visual science, like magic, teaches us to mistrust appearances. His art seeks to interrogate and to disassemble itself. Perhaps he found a warning about this procedure in an essay on Leonardo by Jacob Bronowski, which he enthusiastically recommended to friends. Bronowski saw Leonardo as a Faustian character, who in reconceiving the world menaced our confidence in it and forfeited his own mental composure. He was, in Bronowski's judgement, more than 'an original man, in the sense that he had two or three profound and new ideas'; by reconsidering everything on principle, he became 'a perverse man'. The same could be said of Welles. In fact, he obliquely said it about himself in one of Leland's comments on Kane. Leland pays tribute, strangely, to Kane's 'generous mind', then qualifies the compliment: 'I don't suppose anybody ever had so many opinions . . . But he didn't believe in anything except Charlie Kane. He never had a conviction except Charlie Kane.' Can opinions, however abundant, replace belief? Burckhardt, summing up the Renaissance, lamented a 'general spirit of doubt' that influenced the 'development of the modern spirit'.

Leonardo's self-analysis disclosed to him his own instability. Man, like nature, was composed of four contentious elements – earth, air, fire and water – which made the human body an analogue for the world: our bones, he argued, are the rocks, and the lake of our blood corresponds to the seas and oceans. Renaissance man, seeing himself as a merely physical phenomenon, could not resist tinkering with those elemental constituents. John Donne in one of his sonnets tried to free his 'angelic spright' from his baser carnal nature, and Hamlet prays for the solid flesh to 'melt, / Thaw and resolve itself into a dew'. Welles's imagery shows the human compound breaking down into an elemental flux. His ice sculptures confer a temporary immortality on the human form. But we cannot live at degree zero, and our vital heat is fatal to us: hence the steam bath in *Othello*, with sweaty, sagging bodies laid out on massage tables. After Roderigo is stabbed, a final cascade of escaping water is like a gusher of colourless, transparent blood. Quinlan in *Touch of Evil* staggers into a stream of effluent. 'The sewer', as Welles declared in his narration for *Les misérables*, 'is the conscience of the city'; Valjean, escaping from the barricades, hides in the cloaca like Harry Lime, with a background of sound effects supplied by overworking the flushes in the radio studio's toilets. But the attack on solidity means a return to chaos, the state in which everything is unfixed and unmanageable, like the cavorting mobs at the Rio carnival. Leonardo's fascination with the restless energies of nature brought him to the same admission of defeat: his sketches of a deluge are, in Kenneth Clark's phrase, 'doodles of disillusion'. Lear invites a similar maelstrom to drown the steeples of the churches, and he emerges from the downpour – in Welles's performance for Peter Brook, shown on American television in 1953 – draped in seaweed and swathed in fishing nets, with a starfish gripped in his hand for a sceptre, as if an annihilating wave had swept over him and washed him up on the beach at Dover.

Such a world view could not but be demoralising. The proud Renaissance mind almost immediately reached the limits of its powers and, like the melancholy Hamlet, succumbed to exhaustion. Ideas continued to pullulate, but why bother executing them? Leonardo finished only about a dozen paintings, and Welles completed the same meagre number of films. Both were conceptual artists, for whom accomplishment mattered less than the mental calculation that initially forms an image or conjecturally unravels a possible narrative. Hallie Flagan remembered the disappointment of Welles's Faustus when he conjured up Helen of Troy: 'anticipation had been better than realization'. Interviewed by *Cahiers* in 1959, Welles described Leonardo as 'a scientist who painted and not a painter who might have been a scientist', and therefore cited him as a predecessor. 'I don't enunciate laws but am an experimenter,' he said. 'We who make a profession of experiment have inherited a long tradition. Some of us have been among the greatest artists, but we've never made the muses our mistresses.' That proviso recalls Welles's problems with the domineering white goddess. Leonardo's homosexuality protected him from her; Welles habitually married his muses or consorted with them extramaritally, and – except for his last, enriching relationship with Oja Kodar – he always came to regret it and to repudiate them. He therefore identified his creativity with his sexual susceptibility, and helplessly, unconvincingly contrasted these aesthetic sirens with the solitary masculine practice of science.

He went on to declare 'I'm not ecstatic about art. I *am* ecstatic about the human function . . . It's the act that interests me, not the result.' The interviewers translated his remarks into French, making him sound pompous and unidiomatic: instead of ecstasy and the human function, he probably talked about his delight in inventiveness, the most playful and fantastical of human skills. Even so, there was a brave falsity to his assertion, which made the best of the discouragement he had suffered. 'I write and I paint,' he said. 'I throw away everything I do.' Whether or not this was true, he intended it as an exemplary gesture, like the aristocratic disdain for one's own trifling productions recommended in Castiglione's Renaissance conduct-book *The Courtier*. But this only partly masked his frustration. For Leonardo, the painter could easily summon up beauties or monstrosities with his pen or brush; Welles complained that the cinema was an absurdly expensive paintbox, said that he needed 'another, cheaper means of expression', and looked covetously at the tape recorder of the journalist he was addressing. Talk is a specifically human function and, since all it requires is air, it costs nothing.

Leonardo left few paintings, but made innumerable sketches. Welles too has a long list of phantom credits. Some films were made but have been lost: for instance *Too Much Johnson*, with Joseph Cotten farcically careening across the rooftops of New York, meant for use in a stage production in 1938. Others were never made, like *Cyrano de Bergerac*, planned in 1947, which would have allowed Welles to atone at last for his puny nose, or Pirandello's *Henry IV*, another self-referring account of monarchical delusion. One at least was made but remains unseen: *The Other Side of the Wind*, financed by an Iranian entrepreneur, was impounded by the Ayatollahs after the revolution, and is locked in a bank vault while lawyers lucratively dispute its ownership. Despite the analogy with Leonardo, completion does matter more than conception: it would be better if we could see these notional films.

In *Mr Arkadin*, the Renaissance man acknowledged the superfluity of his own unstoppable thinking. The occasion is van Stratten's visit to Copenhagen, where he interviews the top-hatted professorial proprietor of a flea circus. The role is played by Mischa Auer, but the character's voice belongs to Welles. As always when dubbing a part, he bestowed one of his available identities on whoever he was pretending to be. The professor is an enormous, unblinking eye: a magnifying glass gives him the omniscience Welles intended to claim for himself in his prologue to *Heart of Darkness*, where his script – explaining the subjective narration – described a series of shots identifying Marlow with the camera and diagrammatically equating eye and I. Ideas for Welles were not unlike the 'educated fleas' (as the professor calls them) that perform in the circus. He bred and nourished them: 'Feeding time' says the professor, positioning the fleas on his forearm with a pair of pincers and smiling paternalistically as they suck his blood. Welles's ideas made him itch, and would not let him rest. Their antics, of course, were spectacular, but what did their virtuosity prove, and what remained after the performance? The insects in *Mr Arkadin* play football, fixing themselves to puffy particles which they then pop. The game's conclusion is a row of zeroes, and at each small explosion, the voice of Welles rejoices: 'Allez, allez, poop!'

Demurring when admirers called him a Renaissance man, Welles produced another identity to replace it. He was, he decided, a baroque man. He aligned his work, aptly enough, with the visual culture that emerged when the classical stability of the Renaissance foundered, unleashing an energy that wilfully transmogrified matter, whirled outwards in centrifugal motion, and delighted in disequilibrium. The German composer Ernst Krenek was astonished to discover a style he called 'amerikanisches neu-Barock' when he saw Busby Berkeley's *42nd Street* in 1934. The spectacle, he thought, was galactic: the dance director had choreographed the music of the spheres, performed by tap-dancing angels. During the operatic première in *Citizen Kane*, the camera lifts skywards. It deserts the muddle and mayhem onstage, where headdresses topple sideways and two-dimensional palaces flutter in a draught, and rises into what baroque artists thought of as the heavens. Here, in the scenery store, entire cities hang suspended, as if floating on clouds: a huddle of pitched

Gothic roofs, Venice with its humped bridges, classical columns with no ground to plant themselves on and nothing to hold up. The camera rises higher, following the taut cables which lead up towards the cosmic engineer who controls the show. Two stagehands balance on a beam at the top of the sky. As Susan's mewling drifts up from below like incense, one of them silently comments on her singing by holding his nose. The firmament, as Krenek said of the baroque, is empty, or full only of shadows and echoes. God, in the person of that cynical stagehand, is at best a scene-shifter, who lowers a provisional, flimsy semblance of a world for us to live in.

Welles's French admirers began to call him baroque during the 1950s. They were well aware that the term had first been used pejoratively, as a synonym for mannerism and distortion: baroque meant the writhing bodies of El Greco, or the equally agitated architectural columns – no longer interested in rootedness and support – of Bernini. Domarchi credited Welles with the mind of a Renaissance man, but said that his tormented treatment of space allied him with baroque artists like Titian, Rubens, El Greco and Bernini. Henri Agel found the same morphological anguish in his work, a symptom of the baroque at its most strung-out and delirious. Maurice Bessy described the films as baroque hallucinations, visions of a world falling apart, and Jean Douchet called their style 'visuellement désespéré'. In French interviews Welles took to calling himself 'un cinéaste baroque', though he liked to pretend that his style was nothing more than contrariness. 'If there were other extremely baroque artists,' he said in 1958, 'I'd be the most classical film-maker you've ever seen.' The truth is that the baroque was Welles's instinct, not his choice; it matched both his psychological quirks and his intellectual temper.

Renaissance painters used the new science of perspective to clarify and articulate space. The baroque artists who followed them preferred optical illusions. Two scenes, early and late, reveal Welles's understanding of the baroque and its playful baffling of certainty. In *Citizen Kane*, the newsreel with its booming, authoritarian narrative is suddenly switched off. The beam of light slicing through the smoky air of the screening room, seen from the side, no longer organises itself into legible images. The motor of the projector, dying, groans more noisily than the moribund Kane. In the darkness, an unsynchronised muddle of voices starts to argue. The indistinct forms of their owners are lit from behind; their thrashing arms agitate the shadows in a demonstration of painterly chiaroscuro. What they say makes us mistrust everything we have so far

been told about Kane, and alerts us not to believe anything we subsequently hear or see. The confusion abruptly ends with a thunderclap and
a flash of lightning, as blinding as the glare from the projector before it
was killed. We are now, it appears, buffeted by bad weather somewhere
above Atlantic City. In *The Other Side of the Wind* Welles recreated this
scene as the Wellesian film director played by John Huston, with Bogdanovich and other courtiers at his elbow, makes his way to a screening
through a crush of prattling journalists and photographers letting off
flashbulbs. Multiple news cameras record the jostling from different
angles; microphones compete to catch the gabbled questions and the
director's evasive answers. Both scenes are about 'capriciousness and the
return to chaos' – and these, for the art historian Heinrich Wölfflin, were
the imperatives of the baroque.

Wölfflin, Burckhardt's successor as a professor at Basel, published his
study *Renaissance and Baroque* in 1888; it set out to chronicle 'the disintegration of the Renaissance', and the freakish architectural forms it
analysed – walls that surge and billow, twisted columns, clumps of stone
that look raw and spongy – have their equivalents in Welles's films,
thanks to his steep, looming camera angles, his fondness for dizzy,
whirligig movement, and his jittery cutting. With its ponderous involu-
tions and its indistinct recesses, the staircase in the Amberson house
impedes communication rather than easing it: Fanny and George exchange
angry whispers from different landings, each incarcerated in a separate
darkness. Arkadin threatens van Stratten during Mass in a baroque
church in Munich. Placed at floor level, the camera gives him an
unearned, unsteady grandeur. It aligns his body with that of a contorted,
elongated statue, tips a shell-shaped font sideways so that it seems ready
to spill an undeserved absolution over him, and sets the dome above his
head as if his ego could swell to fill up its emptiness. Wölfflin suggested
that 'all the most prominent baroque artists suffered from headaches', perhaps caused by ceilings so loaded with decoration that they threatened to
tumble out of the air. Welles induces a similar malaise: a motion sickness
that derives from his animation of spaces where we expect to feel
anchored, secure. During a quarrel on the yacht, Arkadin and Mily
stagger around the seesawing cabin as the boat tosses in a rough sea. In
Touch of Evil, Vargas and Schwartz speed in a car through the narrow
streets of the town, its flimsy ramparts lurching and inclining above them.

Wölfflin traced the change from Renaissance to baroque in small geometrical mutations: the square gives way to the oblong, the circle to the

oval. A circle is 'static and unchangeable, . . . self-contained and complete', which is why Leonardo placed his Vitruvian man inside one. But the oval lacks this poised, perfect 'inner necessity', and its instability appealed to baroque architects, who used it for the 'ground plans of halls, courtyards and church interiors'. Welles in his script for *The Trial* invented some dialogue that draws attention to this baroque oddity. The men who come to arrest Joseph K remove the rug in his room and peer at a steel plate beneath it. A dentist's chair used to be bolted to this; the agents first describe it as circular, then decide that it is 'ovular'. K twice tetchily points out that there is no such word. He objects because the misunderstanding is sexually suggestive, connecting the oval with ovulation.

At the end of the film, K accuses the Advocate of 'a conspiracy to persuade us that the whole world is crazy, formless, meaningless, absurd'. Anthony Perkins addresses the charge to Welles, who does not deny it: the baroque was all about amorphousness. This is why Welles looks at home in the baroque Vienna of *The Third Man*. The architecture – bent under the onus of ornament, like the muscular caryatids that hold up the portico of the palace where Harry Lime lived, and further destabilised by bombs – suits his combination of gigantism and vulnerability. Harry emerges from and merges into an inchoate rubble. On his way to meet Holly Martins in the café, he steps down from the pediment of a ruined building like a suddenly animated statue. His first appearance, smirking in a shallow, darkened doorway as the cat nuzzles his leg, illustrates the spatial untrustworthiness of the baroque. Wölfflin, moralising architecture like Ruskin, admired the 'will and vitality' of Renaissance columns, which stand alone and shoulder burdens. Baroque piers, however, always have 'one foot in the wall' and melt into the mass behind them – which is exactly what Harry seems to do, slipping through a door that can lead nowhere because the entrance has been bricked up. The bulk of the baroque is no guarantee of solidity, and when Holly goes to the Josefstadt Theatre to find Anna, the city of oppressive masonry, downcast ceilings and tilted staircases loses all attachment to the ground and turns ethereally rococo: the play he sees is set in a Watteauesque pleasure garden, and the white-wigged actresses agitate their fans and circulate as weightlessly as moths.

Such rococo flitting and fluttering was not for Welles. He agreed with Richard Marienstras that *Macbeth* was 'a baroque film', but added 'That doesn't mean it's at all rococo.' Ultimately, as Wölfflin argued, the baroque succumbed to its own unwieldiness, which had to be alleviated by the lightness of the rococo. Wölfflin contrasted the slender, taut, ideally proportioned forms of the Renaissance with the flabby, supple, awkwardly outsize masses of the baroque. Inertia had taken over: those colossi 'lie, heavy and immobile, completely without tension'. Once Welles had grown a baroque body, which he increasingly wrapped in capes or kaftans or unstructured suits like the overalls worn by babies, he had no choice but to succumb to this lumpish repose. Stumbling into the rivulet at the end of *Touch of Evil*, he enthrones himself for a moment in a velvet armchair discarded among the avalanche of refuse on the bank. In *The Trial*, he conducts his legal business in bed, thrashing angrily beneath the blankets like a leviathan churning up the ocean. Hal and Poins find Falstaff snoring in bed at the start of *Chimes at Midnight*.

Hamlet tries to go on believing in the divinity of Renaissance man, but cannot ignore the evidence of decay: his own slothfulness, the rotting of the unregenerate body. Brooding over this imperfection and trying to reconcile himself to it by making jokes, he has begun to mutate – as Welles claimed – into Falstaff, and the change from one character to the other corresponds to the transition from Renaissance to baroque. In a lecture first given in 1934, the art historian Erwin Panofsky defined baroque as a later, more quizzical stage in the self-consciousness of the Renaissance. Vitruvian man is a paragon, but none of us look like that with our clothes off, and neither could we maintain his geometrical posture for long. As the circle distends into the oval, art comes to register the odd, deviant nature of phenomena and of human faces. That awareness is already evident, for Panofsky, in Leonardo's sketches of grotesque heads, warty and deformed but a source of wonderment not disgust – and the same sense of man's idiosyncrasy and his malleability appears in Welles's marginal drawings for *Everybody's Shakespeare*, as well as in his revisions of his own body. Panofsky saw 'the sense of humour, as it appears in Shakespeare and Cervantes' as proof of this new spirit, which delighted in physical and moral irregularity. Welles might have been acting on this idea when he argued that any approach to Shakespeare's plays must be 'visually baroque', even though they were 'works of the Renaissance'. But style is always dictated by content: the plays had to look that way because for Welles they were psychologically baroque, struggling to balance tragedy and comedy, angel and ape. Is Othello a perplexed idealist or a pitiful cuckold? How can Falstaff be so benign and sagacious, considering that he is also, as

Panofsky points out, 'a liar and a coward'? Such internicine quarrels were the subject of baroque art.

If, as Harry Lime calculates, the Renaissance lasted only thirty years, then its span was equivalent to youth, adolescence and early manhood, the seasons of Welles's prodigious victories. After that, in the second half of his life, came the long dilation or descent into the baroque, when the self-sufficient confidence of Renaissance man became abstruse mannerism. In 1524, Parmigianino painted himself in a convex mirror, which – like a Wellesian camera angle – magnified his hand in close-up but banished his face to a far corner of the background. Sickening reversals and frustrating deferments made Welles, in the same way, question who he was. Baroque figures, like the plump nymphs of Rubens, at last find a refuge from such self-doubt in a comforting plenum of flesh. During his last decades (or ages), Welles's only defence seemed to lie in cultivating the body's soft, bulbous armour of fat.

Welles cuckolded by the bull in *Touch of Evil*.

CHAPTER 12

Sacred Beast

Early in the 1950s, Welles took to announcing that his current projects included a film about bullfighting, to be entitled *The Sacred Beasts*. He had been a devotee of the bullfight ever since his earliest European wanderings. He claimed that in 1932, after his first theatrical season in Dublin, he travelled to Seville, bought a herd of bulls, and indulged himself by skirmishing with them. In another version of the story, he said he paid a fee as a novice and was allowed to appear in the ring at 'several corridas', billed on the posters as The American. This vicarious profession stayed on his wish list – an unrealised life, like an unmade film – and he updated it as he grew older. At first the film he planned was about an ageing aficionado who follows a torero around Spain, pursuing his unattainable younger self. When he returned to California in the 1970s, he applied the title to a new variant of the same wistful tale. Now the film was to be about a superannuated director trying to revive his Hollywood career.

Welles admired Hemingway's story 'The Undefeated', in which a decrepit torero begs for work from a booking agent who says with a shrug 'I thought they'd killed you.' He settles for an insultingly reduced fee, goes out to face one more bull, and is gored. Bullfighting in Welles's last version of *The Sacred Beasts* dwindled to a metaphor, referring to his doughty refusal to accept professional defeat. In *The Lion and the Fox*, Wyndham Lewis likened Shakespeare's failed feudal monarchs to 'degenerate bullfighters'. Welles appreciated the justice of the analogy, but he adapted and corrected it in the preface he wrote for Tynan's *He That Plays the King*. He considered Tynan to be 'shaky on the matter of brave bulls'. Tynan mistakenly saw the bullfighter as the tragic hero, whereas the sacred beast is of course the bull. The 'tragic truth' of the bullfight, as Welles put it in admonishing him, derives from the animal's fight against death; Tynan's error, in his enthusiasm for heroic actors like Welles himself, was to pay attention instead to the 'high glamour' of the bullfighter, who makes the duel look more dangerous than it actually is. Having begun (or so he said) as a bullfighter, Welles ended as the bull. In his own estimation, he had become the sacred beast, the 'perfect

261

cathedral' – as he called one of the muscular calves he supposedly fought in Seville – toppled on the sand.

The beast is sacred because it has been sacrificed. Its death appeases a resentful god, and its blood irrigates the earth. Welles borrowed his catchy, paradoxical title from Cocteau, who called the new glossy, disreputable breed of celebrities – which included Welles himself – 'monstres sacrés'. The film stars, financiers and playboy princes who made up this international pantheon were monstrous because they were outsized, extravagant, uninhibited. Societies with no religion set them up to be worshipped, but decreed that their immortality would be short lived; we reserve the right to amuse ourselves by delighting in their prompt downfall. The notion may have come from Cocteau, but Welles made it his own because the second half of his life demonstrated what it meant. He therefore modulated and re-coined the famous phrase. In his *Cradle Will Rock* screenplay, his first wife proposes a party game called 'The Beastly Bestiary': this substitutes beasts for monsters, and avoids Cocteau's adjective at the cost of a tautology. The game consists of describing people you know 'as mythical beasts', according them – like celebrities – a status at once more and less than human. Virginia first calls Orson an Arab steed and then, with gloomy foresight, 'a one-eyed circus bear dancing in the spring time to show us he's still young'.

Cocteau's monsters, like the Minotaur or the Sphinx, possessed a genuine supernatural strangeness. Welles's beasts were more easily wounded and abused, like the dancing bear or the bull tormented in the arena. He knew from his own experience that the celebrity is a discredited god, a monarch without a kingdom. A character in his *Cradle Will Rock*, remembering *Macbeth*, says 'They call you "The King of Harlem", don't they?' Welles replies 'Two years ago, sweetie. Been a lotta kings since then.' In his synoptic adaptation *Five Kings*, he managed to speed through five successive, disastrous reigns in a single evening. This for Bakhtin was the grim remonstrance of carnival, with its 'mock crowning and decrowning' of a king who, like Rei Momo in Rio, is a lewd impostor: the festivity enforces the temporariness of authority, and of life itself. Spending time in the resorts favoured by sybaritic celebrities, Welles came to feel an affinity with men who were no longer able to play the king: Churchill, voted out of office in 1945, or King Farouk of Egypt, deposed in 1952 by Nasser and his fellow army officers. In the novel based on *Mr Arkadin*, the hero batters paparrazi who try to snap him, and they go off to bother Farouk instead. Exiled in Rome, Farouk devoted himself to feeding and misbehaving, and – like Kane – attempted to promote one of his meagrely talented mistresses as an opera singer. In 1953 he offered to finance a film of *Julius Caesar,* in which Welles intended to present the Shakespearean tragedy as a contemporary newsreel; he withdrew his sponsorship when he found that Mankiewicz and Houseman were making a rival version of the play in Hollywood, so Welles – who intended to play Brutus, with Richard Burton as Antony – lost his chance to assassinate another would-be king.

Wyndham Lewis derided the Shakespearean king as 'a sham god', and linked the acts of regicide in the history plays with the more primitive 'custom of sacrificing the human representative of a god'. Looking back during the 1950s, Welles felt that this was what had happened to him. The god's erstwhile worshippers had lost their faith in him; the king had been killed, or at least disgraced, to gratify his subjects. The collapse of his career reminded him of the bullfight with its ritualised slaughter. He used two of the bad films he appeared in during this decade of uncomfortable adjustments – *Trouble in the Glen* in 1954, *David and Goliath* in 1959 – to ponder his new position. In both, he tried to present his comeuppance as a smiling renunciation. As the South American grandee transplanted to Scotland, he learns the difference between the powers of a lord and the responsibilities of a laird. On the pampas, he looked after what he calls 'my people – for they belonged to me'. (Welles here repeated a line from *Citizen Kane*: Leland accuses Kane the supposed populist of talking about the people 'as if you owned them'.) The highlanders rebel against his feudal bossiness, and he atones by telling them 'I belong to you.' As Saul, he slumps on his throne while the prophet Samuel declares him unfit to reign. 'The Lord hath departed from thee', moans the bearded wiseacre. Saul is destroyed by the instant victory of the Philistines; Welles was tripped up by latter-day members of the same tribe. Reluctant to accept his redundancy, he demands 'Who is that man – who is he? – that shall be king in Israel after me?' Of course he is soon reconciled to his loss of power, and predicts that young David will accomplish great things.

Welles was less generous than Saul when confronted by potential replacements. He accepted Bogdanovich as an acolyte, not as a young rival, an impatient crown prince. He resented his protégé's first successes as a director, and felt (as Bogdanovich surmises) that 'I was in some way playing Prince Hal to his King Henry IV (or Falstaff) . . . It was the role I actually did play to Huston's ageing "king" in . . . *The Other Side of the Wind* – the old director supplanted or, in mythic terms, killed by the younger one.' Welles constructed his later films around this antagonism between a dessicated elder and a sappy challenger: Quinlan against the honeymooning Vargas, Mr Clay against the sailor he hires to make love on his behalf. The same drama had to be acted out in reality, and it caused a breach between Bogdanovich and Welles.

He grudgingly accepted his own relegation, because he knew that kingship was not the only sacred role he could play. He was also a magician, and as such a kind of priest, able to make kings and unmake them – a rare specimen of what Wyndham Lewis called the 'transformed or *shamanized* man', who deployed occult powers no one could take away from him. The shaman was essential to the well being of tribal society, because he presided over the sacrifices that propitiated its gods, prescribed remedies for the ailments of its members, and when the time came, like Mercury, accompanied the souls of mortals to the next world. Welles's fascination with magic convinced him that an actor could perform these sacerdotal functions in the modern world.

In his account of the shaman's professional training, Mircea Eliade describes trials during which the candidate 'is tortured by demons, his body is cut in pieces, he descends to the netherworld or ascends to heaven and is finally resuscitated'. Welles experienced all this when playing Faust, though he preferred the dismemberment suffered by Marlowe's hero to the beatific pardon bestowed on the apostate by Goethe. Having undergone initiation, the shaman can commute between physical and spiritual realms. His 'techniques of ecstasy', as Eliade calls them, allow him 'to leave his body at will'. Welles did so in his radio performances, or in his ventriloquistic dubbing of roles played by other actors in his films. In South American native societies, the shaman is a sorcerer, like the witch doctors with whom Welles consorted in Rio, and can 'change himself into an animal and drink the blood of his enemies'. In North American tribal culture, the shaman professes to 'know future events, expose the perpetrators of thefts', which were the special skills of Nostradamus and The Shadow.

As psychopompos, the shaman is the companion who conducts us on our journey between life and death. In *The Magnificent Ambersons*, Welles the narrator invisibly accompanies George as he walks for the last time through the town that has effaced him. In *The Trial*, more gruffly, he discharges the same duty when playing the Advocate. He waits for K, who has spurned the ministrations of a priest, in a recess of the cathedral, recites to him the predestining fable about the law, then despatches him to his execution. Though he joked to keep scepticism at bay, Welles believed in such immaterial guardians. While making *Chimes at Midnight* in Madrid, he tried to convince Keith Baxter to come to the bullfights with him. Baxter, disapproving, refused, until one night by chance he found El Duende, a bar behind the Plaza Mayor frequented by toreros and flamenco dancers; the atmosphere intoxicated him. 'No-one finds El Duende by accident,' Welles told him. 'You were led there by a spirit-guide.' Baxter then accepted Welles as his spirit-guide, and agreed to be taken to the fights. When he flinched from the bloodshed, Welles – returning to one of the plays that contained the story of his life – asked 'How could there be a production of *Julius Caesar* without Caesar's death?' Baxter retorted that an actor wasn't killed at every performance, which prompted the producer Emiliano Piedra to sigh 'Ah, if only . . .' Welles, as always, knew better. The actor like the shaman undergoes a symbolic death and then, with luck, is instantly resurrected.

Welles and Hemingway had rival claims to the fiesta. For Hemingway, bull-fighting became a credential of the virility he thought Welles lacked. Yet Welles, according to the legend, had stood his ground against a rampaging steer in the ring. Hemingway could not forgive his oneupmanship.

Hemingway travelled to Spain after serving as an ambulance driver with the Italian infantry, because 'the only place where you could see life and death, *i.e.* violent death now that the wars were over, was in the bullring and I wanted . . . to study it'. That outfacing of violent death developed into a stoical creed. Lincoln Kirstein, reviewing *Death in the Afternoon* in 1933, suggested that Hemingway could not forgive himself for having survived the war. Still in a state of shock, he saw the capacity to kill or be killed as the source of vitality, the ground of existence. He failed to understand, Kirstein argued, that in modern society 'physical courage is scarcely a necessity', except for sportsmen, soldiers and steeplejacks. Praising the matador as an artist, Hemingway rapturously declared that 'A great killer must love to kill' and 'The truly great killer must have a sense of honour and a sense of glory.' Are these really qualities we should admire? Welles's view of the bullfight was more humane: he deplored what he called 'bad kills'. Hemingway explained his tolerance of carnage in the bullring by remembering his war work, prising scraps of dead men off barbed-wire fences. His description is aesthetic because anaesthetic: he sees abstractly, without feeling, amazed that 'the human body should be blown into pieces which exploded along no anatomical lines, but rather divided as capriciously as the fragmentation in the burst of a high explosive shell'. There is a rebuke to this view of war in *Chimes at Midnight*, where the battle of Shrewsbury, from which Falstaff sensibly flees, is an exercise in editorially assembling scraps of film like Hemingway gathering up those bloody bits and pieces – but Welles never forgets that the broken limbs, faces slashed by axes and dented heads once belonged to live human beings. Hemingway speaks of 'killing cleanly and in a way which gives you aesthetic pleasure and pride'. *Chimes at Midnight* demonstrates that there is no such thing as a clean, artful kill. The battle begins with a parade of mounted knights, seen in silhouette against the sky. It soon degenerates into a brawl of foot soldiers who churn the ground into mud and are buried in a quagmire.

After the next war, new converts relied on the bullfight, as Hemingway had done, to articulate the abiding violence of the world. It served this purpose even for those who had never been near a ring. The trumpeter Miles Davis (who said that his phrasing was influenced by the vocal inflections of Welles, whom he praised as a 'motherfucker') kept a bullfighting poster on his wall when he recorded *Sketches of Spain* in 1959. For Davis, playing the trumpet was like wielding a sword, and required a risky existential bravado. He was delighted when told that a retired matador in Spain had heard his album and responded to it by hobbling out into the ring to finish off one more bull. In the mid-1950s at a fight in Pamplona, Tynan met Ratna Mohini, a Balinese dancer married to the photographer Henri Cartier-Bresson. Though a Muslim, she was a devout student of Hindu culture, aware that the bull was literally a sacred beast. After the sacreligious kill she said to Tynan 'This is your revenge. Western Europe revenging itself on the East. Very well. Man kills bull – so Shiva creates the atom bomb.' Tynan thought there was no point in trying to explain the spectacle to her. Welles might have accorded her denunciation more respect, since it invoked an oriental version of the white goddess.

Welles worried about the 'moral defence' of the fiesta, and thought that the spectacle was obscene if 'playing the bull' became 'more important than his death'. He had a limited respect for fancy footwork and the twirling of coloured capes, just as he had doubts about his own showy artistry. He disdained the matador's 'labours with flannel and silk' as 'ornamentally purposeless', and warned that 'what can be done with cloth' – as in the obfuscating flourishes of his own magic act – 'can only be justified by what must be done with steel'. At dinner with James A.

Michener, he criticised the vaudevillian trickery of 'fancy passes', and ridiculed a bullfighter who used to bite the tip of the enraged animal's horn. The matador's function, Welles knew, is 'inexcusable without art'; in its absence, he is merely a butcher. Welles could suggest such brutality, even though it repelled him. In Fred Zinnemann's film of *A Man for All Seasons*, he makes it clear that Wolsey is a butcher's son: he looks like a side of bleeding meat, repackaged in cardinal colours, and he even used drops to produce irritable bloodshot sunsets in his eyes. Nevertheless, when artistry results in the shedding of real blood, we are forced to question the value of art and its sneaky falsity. Actors mime death and, like matadors, flirt with danger. Such exhibitions of bravura insult the suffering bull, which does not take a curtain call.

The matador, Welles told Michener, 'must allow the inherent quality of the bull to manifest itself'. His performances as Othello trained him to sympathise with the creature being killed, not the killer. Wyndham Lewis said that Othello was 'of the race of Christs, or of the race of "bulls"' – as resigned to sacrifice as a god, as helpless as a beast. Iago plays the skulking matador who stands in for 'Everyman, the Judas of the world.' The bullfighting metaphor recurred when Tynan reviewed Welles's London *Othello* in 1951. He thought Welles slothful, and also disliked the puny bantam-weight Iago of Peter Finch; the hero, he said, must be 'a noble bull, repeatedly charging the handkerchief' dangled before him by a nimble matador.

In this view of the tragedy, where is Desdemona? Although Wyndham Lewis and Tynan omit her, Welles wrote her into the fight when describing a confrontation between Arkadin, his daughter and van Stratten. In the novel as in the film, Arkadin surprises his daughter and her lover in her bedroom. He defames van Stratten, who retaliates by hinting that he knows the soiled origins of Arkadin's fortune. The novel supplements the film's dialogue by employing the metaphor of the bullfight, which is now a triangular combat. Van Stratten likens himself to a matador, with Arkadin as the snorting aggressor; Raina is cast as the woman to whom the bullfighter has dedicated the kill. Yet her allegiance is divided between the man and the bull, and she is impartially ready 'to keep the score in this ferocious fight to the death'. Van Stratten is not sure whether she will inspire him or distract him. He regrets his audacity in giving away too much of his secret information about her father, because in Spain he has seen matadors 'lose all consciousness of danger . . . when a woman looked at them'. Overeager to impress, they risk foolhardy feints and end impaled on the beast's horns. The game could also, as he knows, go the other way: if his daring exhausts the bull, it might allow itself to be 'mastered, conquered completely'. This is what happens. Arkadin miscalculates and decides to dispose of van Stratten by treating him as a common blackmailer, which provokes Raina to look at her father reproachfully. She has withdrawn her affection, and will countenance the kill.

Cast as the blundering, victimised bull, Welles could not envisage himself as an Iago. In the introductory letter he wrote for Tynan's book, he refused to play the deft picador and merely remarked 'You have . . . some inflated enthusiasms which beg for pricking. I'm not the man for that job.' When MacLíammóir's journal about the making of the *Othello* film was published in 1952, Welles wrote a gamely self-sacrificing preface in which he described MacLíammóir as Iago the bullfighter who 'doesn't slash or slaughter, or even prick' but turns out to be a 'fatal . . . swordsman', wounding with witticisms. This prompted MacLíammóir to go on characterising Welles as the bull, irate but nimbly outmanoeuvred. In his next volume of autobiography, published in 1961, he remembered Welles's fury when MacLíammóir initially refused to sign on for *Time Runs* in Paris: it was like eyeballing a 'dangerous dark-brown Bull', without the benefit of an intervening fence. When Welles was set upon by female autograph-hunters who mistook him for Harry Lime, MacLíammóir saw him give them 'the famous Welles Glare', like the reproachful gaze of 'a dying bull'. Meeting Welles in 1958, Françoise Sagan asked herself what had happened to 'the young black raging bull who raised terror in the rings of America'. She got her answer when she saw him unmanned by Dietrich in *Touch of Evil*. When Tanya tells Quinlan he is a mess, Welles, Sagan said, 'has the look of a wounded bull before the kill'. The analogy is the closer because Tanya's parlour is decorated with souvenirs of the corrida: the picks that weaken the bull's resistance, even the head of a slaughtered beast. The spears point at Quinlan, and a set of horns hover above him. Perhaps, unlike Othello, he deserves this mark of shame. Was he cuckolded by the 'half-breed' who murdered his wife?

Many commentators on the bullfight have noticed that it mimes sex, as the sword makes its conquering thrust. It complicates matters when you remember that both partners are male. Eisenstein accepted the implicit homosexuality of the contest, and when filming a bullfight for his Mexican film in Merida in 1931 he sketched a sweating matador who sodomises his bull, and also had himself photographed in the ring, protecting his rear end from the jabs of a capering picador. In Quinlan's encounters with Tanya, the bullfighter with the killing look and the dismissive turn of phrase is a woman. The bull remains, as Welles said, 'the supreme representative on earth of the male principle', and as such he can only be vanquished – like Graves's poet with his tormenting muse – by a female.

Welles's myths had a way of coming true. In 1945 he decided that Rita Hayworth should learn to fight bulls, and imported a Mexican matador as her tutor; she prettily jousted with a bull's head mounted on a wheelbarrow, its handles controlled by her father. Later, Welles got to know a woman who had wielded the matador's sword professionally. This was the Peruvian bullfighter Conchita Cintron, to whose memoir ¡*Torera!* he contributed an introduction in 1968. His first reaction to her feats was, he admitted, typical of the patronising male: 'The lady must be protected from those fearful horns . . . The truth is, of course, that the horns that worry us grow on our own heads.' Cintron made him uneasy because she co-opted so many masculine privileges. She fought bulls on horseback, reclaiming the chivalric status matadors had forfeited long ago when a royal decree ordered them to work on foot: Welles called her, 'a knight without armour', who slew dragons herself rather than wringing her hands and waiting – as Elsa pretends to do at the start of *The Lady from Shanghai* – for a champion to come to her aid. Welles could not think of Cintron without projecting her into *Don Quixote*. She was, he said in his essay, a Dulcinea who disproved the antique notion that women must be protectively kept at home. She rode away from the family fortress, but did not rely on her horse to keep her above the fray. Moving from South America to Spain, she caused a scandal by dismounting in the arena to stand before the bull she was fighting. On behalf of his entire gender, Welles turned tail. 'As elsewhere,' he wrote, 'men on the Iberian peninsula are clinging to supremacy by their fingernails.' Cintron's career warned of their imminent demotion. The white goddess now deployed a sword, and after laying you low she could signal her triumph by slicing off your ears, your tail, or any other totemic appendage. That is why Welles indignantly asserted that the reason for the bullfight was 'the death of its tragic hero'. At least this privilege of gender remained inalienable: it must be a bull that dies, not a cow.

In 1950, Welles declared that 'what is inevitable in the tragedy of the bull-ring is the death of the bull'. But once he began to identify with the bull, he came to wonder about the possibility of a reprieve for the gallant, doomed beast. Cintron spared the last bull she fought, at Jaen in Spain.

She faced its charge, then dropped her sword and quit the arena. Still, this was a gesture of disillusion, not an offer of clemency, and the bull was instantly felled by a novillero. Welles imagined another ending, both to the bull's strenuous twenty minutes in the ring and to his own longer, more abraded life, even though the story he toyed with was, as so often, taken away from him and completed by others. The segment of *It's All True* directed by Norman Foster was to be about a Mexican boy who rescues his pet bull from the ring. After the project was cancelled, RKO held on to the rights and finally produced *The Brave One* in 1956, with Irving Rapper as the director. Welles approvingly acknowledged the film, mentioning it in a French interview at the time of its release in Paris, and he enforced its connection with his own project by mistakenly asserting that Foster directed it. *The Brave One* used a version of the original story by Dalton Trumbo, a political ally of Welles's who had joined him in signing a petition against the deportation of a union leader in 1941; this led Hearst's newspapers to accuse them of being communist subversives. Trumbo was blacklisted by McCarthy's committee in 1947, and *The Brave One* pseudonymously assigned his credit to Robert Rich. It won him an Academy Award, but Rich could not claim his Oscar because he did not exist.

Trumbo slyly revenged himself by radicalising the story. When the calf Etano bellows, he has 'a voice like the bugles of Zapata'. At school, young Leonardo's lessons consist of political propaganda, dispensed by a teacher who (for the benefit of viewers north of the border) likens Juarez to Lincoln. Running away to Mexico City to save Etano, Leonardo scampers up a staircase past revolutionary murals painted by Orozco. A blonde American floozy comes to visit the bull ranch and squeals squeamishly when told about the fights, which prompts the rancher Don Alejandro to rebuke her cosy, self-deceiving homeland: 'We Mexicans are a different and older race. We know that there is pain in all life, and that death is never very far away. But your people are always outraged at pain – and as for death, I think you may pass a law against it any day!'

The jibe is hurtfully accurate, though comedy passes its own law against the death that is tragedy's fixed penalty. Leonardo's solitary, desperate mission succeeds, and Etano – having evaded the matador's blade by holding his head arrogantly high, which rouses the public to wave white handkerchiefs as a reward for his courage – is put out to pasture to live happily ever after as a stud. In a way, *The Brave One* also rewrote the tragic ending of another story in Welles's South American anthology, the crusade of the jangadeiros. They petitioned Vargas in vain. Leonardo, after a trek from country to city as exhausting as the voyage of the jangadeiros, wheedles an interview with the Mexican President and persuades him to write a letter of intercession sparing Etano. He delivers it too late, but Etano receives an indulgence from the public, so boy and bull can go home together. Etano is more than a sacred beast. Enjoying the charmed life of a comic character, he is sanctified. In Leonardo's village, he is led to the church to receive a benediction (a sequence initially filmed in Mexico for Welles by Norman Foster in 1941), along with a rowdy flock of sheep, mules, pigs, chickens, dogs and cats. He piously drops to his knees before the priest, who calls him 'especially holy, doubly blessed'. Pleading with the President, Leonardo says 'They cannot kill a blessed animal.'

Lincoln Kirstein in his review of *Death in the Afternoon* argued that bullfighters were 'more priests than warriors' because 'the blood on their hands is almost sacrificial'. Welles likewise remarked that Manolete, killed in the ring in 1947, looked like Christ, because 'his long melancholy face was tragic even when he smiled, which he did rarely'. He revered Manolete's 'courage and a nobility', which for him were the cardinal virtues. They are also the attributes of Etano, perhaps even worthier of admiration when they occur in an animal, which lacks self-consciousness and therefore cannot be accused of faking. Etano resists being rounded up for branding, and the foreman on the ranch says that he is 'not only brave, he is noble'. This for Welles was a crucial adjective: in his letter to Tynan, he pointedly insisted that only the bull's 'nobility (this is the word used) . . . raises the festival above mere sport and pageantry'. Etano deserves the tribute, because he places his horns in the service of Welles's own old-fashioned campaign against modernity and mechanical progress. As a calf, Etano charges the ranch-owner's car, bruises its fenders and blinds both of its headlights. Leonardo chides him for being a 'murderer of automobiles'. Once again, *Don Quixote* sets a precedent: butting that car is like aiming your lance at a windmill.

Despite Don Alejandro's joke about American sentimentality, Welles fantasised about averting the ordained end of the rite. In his film of Cervantes' novel, he intended to send Quixote into the ring to take the part of a cornered bull against the matador; and during the running of the bulls at Pamplona, Welles's Sancho is chased into the ring by the stampede, and unheroically clambers over the wall to escape into the ranks of the paying public. Both bull and man are saved. The mandate of tragedy is overruled, and the fight ends – it was Welles's fondest hope for himself – as a comedy.

Meanwhile, thanks to men who only felt alive when they killed something, other bulls were cut down, tigers and elephants shot, and marlin hauled in. The American male in the 1950s repaired his damaged virility by subscribing to what Tynan called a 'religion of toughness'. In 1958 John Huston, himself an intrepid hunter of big game in Africa and foxes in Ireland, cast Welles in *The Roots of Heaven*, about a campaign to stop the shooting of African elephants. He plays a broadcaster who signs up for a safari, then finds that he is a target for the protesters. They pepper his backside with their pellets; lying rear up in a hospital bed, with a tent rigged above his assaulted rump, he undergoes a conversion. When next able to sit in a chair, he delivers a television address condemning blood sports.

Welles himself was never so homiletic, but he looked askance at this war between man and nature. In 1955, visiting the Basque territory for his television series, he was startled to discover that Basque sailors had invented whaling, which he described as 'the fantastic notion that the world's biggest creature could he hunted and harpooned from an open boat'. The notion appealed to his sense of fantasy, not to his craving for conquest; the pursuit tantalised him because the likelihood of success seemed so remote. For him the hunt was metaphysical, a foolishly unequal contest between littleness and infinitude.

In Huston's film of *Moby Dick,* made that same year, the religion of toughness begets a new race of men, invincibly post-human. Ahab (Gregory Peck) with his ivory leg meets another amputee (James Robertson Justice) who has a hook for a hand. When they compare prostheses, the visiting captain thanks the whale for leaving him with an appendage so 'spanking-new and scientific', and remarks that 'Lubbers with four limbs don't know what they're missing.' Ahab pushes the technological quarrel with an outmoded creator and his purposeless creation to its terrifying conclusion. He dismisses Starbuck's complaint about his blasphemy, says he'd 'strike the sun if it insulted me', and prods the map to indicate where the showdown with the white whale (which he refers to as 'Him') will be. His finger, after straying indecisively across the South Pacific, lights on Bikini Atoll. It was here that the United States exploded an atomic bomb in 1946 for the benefit of the press. Welles condemned the test on his ABC radio programme hours before it took place. Even so, the part of him that MacLíammóir likened to a bomb must have been exhilarated by the spectacle of so much liberated energy. Bikini Atoll soon became a locus of forbidden desire, and gave its name to a newly skimpy swimming costume. In *Mr Arkadin,* the dead Mily is identified from a poster for her nightclub act, which advertises her 'Strip Tease Atomique'.

Welles, who played Father Mapple in Huston's film, had a lifelong obsession of his own with *Moby Dick.* In 1946 he played Ahab in a radio adaptation of the novel, and in 1947 in New York he helped plan an oratorio version by Brainerd Duffield and Bernard Herrmann: Ahab was to be a Freudian neurotic, assuaging his sexual hatred by transferring it to the whale. In 1955 he staged his own *Moby Dick – Rehearsed* in London (and talked about founding a repertory company which would perform his dramatisation of Hemingway's bullfighting novel *The Sun Also Rises*). As late as 1973, while working on *F for Fake,* he filmed his readings of Ishmael's opening monologue or the scene in which Ahab remorsefully weeps. The scaling down is sad. The London production set the landlocked stage afloat: the actors reeled as if the floorboards were heaving beneath them, and a jungle of ropes let down from the flies swayed like the rigging of the ship. By 1973, Welles could not afford to dramatise *Moby Dick* and choreograph the movements of its cast and crew; he had to be content with the solitary pleasure of reading, and – lacking technicians – even operated the clapper himself to synchronise sound and image at the start of takes.

As with all the literary texts that preoccupied him, he found himself in the book. But which self did it reflect? At first Ahab, another of his Faustian egomaniacs. Yet by the 1950s he had lived down the compulsion to prove his power, and he said he would happily have handed over the role of Ahab in the London production to Patrick McGoohan, whom he hired to play Starbuck, the critic of the whaler's mad crusade. In 1954 he made Ahab's violence look absurd when, as the embattled landowner in *Trouble in the Glen,* he fends off the peasants by loading a harpoon gun, a souvenir 'from the old days in South America'. He expressed similar reservations about Ahab's vendetta in his single scene as Father Mapple in Huston's film. In a church at New Bedford, Mapple preaches a sermon about Jonah and his regurgitation by the whale. Melville calls Mapple 'deeply devout', which makes him the antithesis of Ahab; he reprimands the disobedience of Jonah, who wanted to sail to a part of the world where God did not reign. The young Welles also ran away from home in order to recreate the world, dicing with its destruction in the process. As Mapple, having rewritten the script of the sermon to suit himself, he reappraised his own hubris. He does not attempt the hectoring delivery described by Melville, who says that Mapple's chest heaves, his eyes flash, his arms flail. Welles is sober, and speaks softly. He looks weather-beaten, eroded like a carved figurehead of a ship, his wispy white beard as stiff as his stoical face. For Melville, Mapple's pulpit is one of his 'engrafted clerical peculiarities': it resembles the projecting bow of a ship, and he climbs into it using a rope ladder which he then rolls up behind him. Aloft, he takes possession of a 'little Quebec' or 'a self-containing stronghold'. Welles, moving through this mannered bit of business, makes it look both arduous and plaintive. It's quite a feat for him to entrust his bulk to that sagging ladder while reserving one hand to clutch his Bible; once in the pulpit, he does not so much command a fortress as occupy an exposed, isolated solitude.

He reduces Mapple's sermon to a few minutes, and resists the opportunity to mimic the voices of Jonah's fellow-mariners. Instead he concentrates on the conclusion, when Mapple describes Jonah's despairing penitence, which entitles him to be rescued from the whale's belly. Part of Welles admired heroes who, like Ahab, refuse to acknowledge that they have any faults to be pardoned. He was puzzled by the capacity for remorse in others, like Mily in *Mr Arkadin* who watches a procession of wailing penitents in Spain and says 'They must have sinned awful badly.' Welles saw such intransigence as the backbone of tragic character, and he summed up its appeal in his preface to Conchita Cintron's book when he remarked that 'Godlike, the bull defies the gods.' Mapple undermines this defiance when, treating Jonah's eventual death as a rehearsal for his own, he says 'mortal or immortal, here I die' and quietly acknowledges his own insignificance. He ends by declaring 'this is nothing; I leave eternity to Thee; for what is man that he should live out the lifetime of his God?'

This hesitation about mortality and immortality offered Welles a choice of his own between accepting human limitation and attempting as an artist to overcome it. Still balancing the options offered by Ahab and Mapple, he played both parts when he presented *Moby Dick – Rehearsed* in London in 1955. But as he moved through the ages of man, at each stage he reassessed and rejected previous incarnations. When he published the text of *Moby Dick – Rehearsed* in 1965, he assigned the role of Mapple to the actor in the nineteenth-century repertory troupe identified as An Old 'Pro', who lists his specialities as 'Eccentric

Character, First Comics and General Utility'. No doubt Falstaff was among his parts. Welles himself had now graduated to another role in *Moby Dick*. Attending the fights, he sympathised with the bull. How could he not feel sorry for the whale, 'the world's biggest creature' speared by little men in a leaky boat? Welles-watchers found the identification irresistible. Even when he played Ahab, Tynan called him 'a leviathan plus'. In 1955, the writer Wolf Mankowitz had a privileged sight of Welles's blubber bared, as he stretched out in a London bedroom, ready to be injected with a day's worth of vitamins: naked, Mankowitz said, he 'looked like a huge white whale . . . beached in St James's!'

Moby Dick, however, is a malevolent whale, whose whiteness denotes the unknowable blankness of the universe that mocks us. Welles could neither represent nor tolerate such cosmic hostility. Just as the story he wanted to film in *It's All True* tamed a fighting bull and turned it into a domestic pet, so he sought to befriend the whale, to calm its homicidal fury, to smile at its lumbering immensity. Melville pays tribute to the genius of the sperm whale, thanks to the phrenological bump on its forehead, and archly upholds this faith although the creature has never 'written a book, spoken a speech': instead his 'great genius is declared in his doing nothing in particular to prove it'. Like Welles, Moby Dick remains a genius even if he is idle. Melville claims that this monster would have been deified by the 'child-magian thoughts' of a primitive culture, as the crocodile was in Egypt, and suggests that if 'any highly cultured, poetical nation shall lure back . . . the merry May-day gods of old; and livingly enthrone them again in the now egotistical sky; . . . then be sure, exalted to Jove's high seat, the great Sperm Whale shall lord it'. This return of May-day gods was what Welles had in mind in his reveries about Merry England, whose lazy, ribald genius is Falstaff. In fact, Mankowitz's joke about Welles paraphrases a comment in *The Merry Wives of Windsor* by Mistress Ford who, aghast at Falstaff's invasion of her bourgeois neighbourhood, asks 'What tempest . . . threw this whale, with so many tuns of oil in his belly, ashore at Windsor?' She hopes to inflame his greed 'till the wicked fire of lust have melted him in his own grease'. Ahab, maniacally ambitious, was replaced in Welles's personal pantheon by the compliant Jonah, who makes himself comfortable in the whale's belly. George Orwell, in an essay written in 1940, saw Jonah as a type of modern man, the unpolitical quietist wanting to be sheltered from reality inside a padded cell of fat. 'The whale's belly', Orwell argued, 'is simply a womb big enough for an adult.' Orwell, early in the war, disapproved of such detachment. But the whale's insulated interior was a natural refuge for Welles's slumbrous Falstaff.

Welles credited *Moby Dick* with a prophetic power, like that which believers attribute to scripture. Wherever and whenever he opened the book, he would encounter a remonstrance, a coded message directed exclusively to him. He might even have found Kane's secret deciphered, if he had looked carefully enough at an exchange between Stubb and the sailors on a French ship that travels past towing two dead whales. The vessel reeks of decay. Stubbs holds his nose, wishing it were 'a wax one' (like those Welles carried in his make-up case). He cannot speak French, but the symbol on the bow wordlessly translates 'the romantic name of this aromatic ship'. A carved bulb with copper thorns is labelled in gilt letters, which he spells out: '"Bouton de Rose," – "Rose-button," or "Rose-bud"'. Stubbs laughs at the idea of 'a wooden rose-bud' and, with a sniff at the stinking whales, adds 'how like all creation it smells!'. Tragedy concludes at the moment of death, which is exactly where *Citizen Kane* begins. What comes after death – mortal decay or perhaps immortality, as creation feeds on destruction and the cycle repeats itself – is the subject of comedy.

Hemingway went to Spain, he said, to see something 'simple and barbarous and cruel', attuned to the cauterised temperament of modern man. He called the bullfight a 'definite action', which is how Aristotle described tragic drama. In the arena, the crisis of a life could be studied under controlled conditions, continuous in time and inescapably concentrated in space. Welles likewise divided the twenty-minute tragic action of the ring into three precise, remorselessly successive acts: first the picadors, then the bandilleros, finally the death. He gave Keith Baxter a dose of gumption before a fight by telling him that 'ferocity was bred into the soul of Spain', and in the *Arkadin* novel had Raina extol 'Spanish harshness' and declare 'I love Spain. And the Spaniards. They're clean . . . hard . . . stern . . . fatalists.' Yet Welles lacked harshness and hardness, and seldom directed his energies towards a definite action: he favoured digressions, diversions, subplots, which is why he understood Shakespeare so well.

The older he got, the further he retreated from Hemingway's cult of stylish killing and taciturn dying. In 1959 he summarised the current version of *The Sacred Beasts* to the screenwriter Peter Viertel: it was, he said, about 'an old man's love affair with youth'. Viertel asked whether the old man infatuated with the matador was Hemingway or Welles himself. 'Both,' bellowed Welles, laughing. Hemingway, who committed suicide with a hunting rifle in 1961, would not have shared his amusement. Welles happily accused himself of 'premature senility', and said that the relationship in *The Sacred Beasts* resembled an elderly grandee 'falling for a ballerina by merely watching her on the stage'. He had aged into Kane, for this was exactly how Hearst fell for Marion Davies: he spotted her when she was dancing in the Ziegfeld *Follies*, and returned to ogle her adoringly from the front row at subsequent performances. Welles, having touched on the analogy, added that his own story lacked any 'sexual overtones, of course'. He exhibited himself subsiding comfortably into corpulence, embedded in his own body, in his 1955 television programme about bullfighting. He arrives at the ring in Madrid sucking on a cigar; clutching a stuffed pillow, he eases himself into a seat on the shady side among what he calls 'the swells'. He had taken no exercise, Tynan calculated, since his apocryphal appearances as a matador in Seville more than twenty years earlier.

In the long run, Welles's body killed him, as everyone's does. But, in the shorter term, it saved him. His bulk marked him as a comic character rather than a tragic one – able to enjoy himself, not obliged to enter into conflict with the universe. Early in the 1950s, Michael Powell offered him what might have been a self-defining role in his adaptation of Johann Strauss's operetta *Die Fledermaus*, updated to post-war Vienna with its quarrelsome quartet of ruling powers, like a musical *Third Man*. He tried persuading Welles to play Orlofsky, the rich, lazy Russian general. Welles negotiated a fee of thirty thousand pounds for three days' work, then debunked after the deal was made, leaving behind a sketch of himself singing Orlofsky's hedonistic anthem 'Chacun à son goût', with a glass of champagne in one hand and a cigar in the other. He already was Orlofsky, so why bother making the film? His role in *Oh Rosalinda!!* went to Anthony Quayle.

Orlofsky's lassitude is a response to his millions: he despairs of ever spending all that onerous money. Welles's weight was the only kind of affluence he could rely on, and it became his valiant boast of superfluity. His cigars, indispensable as props, could be left to smoke themselves, because they served him as symbols of conspicuous consumption. As the tycoon in *Trent's Last Case*, Welles plays a game of hide and seek with the camera: his first appearance is as a disappearing shadow, leaving behind him a fog of cigar smoke as he quits the room. That smoke, like the plume from the chimney at Xanadu as Kane's spoils are cremated, stands for the man. But Welles exempted himself from the thermodynamic law decreeing that the body, like one of Eugene's automobiles in *The Magnificent Ambersons*, wears itself out by exhaling heat. Manderson in *Trent's Last Case* impatiently discards a cigar, then wonders 'How many hours a day would a man like me have to work to throw away more cigars than he can afford to smoke?' The conundrum allows Welles to joke about his own excessiveness: how many hours a day would he have had to talk or think to throw away more ideas than he had time to realise? The issue of what he could afford was best omitted from the equation. Manderson immediately lights another cigar for himself, and offers one to his secretary, who refuses. A wise choice, snarls Manderson: 'Never cultivate a luxury until you can afford to support it as a habit.' Welles of course disregarded this budgetary advice. For him, cigars signified the vital ignition of mind and body. As the dying Wolsey in *A Man for All Seasons*, he looks pallid, deflated, laid out on a rough bed of planks. But Zinnemann remembered him during rehearsals for the scene, flagrantly alive as he lolled on his cot, 'puffing the longest, fattest Monte Cristo cigar'. In *The Trial*, he utters his first lines from behind a billowing cloud of cigar smoke. Then his nurse (Romy Schneider) wraps his head in a hot cloth. When she removes it, vapour continues to coil from his face and hair as he goes on talking: it is as if his head itself were volcanically smoking, or at least steaming.

Proceeding through life, we acquire the faces we deserve. Welles extended this rule to the rest of the body: he saw physique as fate, the flesh as destiny. Others were intimidated by his height, even before he squared himself by putting on weight. Welles, with his fantasies about the great man, knew that the body could be a source of power, but he took care to point out that a body like his was actually unthreatening. In his script for *The Cradle Will Rock*, Virginia comments on his habit of taking 'little naps . . . like Napoleon' rather than sleeping through the night. Blitzstein is alarmed: 'Napoleon? Should I take that as a warning?' Despots are notorious for being night-workers, and Napoleon had himself painted in his office during the small hours, ruling over a somnolent, submissive nation. But Virginia reassures Blitzstein: 'Orson's tall; and he claims that all the dictators in history are short.' So that is why he abandoned his political career! Dictators, according to the theory, are short because they must be dynamoes, projectiles of will. A big man has a more liberal metabolism. He cannot move so fast, or burn off energy so easily. It's a belated plea to be loved not feared, voiced on Welles's behalf by a wife whom he characterises in the film as an indulgent mother. The same odd idea found its way into Graham Greene's script for *The Third Man*. Martins asks Anna whether the play she's rehearsing is tragedy or comedy. She replies 'Comedy. I'm not the right shape for tragedy.' In January 1949, a few days after completing his scenes as Harry Lime, Welles described himself and MacLíammóir as 'chubby tragedians'. Had he appropriated a line from the script, or did the script quote his table talk? Either way, the comment was blue-pencilled before the scene was shot, and what Anna says in the film is 'I don't play tragedy.' The elegant Alida Valli could hardly be expected to deride her own shape. Welles had no such compunction, and was pleased to have aged and thickened into comedy. But he recognised his loss. 'I'm less than I was,' he told Bogdanovich in the 1970s. 'A thin man can play a fat man, and a young man can play an old man, but it doesn't work the other way around.' For his first Falstaff in 1939, he made himself up to look old and padded his costume; when he filmed his performance in 1960, there was no need to pretend. An actor can outwit nature for a while and play tricks on time. Then reality supervenes and reduces the roles he can play to just one: himself.

Aristotle thought that tragedy was about men who are morally and socially elevated, while comedy concerned our inferiors, whose distresses we can afford to laugh at. Regarding tragedy as the prerogative of thin men and comedy of fat ones, Welles seemed to be following the same classical rule about those mutually exclusive genres. But Shakespeare had shown him that the options overlapped: the morbid, mental Hamlet can be coarse and the fat knight Falstaff can sag into melancholy. The choice of genre was not the inescapable consequence of social class or of physical type. It all depended on the mood you were in, or – cinematically – on the angle of vision you chose.

Chaplin, who saw the genres as alternative camera set-ups, called tragedy 'life in close-up' and comedy 'life in long shot'. If the camera retreats to the middle distance, it cannot register the pain on faces and sees only the inane agitation of the body. At a bullfight, we adopt different attitudes to the sufferings of the various creatures involved, as if adjusting our own mental camera. Hemingway argued that the bull's death is tragic, while the death of a gored horse 'tends to be comic' because 'the horse is a comic character': having made this judgement, we decide to see its blood in long shot. The calculation is all the more self-conscious because Chaplin himself was a symbolic presence at the fights, replaying the tragedy as a farce. A comical matador known as Charlot, dressed in the tramp's costume, used his cane to skirmish with harmless bulls in the ring at Barcelona in 1916. Such satyr plays soon became part of the fiesta, and were called 'charlotadas'. The old man in 'The Undefeated' proudly refuses an offer to join in 'the Charlie Chaplins': as a Hemingway hero, he spurns the indignity of comedy. When Bogdanovich cited Chaplin's remark about tragedy and comedy, Welles wisely and ingeniously amended it. 'Comedy is a medium full shot,' he said. 'The true long shot is tragedy again.' Without moving the camera, Carol Reed showed the process at work in the final scene of *The Third Man*. After the funeral, Valli walks down the long straight avenue in the cemetery while Cotten sits on a bench waiting, hoping that she will pause when she reaches him. While she remains in the distance, slowly advancing, there is the possibility of forgiveness. In medium full shot, a happy ending becomes tantalisingly plausible. But as she stalks into close-up she displays a face frozen in contempt, transfixed by pain. Out of sight behind the camera, she disappears into another distance. Cotten's experience is now defined as tragic.

The close-up honours the anguish of the tragic individual. Welles – who pointed the camera away from himself as he delivered Macbeth's and Othello's monologues – mistrusted such solipsism and self-pity. 'Theoretically, I am against close-ups,' he said in 1966, pointing out how few of them there were in *Citizen Kane*. Such shots, like the fuzzy, flattering inserts of Hayworth the studio added to *The Lady from Shanghai*, served the purpose of delectation rather than supplying psychological insight. For Welles, the long shot reveals a tragedy that is more universal, no longer restricted to individuals and their personal tribulations. But the wider the angle, the more indifferently comic this world view seems. O'Hara at Acapulco adopts just such a long view when he reacts to the prospect of nuclear annihilation by remarking that since the world had a beginning, it will surely have an end. Welles's *Othello* begins with close-ups of the dead faces of Othello and Desdemona as they lie on their biers. Then they are carried away, progressively diminished as their story is filed in the long, indiscriminate store of human misery. After Emilia's murder at the end of the film, Othello undergoes another abrupt belittlement. Wyndham Lewis's leonine individual, so intent on demonstrating his own centrality and on proving the poetic distinction of his grief, is seen in long shot as a tiny figure on the other side of a barred gate, beneath a high

vaulted ceiling. The camera similarly retreats from Welles's Lear at the end
of Peter Brook's television production. The final tableau is a
Michelangelesque Pietà with the roles reversed. The dead Lear, a child
once more, has limply collapsed and is fastened to the throne by Kent, who
might be maternally cradling him in his lap. They hold the pose while the
camera backs slowly away, and maintain it while the credits unroll.

The transition between genres, as Welles saw it, followed the laws of
perspective. In close-up, we are confronted by personal tragedy. In medium
full shot, the anguish on faces fades and we notice the continued vitality
of bodies. In long shot, we watch the indifferent world obliterating all
individuals; at the vanishing point, the lines of perspective converge, and
comedy and tragedy are equated. This happens when the contraction of
the iris terminates the winter expedition in *The Magnificent Ambersons*.
The characters are happily singing, but their car coughs and splutters its
way towards a future in which they will die. In *It's All True*, long shots
track the jangadeiros as they make a landfall and search for a place to eat
and sleep, their dwarfed figures toiling across dunes of rippled, sifting sand
beneath curdled clouds like suspended boulders. Exploring Salvador, they
are seen from mid-air, identifiable only by their white hats as they climb
the arduous stairway to a baroque church.

In Welles's television programme about bullfighting, the camera goes on
watching after the conclusion of the tragedy. The matador has been grazed
by the horns. He staggers back to his feet, strides out to face the bull, and
kills it. That, for Hemingway, would have been the end of the rite. Welles
chooses to record the messy epilogue, as the survivors – like Lodovico in
Othello ordering Graziano to appropriate the Moor's goods or Albany in
King Lear arranging to have the dead bodies removed and deciding who
will sustain 'the gored state' – resume the petty business of living. The sand
of the arena is swept, then hosed down. The sword used for the killing is
wiped off, ready for the next death. Unseen, the bull is being carved up as
meat, like the dead Polonius at dinner with the worms. Its sacrifice makes
possible our feast; the sequel to tragedy is comedy. Welles's attendance at
the bullfights forced him to think again about tragedy, comedy and himself. No longer impressed by the autonomy of tragic heroes, he said that
the bull's abbreviated career in the ring must reveal to us 'not *who I am*,
but *what we are*'. For once – unlike those occasions when he listed his
many selves, or indignantly denied that he was one of anything – he was
not using the royal plural.

Welles in the autumnal Tuileries, from *F for Fake*.

CHAPTER 13

Last Man

Welles, hardly a representative specimen of a human being, began to fret during the 1950s about the fate of the species he did not quite belong to. He often called people dinosaurs: Hearst, for instance, or the obstructive Hollywood moguls who ruined his career. But he also felt himself to be an outsize anachronism, and when he looked at the society whose conformist values he continued to flout, he wondered whether the human race might not be blithely plotting its own extinction. In 1938 he found it easy to frighten America. In 1982 he lamented that his countrymen 'can no longer be scared', even though they now had good reason to panic: he foresaw 'the end of the planet, the extinction of humanity'.

Ahab in *Moby Dick* broods about modifying the human template. He likens the ship's carpenter to Prometheus, the blacksmith who first galvanised man with a vital spark from the hearth of the gods. Now he orders the carpenter to carve and saw 'a complete man after a desirable pattern': a totem pole fifty feet tall, with 'no heart at all, brass forehead, . . . about a quarter of an acre of fine brains' and instead of eyes 'a skylight on top of his head to illuminate inwards'. Ahab's prescription for revising the human body makes immediate sense to the actor. Olivier padded his scrawny legs, and Welles had his collection of noses, which sometimes came loose in performance and left him resembling a leper, about to lose an appendage. But because Ahab prefers wood and metal to vulnerable flesh and blood, his recipe for the complete man looks beyond the makeshift pretences of the stage. His manikin will be an invincible killing machine, a prototype for the Martians described by the dying announcer at the end of Welles's *War of the Worlds*. 'Five great machines', as he calls them, wade across the Hudson River from the Palisades and stride ashore, their heads butting the skyscrapers; their 'metal hands' swat the frantic citizens like flies. 'This is the end now,' gasps the announcer.

The end comes when machines appropriate the creative and destructive capacity that once belonged to gods. In doing so, they render men redundant, dismissing the idea of the individual – that proud Renaissance invention – and seeing only dots in jerky, pointless motion like those Kindler and Harry Lime look down on, or a mass pulped by contagious terror like the New Yorkers fleeing from the Martians. Reflecting in 1966 on his Hollywood career, Welles interestingly said that he was the victim of 'a machination': accountants – or their adding machines – decided that he was a spendthrift. Yet, though he blamed machines or mechanised men, he still coveted the mechanical toys he was no longer permitted to play with. His interviewers reminded him that European film-makers were freer from such interference. 'But they don't possess the American technical arsenal,' said Welles, 'which is a grandiose thing.' Arsenals, however, are used for making war, not art.

In the *War of the Worlds* broadcast, a government official with a voice like that of F. D. Roosevelt pleads for calm so that America may respond to the invasion as a nation 'consecrated to the preservation of human supremacy on earth'. Put that way, it already sounds like a doomed project, or an unworthy one. Is our supremacy a sacred right or an evolutionary accident? Do we deserve preservation? As the astronomer Pearson, Welles wanders through the smoking remains of New Jersey, 'obsessed by the thought that I might be the last living man on earth'. A stark choice is proposed for humans: mutation into machines or regression into beasts. 'It's all over with humanity,' Pearson concludes. The National Guardsman accepts that 'we men – as men – are finished'. To survive, he recommends living in the New York sewers, like Lime or Valjean in *Les misérables*, who seeks refuge from the police in the cloaca beneath Paris. Mary McCarthy, who admired Welles's Harlem *Macbeth*, saw Shakespeare's play as a preview of this extremity. *Macbeth*, she said in an essay written in 1962, 'shows life in a cave' (which is where Welles set his film version). Primitive man hid there to escape the hobgoblins that assailed him; modern man has gone back into this atavistic hole, retreating in terror from an outer world ruled once more by the irrationality of what McCarthy called 'the Fascist nightmare' or stalked by 'new spectres in the form of Communism and Socialism'.

Pondering *Touch of Evil*, Welles found in it a prophecy of this comfortless future, at once inhumanly technical and bestially crude. The detective story became, in his commentaries on it, a social allegory, with Quinlan and Vargas as philosophical opposites. At first in 1958 he deplored Quinlan's betrayal of the law and called him 'the incarnation of everything I struggle against, politically and morally'. But just who had incarnated Quinlan? Despite the contradiction, he went on to treat Vargas as his 'mouthpiece', as if the man were a microphone, and said that 'he speaks as a man of dignity according to the tradition of classical humanism, which is absolutely my tradition as well'. By 1974, Welles had changed his mind. In an interview with *Positif*, he now disparaged Vargas as one of the post-human freaks invented by contemporary society. He called him 'the new man' and 'the modern man', which was tantamount to saying that he was not a man at all but merely 'a well-programmed organizer' like the suburban humanoids and corporate wage-slaves described in popular sociological treatises such as William H. Whyte's *The Organization Man* or David Riesman's *The Lonely Crowd*. Welles now called Vargas's interpretation of the law techno-cratic, and saw him as a bloodless being, more intimate with his elec-tronic aids than with any other human being. The interviewer pointed out the oddity of Vargas's nationality: wasn't Welles describing a type specific to the United States (like the buttoned-down Schwartz) and forgetting that Vargas is supposed to be Mexican? In discussions with Heston, Welles had decided that Vargas was educated north of the border. Devising an imaginary curriculum vitae for him, they agreed that he graduated from the University of Southern California and Harvard Law School. In 1974, Welles had no compunction about sending Vargas back home. In response to the interviewer's objection, he immediately adjusted his argument and called Mexico 'a country born from the fermentation of a deliciously corrupt humanity, which enters a technocratic stage of development and produces men like Vargas'.

Welles, of course, preferred delicious corruption to robotic rectitude. The relationship between Quinlan and Vargas is, as so often, that of Falstaff and Hal: pleasant, gratified vice is set against a shrewd, ruthless selfishness that claims to represent virtue. Filming *Touch of Evil* on location, Welles showed the new world that came into existence when machines trampled nature. In a wasteland of inconstant dunes and drifting smoke, oil derricks as insatiable as the blood-sucking Martians in H. G. Wells's story drill the soil, intently trying (as Quinlan says) to 'pump up money' although there is no one left to spend it. A carved frond of leaves on the side of the bridge is a reminder of what nature used to look like. Beneath a crumbled balustrade, the leavings of civilisation putrefy in a valley of ashes: broken chairs and tables, the springs of an upended bed, padding from a gutted mattress, fouled, twisted rags. Ancient explosions still ricochet through the air as a tape recorder replays a shooting, and blood slowly drips into the dank sluice of a stream. A last man tumbles into the sluice and is swilled away between bobbing crates and a gobbet of indestructible plastic. It is indeed all over.

In 1515, a rhinoceros arrived in Lisbon from India. Valued as a curio, evidence of the worlds elsewhere opened up by Renaissance navigators, it was sent on to the Pope as a gift. The ship sank during the voyage to Italy, and the precious monster drowned; the Pope's present reached him stuffed. Dürer, who never saw the beast, made a woodcut of it, giving it a hide of plated metal. For Renaissance connoisseurs, the rhinoceros, like Pico della Mirandola's chameleon, demonstrated the quirky oddity of nature: Dürer had heard that it was 'fast, cunning and daring', and could gore elephants. Its singularity made it a prize. By the 1950s, such a glorious exception to nature's rules was inconceivable, or not allowable. Society – whether in the softly conformist West or in the harsher regimes of Eastern Europe – had outlawed the Wellesian spirit of idiosyncrasy. Now the rhinoceros, in league with a horde of fellows like a formation of armoured vehicles, symbolised the herded conformity of the mass.

Early in 1960 at the Royal Court in London, Welles directed Ionesco's *Rhinoceros*. Olivier played Berenger, the bureaucrat who obstinately refuses to follow fashion and become a blundering rhinoceros, even though the change would secure him a better job. As his courage falters, Berenger reflects that 'People who try to hang on to their individuality always come to a bad end!' But he regains his confidence and ends by asserting 'I'm the last man left, and I'm staying that way until the end.' Charles Marowitz described Ionesco's conceit as 'a cartoon-enlargement of Kafka's cockroach' in *Metamorphosis*. Logically enough, Welles went on in 1962 to film Kafka's *The Trial*, working first in Zagreb and later inside the derelict Gare d'Orsay in Paris. As K, Anthony Perkins is another version of the last man – although whereas Berenger fights the stampede, K surrenders to the arresting officers and allows them to lead him to a crater in another suburban junkyard, where they blow him up.

The hangar-sized clerical factory with its columns of workers in Welles's *The Trial* looks like an expansion of Ionesco's stage directions for the second act of *Rhinoceros*, set in what we take to be a government department or the headquarters of a firm that publishes law books: the shelves, Ionesco specifies, are marked with signs denoting sections on jurisprudence, judicial codes and fiscal rules, any of which might be useful to K in researching his case. At least Ionesco's stage architecture is solid, cluttered with equipment and vouching for the substantiality of the world. Welles made it more permeable, outfitting the stage at the Royal Court with glass doors that were constantly swinging open and shut. In his set for the corresponding scene in *The Trial*, the abolition of private space is explicit. K invites his uncle into his office for a confidential talk. The office, however, is just a raised platform, lacking walls. There can be no escape from surveillance in this regimented, neon-lit factory.

Both here and in his adaptation of Kafka, Welles's sympathies ought to have been with those harassed last men, gallantly standing up to the collectivised majority. But as always he turned the stories he retold into personal psychodramas, and with his multitude of contradictory selves he found that he was on both sides of the argument. He claimed to hate *Rhinoceros*, and said he only took it on as a favour to his friend Larry, who (according to Welles, again cast by himself as the hapless victim of treachery) sabotaged his direction, bad-mouthed him to the other actors, and banned him from the last few days of rehearsal. He was allowed back for opening night, and choreographed the rhino charges by loudly muttering into a microphone from the back of the theatre. It was Welles who did the machinating: he assembled the battery of technological tricks – thunderous sound effects, strobe lighting, a television screen to relay the latest images of rhinos mobilising in the streets – which assailed Olivier.

He had a prior philosophical disagreement with Ionesco, vented in a letter to *The Observer* in 1958. Tynan had criticised Ionesco's *The Chairs*, then being performed at the Royal Court, for ushering in a 'bleak new world from which the humanist heresies of faith in logic and belief in man will forever be banished'. Welles intended to support Ionesco, then found he shared Tynan's dismay. *The Chairs* ends with the literal dumbing-down of words: an Orator who is a deaf mute delivers a speech consisting of inarticulate guttural moans. Welles warned that by 'proving the incapacity of language, [Ionesco] also proves the incapacity of man himself'. His letter condemned this helpless political apathy, and maintained a resilient American faith in freedom of speech and other freedoms that were worth fighting for. To Welles, Ionesco was a treasonous clerk, who advised the rest of the world to abandon liberal values just because they had been suppressed in his native Romania. Interpreting *Rhinoceros* as a political tract, he missed or chose to overlook another implication that is even more threatening. Ionesco once confided that, when he first went to the theatre, the performances embarrassed and upset him, because he felt that the actors were engaged in a reprehensible activity: 'They gave up their own personalities, repudiated themselves, changed their own skins.' Welles knew all about such transmigrations. Though Wyndham Lewis thought of him as a lion-actor, he made himself look like a bear in *Macbeth* or a hog in *Touch of Evil*, and in 1979 he happily fraternised with humanised frogs and piglets in *The Muppet Movie*.

He had good reason to feel uncomfortable about *Rhinoceros*, because he had a share in creating it, or in demonstrating the accuracy of its comments on the 'collective psychosis' of a mass society. Ionesco specifically alludes to the *War of the Worlds* broadcast in his play, forcing Welles to confront his prank all over again. Botard dismisses the first rhino sightings as 'a myth – like flying saucers', which he attributes to popular hysteria. His mockery hardly disposes of the problem: there were no Martians in 1938, but listeners still had nervous breakdowns as they ran away from them. Near the end of the play, the noise of trumpeting blares from a radio. Daisy cries 'They've taken over the radio stations!' Berenger's dispute with his colleague Jean recapitulates the dialogue between Pearson the Princeton academic and the National Guardsman. Jean favours capitulating to the mob. When Berenger accuses him of replacing moral laws with the imperatives of the jungle, he declares 'We must get back to primeval integrity' and snorts 'Humanism is all washed up!'

The same argument recurs in Welles's adaptation of *The Trial*, when K stands up to the Advocate in the cathedral. Welles wryly explains that the universe is absurd, which makes protest pointless. In the novel, K vainly cites our shared humanity: 'How can a human being ever be guilty? We are all human beings here after all, each the same as the other.' Welles knew that this appeal was no longer possible, given recent revelations of man's inhumaneness. In the new dialogue he wrote for the scene, the Advocate deprives K of self-pitying options. K denies that he sees himself as a martyr. 'Not even a victim of society?' sneers the Advocate. 'I am', K says with pathetic, deluded dignity, 'a member of society.' In Welles's judgement, K is too keen to behave conventionally, too proud of his own rank and status, more like a corporate hireling in modern America than Kafka's blameless nobody. Addressing the court, Welles's K borrows the sociological jargon of the 1950s and points to the 'vast organisation' behind his accusers, 'an establishment which contains a retinue of civil servants: officers, police and others – perhaps even hangmen'. As officious as any of these officials, he lives in hope of being promoted to deputy manager of his department. He boasts that sometimes petitioners have to wait for a week before he grants them a private appointment, which turns him into the kind of studio functionary who humiliated Welles.

In a 1965 interview Welles called K 'a petty bureaucrat', and said that he was guilty because 'he belongs to a guilty society, he collaborates with it'. Nevertheless he rewrote the end to give K, who in the novel resigns himself to dying like a dog, the benefit of Berenger's recalcitrance. After Auschwitz, Welles worried about showing a victim of totalitarianism succumbing so meekly. On the way to his interrogation in the film, Perkins passes a crowd of naked, numbered elders, dejectedly awaiting deportation beneath a muffled, blinded statue of some defunct civic virtue. They do not resist; obstreperous, given to answering back, he does so on their behalf. Welles made Perkins defiantly laugh at his assassins, who then have to dispose of him by hurling dynamite into the pit. In 1982 he justified this change by explaining his own code of conduct, which differed from that he found in both Kafka and Ionesco. 'I am a complete pessimist,' he said, 'but I'm allergic to despair.' He therefore habitually guffawed when remembering his own professional downfall. In 1958 he chided Ionesco for his political neutrality, and pointed out that other artists had pondered the consequences of such defeatism in 'the only effective ivory tower to be erected in our century – the concentration camp'. He may have been making the same dangerous joke in *Touch of Evil*, which opened a few months before his article in *The Observer*. The motel where Janet Leigh is deposited is called the Mirador, which means a scenic lookout. But the only scenery is a dusty waste, and the low, shoddy cabins look disturbingly like a concentration camp. The walls are thin, and Orwellian loud speakers relay a tormenting musical din to every room. Solitude and peace are disallowed: this is a world, as Welles said in his reply to Ionesco, 'where privacy is a crime, where the sovereign individual is an outlaw'. In the film, K accordingly charges the police inspectors with 'invasion of privacy'.

Feeling like the last man, Welles twisted Kafka's fable into an explanation of the social forces that had conspired against him. He said that the dialogue between K and Miss Pittl, the crippled friend who removes Miss Burstner's trunk after her eviction, was his 'war horse', using black comedy as a weapon 'directed against the machine and in favour of freedom'. Miss Pittl, played by Suzanne Flon, is stiff, censorious, almost mechanomorphic thanks to a surgical brace on her leg which creaks and clanks as she lopsidedly drags the trunk through another bleary waste, pursued by K. The character was invented by Welles, expanding the novel's glimpse of a German girl called Montag who takes over Miss Burstner's room and suffers from nothing worse than 'a slight limp'. Like Ahab's ivory appendage, her metal contraption is a sign that she is no longer an organic being. Her body has been retooled, and on the soundtrack, the whirring and clattering of the brace is conjured up by a telephone dial. If Perkins is the warhorse, he is not exactly bellicose, since he chases after the woman rather than attacking her, and lets her get away. Welles said that the subject of the scene with Miss Pittl was 'free will'. K freely asks Miss Pittl questions, but she hobbles off, hauling her burden, without answering them. The man cannot keep up with the machine, despite its impediment.

Welles exposed the same anxiety in inventing another character, the computer scientist played (in a scene he cut) by Katina Paxinou. Men had become expendable in a society run by machines. Except for their role as inseminators, they were equally expendable in a society of liberated women. An alliance between woman and machine doubly alarmed Welles. In *F for Fake* he assailed technocrats and their priestly prestige: 'Experts are the new oracles. They speak to us with the absolute authority of the computer, and we bow down before them.' With what the script for *The Trial* calls her 'aged, simian features', Paxinou put a personal face on that expertise, unmanning the worshippers who bowed down before her. For Welles, this 'venerable lady of science' inevitably recalled another coolly omniscient oracle, Tanya the fortune teller. In the deleted scene, K asks her if computers will one day be entrusted with making legal decisions. 'You don't really think we're going to start telling fortunes, do you?' she replies. In *Mr Arkadin*, however, Paxinou – playing the raddled consort of a Mexican warlord – pores over her cards like Tanya, and might be a Norn juggling human fates as she shuffles the pack. When K asks the scientist what crime he would be most likely to commit, she says 'Suicide.' Not an accurate guess, because Welles made him challenge his executioners. But her comment is meant to convey scorn for the weakness of men, who lack the secret of immortality.

Actors at the start of the 1950s, responding to the challenge of technology, tried to show that human beings could reassert their physical power by taking suicidal risks, or demonstrate their heroism by bloodily suffering: hence, James Dean's participation in the chicken run in *Rebel Without a Cause*, or the beatings Marlon Brando withstands in films like *On the Waterfront*. *The Trial* looks back at such tests of masculine valour when it peeps into the closet where the corrupt policemen are being flogged by a man in leather. But these miscreants do not relish their punishment, and tape their mouths to stifle their screams. K, their accuser, tries to get them pardoned, though only because he is distressed by their whimpering. Perkins's twitchy, flustered revulsion marks him as a new kind of actor, exactly suited to Welles's purposes here. He lacks Dean's animal grace and Brando's brutish bravado; rather than defending masculinity, he deserts it. He spends most of the film squirming as he resists the entreaties of fussily possessive or rapacious women, and finally flees from the posse of little girls who gather outside the studio of the painter Titorelli. Here Welles reverses and inverts an image from *Psycho*, in which Perkins first exhibited his androgynous persona. There his eye in close-up stared through a hole in the wall at a woman as she undressed. Despite Norman Bates's sexual uncertainties, the male eye still does the looking, while the woman is looked at. In *The Trial*, the eyes of the girls lewdly peer through crevices in the wall, and it is the men inside that wooden cage who nervously undergo appraisal. Because of Perkins, K's predicament seems biological rather than judicial. He is the last of his species, and of his gender: what further use does this gynocracy have for a man? All the females in *The Trial* are manifestations of the white goddess, from the scientist who looks 'old as the world' to the predatory gang of giggling, barely pubescent girls. The goddess, according to Graves, presides over 'Life-in-Death and Death-and-Life'. She directs the progress of men from one stage to the next, ordaining deaths and sometimes (though not for K) permitting resurrections, and she constructs subterranean castles – mazes or labyrinths like those Graves identified in Wales or Ireland – in which these mysterious changes take place. This is the topography of Welles's film, evident in the apartment of K's landlady with its draughty corridors and indiscreet connecting doors, in the tenement with its warren of tunnels through which the shrieking girls track K, or in the offices of the Advocate where the nurse stirs stewing pots in a candlelit kitchen, dumps discarded postulants like Bloch in spare bedrooms, and copulates with K on a bed of legal papers.

In his 1965 interview about *The Trial*, Welles noted that his films often took place in labyrinths, because this was the kind of space best adapted to a search. He might have been thinking of Kane disconsolately prowling around his own opulent tomb, with visitors from a recent house party still hibernating in the west wing. The labyrinth can be outdoors, open to the air, but it is no less treacherous for that. In *The Stranger*, Kindler conceals a body in a birch wood and hastily rearranges the paper trail left by the athletes, which should have functioned like the thread that guided Theseus through his labyrinth. If Welles's labyrinth seems to have no centre, as Borges claimed in his criticism of *Citizen Kane*, that is because his characters are running away from that centre, not groping towards it. In the centre they would find a revelation of their own insignificance: the furnace that gobbles up Kane's possessions, the ovens into which Kindler shovelled beings he considered less than human, the brazier at which Falstaff keeps himself warm and alive for a little longer, or the computer in K's office, with cooler lights flickering on its metal panels as it chatters to itself and decides what should be done with the remnants of the human race.

Before being escorted to his execution, K accuses the Advocate of trying to undermine his confidence in normality. Perkins stands in front of the blank screen after the slide lecture in which Welles demonstrates the law's inaccessibility. 'It's all lost, lost,' he cries. 'So what? Does that sentence the entire universe to lunacy?' In the novel, Kafka's hero simply says to the priest: 'Depressing thought. It makes the lie fundamental to world order.' That reference to world order makes clear Kafka's challenge to politicians and their 'dirty game'. But the film's implication is not political; the outburst Welles wrote for Perkins is aimed at the insanity of modernism and its desire, as André Breton put it in a surrealist manifesto, 'to escape from the human species'.

The attack is all the more pointed because of Welles's own complicity in that 'conspiracy', as K calls it. In his adaptation, he claimed for himself an authority that no one commands in Kafka's novel. He even supplanted the author. In his introduction, he comments that the parable about the law is told 'in the course of the story called *The Trial*', without mentioning Kafka's name. Having recited it first as the narrator, he delivers a second reading of it in the cathedral. Vocally omnipresent, he dubbed the roles of all the authority figures: K's boss, the examining magistrate, the man in leather who conducts the flogging in the cupboard, the painter with privileged access to the court. Welles, imagining himself inside Kafka's bad dream, wanted to show how a modern vision warps and disfigures the world we recognise. Picasso wracked bodies into new shapes, Dalí caused them to melt or spontaneously combust. Both, like Welles, were specialists in metamorphosis, the Kafkaesque magic that can turn a man into a beetle.

The blinding eye of the slide projector at the beginning is an electrified version of Welles's gaze. Looking through the camera, he saw a world refracted, deformed or at least rearranged by the lens. Grisby in *The Lady from Shanghai* uses his spyglass to watch Elsa diving, telescoping distance to award himself a lecherous close-up. In Welles's *Don Quixote*, Sancho Panza pays a fee to squint through a telescope in the marketplace 'Stick your eye up close! Only one eye!' barks the proprietor, as if it were a camera. In *Mr Arkadin*, the proprietor of the flea circus uses a magnifying glass to inflate his own eye until it is bulbous, grossly dilated. The dealer in antiques who sells van Stratten a telescope supplies it without a lens. The eye that looks through it will have to bring its own visionary stigmatism to bear. The idea is not so odd, since Welles introduced *The Trial* by using a camera without a lens: the pin-head images by A. Alexeieff that narrate the allegory of the law were made by pricking patterns in a white cloth and shining light from behind through the patterned holes, with the fabric acting as a camera obscura. After this slide lecture, the film goes on to study the kind of eye that surrealises reality. K is asleep; we see his head upside down, like that of Othello on his bier or O'Hara when he returns to consciousness in the crazy house after the overdose of pills wears off. Fuzzily out of focus, K's eyelid jerks, his eyelashes flutter. When his eye opens, its semicircle blurs into a halo of light around his bedroom door. This door, like all the others in the film, is the portal of reverie, granting entry to the unconscious mind. When quizzed about the connection between his room and Miss Burstner's, K says 'That door is kept firmly locked, Mrs Grubach keeps the key.' The camera topples such barriers by rendering them transparent.

In the crazy house, O'Hara stumbles through a series of theatrical sets designed by Welles to exemplify modernism and its varieties of ocular madness. On his way through this deranged museum, he resembles K groping for an exit from the paranoid catacomb in which the court has its headquarters. 'Can you tell me how to get out of here?' K asks a guard. 'I've seen enough of this place.' When Miss Burstner says 'I think you're crazy', he first agrees with her, then orders himself, like O'Hara, to cling to realities: 'I must reject everything but facts.' But what reassuring facts are there in a crazy house?

As the scene begins, O'Hara's inverted head swoons out of focus like K's. He struggles to his feet, insisting 'I was sane' though he is surrounded by graphic insanity. He reels through a room that looks like the set for Robert Wiene's expressionistic *The Cabinet of Dr Caligari*. Angular perspectives taper to a sharp point; the jagged crucifying beams and impassible slopes are roofed by a painted face, as if the space – like Wiene's asylum – were under the supervision of a mad deity. Next is a surrealistic chamber, where the skulls of cattle serve as light brackets, with bulbs protruding from their horns. Skidding down a grooved channel, he tumbles into the mouth of a dragon. The chute is its projecting tongue; he has been sucked into its head, imprisoned within another demented imagination. Next, oval blobs and triangles jostle a cubistic pile of building blocks that might be materials for constructing a world, or perhaps the debris of a world that has been knocked down. Mirrors elasticise or compress his body as he lunges across a moving floor. At the exit, a compass is painted on the wall, its arrows bisecting an open eye: a reference to the mathematical equation between an eye and the narrator's subjective I with which Welles intended to begin his film of *Heart of Darkness*, and also an ironic joke about the visual disorientation of modern art. Elsa, pinioning O'Hara against another wall with her torch, stands beside a patch of scribbled graffiti, doodlings that recall art's primitive or childish impulse – so prized by the modernists – to make a mark or a mess.

K goes on the same accelerated journey through the history of modern art. Reproductions of Renoir nudes and van Gogh sunflowers hang in his bedroom: shockingly unacademic in their day, tamely decorative now. In the painter's studio he catches up with what still, in the early 1960s, counted as the latest affront devised by the avant-garde. Titorelli exhibits a canvas and explains 'It's modern you know, action painting – I call it *Wild Nature*.' Actually it looks like an inferior Dufy, but K buys it to hang in his office, even though his cubicle has no walls. Titorelli's stylistic name-dropping suits Welles's purpose, because it enables him to suggest the continuing relevance of Kafka's parable. Tynan, during the triangular discussion he and Welles had with Ionesco in 1958, lamented modern art's abandonment of our visible, habitable world, and recalled the recent case of 'a French painter who declared that, since nothing in nature exactly resembled anything else, he proposed to burn all of his paintings which in any way resembled anything that already existed'. Tynan concluded, unjustly, that 'The end of that line, of course, is action painting.' Titorelli's canvas may not be an action painting, but what follows when the dizzy K leaves the studio is Welles's attempt to mimic that pictorial manner – hasty, unstable, improvised, scattering projectiles of paint – by using the camera rather than a brush. The coven of girls chase K through a Wellesian labyrinth boarded with wooden slats or walled with dank bricks; as he runs he is stroboscopically assaulted by flashes of light that glare through the slats, or by his own shadow cast on the bricks. This flickery agitation is precisely what alarmed Kafka about the cinema, with its bombardment of imagery like sunspots. In 1924 he complained that 'the quickness, the rapidity of the succession of images . . . appropriate our gaze. They inundate consciousness.' The girls run behind K, but Welles's camera – mounted on a wheelchair pulled by a runner – speeds ahead of him. Its mobility matches the tactics of the action painters, who wanted to stage an event rather than replicate a scene, and the striations of light and shade in the narrow tunnels, as jerky and spasmodic as ammunition from a machine gun, recall a comment by the critic Harold Rosenberg. An action painting, Rosenberg said in 1952, is 'apocalyptic wallpaper'.

Welles's action paintings, made with light, are blurred or erased as soon as they are seen, or else shot to smithereens. The showdown at the end of *The Lady from Shanghai* occurs in a hall of mirrors, where there is no way of telling the real person from his or her simulacrum. Those mirrors, like the camera, reproduce people and multiply them indefinitely. The facsimiles of Elsa and her husband fire at each other and shatter the maze of optical illusions. As O'Hara, Welles looks on without regret. The iconoclastic scene recurs in *The Trial*, when K edges down a corridor panelled with mirrors in the Advocate's apartment. The seductive nurse, her body apparently depthless, stands in a niche from which the mirror is missing. 'I broke the glass,' she tells K. 'I wanted you to come to me.' K – like Orphée entering the underworld through the surface of a mirror in Cocteau's film – steps in to join her. In his *Don Quixote*, Welles sent the knight charging down the aisle of a cinema to slash the screen with his sword. Quixote wants to rescue a starlet who is being mistreated in the film. K, however, happily accepts the invitation to live in the nurse's looking-glass world. In *Touch of Evil*, one of Grandi's thugs spies on Susan as she dresses in her hotel room, shining a torch into her darkened refuge from a building across the way. Her window has no shade, but she does not consent to be picked out and caressed by that darting spotlight. She comes to the window and, as if leaning out of a cinema screen into the third dimension, tells the voyeur not to waste his batteries. She then unscrews the bulb in the ceiling light and hurls it at him. When Vargas arrives he asks 'Can we turn the light on now?' 'No,' she says flatly, 'we can't.' You cannot make a film without electricity: Welles has once more pulled the plug on the art he practised.

Rosenberg said that the action painter depicted 'his own daily annihilation'. So did Welles. Morally, he deplored the conceptual violence of modern art, which disclosed the instability of our world. Artistically, he found it scarily exhilarating. Montage dynamises reality, as does dynamite. *Touch of Evil* shows that process of fission at work during the ticking countdown to detonation. Convertibles, push carts, farm animals and ambling pedestrians eddy about, defeating the efforts of policemen and border guards to impose control. The overarching camera on its crane interconnects these disparate beings, but when the bomb goes off they are hurled apart again by its unleashed energy. Rudy Linnekar, a man of substance a moment ago, is 'blown to jelly' and could now be strained through a sieve. 'You have to get outa here,' warns a member of the road construction gang later in the film. 'We're gonna blast again.' Physics shows how volatile our world is, and chemistry demonstrates its combustibility. A flask of acid aimed at Vargas splashes on to a nightclub poster. Above the door a neon sign advertises '20 SIZZLING STRIPPERS 20', and one of them actually sizzles as the chemical corrodes her image on the paper and makes her body smoulder. The girl in question has already gone up in smoke: it was she who died in the car with Linnekar. Quinlan rightly observes that the choice of dynamite as a weapon was crucial, since 'the killer didn't just want Linnekar dead, he wanted him destroyed, annihilated'. The method is nihilistic, and Welles in 1966 underlined the point by questioning the left-wing intellectual revolt of 'a new generation of Nihilists'.

Quinlan's forensic technique depends on collating whatever is left behind after the big bang, piecing together the fragments of a disintegrated world. 'An old lady on Main Street picked up a shoe last night', he remembers. 'The shoe had a foot in it.' The foot, of course, was no longer attached to Rudy Linnekar's body. Quinlan makes good that dismemberment with a joking substitution of his own when he incriminates Sanchez by depositing two sticks of dynamite in a shoe box in the bathroom. Meddling at crime scenes, he plays with bits of bodies or prosthetic substitutes for bodily parts: Vargas mentions 'the dentures in the Ewell case'. *Touch of Evil* confirms Sartre's suspicion about the 'false disorder' of *Citizen Kane*: Welles purposely created confusion, distraction, discomfort, because these – as he saw it – were the imperatives of modern art. A mangled phrase used by Grandi plays with a gruesome metamorphosis of the body. He warns Quinlan about what will happen 'if Vargas goes on . . . shooting his face off'. He means shooting his mouth off, firing accusations like guns. But the mistake suits the film's mood of dangerous experimentation: it is as if Vargas had shot himself in the face, literally effacing his own identity.

In a fifty-eight page memo written after Universal sacked him and recut the film, Welles felt no need to apologise for the overlapping dialogue during Sanchez's interrogation: the scene was intended to ensure that 'the audience's ability to follow everything that's being talked about is strained to the utmost point of safety'. *Citizen Kane* began with a sign ordering us to keep out; Welles here warns that a film may be unsafe to watch or listen to. He explained his aims by appealing to the tenets of cubism in literature, painting and even music. Cubism showed objects from a succession of jarring, inconsistent angles. This is how Welles intended to present his characters, and he regretted the way that the marriage of Vargas and Susan, who are drawn together sexually but divided in every other way, had been softened by the studio's addition of cute, smoochy scenes he had not directed. He thought that 'reducing the peculiar angles and sharp edges . . . eliminates whatever might be interesting about the couple'. The graphic contours of cubism are here applied to the physical and psychological adjustments two newlyweds must make. And if the angles and edges fail to cohere? The cubists relied on glue, the essential ingredient of collage. During the early scene in which Grandi menaces Susan, who laughs off his threats, Welles planned a brief 'contrapuntal' cut back to the explosion. The interruption was meant to make the quarrel 'inconclusive' or 'deliberately anti-climactic', defusing Grandi's threats. The studio's editors, he noted, had removed the interruption, 'welding' or 'gluing these two parts together'. For once, the glue was being used to paste a jumbled collage into a kind of logic, but at least its presence indicated that nothing cohered naturally: episodes had to be forced together, held in place until the adhesive hardened.

On the soundtrack, Welles wanted a similar cubist pile-up of music. During the opening crane shot, he wanted to use a selection of the juke-boxes and honky-tonk bands that broadcast their wares into the street from the town's bars and cantinas, contrasting mambo with rock and roll and 'Afro-Cuban jazz' in their competition for aural space; this brassy Babel was replaced by the continuous, unifying percussive beat of the score the studio commissioned from Henry Mancini. On the way to the Mirador, Welles also planned to cut back and forth between the radios in the two cars. Garbled news broadcasts in two different languages would have been mixed into an aleatory symphony – a Mexican waltz, a schmaltzy lullaby for Susan, police sirens, the thunder of dynamite at the construction site – as Vargas fiddled with the dial to change stations. In *The War of the Worlds*, the radio transmits reports of alarms in outer space while the orchestras in hotel ballrooms try to maintain melodic normality. Twenty years later, Welles was still listening in to the atonal music of the spheres.

When he planned the score for *The Trial*, Welles sought the same clash of idioms and ages, speeding through the history of music like O'Hara as he tours the deranged museum of modern painting. K's predicament is represented by a baroque threnody taken from the first bars of Tomaso Albinoni's *Adagio*. Albinoni's organ funereally announces that a solemn, implacable ritual is underway, conducting men from one world to the next; its dead march is heard when K crosses the square where the deportees are huddled, when he staggers away from the flogging in the closet, or as he is conducted towards the crater where he will be killed. Albinoni escorts him to the Advocate's door, but once he is inside, the soundtrack instantly jumps forward two centuries: he chases the nurse and the undressed Bloch through the rooms to the sound of a jazz trio. Jazz – irregular and offbeat, disrupting steady rhythms and risking blue notes – starts up when Miss Burstner woozily returns from her nightclub, and it follows K to and from his rendezvous with Titorelli. Albinoni's organ sounds when he accepts the story's determinism, but whenever he attempts to amend or outrun his fate the piano, bass and drums urge him on. The syncopation of jazz expresses a slangy American liberty, a refusal to accept hallowed, customary rules.

Irmie scoffs when she tells K that her father is worried about 'the honour of the family and all that jazz'.

Welles does not ease the transition between musical styles: the principle of collage emphasises those dissonant angles and edges. The film's settings are equally jumbled. K walks out of the riveted industrial ironmongery of the court's headquarters on to a baroque staircase where Irmie awaits him beside a statue in billowing stone robes. He then wanders away into an office precinct of concrete and glass boxes lit by neon strips. The scene begins in the nineteenth century, takes a detour into the eighteenth, then advances into the twentieth. In their 1909 manifesto, the Italian futurists declared that the spirit of modernity had cancelled both time and space, the familiar co-ordinates that once enabled us to date and locate ourselves. Welles photographed that future, in which people without identities wander for all eternity through a city that is Zagreb, Paris, nowhere and everywhere.

K's landlady cheers him up by remarking that his arrest is nothing personal. 'I get the feeling of something abstract,' she says. K glumly agrees that 'It's so abstract I can't even consider that it applies to me.' Their use of that word, a talisman of modernism, is telling. What did the modernists abstract us from? From ourselves, and from a reality that owed its appearance of rationality to the conscientious lies told by art. In 1942 in *The Myth of Sisyphus,* Camus summed up the revelatory moment when man, suddenly aware of how absurd his life is, comes to reject the routine of rising, travelling to the factory, working like an automaton and doing the same journey in reverse before repeating it tomorrow. This is the mental drill that Jean forces on Berenger in *Rhinoceros* when he orders him to shave, stop drinking, wear a clean shirt, polish his shoes, and arrive on time for work. Abstracted from such chores, the awakened man looks back on an existence that has no point. Camus likened this sorry inhuman spectacle to the sight of someone talking on the telephone on the other side of a glass partition. Welles, as if concurring, included such a scene in *The Trial* when Irmie comes to visit K at work and, debarred from the office itself, stands behind a thick glass wall, mouthing inaudible, meaningless words.

'It happens,' Camus said in describing the advent of truth, 'that the stage sets collapse.' Welles's initial designs for *The Trial* acted out this vastation. 'The sets', he explained in 1965, 'were to gradually disappear. The number of realistic elements was to gradually diminish . . . until only open space remained, as if everything had dissolved away.'

As usual he ran out of money, and could not build the sets that were to vanish. He therefore made do with the lumber room of the Gare d'Orsay. This did not mean that he accepted those false fronts – what Camus called 'the stage scenery masked by habit' – that cover up shaky absurdity. In fact, he literalised Camus' metaphor by sending K to the theatre, then denying him the chance to watch the show. In the novel, a telephone call at the office summons K to his first appearance before the court. In the film, he goes to the theatre (or perhaps the opera, since Welles originally wanted the orchestra to be playing the overture to *The Merry Widow*) and is beckoned from his seat to be told the news. The detour allows Welles to imply that social life is a shabby, unconvincing theatrical performance. His camera turns the auditorium back to front: instead of looking at the stage, we look out from onstage as the curtain parts and sheds an artificial glare on the tiers of boxes. The excited patrons applaud – or are they laughing at us, while we, members of another audience, hold the mirror up to them? K leaves without disturbing the pudgy woman beside him, who is fast asleep.

Thanks to Welles's metaphysical magic, the stage sets neither collapse nor disappear. They do not need to, because they never existed. As K and the Advocate continue their dispute after that disillusioning slide show, a bright, empty screen stretches between their faces, still lit by the beam from the projector. Here is the final destination of modern art, as bleakly averse to human feeling as the whiteness of Moby Dick. Discussing 'the end of Art' in the 1950s, Rosenberg said that 'the American vanguard painter took to the white expanse of the canvas as Melville's Ishmael took to the sea'. Enlightenment is the absence of images: a white canvas, a blank screen, confronted – as in the film's unwritten final credits – by the burning lamp of the projector.

In 1967, Welles brought his earlier Faustian persona up to date when he played the advertising executive Jonathan Lute in Michael Winner's *I'll Never Forget What's 'Is Name*. Once more he is a man who promotes himself to the status of a god. He enjoys the same aerial perspective as Harry Lime: he has a penthouse office in Bloomsbury, and practises golf on a roof terrace, idly smashing the windows of neighbours in adjacent buildings. He shares Lime's amused incapacity for human feeling. While Oliver Reed – as a copy-writer who tries to escape from his spell – grapples with the mistress who maligns him, Lute looks on impassively, a cigar plugged into his mouth. He also paraphrases Arkadin's anecdote about the scorpion. After a rally with toy cars on a miniature speedtrack, he says 'I always seem to win. It's my nature.'

Lute keeps society going by telling lies, but he absolves himself from having to believe in them. He samples a breakfast cereal which his firm advertises, spits it out in disgust, then demands why the flakes don't make squeaky noises in the bowl. He knows that the right true end of consumption is excretion, since advertisers persuade people to buy things they do not need and probably cannot stomach. Like Lime, he is an authority on the lower depths where an affluent society's excess is flushed away. Pouring the contents of an ashtray and a champagne bottle into a greedy trash mill, he says 'In the twentieth century, the main product of all human endeavour is waste . . . A whole new industry's grown up just to dispose of it – millions of sewage farms and rubbish pits', where unread poetry is churned together with 'the outer wrappings of processed cheese'. He might be referring to the windblown detritus in *Touch of Evil*, or the bulldozed dump outside the city in *The Trial*. Lute ventures a prophecy for his protégé's benefit, like Lime with Holly Martins or Borgia with Orsini or Arkadin with van Stratten: 'In two centuries, dear boy, there will be five people to every square yard of ground, and all of them standing on a great mountain of garbage. It's up to you and me to see that we're standing on it and not under it.' The line recurs in a subversive commercial filmed by his acolyte, over images of corpses being shovelled into a trench at a concentration camp.

By this time Welles himself was a waste product, discarded by his own industry, and Winner makes him suffer again the indignity of having a film taken away from him and re-edited. Reed orders him out of the cutting room where the commercial is being spliced together. He goes quietly, murmuring 'Round here, you're God.' He is further humiliated when the tinny voice of a Speak Your Weight machine on a railway platform announces 'You are 30 stone 7 pounds', causing him to shudder. Once proud that there were so many of him, Welles now acknowledged that there might be too much of him. During his vigil at Chartres in *F for Fake*, He recalled Lute's vision of the bloated, cloacal economy, and extended it to the cosmos. 'Ours, the scientists keep telling us,' Welles said as he looked up at the cathedral, 'is a universe which is disposable.' He contrasted this monumental tribute to 'God's glory and the dignity of man' – a rose window that brought heaven down to earth, and the columnar forest of sages and elders around the portals – with the paltriness of the contemporary world-view. 'All that's left, most artists seem to feel these days, is man – naked, poor forked radish': the line is delivered with a breathy rumble, like the elegiac sigh made by the retreating sea of faith in Matthew Arnold's poem 'Dover Beach'. At least Welles, speaking beneath leafless shivering trees in a chilly fog, has found a use for his physique, which plumps up the starved, diminished human image. Whatever else he might have become, he was no forked radish.

In 1975, a few months after the opening of *F for Fake*, he accepted an award from the American Film Institute in Los Angeles. At the ceremony he issued another bulletin on his own advance towards obsolescence and mankind's concurrent extinction. 'We are a vanishing breed,' he said. As it happened, the breed in question was a tiny minority of the human race: he was bemoaning the treatment of independent film-makers like himself in 'this conglomerated world of ours'. In his speech he looked askance at the economic system of mass production, indiscriminate consumption and conspicuous waste whose rules are promulgated in Winner's film. He likened himself to a family farm, with a smaller output than the agricultural factories of the day, or to a friendly neighbour-hood grocery store whose owners hold out against the monopolistic supermarkets. Reversing history and returning – in smoggy, motorised Los Angeles – to the pastoral idyll of *The Magnificent Ambersons*, he said he was a traveller on a side road, content to move more slowly than drivers on the freeway.

It was an endearing performance, guilefully concealing his intransigence. In retreating to the past, Welles found a way of combating the present. Already, in Ionesco's version of the last man, he discerned traces of the two earlier men who for the rest of his life were to conduct his insanely idealistic, teasingly seditious campaign against modernity: Don Quixote and Sir John Falstaff. He had been filming his own *Don Quixote* on and off since 1957, and he presented *Chimes at Midnight* on stage in Dublin just before he began rehearsals of *Rhinoceros*. When Berenger refuses to join the pack and calls for 'international solidarity', his fellow-worker Dudard says 'You're a Don Quixote.' He adds that he does not mean to be insulting. Berenger is even more like Shakespeare's wily sluggard. He is slothful, fond of drink, physically and mentally sloppy. The bureaucrats he has to deal with treat these qualities as demerits, but Berenger's vices become what Jean calls 'the weapons of patience and culture, the weapons of the mind', as wittily poignant as Quixote's lance or Falstaff's verbal retaliations. Allegorical to the end, Welles saw his own victory or defeat as a verdict on faltering humankind. He worried that man had been superseded by the quicker calculations of machines, or by a technological society that had compressed individuals into interchangeable, anonymous units. As valiant as Quixote, as sly as Falstaff, he was therefore determined to remain himself.

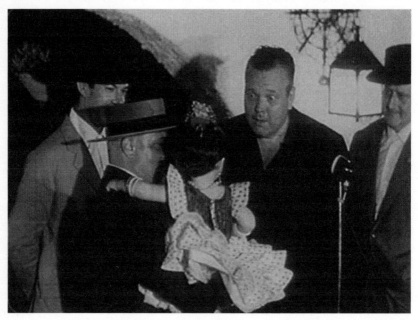

The sherry-makers of Jerez pay tribute to Welles in the
television newsreel from *Don Quixote*.

CHAPTER 14

Quixote

According to Cervantes, the neighbours of the senile backwoodsman whose name was either Quixada, Quesada, Quexana or Quixano were taken aback when he grandly rechristened himself Don Quixote and set off to 'roam through the whole world, armed from head to foot and mounted on his steed, in search of adventures'. Welles, aware of how disastrously the journey turned out, chose all the same to follow Quixote's example, and conducted his career as a picaresque romance. In the screenplay for *The Cradle Will Rock*, his young self indignantly denies being a theatre professional, and declares 'I'm an adventurer.' He admired the same buccaneering spirit in Arkadin, whom he described in 1958 as 'a pure adventurer'. Joan Plowright, recalling her role as Pip in *Moby Dick – Rehearsed*, has said that the production was the most exhilarating she ever took part in; it was also, she added, a 'quixotic adventure'. In the narration for his film of *Don Quixote*, Welles hinted at the resemblance between himself and Cervantes' hero. The broken-down quester, he said, possessed 'so much heart – and so few means'.

In the novel, Quixote pays homage to the carved image of St George on an altar and calls his predecessor 'one of the best knights errant the divine warfare or church militant ever had'. Welles had no such lofty sense of spiritual vocation, although during the 1940s he campaigned for the UN Committee to Win the Peace or the Soviet-American Congress and editorialised in a monthly political magazine called *Free World*. His own quixotic mission was his film of *Don Quixote*, too high-minded for the mercenary culture in which he had to operate. He first tested Mischa Auer for the role of the knight in 1955, and later pleaded with Charlton Heston to take the part. Finally he settled on Francisco Reiguera, exiled in Mexico because of his opposition to Franco. He worked on the film intermittently in Mexico, Spain and Italy, using haphazardly assembled crews and assigning technical chores to his wife and other household helpers. In 1971, juggling the inconsistent footage, he decided to recast the adaptation of the novel as a documentary essay on Spain. He sympathised with the country's ancient mood of stylish, haughty morbidity. 'Nowhere,' as the philosopher Georges Bataille put it, 'does humanity lean over the empty depths of life with greater obstinacy than in Spain.' Even so, the project came no nearer to completion, and Welles began devising excuses for his postponements. The producer Dominique Antoine asked when he intended to finish it. On the day that he decided never again to set foot in Spain, he said. This implied that his account of the country's fall into pragmatic, ignoble modernity would make him unwelcome there. Behind the radical bluff, he was admitting that there would be no end. He refused to retire from the crusade, or repentantly admit his insanity like Cervantes' dying hero. Welles was proud to be more quixotic than Quixote himself.

Others independently developed the idea he could not realise. In 1960 John Steinbeck, imagining a contemporary American Quixote whom he called Don Keehan, loaded up a camper van which he nicknamed Rocinante and set out on a tour of the United States, chronicling the trip in *Travels with Charley*. Arthur Miller's script for *The Misfits*, filmed in Nevada by John Huston in 1960, began as a short story subtitled The Last Frontier of the Quixotic Cowboy. Rocinante is here as obsolete as the knight who once rode on her. Miller's cowboys round up mustangs to be slaughtered for dog food; the horses can't even have careers as children's ponies, because 'kids ride motor-scooters now'. In 1982, in *Monsignor Quixote*, Graham Greene described the adventures of an unworldly village priest in a Spain whose mock-medieval social stasis had ended with the death of Franco. The Sancho Panza who accompanies him is a communist, and they ride in a battered car called Rocinante. Quixote refuses to ditch the vehicle, and imagines Rocinante reproaching him by declaiming Wolsey's lines, delivered by Welles in *A Man For All Seasons*: 'Had I but serv'd my God with half the zeal I serv'd my king, he would not in mine age have left me naked to mine enemies.' He and Sancho share an interest in the cosmonauts then exploring space, just as Welles's Quixote was to make a trip to the moon. In Vallodilid, Greene's Sancho takes Quixote to the cinema. 'So that's what they call a film,' the Monsignor sighs, never having seen one. He sits through a pornographic romp entitled *A Maiden's Prayer*, and though he does not try to rescue the heroine – like Welles's Quixote when he slashes the screen – he worries about her apparent suffering, since she spends so much time groaning and screaming.

Quixote, the blinkered enemy of modernity, is omnipresent in our modern world, whose shoddy values he challenges with his lance. Jorge Luis Borges transposed him to the twentieth century in a fable about an imaginary novelist called Pierre Menard, whom he describes as 'author of the *Quixote*'. Of course this honour belongs to Cervantes, but Borges claims that Menard contested it by rewriting the original book. He did so without changing a word, and in the process produced a new work that Borges – on the basis of two and a bit completed chapters – judges to be 'verbally identical' with the original but 'infinitely richer', because it takes account of the changes in consciousness during the three centuries since Cervantes. Welles, retelling the story in his film, also made Quixote travel in time. Cervantes' hero yearned to live in the past; Welles ejected Quixote and Sancho into the uncomprehending present. Sancho, watching television for the first time, scratches his head over a report of Franco's visit to a new reservoir. The same broadcast reports on the scientific desecration of the heavens: it includes a demonstration of sea-to-air missiles developed by the United States for use in a holy war against the Soviet Union. Down on earth, ancient bonds of deference and service have been cancelled by an insistence on equality, which leaves no room for the exceptional individual. When Quixote gets lost, Sancho approaches a group of foreigners – actually members of Welles's film crew – and asks if they have seen his master. 'You mean your boss,' snarls one of them. 'There's no masters any more.' Borges, in another essay on Cervantes, found a contemporary analogy for the novel's dusty tracks and flea-bitten inns: 'imagine a novelist of our time centring attention for the purpose of parody on some filling stations'. This is just what Welles did, for the purpose of elegy rather than parody.

Summarising Menard's career, Borges curtly lists the '*visible* work' he published, and assigns his *Quixote* to the larger, more tantalising category of 'the subterranean, the interminably heroic, the peerless. And – such are the capacities of man! – the unfinished.' Welles's *Quixote* remains unviewable, at least in the form he envisioned (though two hours of the footage were shown at Expo 92 in Seville). Yet perhaps there was no need for him to complete his *Don Quixote*. Hadn't he made it already? The hero and his inane, shiningly beneficent exploits recur in the stories he told.

In 1940 he adapted *Huckleberry Finn* for the radio. At the beginning of Mark Twain's novel, Tom Sawyer recruits Huck to help ambush a contingent of 'Spanish merchants and rich A-rabs' whose cavalcade of elephants and camels are allegedly 'loaded down with di'monds.' Instead, they only manage to disrupt a Sunday school picnic. When Huck complains, Tom says that if he had read 'a book called *Don Quixote*' he'd know that the substitution was 'all done by enchantment': magicians turned the army and its treasures into that meek churchy outing. Though Huck is sceptical, Tom's brave pretence is the manifesto for an American romanticism which Welles inherited. There is no need to rub battered tin lamps and summon up genies; young genius has a visionary power to transfigure the world and recover the wonderment of childhood.

In Booth Tarkington's *The Magnificent Ambersons*, Eugene is said to be 'a knight, . . . – a crazy one, perhaps, if you've read *Don Quixote*'. The tribute is ambiguous: Eugene's impossible dream is the motor car, which destroys the equestrian society of chivalry. In his script for *The Cradle Will Rock*, Welles referred to the nag that draws Kildare's ice cart as this 'spavined Rocinante'. Belonging to 'an endangered species' like the hero himself, the horse has to wait for a Manhattan traffic light to change. But for Welles, more was at issue in *Don Quixote* than a change in the means of transport. Cervantes described the transition from an age of faith to an age of doubt. In some dialogue at the Amberson ball, filmed by Welles but deleted by the RKO editors, Eugene tells Isabel that 'the deepest wrinkles are carved by lack of faith. The serenest brow is the one that believes the most.' In modern times, can such unquestioning belief be anything but self-deceptive?

John Ford's *Stagecoach* showed chivalry improbably flowering all over again in the American West. The Ringo Kid (John Wayne) has been in prison since the age of seventeen, which has quaintly conserved his innocence. He mistakes a saloon floozy for a respectable lady, and doesn't notice the squalor of her home in the red-light district; he proposes marriage and rides away with her to live on a farm. To maintain the chivalric fiction demands virginal credulity, or else an unlimited expenditure of funds. Hearst loaned his guests armour and medieval motley for fancy-dress balls at San Simeon, and in 1922 cast his pert Dulcinea, Marion Davies, as Mary Tudor in a film entitled *When Knighthood Was In Flower*. Welles pointed to the risks of the courtly lover's besotted worship in *The Lady from Shanghai*. Before the brawl in Central Park, O'Hara remarks that 'In this story I start out a little bit like a hero – which I most certainly am not.' Usually knights errant perform feats of valour to earn the lady's esteem. The task Elsa sets O'Hara is murder.

Welles lacked O'Hara's naïveté. *Touch of Evil*, for instance, could be described as *Don Quixote* without the benefit of magic or madness. Quinlan is Quixote, a wandering knight turned detective, who rights wrongs and solves crimes by corruptly tampering with evidence. His helper and admirer Menzies serves as Sancho the squire, but is prevailed upon to betray and eventually kill his master. Tanya is Dulcinea, now ageing and in charge of a bordello: she alone, seen in softer focus through the cloud of cigarette smoke she exhales, preserves the aura of romance stripped from the other characters. Though Welles allowed Dietrich to retain her mystique, he did not share Quixote's reverent attitude to the goddess who inspires the chivalric quest. In his diary about the filming of *Othello*, MacLíammóir remembered an incident in a Montmartre nightclub when Welles received an injection of poison from the varnished talon of a Spanish woman who clasped his hand. 'Like all people with intellectual scorn for The Sex,' MacLíammóir commented, '[Orson] is a born Quixotic.' He passed this misogyny on to Pistol (Michael Aldridge) in *Chimes at Midnight*. Aldridge has Quixote's boney physique, battered armour, floppy hat and fustian rhetoric. The Doll Tearsheet of Jeanne Moreau is his Dulcinea: she bludgeons and abuses him, and her tirade drives him to take refuge in the privy. Welles proved the truth of MacLíammóir's analysis on another occasion when he elaborated a theory about 'the Inequality of the Sexes'. Women, he argued, were uncreative, and had 'invented Nothing – not even hats, the best designers being men'. MacLíammóir responded that women, with their down-to-earth view of things, probably invented comedy. They did so, said Welles, only to ridicule and belittle men. Was Quixote another of his sexual neurotics, idealising women who actually terrified him?

Identifying himself with Quixote, Welles took advantage of the self-referentiality built into the book by Cervantes. In the second volume of the novel, Quixote indignantly discredits a spurious sequel to Cervantes' book published by Alonso Fernández de Avellaneda in 1614. The faker, he complains, gets the names of characters wrong, and libellously intimates that he is no longer in love with Dulcinea. Welles's Quixote takes his reputation less seriously, and signs on to play a caricature of himself in the film. He avoids disgrace because no one recognises him: as he rides through the streets, passers-by take him for Don Camillo, an affable priest in a series of comic novels by Giovanni Guareschi, popular in the 1950s. Sancho too gets on to Welles's payroll as an extra, and is directed to amble on his donkey down a dusty track. Welles himself, smoking a cigar beneath a clump of Mexican cacti, calls 'Cut' at the end of the shot. In a letter home, Sancho warns his family that the film crew might be coming to do some location work. If so, he advises them to 'grab the fattest guy and ask him for a few pesetas'. He naturally imagines that a man who is so fat must be wealthy.

The remark illustrates Welles's perplexity: like Quixote, he had to compete with his own myth. But they dealt with their quandary in different ways. In the novel, Quixote hastens to Barcelona to prove Fernández de Avellaneda a liar. Welles, the incorrigible romancer who beguiled interviewers with fanciful stories about his early days, was more likely to expose himself as a liar; he happily disowned the myth by acknowledging its fraudulence. A television newsreel in *Don Quixote* shows him bartering and cheapening his personal mystique at a ceremony in Jerez, where he receives a fraternal medal of honour from the makers of sherry – a reward for agreeing to be associated with their product. 'The book of chivalry retains the characteristics of epic,' as Ortega y Gasset pointed out, 'except for the belief in the reality of what is being told.' Modern novels, of which *Don Quixote* was the first, do not even pretend to veracity: F also stands for fiction.

The role Welles awarded himself in the film was that of the narrator, a surrogate for Cervantes. He cast the child actress Patty McCormack as an American tourist called Dulcie, and propped her on his knee in the lobby of a Mexican hotel where she listened to him deliver an eight-minute synopsis of the book. Welles could hardly aspire to the eroded body of the gaunt knight. He admired the aristocratic hauteur of the Spanish character, which he found in El Greco's saints, in the brooding kings painted by Velasquez, and in the doomed bullfighter Manolete whose 'purity and courage and nobility' he extolled. Affecting a black cape and sombrero, Welles managed a personal version of the costume that suited such gloomy grandees. Still, he was too bulky to play a character whose emaciation is proof of both his moral refinement and his pitiful vulnerability. Hence his choice of the cadaverous Reiguera, whose frailty is laid bare when he swims naked in a stream or is bathed by Sancho Panza in a tin drum.

In his narration for the film, Welles said that 'If Don Quixote is the great myth, Sancho is the great personality.' All the same, the etiquette governing the actor who plays kings prevented him from taking the part of the demotic squire, whose surname means paunch; he therefore cast Akim Tamiroff in the role. But he staked a claim to both characters when preparing a rough cut of the film, and chose to dub the voice of the extravagant, altruistic master and also that of the lowly, greedy servant. The double act was a psychological necessity. Welles possessed the mind of Quixote in the body of Sancho.

For four centuries, commentators have argued about Quixote. Was he a creator or a destroyer, an idealist or a buffoon, a wild-eyed revolutionary or a nostalgic reactionary? The dispute, in retrospect, is like a discussion of Welles.

Soon after its publication, Cervantes' novel was accused of killing Spain by devaluing its noble national lore: he began to write less than a decade after the loss of the Armada in 1588, so Quixote's embarrassments coincided with the collapse of the country's empire. In Welles's film, Sancho repeats this superstitious charge when Quixote breaks up a religious procession in Seville, believing that the penitents have been bewitched. Sancho protests that he is making war against 'our faith', and kneels to pray for forgiveness while the monks fight Quixote off with their staves. Although Welles's Quixote found himself disoriented and homeless in contemporary Spain, it was he who first prodded the country to cast off feudalism: in the novel, he unchains the galley slaves. Welles omitted that incident from his film, perhaps because he was still not entirely sure that he approved of it. Playing himself in Henry Jaglom's *Someone to Love*, made just before his death in 1985, he likens women's liberation to the freeing of slaves, then warns the gathering of unshackled Californians that 'No civilisation, even Periclean Athens, has survived without slavery.' He invites them to consider the condition of feudal women, who enjoyed – as Dulcinea might have done if she had accepted Quixote's suit – 'a very privileged slavery: the difference between the full slave and the house slave'. He was lucky not to have been massacred by the female members of Jaglom's cast.

Modernity at first demanded the renunciation of romance; but romanticism soon reappraised Quixote. Seeing giants in place of windmills – or, in Welles's adaptation, steam-powered shovels – Quixote views the world metaphorically, overcoming its shabby materialism. He is protected by his innocence, or by the intensity of his imagination. During the nineteenth century, a Christ whose divinity seemed questionable began to merge with the absurdly noble Quixote. In 1876, Dostoevsky called Cervantes' novel 'the ultimate and greatest word yet uttered by human thought', a secular scripture. Dostoevky's own quixotic Christ is the epileptic Myshkin in *The Idiot*, a good man incapable of reforming his venal society or preventing the murder of his Dulcinea, Nastasya Filippovna. Søren Kierkegaard, struggling like Dostoevsky to reconcile the idea of goodness with an ungodly civilisation, admitted that, for him, faith remained a sad and solitary vocation. Haunted by Quixote, he admitted that 'I only understand the Knight of the Doleful Countenance.' In 1914, Ortega y Gasset called Quixote 'a Gothic Christ, torn by a modern anguish; a ridiculous Christ of our own neighbourhood'. Welles, despised and rejected, was happy to see himself as a beatified victim.

Mythic characters are available for hire, and accept whatever meanings commentators and recreators wish on them. Quixote was therefore conscripted by both sides in the ideological disputes of the twentieth century. The national ideology Cervantes supposedly demolished was rehabilitated by Franco, whose regime revered God, Spain, Chivalry and Death. In this line up, death did not signify political failure; it offered the chance of self-sacrifice, admitting the fallen warrior to the valley of tombs outside Madrid where the country's heroes were interred. In Joris Ivens' *The Spanish Earth*, the treasures salvaged from the Duke of Alba's palace in Madrid – bombed by the rebels in 1936 – include an illustrated edition of Cervantes' novel. The next shot in the film is a statue in Plaza de España, with Quixote the standard-bearer accompanied by the stout Sancho; the same monument, encircled by traffic, reappears in Welles's *Don Quixote*. Combatants in the civil war squabbled over the interpretation of this statue. Republicans insisted that Quixote's commanding arm was a radical summons, with Sancho as the vanguard of a proletarian army. Nationalists read the gesture as a fascist salute. Nabokov, lecturing on the novel in Harvard in 1951–52, proposed an analogy between Quixote and Churchill, arguing that the knight errant had chosen a life of '"sweat, tears and blood" as another much fatter gentleman put it on another much more tragic occasion'. But if Welles had agreed to appear in Hochhuth's *Soldiers*, he would have encountered a Churchill

accused of slaughtering a true Quixote. The play is about the concession
Churchill supposedly made to Stalin in agreeing to the assassination of
the Polish freedom-fighter Sikorski, 'the noble Voyevod Quixote of the
Sjem'. Out-argued by Churchill, who refuses to jeopardise his alliance
with Stalin by denouncing Russian war crimes in Poland, Sikorski
remarks with 'a touch of quixotry' that he will persist in calling for
justice.

In reality, those who inconveniently adhere to principles are usually
sidelined or killed off, as Sikorski was. Welles, however, fantasised about
finding room in the modern world for Quixote and his old-fashioned
creed. Menakar in *The Big Brass Ring* reminds the presidential candidate
Pellarin that his romantic wanderings are over by chanting a song
whose refrain is 'The days of chivalry are dead.' Though Welles's notes
call the song 'inconsequential doggerel', it was written by P. G.
Wodehouse for Jerome Kern's 1917 musical *Leave It to Jane*; it
describes Sir Galahad and his colleagues fatuously scrapping in iron
BVDs to please their Janes, and reports that now you can impress a
mistress by buying her jewels, without needing to climb on horseback
and get yourself punctured by a lance. Pellarin ignores the warning and
continues to behave chivalrously, which means quixotically. After all,
he owes his name to Isak Dinesen's Pellegrina in *The Dreamers*, who is
also known as Donna Quixotta de la Mancha. He pardons a maid
when he catches her stealing from his wife, and bets all his money on a
horse fancied by an Asian girl, which happens to be called Cavalier. He
and Menakar deliver another verse of the song as they abscond at the
end of the script. Though chivalry is officially dead, they are intending
– with the help of a briefcase stuffed with stolen money and a large
bottle of brandy – to revive it.

Welles once told a college audience that he worshipped bravery and
believed it to be 'one of the greatest virtues'. But he qualified the heroic
ethos by warning the students 'Don't call me a macho, that's not what
I'm talking about.' So what exactly was he talking about? His notion of
bravery entailed making sacrificial concessions to his enemies; it was a
mode of moral bravura. In 1958 he explained why, as an actor, he exerted
himself on behalf of his Faustian villains: 'Since I believe very strongly in
the quality of chivalry, when I play the role of someone I detest, I put
great value on being chivalrous in my interpretation.' Though Quixote
championed lost causes, this is not a practice he would have understood:
he wanted to rout his foes, rather than to imagine what it felt like to be

them. Welles interpreted the knight's mission as an injunction to contradict his own professed values, to transform himself into his antithesis.

In 1959 he chivalrously bestowed his sympathy on two characters he detested when he delivered the defence attorney's plea for mercy in *Compulsion*. The story of Richard Fleischer's film is based, like Hitchcock's *Rope*, on the case of Leopold and Loeb, college boys who in 1924 murdered a friend as a Nietzschean experiment, defying a non-existent God to punish them. They were defended by Clarence Darrow, whose final speech to the judge requesting leniency took up two days of the court's time. As Jonathan Wilk, Welles is given an abbreviated version of Darrow's plea, which lasts twelve minutes. This was the longest speech in the cinema's history to date; released on record, it added to the catalogue of libertarian orations by Tom Paine, Patrick Henry and John Brown that Welles performed for the gramophone in 1945. He persuaded E. G. Marshall, cast as the prosecutor, not to look him in the eye as he delivered the lines, because that would have made him self-conscious: he wanted to speak the truth rather than showily acting.

As Wilk, Welles has the doleful countenance of the long-suffering knight: tousled, weary, sweaty, his tie askew and his collar loose, with lank greasy hair and appliquéd worry lines beneath his eyes. He does not rumble rhetorically, but toils through his summing-up with an almost depressive lethargy, conscious of how difficult it will be to oppose public opinion by appealing for clemency. Wilk admits the guilt of his clients; he therefore takes a moral and philosophical risk in arguing against the death penalty. By contrast, the concluding tirade of James Stewart in *Rope* seems illogical and evasive. Stewart, the mentor of the homosexual killers, has encouraged the atheism that makes possible their crime; he discovers the body, denounces them, summons the police, and disposes of his own responsibility by declaring that, though he may have talked about such a gratuitous outrage, he would never have committed it. How can this excuse hold up in a film by Hitchcock, who wickedly incites us to imagine murder and grants our fantasies immunity from prosecution?

Wilk transfers the blame to society, which is easier to do when criminals are downtrodden, unlike his pampered clients. He therefore inserts a hesitant, self-disbelieving pause at the end of his claim that the rich should be pitied as much as the poor. 'All parents', he says, 'can be criticised, and these might have done better if they hadn't had so much . . . money.' Aware that wealth hardly qualifies as an extenuating circumstance, he chooses instead to rely on charity or caritas, an unconditional Christian or quixotic love which overlooks our faults and our evil-doing. He addresses a series of rhetorical questions to the judge, who must decide on the verdict without recourse to a jury. 'Can Your Honor tell me what I deserve?' he asks. 'Can Your Honor appraise yourself and say what you deserve?' The judge shifts uneasily in his seat. Later, paraphrasing Portia's intervention at the trial in *The Merchant of Venice*, Wilk says that 'Mercy is the highest attribute of men . . . In this court of law, I am pleading for love.' He explicitly invokes a religion that can be relied on to uplift the beleaguered Quixote or to pardon Falstaff and write off his debts: 'This is a Christian community, so-called. Is there any doubt that these boys would be safe in the hands of the founder of Christianity?'

Again the rhetorical question, dangerously dependent on bluff, goes unanswered. Irony and honesty both dictate that the doubt should remain, because the response might not be the one Wilk hopes for. The young Nietzscheans do not thank him for his intercession, or – as he points out – express any gratitude to God for sparing their lives. When they sneer at Wilk's piety, he can only restate the agnostic dilemma of the liberal, which Welles had known about ever since his vacillating Brutus in 1937. 'A lifetime of doubt and questioning', Wilk says, 'doesn't necessarily mean I've reached any final conclusions.' His mental quest is open-ended, which is another reason why Welles's *Don Quixote* could reach no final conclusion.

Welles lived parallel lives, which required him to commute between parallel projects. Unable to play Quixote, he reverted to one of his earlier Shakespearean performances. Though he abandoned the film of Cervantes' novel, he did complete *Chimes at Midnight*, aware – as Wyndham Lewis argued in *The Lion and the Fox* – that 'Falstaff is [Shakespeare's] Don Quixote'.

Welles spoke of the two characters interchangeably. 'A great figure of myth like Quixote, even like Falstaff,' he said in 1966, belongs to no particular time or place but stands as 'a silhouette against the sky of all time'. The phrase eloquently recalls the Eisensteinian vantage points he used to ennoble the jangadeiros: he dug a sandpit for his camera and from inside this trench looked up at their weathered faces as they withstood the assault of sun and sea or measured their resolve against the thundery clouds. But Quixote and Falstaff, being mythic, have an extra power denied to the overwhelmed jangadeiros. They can change the sky's complexion, alter our spiritual weather. The thin, woebegone knight redeems the world by thinking better of it than it deserves and fighting to improve it. The fat, witty knight loathes the very notion of warfare, but he achieves the same result using different methods. His humour, his verbal invention and even his audacious lying magnify and multiply our sense of human possibility. Not only witty in himself but a source of wit in others, he distributes this grace as generously as Quixote, while doing less physical damage. When Welles called Falstaff 'Shakespeare's good, pure man', he transferred to him the sanctity Dostoevsky and Kierkegaard had discerned in Quixote.

To step sideways from one project to another was logical, since Cervantes and Shakespeare also had parallel lives and even died on the same day (calculated by different calendars) in 1616. Wyndham Lewis argued that Brutus, Coriolanus, Timon of Athens, Hamlet and Othello were versions of Quixote or specimens of the 'quixotic attitude' – though seen with a cold eye, because Shakespeare unlike Cervantes was a positivist, sceptical about the 'great spiritual creation' of chivalry and aware that it had been replaced by the mercantile egotism of Iago. Making these connections, Welles wishfully reversed the moral history that led from medieval to modern times. In 1860, Turgenev delivered a lecture in which he contrasted Quixote and Hamlet as eternal human types. He saw the transition from pious knight to brooding prince as a philosophical catastrophe: Quixote possesses an ardent capacity for belief, whereas Hamlet uses his probing, experimental intellect to promote a Mephistophelean 'doctrine of negation'. In the modern world, the Hamlets have come to outnumber the Quixotes. For Turgenev, that is our loss, because Quixote not Hamlet is the true innovator. 'The Don Quixotes discover; the Hamlets develop,' he said. 'How . . . can the Hamlets evolve anything when they doubt all things and believe in nothing?' Paying tribute to Quixote, Turgenev claimed that 'without such comical crank-pioneers, mankind would not progress, and there would be nothing for the Hamlets to reflect upon'.

Welles, himself a tragicomic crank-pioneer, extended Turgenev's fanciful theory, and in doing so overcame the decline built into it. He avoided Hamlet, even when young. He waited instead for the character

– having peacefully settled in England, as he imagined – to ripen into Falstaff; when that happened, he implicitly equated Falstaff with Quixote by filming *Chimes at Midnight* in Spain. As always, this decision was fortuitous – accidental but inspired. Welles's financial backers were Spanish, and he was living in Madrid at the time. The result ought to look incongruous, as it does when the baked earth of Spain and some stunted olive trees appear in the battle at the end of Olivier's *Richard III*. But Olivier had gone to Spain merely because of its sunshine and cheap labour, and hoped that no one would notice the discontinuity; Welles justified the location by repatriating Falstaff, rooting him in a culture he shares with Quixote. In his homily about Falstaff, he claimed that the character possessed the sustaining, rudimentary goodness of 'bread and wine'. He specified wine, not beer (or the sack which is Falstaff's preferred drink). Bread and wine are staples of a Mediterranean diet, and they function as symbolic representations of Christ's body and blood. Welles's identification with Falstaff was a kind of communion.

He knew that a geographical gulf separated Falstaff and Quixote. Attempting to bridge it, he was once more struggling to unify his disparate selves. In a conversation with MacLíammóir in 1949, he contrasted northern and southern myths. The north, he said, treasures the idea of a golden age, a Merry England which 'only the oak trees and the flowering chestnuts remember truly'. The south is less blithe in its emotional mood. Its landscape is arid, eroded, punished by a lacerating sun. Mediterranean cultures, like the Haiti of the Harlem *Macbeth*, venerate 'Death, the Goddess, the malevolent womb'. Spain alone, MacLíammóir added, still adheres to this cult; and Welles hoped to save the country from its grim fatalism by locating Falstaff's Merry England there. Though he smuggled the reverie south for safekeeping, he could not protect it from the incursions of history. He argued that in *Chimes at Midnight* 'it is more than Falstaff who is dying. It's the old England, dying and betrayed' – rejected by the foxy duplicity of the new king, left behind by the advance into a brutal, pragmatic future. At work on his *Don Quixote*, he saw the same changes overtaking Spain. In his narration for the film, he said that the characters of Cervantes 'express a landscape', and illustrated the remark by a vista of cheap hotels marring the Spanish coast; he adds that this landscape, 'despite being assailed by tourism and development plans, is still alive'. Talking to Peter Viertel, he measured the distance between

Spain's past and its present by contrasting two bullfighters. Antonio Ordóñez, humbly self-effacing, had the traditional virtues, whereas the celebrity matador Luis Miguel Dominguín, a friend of Viertel's and for a while Ava Gardner's lover, stood for 'the Spain of today', and was 'as close to an upper-class torero as you'll ever find'. As a liberal, Welles could hardly bewail what he called 'the falling away of the old shackles', or deny bullfighters their meritocratic right to fame and fortune. But he took sides by choosing to have his remains interred at a farm in the Ronda owned by Ordóñez.

When he transplanted Falstaff to Quixote's home ground, Welles gave him a mythical terrain to inhabit. In *Chimes at Midnight*, he returned to the primal scenery of epic, which – as Ortega y Gasset put it in his essay on *Don Quixote* – deals with 'the past as such' and 'speaks to us about a world which is no longer'. The first words heard in the film are Shallow's chortling recollection of that glorious, disreputable time: 'Jesus, the days that we have seen.' Falstaff, snoring in bed or snuggling up to the fire, dreams of another 'world which is no longer' – though he does not risk himself, like Quixote, by venturing forth to find if it still exists. That world is Eden or Arcady or Grand Detour or perhaps the Basque country where, as Welles chuckles in his television film, the local dialect is supposed to be the language spoken by Adam and Eve in paradise. Wherever it happens to be, we think of it as the setting for our childhoods. During the Gadshill robbery in *Chimes at Midnight*, bandits disguised as friars scamper through an autumnal forest, like the schoolboys in *The Stranger*: crime is harmlessly redefined as play. On Shallow's estate, where the film begins, the remembered garden is preserved, as if cryogenically, beneath a counterpane of snow. While the dying Quixote guiltily regrets his past, Falstaff dies happily, babbling of green fields. Welles too pined for an idyllic past, even though the misadventures of his two derelict knights demonstrated that it was gone for ever. He spent his boyhood, he said in 1982, in an 'old-fashioned, early-Tarkington' society, with horse-drawn buggies and no electricity; Grand Detour was 'one of those lost Edens you get thrown out of'. In fact, like Quixote quitting his dreary village in the barren province of La Mancha, he chose to leave. But he preferred to think that he had been expelled – though for what secret, guilty act of transgression? Then, wandering around Ireland in his donkey-cart in 1931, he described the country as 'a kind of lost Eden rich in romance'. He needed to believe in the existence of such a happy state, from which he then excluded himself. Eden was the age of innocence; he belonged, as he said in 1934, to 'the age of insolence'. In his interview about *Chimes at Midnight*, he declared that 'the central theme in Western culture is the lost paradise'. It was also the theme of his own life.

Welles directing his own rejection at the end of *Chimes at Midnight*.

CHAPTER 15

Falstaff

Hazlitt asserted 'It is we who are Hamlet', while Coleridge confided that 'I have a smack of Hamlet in me.' For Hazlitt, the identification derived from our collective lassitude and misery, which we shake off by going to a play. Coleridge, in a more private confession, was likening his own creative irresolution to Hamlet's interest in detour and digression rather than duty. Welles did not need to declare the likeness between himself and Falstaff: his performances of the role, from *Five Kings* in 1939 to *Chimes at Midnight* in 1966, made it self-evident. A French poster for his film of *Henry IV*, its title simplified to *Falstaff* for that market, solemnised the fusion between them. It depicts Welles as a silhouetted blob, amorphous like a Rohrshach blot, black on a ground of white paper – except for a single glowing point of red, which represents the phallic tip of the cigar he grips in his right hand. This alone distinguishes director from actor: despite his other addictions, Falstaff could hardly smoke, since tobacco was a bequest of the Renaissance, imported from the Americas by Elizabethan mariners. It is Welles himself who is branded with a symptomatic weakness by being given this modern prop, which he wields as a commanding baton. Coleridge owned up to only a smack of Hamlet. Welles, from brain to belly, was Falstaff, and his later life might have been extrapolated from Shakespeare's plays about the corpulent, unreliable, ingenuous scapegrace.

Indirectly defending himself against detractors, he allegorised Falstaff as 'the greatest conception of a good man' or 'the most complete good man' in literature, just as, in the narration for his *Don Quixote*, he called the knight 'the most perfect gentleman that has ever existed'. In 1967, Tynan asked Welles his opinion of Auden's claim that Falstaff is a type of Christ, the god who is lovingly made manifest to humanity in the guise of 'a real man' and is promptly condemned as 'a blasphemer and a Lord of Misrule'. Welles said he had no argument with the theory, and wittily improved on it by adding that he preferred to think of Falstaff as 'a Christmas tree decorated with vices'. As he saw it, those vices, which he shared, were virtues according to another moral code. In

1958 he had chosen to overlook Macbeth's crimes by calling him 'a great man, who likes good wine'. Greatness and goodness are alike humanised by the possession of a hearty appetite.

Welles's fellow-diners, when describing his repasts, enviously magnified the quantities he ate: myth-making is a collaborative activity. In 1952 in Paris, Michael Powell watched him tackle breakfast, one course of which allegedly comprised 'eight boiled eggs, shelled and then beaten up with ground black pepper, sea salt and butter in a bowl'. In 1955 in London, during rehearsals of his *Moby Dick* adaptation, he periodically disappeared, apparently to evade men serving writs. He usually returned with a Fortnum & Mason hamper, from which – according to Joan Plowright – he would pick out 'two chickens, pâté de foie gras, quails' eggs and succulent pastries', washed down by 'a bottle of Chablis or two'. In his last years, the Los Angeles restaurant Ma Maison served him lunch every day, and accepted his presence – like a sideshow for out-of-towners – as reimbursement. Falstaff, chided for not paying his bill at the Eastcheap tavern, would have relished the arrangement. In 1982, French film critics laid on a banquet for Welles at Fouquet's restaurant in Paris. They ate their way through a digest of his screen credits: crayfish salad in homage to the monsters of the deep dredged up in *The Lady from Shanghai*, asparagus that grew in Falstaff's green fields, a recipe for turbot borrowed from Arkadin's kitchen, and a dessert previously served in the Amberson mansion. Even the bread rolls were embossed, like the gates of Xanadu, with Kane's initial capital.

Greed and gluttony are unthinking, uncontrollable. Welles's gormandising was more premeditated, and he had good reason for his Falstaffian blowouts. Asked by a colleague how he had become so fat, Welles replied that eating had replaced creativity in his life. When young, thin and bankable, he had been able to make works of art. Now, unable to direct, he passed the time by turning himself into a work of art. Thanks to Shakespeare, he was able to consider his weight as a moral prerogative. In *Henry IV*, Falstaff mistrusts Prince John because he is so abstemious, just as Caesar is rightly suspicious of the lean, hungry Cassius. A man with no liking for food and drink probably dislikes himself, which makes him dangerous to others. Meals are fuel, like the oil which Eugene Morgan's automobiles guzzle, but they are also ballast. They make us feel secure, safe, comforted; gorged, we are happy, peaceful, a threat to no one. Peter Sellers walked off the set of *Casino Royale* after a neurotic punch-up with the director, and stayed away for three weeks. Welles, arriving for work every day, made a habit of pointedly asking 'Where's our thin friend this morning?'

This justification of appetite underlies two of Welles's projects, in roles that are ancillary Falstaffs. In 1941 he wrote and narrated *His Honor, The Mayor*, broadcast on CBS in a season of 'plays about the meaning of America' performed by The Free Company – a propagandist series to which Sherwood Anderson, Archibald MacLeish and William Saroyan also contributed. Ray Collins as the mayor spends a tense day coping with a putsch by a gang of white supremacists. He fortifies himself for the moral fight with a series of gargantuan repasts. Welles's narration tallies his intake: pancakes with maple syrup for breakfast, two nut bars before a lunch that includes potatoes, bread and butter and custard pie, and a dinner of creamed chicken, baked potatoes and hot bread, followed by chocolate cake and ice cream. 'Take my word for it,' says Welles as narrator, 'when responsibilities get to be almost unendurable, a man on a diet takes to his sugars and starches as an addict retreats to his opium-pipe, or a drunkard to his bottle.' By the end of the day, the mayor has gained five pounds, which partly makes up for losing ten years of his life in the crisis. *His Honor, The Mayor* is a Brechtian parable, and it might be expected to share Brecht's attitude to such conspicuous consumption: in *Mahagonny* an affluent citizen eats himself to death, and in *The Seven Deadly Sins* the chorus sarcastically sings the praises of bingeing. But the meals console Welles's mayor, steady him, and supply him with a means of diplomatic avoidance, enabling him to dodge an importunate caller by saying he is out to lunch.

In 1968, Welles conscientiously snacked his way through *Is Paris Burning?*, directed by René Clément. His role here was the Swedish consul Nordling, who – as the representative in occupied Paris of a neutral country – negotiated with the Nazis in the hope of handing over political prisoners to the Red Cross. Sweatily overweight, Welles squeezes in and out of small cars as he speeds on his persuasive errands. Demanding sustenance at every stop, he seems, in the rationed city, to be driven by selfish appetite. But his campaign is disinterested, and the food and drink he calls for are reminders of human values more profound and nutritious than the blood and soil worshipped by the Nazis. He agrees to plead the case of one prisoner because in peacetime he visited the man's country house and there ate a trout mousse which he still remembers fondly. Feeling faint, he asks von Colditz (Gert Frobe) for some brandy. The military commander offers water instead, which is better for you than fermented grain. 'Couldn't agree with you more,' says Nordling, and sourly smiles at von Colditz like Falstaff summing up Prince John. Of course it's because water is so good for you that he detests the stuff. Abstinence seems morally unhealthy to him: the Nazis train the body as a lethal machine. During a bargaining session in the kitchen of the Hotel Meurice, Nordling picks at shavings of the chocolate flowers that decorate a cake. 'Why', he asks as he does so, 'has Hitler ordered the destruction of Paris?' The cake and the imperilled city are momentarily equated. Civilisation is about surfeit, sensuous luxury, which gives an extra value to Welles's magnificently useless bulk.

The equivalence between Welles and Falstaff was mental as much as physical. They shared an irrepressible inventiveness. This enabled Welles, like Falstaff, to squirm out of trouble or improvise a way around obstacles. He complimented himself on this talent at the end of *Touch of Evil*. After Quinlan weeps a single tear of remorse for his murder of Menzies, Vargas comments that this is one thing he won't be able to talk his way out of. 'You wanna bet?' says Quinlan. Vargas smiles for a second, like Hal beguiled by Falstaff's effrontery. Then at once – just as Falstaff instantly elaborates a self-defence when Hal and Poins accuse him of running away from the Gadshill robbery – Quinlan starts to tell a story and transfer blame: 'You killed him, Vargas.' Condemnation and wonderment do battle here.

During the interview in which he insisted on Falstaff's supreme goodness, Welles acknowledged that the character's downfall was inevitable and perhaps deserved. Goodness must fail: the world, as currently constituted, cannot tolerate it. 'Almost all serious stories,' he said, 'are stories of a failure', and they entail a death. But that death, he added, 'is more lost paradise than defeat'. For Shakespeare, Falstaff was a participant in history, exploiting the military and political disputes and rivalries of his time; for Welles, the character belonged in myth – a universal myth about our expulsion from paradise, and a personal myth which hallowed Welles himself as a rejected saviour, a lost leader, an abused, overgrown infant.

On location in Spain in 1964, the photographer Nicolas Tikhomiroff documented the metamorphosis. In some of Tikhomiroff's shots, Welles, behind the camera, is still wearing the monastic robes which are Falstaff's disguise during the robbery: if we didn't know the story or anything about Welles, we might take him for an unworldly, rubicund abbot. In the mountaintop castle at Cardona, where he filmed the opening scene at court, a chance lighting effect confirms Welles's godly status. He stands in profile between a high, narrow window; light streams through, bisected by bars, and in a long slanting ray targets his head, like a signal of divine favour in a nineteenth-century biblical illustration. But the portent remains ambiguous, because Welles inevitably has a cigar plugged into his mouth, which adds a cloud of brighter smoke – as dazzling as steam from a whistling kettle, thanks to Tikhomiroff's skill in the darkroom – to the beam of sunlight from the window. The nimbus behind Welles's head, sharpening the outline of his face and restoring his youthful features, looks divine; the fumes of the cigar could just as well be diabolical. Despite its aura of sanctity, the image contains an inadvertent joke which drags the god down to ground. Welles has been made to hold the pose for so long that the accumulated ash on the tip of his preposterously long cigar is drooping, about to drop off: a reminder of declining potency, of a failure that is shamingly physiological.

Self-parody saved Welles from the sanctimoniousness that deifies elderly actors. Olivier played Zeus in a vacuous romp called *Clash of the Titans*, and in his late eighties Gielgud read Genesis on the BBC. If Welles was a god, he was one who knew himself to be unworthy. He was also one who made himself manifest in the loose and baggy form of a monster. 'You're a mess, honey,' Tanya says to Quinlan, whose bloated physique, inside a greasy coat and beneath a dented hat, is the same as Falstaff's. But why should a higher being have the trim build of an exemplary human specimen – of Charlton Heston as Vargas, or Keith Baxter as Hal? Edgar Wind explains that, for Renaissance mystics, 'the monstrous is higher and more divine than the normal'. That applies to supernatural apparitions and Martians, to circus freaks and white whales, and also to actors, whose bodies are so mysteriously and terrifyingly mutable. Welles as Falstaff positioned himself midway between the monster and the god.

The world Welles created for Falstaff to live in never existed, except in the imagination. He attributed to Shakespeare, with very little justification, a 'preoccupation with Camelot, which is the great English legend'. That preoccupation, in fact, was American rather than 'arch-typically English', which may be why Welles so insisted on it. Late in the 1950s, John Steinbeck embarked on a modern translation of Thomas Malory's Arthurian legends, and tried to find the spirit of 'gallantry' in cynical

America. He paid tribute to knightly organisations like the Elks or the Masons, said they were 'all, all noble', and argued that their exclusiveness proved the 'need for grandeur against a background of commonness, for aristocracy in the midst of democracy'. Catering to that need, the Lerner and Loewe musical *Camelot* opened at the end of 1960, the year in which Welles tried out *Chimes at Midnight* on stage in Dublin. Contemporary history demonstrated the resilience of the myth. After the assassination of President Kennedy, which occurred during Welles's first stint filming *Chimes at Midnight* in the autumn of 1964, the idealistic experiment of Arthur's round table was regretfully linked with the early hopes of the Kennedy administration. Lancelot in the *Camelot* refers to his 'training programme for knights', which makes it sound like an advertisement for Kennedy's Peace Corps. Two early memoirs of Kennedy used phrases quoted from Arthur's elegiac song about Camelot in the musical – 'a fleeting wisp of glory' and 'one brief shining moment' – as their titles.

Welles, at the end of his musing on Camelot, called Falstaff 'a kind of refugee from that world'. The myth has amended and softened the facts of the case. Actually, Falstaff is not a refugee from that world, or from any other. He profitably operates in the present, using the wars to make money, and calculates that Hal's ascent to the throne will mean further enrichment. Welles treated him as a displaced person because he was one himself: a rootless refugee from America, a sorry, decaying evacuee from childhood and the blissful garden. In Mistress Quickly's malapropistic obituary, Shakespeare sends Falstaff to 'Arthur's bosom' after his death. The destination is the wrong one: she means Abraham's bosom. Welles, rather than waiting to reunite them in death, saw Falstaff as Arthur's offspring. Emerging from the privy in *Five Kings*, the character's first utterance is an unShakespearean snatch of song, 'When Arthur first in court'. Later, in the scene when Falstaff impersonates the king and royally compliments himself as 'a good portly man, i' faith and a corpulent', Bardolph sings another song about the time 'when good King Arthur ruled this land'. It is his reminder that the round table was used for eating as well as for political deliberations. Arthur is here a cook, who steals three pecks of barley meal and makes a suet pudding stuffed with plums:

> The King and Queen did eat thereof,
> And noble men beside.

> And what they could not eat that night
> The Queen next morning fried.

Welles's interpolation has an echo when Hal, assuming his father's voice in the charade he and Falstaff act out, denounces his companion as 'that stuffed cloakbag of guts, that roasted Manningtree ox with the pudding in his belly'. Falstaff, the 'big pudding' in the song, is here literally created by Arthur, who gobbles him up, reheats him and eats him again as leftovers, just as Welles fed on Falstaff, nurturing himself whenever he returned to the character.

Transforming Shakespearean history into myth, Welles also changed the chronicle plays into something more like a novel. He looked out through the back wall of the theatre to the society and the landscape beyond it, releasing the characters into that larger setting as novels do: hence the gutted castles of *Chimes at Midnight*, the bare mountains planted with gibbets not trees, the muddy open grave of the battlefield, the laving snow on Shallow's estate, or the open country into which Falstaff's coffin is dragged. He approached the plays obliquely, using a favourite novel as an intermediary. His view of Falstaff as a lapsed Arthurian knight was prompted by T. H. White's *The Once and Future King*, which he treated as a substitute for and an amplification of Shakespeare. In Dublin, he sometimes cancelled stage performances of *Chimes at Midnight* and gave readings instead, taking White's Arthurian epic as one of his texts. The novel served his purpose because it reversed the conventional relationship between present and past. Though White's Lancelot and Guinever, like Welles's Hotspur, live through 'the sundown of chivalry', theirs was still an age of gold. Ours, White argued in the middle of the twentieth century, is the dark age, befouled by a mechanised brutality. Welles adopted the same duality when describing *The Magnificent Ambersons*. The point, he said, was 'to make this golden world' and then show its destruction by 'the bad black world that came'.

White defended feudalism, as Welles was to do when castigating the women in *Someone to Love*, because its social and economic system authoritatively informed people who they were, and dispensed them from the anguished, indecisive journey of self-discovery and self-definition which modern men must embark on. It was a regressive argument, dangerously and culpably so when White began to publish his Arthurian sequence in 1939. Though Merlyn, living backwards, remembers Hitler and disparages his policy of 'reformation by the sword', this is not quite enough to differentiate White from those political fantasists who – like the recruits to the English Banner in *The Smiler with a Knife* – were simultaneously attempting to remedievalise the world. The young Welles, a Renaissance man and thus a self-invented being, would have had little sympathy with this nostalgia. But the middle-aged Welles thought differently, which is why he revived his compilation of the history plays, giving Falstaff precedence over the five kings. The 1939 version ended with Henry V's French victories. In 1960, Welles omitted this triumph and chose to conclude with Falstaff's death. Kafka's cowed bureaucrats and Ionesco's marauding rhinos had shown him what became of the individual in a society that agglomerated men into masses. For the purposes of his myth, he decided that the decline began when Hal killed Hotspur and spurned Falstaff: here was a dual warning that – in the starkly functional world to come – idealism and idiosyncrasy would not be tolerated.

'What an amazing time the age of chivalry was!' White remarks in his last volume, published in 1958. 'Everybody was essentially himself – was riotously busy fulfilling the vagaries of human nature.' He calls this era 'the age of fullness', of rowdy enjoyments like the romp Welles choreographed in the tavern dormitory in *Chimes at Midnight*, and he sees that fullness embodied in a 'coruscating mixture of oddities who . . . possessed the things called souls as well as bodies': gargoyles such as those Welles admired at Chartres in *F for Fake*, or those with whom he populated his film about Falstaff – Norman Rodway's undersized, rambunctious Hotspur, who drops his bath towel to reveal a naked rump and lets a letter about the rebellion drop into his tub; Michael Aldridge's spindly Pistol and the Mistress Quickly of Margaret Rutherford with her pursy, indignantly quivering jowls; Walter Chiari's Silence, convulsed by his stammer, and the Shallow of Alan Webb who is a senescent, capering sprite. Reviewing a panorama of 'the fabled Merry England of the Middle Ages', Lancelot and Guinever gaze on what White calls 'the Age of Individualism'. God moulds clay into quirky, unrepeatable forms, rather than mechanically applying a formula and duplicating men as if in a factory. Rejected by factory managers, Welles like Falstaff was a relic of Camelot. Writing in *Esquire* in 1958, he dismissed the industrial organisation of Hollywood, arguing that theatre and film belonged outside bourgeois society with its pettifogging discipline. He dated the loss of artistic autonomy from the moment when the actor and director Henry Irving was knighted by Queen Victoria. Great artists, he said, did not deserve to be promoted to minor nobility; they deserved much more. Rather than hoping for political preferment from the new king, Falstaff would have done better to renounce his knighthood.

As Lancelot and Guinever gaze down from their solar window at the outstretched ground of their bright Eden, they sing about 'the moneth of May'. In Merry England, it is always spring. Welles was right to say that the oaks and chestnuts were the true historians, conserving a memory of Merry England in their subterranean roots even while their upper halves look bare, skeletal and blackened; trees are undying gods, annually reborn. He returned to these metaphors throughout his life, because they enabled him to think about the mysterious resurrections of theatrical performance and his own periodic acts of self-regeneration. A reviewer in 1938, praising his boisterous production of *The Shoemaker's Holiday*, pointed out that Welles had treated the proletarian comedy as a rite of spring, 'a lusty May-Day hymn to the joys of procreation'. In *Everybody's Shakespeare*, Welles said that the plays addressed 'every mood and minute of a man's season'. But a man, as he discovered in growing older, has more than one season, and should try to be a man for all of them, adjusting to each new stage in life as it arrives. Wolsey, played by Welles in the film of Robert Bolt's play, does not manage it: he dies in icy, paralysed winter. In his interview with Marienstras in 1974, Welles doomed his own art to the same fate. 'The theatre', he said, 'is like the seasons. It's now in its winter, but I don't foresee any real spring.' Suffering through the change from one life and the next, he often had such doubts. As Rochester in the film of *Jane Eyre*, Welles explains his bad humour to Jane by remarking 'I was as green as you once – aye, grass-green. But now my spring is gone.' A deleted line from Graham Greene's script for *The Third Man* perhaps underlines the irony in Harry Lime's odd surname, which is an acid variant of the novelist's: Martins says that Lime 'couldn't bear the colour green'. Though Lime recovers from his own reported death, he lacks comedy's faith in nature and its renewal. In freezing Munich, with a band playing Christmas carols outside, Arkadin pulls back the bedclothes and smirks at the cowering Zouk. Asked what he's laughing at, he replies 'Old age . . . old age.' Once more, the individual's death coincides with the death of the year, and no saviour is born to console us. But as Falstaff, Welles plays a timeless man, an elderly baby who experiences all the seasons at once; a highly-seasoned creature who exemplifies the tragicomic wisdom propounded to Gloucester in *King Lear* and demonstrates that 'Ripeness is all.'

Chimes at Midnight introduces him by having Hal, in a line written by Welles not Shakespeare, ask 'Where's Falstaff?' In the theatre he would have to walk onto the stage, but a film can go to find him, so the camera races through the inn on a labyrinthine search. He is discovered in bed; he heaves beneath the covers and shakes himself awake, as if he had hauled himself out of an overnight death. The scene recalls the opening of *Citizen Kane*, where the camera more surreptitiously closes in on a bedridden hero. The dying Kane, like Falstaff, is an old man who has regained his childhood, encased in that snowy globe. Falstaff's rosebud is his page, played by Welles's daughter Beatrice. A child is his younger self; the page announces Falstaff's sickness at the end of the film, declares 'Falstaff is dead' when Poins casually queries whose coffin it is, and it is he (or she) who weeps for him.

Welles supplemented Shakespeare's political history with a natural history of his own. He wanted to chronicle the remorseless narrative of seasonal change, and intended to start filming during summer and conclude in winter. Such orderly chronology proved impossible, given his haphazard, scrambled working methods. But the inconsistencies prove poetically apt. The battle of Shrewsbury begins in a leafless forest which is newly affoliated by the time Hotspur dies, as if the fighting had lasted several months. Perhaps it is true, as Westmoreland says to Prince John in discussing the state's distempers, that 'the seasons change their manners, as the year / Had found some months asleep and leaped them over.' Revising his initial scheme, Welles chose to have the film both begin and end in winter: Falstaff and Shallow totter through snow in the first scene, and Henry IV holds court in a denuded castle, with John Gielgud's breath congealing in the frosty air. When Shallow reminisces, a bell tolls to make audible that midnight chime which is a memento mori, and another tocsin starts up when the narrator (Ralph Richardson) mentions the murder of Richard II. A distant organ sounds during Hal's first monologue, in which he whispers his determination to reject Falstaff: an instrument as mournful as that funereal bell. Hal's address to Falstaff as 'the latter spring' and 'All-hallow summer' is removed by Welles from the second scene of the play and placed later, when Hal quits the inn to go to court. This makes it a definitive breach. Hal – who intends to 'imitate the sun' – is abandoning those belated seasons, which have outlived their time. During the Gadshill robbery, he scatters a shroud of autumn leaves on Falstaff, treating him as the corpse of a moribund year.

Near the end Falstaff is depressed, melancholy, off-loading his retainers because he is penniless. Jean Moreau's Doll Tearsheet tries to revivify him. She enters the inn wrapped in a black Spanish cloak with a broad-brimmed hat worn aslant, a patrician costume Welles himself favoured. But she is barefoot, and she shrugs off her gloom in discarding the cloak. Falstaff slumps wearily onto the unmade bed and calls for a bawdy song to make him merry. Doll clambers on top of him, chafing his exhausted flesh back into sentience with her hands, squirming across his belly like a mountaineer. He lacks the energy to make love to her; it is she – another manifestation of Graves's 'White Goddess of Life-in-Death and Death-in-Life' – who tries to fertilise him. He moans 'I am old', while Hal, watching from the rafters, comments on desire outliving performance. Doll, unable to manage an arousal, later falls asleep on Hal's chest. The scene notices a double sexual defeat: Poins stares bitterly at Hal – aware that their affair has also terminated, though for diplomatic not biological reasons – and accuses him of hypocrisy. When Doll waves to Falstaff as he leaves for Gloucestershire and tells him to patch up his body for heaven, she speaks, he says, like a death's head. Decamping for London when Hal inherits the throne, Falstaff expects renewal and rebirth. But it is the wrong season for comedy, and he departs across snowy fields, with bells tolling. The winter in this scene was Welles's improvised set-dressing: the weather had changed, and he suppressed the signs of spring by spreading bed linen on the turf.

Chimes at Midnight ends with Falstaff's coffin trundled off for burial. Of course the box is empty. Like Arthur, the once and future king, mythical heroes never irrevocably die. Falstaff has already bounced back from a sham death in battle; and Welles, though following Falstaff's movement towards death, intended to reverse that history by simultaneously making another film about a latter-day Falstaff who escapes from his accusers and from mortal penalties, rowing a boat towards freedom. Determined to demonstrate how many of him there were, he planned to direct and act in a version of Robert Louis Stevenson's *Treasure Island* while filming *Chimes at Midnight*. It was the pirate story the Spanish producers wanted; Welles persuaded them to pay for the Shakespeare adaptation as well, claiming he could use the same actors and some of the same sets. Taverns were easily interchangeable, so the set for the Eastcheap bawdy-house could thriftily serve as the Admiral Benbow Inn. His casting elicited analogies between Shakespeare's characters and those of Stevenson, identifying parallels between different retellings of the same myth. Falstaff had his equivalent in the cynical, irrepressible old buccaneer Long John Silver, which was to be Welles's role. Baxter agreed to play Dr Livesey. Tony Beckley, engaged as Poins, reluctantly took on extra work as Israel Hands, a member of Silver's crew. Gielgud (though nobody told him so in advance) was expected to pitch in as Squire Trelawney. Welles's nepotism didn't quite extend to casting Beatrice as Jim Hawkins, who is beguiled and terrorised by Silver. A younger Baxter would have been ideal, since his relationship with Silver corresponds to that between Hal and Falstaff. In the novel Silver calls Jim 'my son', and says he is 'the pitcher of my own self when I was young and handsome'. He protects Jim from his fellow pirates, but only as insurance in case he needs a character witness at a trial. Jim eventually betrays him and surrenders him to the law. Even so, Shakespeare's stern Lord Chief Justice melts into Stevenson's squire, who – though he condemns Silver's villainy – declines to prosecute him, enabling him to escape with some of the treasure. This is *Henry IV* with a happier ending.

This doubling-up proved impracticable, and *Treasure Island* was soon abandoned. In 1973, however, Welles played Silver in an internationally financed *Treasure Island* directed by John Hough; he also took partial credit for the screenplay, using the pseudonym O. W. Jeeves in homage to P. G. Wodehouse's apparently obsequious but actually manipulative butler. His performance as Silver is self-referential, exposing the underside of Falstaff and a darker and sadder facet of Welles himself.

In a straw hat, lolling among barrels in his grog shop, he looks like Falstaff put out to pasture. His wife is a Caribbean woman in a turban: he has married a Doll even more far-fetchedly exotic than Jeanne Moreau. He lacks Falstaff's resilience, and is a moody, maudlin, self-scourging drunk. His physical debility is woefully evident. Silver is supposed to possess a peg leg; Welles had two legs, but by the 1970s they could scarcely support him, so he could not be expected to balance on a prosthesis. His lower half is therefore concealed by baggy culottes or a tattered floor-length cloak, and the camera tactfully avoids looking downwards. Once, photographed from behind, Silver hops nimbly on his wooden limb. For this scene, Welles was replaced by a stand-in who did not resemble him. In the cave, one of the pirates jeers at Silver as a 'fat old cripple'. To mention Welles's infirmity must have been a capital crime: Silver shoots him dead.

The cane used by Quinlan and by Mr Clay in *The Immortal Story*, a prop that punningly evokes Charles Foster Kane, is here a crutch, which must do heavier duty. Along with this shaming aid, Welles's Silver has two familiars: a black monkey and a foul-mouthed parrot. The bird is his ribald, rebarbative alter ego. In the novel Silver describes it as an almost Mephistophelean creature. He calculates that it is two hundred years old, and says that 'if anybody's seen more wickedness, it must be the devil himself'. It recalls the white cockatoo that raises its crest and screeches mockingly at the break-up of Kane's second marriage, or the parrot that nips the runaway Holly Martins in *The Third Man*. A parrot can be cheeky with impunity, like a ventriloquist's dummy. In reality, Welles was too mild-mannered to tolerate such a companion; he preferred budgerigars, though once in Spain he did own a macaw. Instead of Silver's menagerie, he took up, during the last years of his life, with a sheep dog, a Newfoundland puppy, and finally with a pampered, obnoxious white poodle called Kiki, which he cradles in *Someone to Love*. Kiki was as highly strung and petulant as the poodle that trails Roderigo in Welles's *Othello*. He catered to her every whim: she shared his bedroom, occupied a chair of her own at Ma Maison where she lapped water from a butter dish, and used the balcony of his Paris hotel suite as her private toilet. Friends wondered at his devotion. If Falstaff was, as Auden called him, 'the prince's dog' – an indulged and secretly despised clown – then the Falstaffian Welles in turn needed an absurd pet to dote on him. Kiki expected only to be fed and caressed, and could be relied on never to ask him when he was going to finish *Don Quixote*.

Welles fitted his role in *Treasure Island* into the intervals of work on *F for Fake*, in which he elaborated a sunnier, more optimistic variant of the seasonal narrative that condemns Falstaff. *F for Fake*, like *Henry IV* and every other Shakespearean play, has a double plot. The supposed protagonist is the forger Elmyr de Hory; but, just as Falstaff upstages the contentious politicians, the real hero turns out to be Welles himself, who bought a television documentary about Elmyr made by François Reichenbach, re-edited it, added some passages of personal reminiscence, and turned Elmyr's biography into another instalment of his own autobiography. Older now than he was when he played Falstaff, Welles here resurrects himself and takes up residence in a lingering spring and a protracted, blazing, sensually glutted summer.

At his first appearance in *F for Fake*, he confesses his charlatanism by remembering the lies that got him his job in Dublin. He recalls his vagabondage in Ireland, trailing around in a donkey cart and painting landscapes. 'It was a very nice summer,' he says as he strolls through the

Tuileries beneath thickly leafy trees in another summer. But summer's end in 1931 provoked a crisis: 'Winter was coming in', and how would he survive it? Immediately Welles fits a frosty blue filter to the camera, and returns to the Tuileries to show the same trees naked and shivering. The moment he describes how he saved himself from cold and hunger by persuading MacLíammóir and Edwards to employ him, the scene switches back to the Tuileries in summer, with long violet shadows and an impressionistic glare from the setting sun. But because the seasonal cycle is a wheel of fortune, Welles soon reverts to misty spring, with fewer leaves on the trees. Occupying a park bench, which for Charlie Chaplin was the very symbol of bereft urban misery, he reflects on the vagaries of those twin wheels: 'I began at the top and have been working my way down ever since.'

His detour to Chartres happens during mortified winter, after which he returns to fog-bound Orly airport to collect Oja Kodar. Then the cycle speeds up, instantly transporting Kodar to a Mediterranean resort in torrid summer, where she tantalises Picasso by parading beneath the window of his studio on her daily walks to and from the beach. At Chartres, Welles contemplates the mouldering of our works and our bodies. But thanks to Kodar – promenading in her bikini, or posing naked when Picasso lures her inside – the body enjoys a sleek, sunned, brazen rejuvenation. Cicadas whirr on the soundtrack, to evoke the sweltering southern night. A boy called Olaf from Oslo jazzily serenades Kodar on his trombone, a steel phallus. Welles, entertaining the notion of cuckoldry with a good humour Othello could not manage, says he does not know what happened between Kodar and Picasso in the studio, but he is sure that the results were 'to say the least of it . . . fruitful'. The ellipsis marks a suggestive pause, and his utterance of the word 'fruitful' coincides with a zoom out from a close-up of the cleft in Kodar's buttocks. Picasso's brushes, propped in a pot, seem to be stroking her flanks. As penile substitutes, they have ousted the Norwegian boy's trombone. Welles goes on to describe a Keatsian season of surfeit: 'Figs sweetened on the tree, grapes burst into ripeness on the vines, and twenty-two – twenty-two! – large portraits of Miss Oja Kodar were born under that virile brush.'

The story of Kodar's period as Picasso's muse, invented by Welles, rewrites *The Immortal Story*, the Dinesen fable he filmed in 1968, and supplies it with an optimistic outcome. This time, the suborned woman – Kodar here, or Virginie in the Dinesen film – renounces union with the young blonde traveller: the Norwegian tourist Olaf or the Danish sailor

334

Pierre in *The Immortal Story*. Like Doll clinging to Falstaff, she chooses the brooding voyeuristic tycoon, whose potency she restores: Picasso, seen staring through a shuttered window, or Welles's Mr Clay. Kodar too leaves with a reward worth more than the harlot's fee paid to Virginie. She extorts the twenty-two canvases from Picasso in exchange for her forfeited days at the beach, and takes them to Paris to be sold for her own enrichment. Welles has slipped into the story and assumed Picasso's role: Kodar was his legatee, and she inherited his unfinished films.

'She gave you a whole summer,' Kodar's bedridden grandfather tells Picasso, as if she had bartered her youth by agreeing to spend her days in the studio not on the beach. Picasso, allegedly disgruntled by Kodar's hard bargain, denounces the portraits as forgeries, and is enraged by a newspaper review declaring that he 'has been born again' because of the 'fecundity' of these new works. Welles so relishes this word that he even takes his cigar out of his mouth to enunciate it. Then, showing off a talent for self-regeneration as imperious as Picasso's, he concludes the story by raising the dead. Kodar's sickly grandfather, who languishes in bed during the spurious interview with Picasso, is seen stretched on the grass, like Hamlet's father dozing or dead in his orchard. Welles covers him with a shroud, then causes him to float upwards, like a spirit on its way to the afterlife. Arresting the corpse in mid-air, he whips the sheet off and reveals that there is nothing beneath it. For a moment it looks as if Welles has performed a miracle, defying the gravity that tugs us to earth and into the grave. But the sheet is cladding for a ghost, who has already evaporated.

In 1934, Welles envisaged Shakespeare as an energetic stripling like himself, who helped England get 'up on its hind legs' and pushed it towards a modern mental awareness. In his society, 'all kinds of old established convictions were being questioned'. By the time of *Chimes at Midnight*, Shakespeare had grown old along with Welles, and stared grumpily backwards not ambitiously forwards. Welles now decided that 'Shakespeare was profoundly against the modern world, as I am. I am against my modern age, he was against his. His villains are modern people.' Sliding sideways from *Henry IV* to *King Lear*, he claimed that modernity meant 'gouging out eyes and sons being ungrateful to their fathers'.

Welles's new allegiances were scandalously retrograde. Chivalry could hardly be reconciled with American democratic values. 'The mass of mankind has not been born with saddles on their backs,' Thomas Jefferson declared in 1826, 'nor a favoured few booted and spurred, ready to ride them legitimately, by the grace of God.' Mark Twain despatched his Connecticut Yankee to King Arthur's court to 'undermine knighthood' and install 'a better order of things', which he does by mechanically massacring 'the chivalry of England'. Welles mounted a lone defence, standing up to the massed might of his own country. In his documentary about the Basques, he praised the American woman who had brought her young son to live in this enclave, depriving him of the 'mechanical aids to amusement' to which American teenagers were addicted. He promised that he was 'not going to make a speech against the machine age' but did so all the same, blaming machinery and its 'softening of life' for reducing us to passivity and provoking a 'moral crisis'. Among the amenities Welles disapproved of was the camera, which he once called 'a vile machine'. He passed on this self-spiting opinion to Don Quixote, who in his film calls the camera 'a demonic instrument' and says that its inventor is surely in hell. He then attacks Welles's own camera with his lance. In *Orlando Furioso*, Ariosto warns that Alfonso d'Este's cannon foundry put an end to chivalry and its choreographed jousting, and has Orlando perform a pardonable act of sabotage by pitching the 'murderous engine' into the sea. In *Don Quixote*, Welles made the knight skirmish with a sputtering motor scooter, which he denounces as a dragon. His campaign against the internal combustion engine proves unsuccessful; he and Sancho repair the damage to themselves while sheltering in a junkyard of gutted cars.

Contrasting America with the Basque country, Welles pondered the difference between restlessly 'moving somewhere' with the help of technology and contentedly 'living in a certain way' or 'being a certain thing'. 'I don't think that progress and civilisation go together,' he said. 'The most civilised countries are those where progress is not considered a very important preoccupation.' Narrating *The Magnificent Ambersons*, Welles notices the relativistic quandary of the passengers on the streetcar: 'the faster we're carried, the less time we have to spare'. At the dinner party, Eugene admits that automobiles 'with all their speed forwards . . . may be a step backwards in civilisation'. For all his snobbery about horseless carriages, George too is one of those compulsive, driven 'modern people' who, according to Welles, are classified as villains by Shakespeare. When Lucy (Anne Baxter) asks him what he intends to do with his life, he says he will probably 'take part in movements'. 'What kind?' she enquires. 'Whatever appeals to me,' snorts George. Mobility is an end in itself.

Rather than being hustled through life, Welles argues in his Basque film that we should pause 'to examine the things that our fathers and grand-fathers knew and valued, and which have helped to make our civilisation' – for instance those great books, often first encountered in childhood, which Welles spent his life reading, retelling and dramatising: *The Odyssey,* Shakespeare's plays, *Don Quixote, Treasure Island, Huckleberry Finn,* or any of the other volumes that were piled in the bathtub of his house in the Hollywood hills on the night he died. Having enunciated this principle, he stops to wonder whether the Basques themselves actually exemplify it. You can only be proud of your accumulated, storeyed wisdom 'if you have a library of books to show for your past', and the Basques have none. They even lack the congregation of stone ancestors he filmed at Chartres. Though the young Welles summarily rid himself of his own father, this homage to a paternal inheritance became basic to his sentimental medievalism. Eitel, the landowner in Dinesen's 'A Country Tale' – one of the stories Welles fancied filming – explains the logic of this ancestor worship when he volunteers to atone for a crime committed by his dead father. Christianity, the gospel of proletarians, insists on the equality of all men. But feudalism attends to the bonds of fealty and service that Christianity ruptured, and 'speaks not of brothers and neigh-bours but of fathers and sons'. Therefore, while a Christian would worry first about the care of the living, Eitel attends to the needs of the dead. Aristocrats exist so that 'the past, and the dead, may put their trust in us ... If we are not there, who will look after the past?' Welles assumed that curatorial task in his excursion to Chartres, where he overhears the consoling song of the statuary, voiced by 'dead artists out of the living past'; it also prompted *Chimes at Midnight* in which, as he said to Baxter, he wanted to 'call down the corridors of time'.

Character, Welles declared in 1958 when expounding his theory of chivalry, is 'an aristocratic conception'. Baroness Blixen naturally adhered to this patrician sense of duty. The creed seems stranger when adopted by an American, who decides to disregard his country's poor, tired, huddled masses and replaces the future – America's favourite tense – with the past. As the narrator in *The Magnificent Ambersons,* Welles adds an ironic inflection to the phrase introducing the ball given for George as 'this pageant of the tenantry'. But the deference of the tenantry is preferable to the go-getting selfishness of the motorist who runs over

George and instantly vows 'He ain't goin' to get not one single cent out of me!' Sooner the pageant than the violent, competitive dynamism of traffic. At Shrewsbury in *Chimes at Midnight*, Welles's knights are outfitted like impervious machines. Clothed in metal, they are winched onto horseback by teams of foot soldiers, who tug ropes to haul them into the air and then drop them onto their saddles. They resemble tin men, or armoured vehicles. Jack, in a passage of dialogue deleted from the ball scene in *The Magnificent Ambersons*, remarks that Isabel regards George as 'a little tin god on wheels'.

This regretful interpretation of history contrasts with the progressive view of Shakespeare advanced by Grigori Kozintsev, whose film of *Hamlet* was released in 1964. The *Henry IV* plays, Kozintsev thought, were 'a tale of sick times'; he noted that Engels described the decay of the idle, parasitical Middle Ages as 'Falstaffian'. While Welles sought to delay the arrival of modernity, Kozintsev was determined to force the pace of social change. He wanted people who saw his *Hamlet* to feel that they were smashing 'the very foundations of Elsinore'. The castle – which closes around Hamlet at the beginning of the film, raising its drawbridge and closing its gates to immure him – must be besieged and breached. Its imagined collapse marks the end of feudalism, and allows Kozintsev to hint at the fate of the totalitarian Russian state. He felt briefly ashamed of using a rich merchant's showy Crimean dacha in *Hamlet*, and hoped no one would recognise the shadow the plutocratic palace cast on the sea. Welles possessed no such scruples, and wanted to rebuild the feudal castle: hence Xanadu or Macbeth's humid catacomb of tunnels or the Mogador fortress. Arkadin occupies a Spanish castle perched on a crag, which frowns over the hunched village below: 'That castle's kind of hard to get away from,' says van Stratten. A more democratic apportionment of space, subdividing the castle, is a baleful sign of the family's decline. In another deleted scene, George shouts 'Holy cats!' when he sees excavations for shoddy rental homes in the back garden, and during his last night in the mansion Welles's narration imagines a time when Isabel's bedroom, where George now prays to be forgiven, will have been sliced up, partitioned and pressed into service as some overworked young woman's kitchenette.

Quixote promised Sancho a private island, where he could govern as he saw fit. In *F for Fake*, Welles envies Elmyr his small fiefdom on Ibiza, where he presided over a court composed of art dealers, partygoers, catamites and fellow fakers like Clifford Irving, who forged the autobiography of Howard Hughes. A comment made by Irving in the film associates Elmyr's empire of illusion with the battlemented personal worlds that Welles so often used as sets: 'Elmyr', he remarks, 'has developed a fiction about his life, and to destroy that fiction would tear down the whole castle that he's built.' Welles searched the map for such monopolistic realms, cast away by history like the inaccessible terrain of the Basques. He dreamed of a place as elusive as Merry England or Neverland or Erewhon or Utopia, where a man could perhaps live outside the flux of time, 'erect, silent and alone' like Mr Clay in *The Immortal Story*. In one of his reveries he located this sovereign, imagined state on the island of Maliñha, situated somewhere in the vicinity of Ibiza – between Gibraltar and Corsica, close to the North African coast. Fishermen lost at sea made the first landfall there, attracted by the scent of its flowers (as if the jangadeiros had happened on an undiscovered Eden while sailing down the Brazilian coast). Welles added immediately that this was mere legend, and admitted that most people had never heard of Maliñha. That was because it did not exist.

The imagining island is the setting for *Une grosse Légume*, a novel published by Welles in 1953. It derives from *V.I.P.*, a film treatment he prepared for Korda, which derived in turn from one of Harry Lime's posthumous adventures on the radio. Korda paid Welles's fee in cigars, but never made the film. Maurice Bessy adapted and translated the script, incorporating swathes of Wellesian table-talk about the opposition between tradition and modernity. The V.I.P. or big vegetable or (more colloquially) big cheese is the innocuous Joe Cutler, sent to Maliñha from Mobile, Alabama at the behest of Fresco, a soft-drink firm whose global marketers have noted that the company lacks a franchise on the island. Maliñha's scheming politicians, led by the dumb despot Admiral Massimiliano-Cuccibamba, take Cutler for an envoy sent from Washington by the American President. They expect him to dispense financial aid, in return for ideological concessions and free elections. This is Gogol's *The Government Inspector* relocated to the Mediterranean. Farcical misunderstandings ensue as the islanders fawn over the salesman, but the plot matters less than the exchange of ideas between two continents and two temporal eras. Cutler is a transatlantic muddler like Holly Martins; the Harry Lime of the story is Maliñha's elderly Archbishop, as politically cynical and fruitily corrupt as Welles's Wolsey in *A Man for All Seasons*. The missionary capitalism of America – convinced that progress means mechanised velocity and exponential riches, its high spirits topped up by doses of fizzy drinks – confronts the ancient, wily, insidious genius of what Welles called 'Latinité'. Maliñha is a balmily decadent redoubt of the Latin culture that bred Quixote and Falstaff, and in which the exiled Welles had made himself at home.

The novel begins with a lecture on 'le rançon romanesque de notre caractère latin', delivered by the sly Joachimo Figureido for the benefit of his naive American fiancée Susie Krauss. Susie has her own deluded image of the Latin world, and fantasises about wooers on hot nights playing mandolins beneath balconies. Joachimo corrects her. The Latin character invented the cult of courtly love or 'l'amour romanesque', which arrived in the world at the end of the fourteenth century and impelled the knightly quests of Lancelot, Orlando Furioso, Quixote and Dinesen's old chevalier. But this disinterested ardour should not be confounded with the sentimental, slurping, connubial fidelity Susie has in mind. The balcony, Joachimo explains, exists to make the woman visible but to keep her unattainable. In his country, Juliet does not unfurl a rope ladder so that Romeo can climb up to her – or at least she only does so after taking the precaution of marrying someone else, so that (like Guinevere in the Arthurian story, or the lady from Shanghai) she can enjoy her Romeo as an illicit, adulterous diversion. American women are too co-operative for Joachimo's taste: they take the initiative, and clamber down the rope ladder themselves. The goddess forfeits her sanctity if – like Jeanne Moreau's bedraggled, bleary, hungover Doll – she condescends to behave affectionately. Joachimo's exposition suggests that a double standard enabled Welles to rationalise his own emotional limitations. In his preface to the novel, Bessy succinctly comments on this aspect of Welles's character, and says that he was always a lover but never in love.

The Archbishop's political doctrine measures how far Welles had travelled from his youthful, principled Brutus. With Wildean irony, the priest – whose lips curl in a permanent smile, and whose eyes shine with joyful malice – derides the callow American campaign to impose democracy on the island, and defends the 'classic Mediterranean allure' of dictatorship. Latins, he argues, are incurable anarchists, which is how Welles saw himself; they live behind high walls – castellated, like all those Wellesian heroes – and therefore have no conception of organised community. Their irresponsible individualism is integral to their culture, like olive trees or the midday sun: here the Archbishop anticipates Welles's homily to Falstaff, whom he associated with the sustaining goodness of bread and wine. Northerners engender dictators in a spirit of gloomy penitence, but in the south men applaud a tyrant for more childishly amoral reasons, because they love noise and adore parades. The Archbishop indulgently scoffs at Mussolini as a 'little Caesar', which is what Susan calls the incompetent Latin-American gangster in *Touch of Evil*. The Italians, he claims, never believed the Duce's militant bragging, because they never believe in anything. They simply admired the megaphonic skill of a man who could make his voice heard in more northerly latitudes. Thanks to his days on the radio, Welles understood the affinity between dictators and loudspeakers.

The Archbishop might be a Falstaff who has enjoyed a different future – not rejected by Henry V but granted the promotion to high office he expects, improbably enrolled in holy orders and given a cathedral as his playground. His values are wisely Falstaffian. Susie consults him about a spiritual problem: she has grown to dislike Joachimo and loves Joe Cutler instead, but Joachimo is energetic and Joe is lazy, which she, as a good, industrious American, cannot tolerate. The Archbishop consecrates idleness, repeating Welles's conviction about the incompatibility between progress and civilisation. Later he elaborates a theory to explain the development of the English character, which incidentally reassigns blame for the decline of Merry England. Until the eighteenth century, the Archbishop says, the English were renowned as exuberant, violently passionate creatures, the wild men of Europe. How did they turn into bywords for punctilious self-control? He argues that the steam engine and the industrial revolution caused the change (just as the motor car destroyed paradise in *The Magnificent Ambersons*). English society suddenly required an élite of managers and sober cost-counters to run its factories, like the white-uniformed computer scientist Welles added to Kafka's cast in *The Trial*; public schools were set up to train the young in behaviour that was prudent and commercially reliable. The hobbyhorse was forgotten, and Falstaff was belatedly reinterpreted as a villain and a wastrel. In an essay for Bessy's volume of tributes to him, published in 1963, Welles surmised that England underwent a spiritual change during the eighteeenth century, when alcohol and wine gave way to the thinner, more genteel tipples of tea and coffee. This dietary myth paraphrases Falstaff, who thinks Hal's brother Prince John cold-blooded because he refuses to drink liquor.

The Archbishop's final sermon is reported by Susie, now a convert to his world view. She decides to marry Joe, who knows the precious chemical secret of the Fresco formula: why shouldn't they cash in? To possess knowledge, she tells him, is the contemporary equivalent of being born into the aristocracy, and he would be a fool to squander his birthright. The trouble is that he despises the sugary, carbonised concoction. She tries to persuade him to believe in it, since he is living off the profits from its sale. She is welcome, he sneers, to put her imagination to work by thinking up slogans to advertise Fresco. This provokes her to quote the Archbishop, who considers that the economic hegemony of the Anglo-Saxons depends on their hypocrisy, which always accompanies protestations like Joe's. Latins, having no faith in absolutes, cannot be bothered dissimulating. If they are two-faced, it is only because they want to please, not because they intend to deceive. The Archbishop has told her why she dislikes the truth: she suffers from the ailment of idealism, which she must attempt to cure. The advice was Welles's futile remonstrance to himself.

When Maliñha stages its supposedly democratic election, the admiral's sly, wheedling mistress Lola assures the American investors in Maliñha that 'la féodalité est morte'. Her comment is a lament, not a proud announcement of progress. Feudalism expires all over again at the battle of Shrewsbury, which Welles filmed in the Casa de Campo, an expanse of pine woods and scrub that used to be a royal hunting ground on the western edge of Madrid. *The Spanish Earth* includes a battle there, with the rebels defending the university which they occupied; Welles's narration points out the commander, a former lawyer, who was killed on the very day that Ivens filmed the fighting. By the 1960s, the Casa de Campo was criss-crossed by roads. Welles set the recriminatory dialogue between Hal and Poins beside a shallow, stagnant pond, with cars shuttling past at the edge of the water. Luckily a morning mist obscured them, and gave the scene an aptly mournful look. Once the mist lifted, as Baxter commented, 'the whole ugliness of the place was revealed, but not to the camera'.

At Hotspur's death, the camera was less successful in filtering out the evidence of modernity. As the last of the chevaliers collapses, a motor car can be seen driving through the leafy distance. It's scarcely visible, and in the haze it can easily be taken for a horse, though its pace is too even. Welles may not have noticed, or have relied on us not to notice. Hotspur goes on to say that 'Time, that makes survey of all the world, must have a stop.' Time then stops for him, but for the rest of us it has speeded up, transporting us into the future. In 1981, with downcast gaze and shifty eyes, Welles reflected ruefully on the foresight of Nostradamus in *The Man Who Saw Tomorrow*. 'Do we really want to know about the future?' he asked. 'Maybe so, if we can change it . . . But can we change the future?' Of course we cannot. The intrusion of that car represents the start of a new time, which unseats the caste of horse-riding nobility and consigns Welles himself to oblivion.

Falstaff dares to play the king, and is promptly dethroned. During his first scene in the tavern, Welles cheekily impersonates Henry IV, with a lopsided kitchen pan for a crown. Hal elbows him aside, assumes his father's role, and rehearses his eventual banishment.

At the end of *Chimes at Midnight*, when the news of the accession arrives in Gloucestershire, Falstaff delightedly demands 'What, is the old king dead?' Welles filmed Falstaff's reaction from a low angle, like that he used for Quinlan's entrance as he spills out of his car. He looms in the air, lofty but unsteady, poised for a fall. The film's opening scene, which according to the play's chronology happened just moments before, has already deprived him of this fanciful eminence: he and Shallow are insignificant specks in the bleak, blank, snowy landscape. At court, after despatching Falstaff to prison, the new king retreats into a long shot, his back turned. Falstaff too visibly dwindles, tottering into the draughty shadows towards a small arched doorway in the castle wall. This is the straight gate and the narrow way, which he must squeeze through in making his exit from existence. In *Henry IV* his immediate future remains open to question, since his death is only reported in *Henry V*. Welles's contraction of the plays leaves no such interim. The page remarks on Falstaff's sickness during the court scene, and his coffin is instantly placed on view. Welles gives the last word to a narrator, the voice of the chronicles that were Shakespeare's source. 'For conclusion' this unseen historian commends Henry V's reformation, and guarantees that he will remain 'famous to the world alway'. Ralph Richardson, whose voice constructs this version of the past and anticipates the verdict of the future, was renowned for his Falstaff – he played the part at the Old Vic in 1945, with Olivier as both Hotspur and Shallow – though he is here enlisted to pass judgement on the antique reprobate. Welles knew this flattering preview of the new regime to be untrue, and advised Baxter against playing Henry V who was, he said, a shit. But history is written by the winners, whether or not they owe their victory to money or industrial might or slick public relations.

Falstaff's rejection stuns him; Welles, after long experience, was better prepared. In a contribution to the celebratory volume edited by Bessy, he accepts the justice of this comeuppance. A great actor, he says, like Oedipus or any other classical king, must kill his father, outdo his predecessor. But the upstart should not be surprised when he too is killed off by the next precocious contender. The regicide may even be a contemporary, not a representative of the next generation. 'He *had* to destroy me in some way,' Welles said when he told Barbara Leaming about Olivier's behaviour during the *Rhinoceros* rehearsals. He bore no grudge, and saw this lethal struggle as an orderly succession: winter dies, spring comes, and 'summer's lease' (as Shakespeare's Sonnet 18 puts it) 'hath all too short a date'. The whimsies of fashion in *The Magnificent Ambersons* enforce the same law. You outgrow your clothes even faster than your youth, and overcoats have to be lengthened, according to Welles's narration, 'after a season or two'.

The cycle has continued, even in Welles's absence. In 1991, Gus Van Sant brought *Chimes at Midnight* home to modern America in *My Own Private Idaho*. Van Sant's film begins with a shot-by-shot duplication of Welles's opening scene, slangily amending the initial line. 'Jesus the things we've seen, ain't I right Bob?' says an adolescent hustler. He is addressing Van Sant's Falstaff, an indigent alcoholic who camps in a derelict hotel in Portland, Oregon, attended by a gang of dropouts. Keanu Reeves plays Scottie, who corresponds to Hal. The son of the city's mayor, he rebelliously dresses in black leather and distressed denim, adopts Bob as his 'psychedelic poppa' and 'street tutor' and, when not snorting cocaine, swigs from a bottle of Falstaff beer. He is also yearningly in love with Poins (River Phoenix, whose character is called Mike), making visible a subtext that *Chimes at Midnight* can only hint at. Welles's Merry England has its diminished equivalent in Mike's private Idaho, the flat, featureless waste he retires into whenever he suffers a narcoleptic fit.

Each time a story is retold, we are allowed to hope for a different ending. Van Sant, however, refuses to mitigate the story he retells. Scottie rejects Bob and leaves him to die, then assuages his guilt by charging the funeral expenses to his American Express card. Welles, in his retellings, looked for a way to pardon crimes or even suspend mortality. What if Hamlet aged into Falstaff, and escaped death in the sword fight with Laertes? What if Falstaff was not rejected by Hal but rewarded with a Mediterranean bishopric? Or, as in *The Big Brass Ring*, perhaps the

344

prospective king could give up his throne and run off with Falstaff? Imagining alternative outcomes, Welles amended his own story and permitted himself a more propitious future. 'Only on repeated hearings of a fairy tale', as Bruno Bettelheim put it, 'is a child able to profit fully from what the story has to offer him.' Welles was that listening child, like Patty McCormack in *Don Quixote*; he was also the storyteller, able to gratify his own wishes by changing the narrative and magically forstalling tragedy.

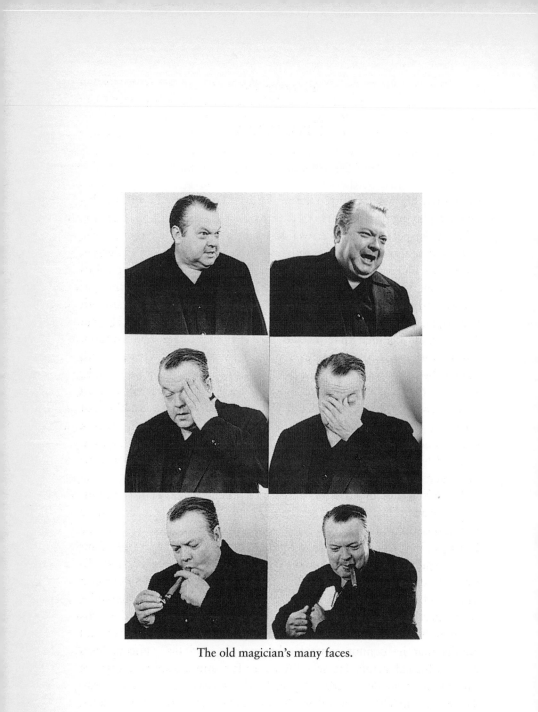

The old magician's many faces.

CHAPTER 16

Prospero

In his early life, Welles skirted the role of Hamlet. At the end of it, he also avoided playing Prospero. He said he loved *The Tempest* more than any other Shakespearean play – as well he might, since it could have been the last instalment of his autobiography: it is about the autocracy of illusion, though its magus voluntarily lays down the staff with which he raises spirits. But Welles never directed the play or acted in it. The omission was so odd that he sometimes hardly believed it, and filled the gap with imaginary productions. In an interview to publicise the Harlem *Macbeth*, he claimed that he had directed *The Tempest* in London. During the 1970s he remembered planning a version of the play with designs by the surrealist painter Pavel Tchelitchev; it was actually *King Lear* that they briefly worked on in 1937. Gielgud once tactlessly offered him the role of the bestial Caliban. Welles refused, preferring to think of Prospero as his ideal self-image. In 1974 he denied that he was a Renaissance man, but said that Prospero certainly was one, and commended him for rejecting the arrogant atheism of the Renaissance by drowning his book of spells and renouncing his black art.

Though Welles bypassed *The Tempest*, he crept up on it by round-about means. *The Immortal Story* in 1968 and *F for Fake* in 1973 were reflections on Shakespeare's play, and in both he played a would-be Prospero. In the Dinesen fable he is Mr Clay, the misanthropic merchant whose walled estate is a domain as solitary as Prospero's island. To translate the immortal story from fiction into fact, he brings together a sailor and a woman. These hirelings are his Miranda and Ferdinand – kept apart by Prospero, but bribed to make love by Mr Clay. His motives, however, are not generous. Prospero in laying down his wand admits that he cannot control other people, and his ineffectualness ensures his salvation. He sees life as a play, and a play as a fugitive formation of shadows. Mr Clay lacks this chastening self-awareness. The woman in *The Immortal Story* criticises his notion of drama. Actors, she says, are supposed to be pretenders, merely simulating love or death, but he resembles 'the Emperor Nero of Rome, who, to amuse himself, had people eaten up by lions'. Even so, the result of his experiment is fatal for him, because he has committed Faust's crime, behaving as if he were a god.

In *F for Fake*, Welles's identification with Prospero is even closer because he plays himself. Swathed in a cabbalistic cape, He exposes himself as a trafficker in illusions like the forger Elmyr de Hory. Again there are suspicions of a Faustian pact. The film includes a quote from a French newspaper, declaring that Elmyr had sold his soul to the Devil in exchange for the devious technical facility that enabled him to imitate Matisse or Picasso. Welles likens him to Paganini, the romantic violinist whose virtuosity was rumoured to be the result of demonic possession. From the margins, he ruefully notices that someone else has improved on his impersonation of Prospero.

The film's other protagonist is Clifford Irving, Elmyr's biographer, himself a skilfully devious faker. After disentangling Elmyr's deceptions in his biography *Fake!*, published in 1969, Irving outdid them by forging the autobiography of Howard Hughes. Claiming to have interviewed the recluse a hundred times in parked cars and motel rooms, Irving presented himself as Hughes's appointed ghost. He duped the publisher McGraw-Hill and *Life* magazine; when Hughes denounced the fraud, Irving went to jail, where Elmyr had also spent time. Welles could only admire such effrontery. Irving was, he claimed in *F for Fake*, 'a much better magician than I am'. He surely did not believe it, since the film's incriminating montage of snippets demonstrates his own technical wizardry. But the comment shrewdly served as insurance. Welles, forever scheming to mitigate the unavoidable doom of tragedy, rejoiced that Prospero had escaped the punishment of his fellow-conjurer Faust.

Dinesen's 'The Immortal Story' was first published in 1958 in a volume entitled *Anecdotes of Destiny*; here it was immediately preceded by 'Tempests', which describes a visionary production of Shakespeare's play directed by the demoniacal Herr Sørensen, who casts himself as Prospero. He finds himself turning into the imperious fantasist, and discovers that the play has spilled over into reality. The next anecdote of destiny in Dinesen's collection – another tale about the predestining power of stories, which lay out the course of our lives in advance – extends this commentary on *The Tempest*. Mr Clay is a hard-headed, unimaginative Prospero who, unable to recognise the difference between art and life, wishes 'to do the thing which cannot be done'. He insists that the story told by so many sailors must be willed into truth, performed for a fee by a Ferdinand and Miranda who are his 'young and lusty jumping jacks' (as Welles gloats when he spies on their copulation). Mr Clay relies on a rancorous, demoralised Ariel, his clerk Levinsky, who recruits the woman. The enactment immediately begins to go wrong: this is a fable about the profane folly of making life imitate art, and as such it was a personal reproach to Welles, who had always conducted his private life as if it were an extension of the roles he played on stage or in film – Faustus, Kurtz, Kane or Falstaff. Levinsky is content in his lowly position, though he lacks Ariel's grudging fondness for Prospero. Ariel wants to regain his liberty, but Levinsky dreads unemployment; nevertheless he facilitates the experiment which, as he knows, will kill Mr Clay and lose him his place.

The woman he suborns, Virginie, both is and is not Miranda. Her name places her in another story: she and the sailor Paul ironically allude to the protagonists of Bernardin de Saint-Pierre's romantic novel *Paul et Virginie*, about a couple who escape from society into an innocent Eden. There is no such 'brave new world' for Dinesen's pair. At dawn the virginal sailor Paul asks Virginie how old she is, and she pretends to be seventeen. Then they are the same age, he replies. It is his infatuated error: she – as played by Jeanne Moreau in the film – is middle-aged, rouged, puffy-faced, cynically experienced, almost a colleague of Doll Tearsheet. And Virginie is not Mr Clay's daughter but the daughter of the business partner he betrayed, bankrupted, evicted from his house, and drove to suicide. She consents to take part in the story because, like Levinsky, she wants revenge.

At least the sailor, played by Norman Eshley, naively and unquestion- ingly fits into the role of Ferdinand (though since all stories overlap he is also Melville's Ishmael, having been the sole survivor of a shipwreck, cast up alone on an island). He tells Virginie that his father drowned before he was born, and wonders what he felt when the sea took him. This might be a cue for Ariel's song, which in Shakespeare's play rings a knell for Ferdinand's father Antonio and describes his mutation into pearls and coral. In 'The Immortal Story', the corpse's underwater fate is transferred to Mr Clay. He has amassed his pile of hard, solid gold, he says, as 'proof against dissolution'; he explains that he turned on Virginie's father because he feared that love, friendship, loyalty and all such soppy, infirm notions would 'dissolve my bones'. Welles utters this phrase with a sepulchral shudder. The resonance of his voice came from emptiness within. Is a man just a wind tunnel, with clayey flesh waiting to be mixed with the soil and brittle bones ready to snap (as Welles's ankles, so overburdened, were liable to do in his last years)? The diplomat's memo in *Mr Arkadin* describes the tycoon as 'a phenomenon of an age of dissolution'. Mr Clay physically experiences that dissolution. This immobile man, who thinks of himself as an unassailable pile of ingots, discovers – like Quinlan top-heavily subsiding into the stream – that he is merely a waste product. Mr Clay turns out to be more tragic than Prospero. Before the end of *The Tempest*, the magician resigns himself to failure, and anxiously prepares to save his soul. Mr Clay's experiment succeeds, so he must be punished for it, and Levinsky finds him dead the next morning. In the story he sits rigid in an armchair in the dining room. In the film, the chair is moved onto a verandah, where Welles watches the epilogue – Paul's farewell, Virginie's cool indifference, Levinsky's acquisition of freedom – with staring, sightless eyes, his face hardened into its last expression of baleful dismay. Dinesen calls Mr Clay 'the old stone-man'; Welles shows him petrifying.

Stories like Dinesen's are immortal because they are perpetually being retold, reinvented. This is true of the sailor's tale, and also of the story about Mr Clay's rivalry with Virginie's father. 'In the course of time', Dinesen comments, 'this story had taken on the character of a myth', just as Kane acquires mythic status as we watch and listen to people talking about him. Welles eavesdrops on the process of myth-making when he rounds up a group of merchants to gossip about Mr Clay as he drives past in his carriage, like the citizens exchanging rumours in *The Magnificent Ambersons*. One of these choral voices has a cockney accent: it belongs to Warren Mitchell, hired by Welles to dub the role of Levinsky, played by Roger Coggio. The incongruity is somehow appropriate, because stories like this are told all over the world. Welles adds to the universal store of variants by choosing pseudo-classical music to accompany the telling: the *Gymnopédies* and *Gnossiennes* for piano by Erik Satie, which are slow, solemn evocations of Greek exercise routines, with figures freezing into statuary as we listen. Spartan athletic festivals were called gymnopaidiai because naked youths performed in them. The music subliminally suggests innocence and also – because it is so archaic – the loss of paradise.

Stories lapse into mortality only when they are limited to a single, authorised version, which is what Mr Clay attempts to impose. If a story is acted out, its human actors can adapt it to suit themselves, as Virginie does. To write it down condemns it to a single, limited meaning. Books inter stories, rather than allowing them to grow, reproduce themselves, recombine: Levinsky entertains Mr Clay during his insomniac nights by reciting from ancient bills, contracts and estimates, toiling through the records of long-defunct, incorrigible business deals. Dinesen escapes from this dead end by encouraging her stories to multiply in the telling. Thus 'The Immortal Story' extends to encompass *The Tempest*, *Paul et Virginie*, even *Moby Dick*. Welles claimed the same liberty when he retold the story. He respected the text and transcribed most of the dialogue from it, but he felt entitled to customise it, making it a story about himself. In his 1982 interview with Bill Krohn, he claimed that during the 1930s, when he was meandering around on a cargo boat, he too had been told the immortal story by a sailor. His annexation began by altering the location. Dinesen's setting is Canton; Welles moved it to Macao (though, as always, he relied on a collage of disparate places, combining a house in Rueil, outside Paris, with some dusty squares in the Spanish coastal village of Pedrazza). This was one of the places he claimed to have visited with his father during those fanciful travels when, like the sailor, he lost his innocence. Whether Welles himself had been there or not, one of his characters had. O'Hara in *The Lady from Shanghai* nostalgically calls the Portuguese colony the wickedest place on earth.

In Dinesen's story, the storyteller is the clerk. He is the bardic figure who spends his nights reading aloud, and his own life-story is a series of reincarnations as he, a wandering Jew, makes his way from Poland to China. Dinesen's Levinsky is a self-destructive Iago, who despises 'the goods of this world' but panders to Mr Clay's greed because it secures his own employment. The story ends as he picks up the shell the sailor has left for Virginie, holds it to his ear and listens to the surging of a bottled ocean. Like the story, he feels he has 'heard it before, long ago. Long, long ago. But where?' In the film, Welles of course took over as narrator as well as playing the protagonist. But he remained in two minds about the story's relevance to him. Interviewed by Gavin Millar on the BBC, he agreed that Mr Clay is 'a kind of director', though he added that 'he shows the total uselessness of the director's job'. However, when Bogdanovich asked if what interested him in the story was 'the notion of a director making things happen', He gruffly replied 'No.' Bogdanovich tried to persuade him that 'a director basically does what Charlie Clay tries to do in the movie'. 'The name's *Charles*,' snapped Welles. 'Certainly no one ever called him "Charlie" in his life.' He was as indignant as if he himself had been impolitely addressed; in fact it is Welles, appropriating the story, who gives him this first name, since in Dinesen's story he is simply Mr Clay. A Charley is mentioned, but he is the young accountant who keeps Virginie as his mistress and sends Levinsky to her with a selection of shawls. Welles's small mistake contains its own revelation. Kane's first name was Charles, though Susan familiarly calls him Charlie.

Welles crucially amended Dinesen's conclusion, extending Mr Clay's role even after his death. In the story, Levinsky waits outside the bedroom, and the sailor leaves Virginie's shell in his care. Welles sidelines Levinsky, so that the transaction can happen between the sailor and Mr Clay, who is already dead. The sailor tells him about the shell, and makes him promise to pass it on; Mr Clay, his face sculpted by rigor mortis, mutely agrees. The sailor places the shell on his lap before he leaves. It is next seen gently rocking on the floorboards beside the chair. Mr Clay's retentive grip no longer functions, but somehow the shell's passage to the ground must have been magically cushioned, because it has not shattered. Seen, it has a beauty and a symbolic allure necessarily absent from Dinesen's glancing reference to 'one big shining pink shell'. Welles turns it into a Nautilus, and when the sailor holds it up, the morning sun catches its thin translucent wall and makes the interior glow, as if it contained light as well as the song Paul says he hears in it. Like the dome in 'Kubla Khan', it is 'a miracle of rare device', properly belonging to the artist who imagined it. Welles therefore awards it to himself, and takes delivery posthumously. Finally, as in Dinesen, the clerk picks it up and listens to it. At this instant, the film fades to white: surf seems to foam across the screen, effacing the characters. It is one of Welles's most lyrical moments, recalling the blizzard inside Kane's globe or the excursion in the snow in *The Magnificent Ambersons*. The song inside the shell is made visible, if not audible.

'I want to see it all with my own eyes,' says Mr Clay as he pays for the story to be played out, like Othello demanding the 'ocular proof' of Desdemona's infidelity. What we see, through his dead eyes as he keeps his vigil on the verandah, is a retrospective review of previous Welles films. The staircase is a smaller-scale replica of the one in the Amberson mansion, and its stacked landings allow for a vertical conversation between the clerk and the sailor, staged like the argument between George and Fanny. When Mr Clay picks up the sailor at the harbour, it is impossible not to remember Bannister's recruitment of O'Hara at the shipping office in *The Lady from Shanghai*; Mr Clay envies the sailor his 'juices', just as Bannister reflects on his young sailor's vitality and manoeuvres him into a liaison with Elsa. Virginie's father left the mirrors behind in the house Mr Clay took from him, so that his murderer should always have to face an image of the hangman. Welles's narration comments that Mr Clay dines alone, grimly confronting his portrait in the glass. In *The Lady from Shanghai* and *The Trial*, those accusing mirrors are shattered. Here the intact mirrors make the house a purgatory where the occupant is tormented by mementoes of his past.

Welles retold the stories of his life to see if he could evade their determinism. 'Echoes', the second of the Dinesen stories about Pellegrina that he began filming near the end of his life, describes a happy, liberating repetition. The opera singer who has lost her voice discovers a boy chorister in whom that voice, she believes, has been reincarnated. But once again the story does not go according to plan. Pellegrina – like Prospero, like Kane bullying Susan into a career as an opera singer, or like Mr Clay playing with Paul and Virginie as if they were dolls – toys with life, forcing it to mimic art. Emanuele rebels, calls Pellegrina a witch and a vampire, and says she wants to enrich herself by selling him to the devil. *The Dreamers* was never completed; the dream – like the masque which Prospero curtails – vaporises in brutal daylight.

In *The Immortal Story*, Welles first indulges and then condemns the conceit of Prospero, who uses magic to gain supernatural power. Gloating over his scheme, Mr Clay enters what Dinesen calls 'the heaven of his omnipotence'. In *F for Fake*, Prospero is less threatening. True, Welles whips up a splenetic tempest, using stock footage of a tropical storm to illustrate the rage of Picasso when his faked portraits are put on sale. But otherwise the Prospero played here by Welles resembles the character at the end of the play – a self-confessed mountebank, who hopes that the failure of his enchantments will earn him forgiveness, or at least pity.

He begins by playing tricks on children at a Paris station, making a coin vanish and then causing it to pop up again in another place. He asks if his young audience has heard of Robert-Houdin, from whom Méliès received lessons in illusionism. The children look blank, but Welles quotes Robert-Houdin anyway: he said that a magician is just an actor. If Prospero's marvels – the tempest itself, the vanishing banquet, the interrupted masque with the aerial goddesses – are merely entertainments, there is no moral harm in them. Of course the customers have been conned, but that is what we pay for when we go to the theatre. 'We hanky-panky men', Welles says in *F for Fake*, 'have always been with you.' At the end of his wartime performances in the tent on Cahuenga Boulevard, he thanked the GIs for their good-humoured gullibility: 'We trust you like to be fooled, and we hope we fooled you.' In *F for Fake* he admits that stories usually tell lies, but promises that 'For the next hour, everything you'll hear from us is really true, and based on solid facts.' He knows that we will not consult our watches, so as soon as the hour is up, the film – which then digresses to tell the story about Picasso and Kodar – becomes flagrantly fictitious.

This ingratiating Prospero has a surrogate, through whom Welles is able to explore the character's more devious or devilish side. Elmyr de Hory is his Ariel – a dapper, androgynous sprite, wizened and weighed down by his jewellery. Like Prospero sending Ariel to do his dirty work, Welles allows Elmyr to make manifest an ulterior identity that disturbed and even terrified him. His tragic heroes are great men who turn out to be hollow, like Kurtz or Kane. In Elmyr's case, the tragedy is replayed as impudent farce. Mincing through the streets of Ibiza or dispensing kisses at parties, Elmyr flaunts his fraudulence; this is the practical joke he played on a credulous world. When he first appears in the film, he cites two of the great men Welles had brooded about throughout his career. 'We're not talking about Napoleon or Julius Caesar,' he says, 'we're talking about Elmyr!' Though he seems to be distinguishing his own petty larceny from the exploits of more notable figures, the comment is actually a boast. Welles in his commentary calls Elmyr 'the emperor of the hoax'. Like Napoleon, he is an insidious revolutionary, who unsettles society by subverting its hierarchy of value and questioning its definition of legality. Like Caesar, he ponders his own coronation, smirking at his success in convincing museums that his forgeries are authentic, which must make him – he concludes – a great artist in his own right. However much Welles might have deplored Elmyr's activities, he could not dissociate himself from them. Showing off his fluency of line, Elmyr claims at one point that he is more Matisse-like than Matisse himself. He might be Pierre Menard transcribing *Don Quixote* and in the process improving on Cervantes; but he might also be Welles, retelling stories by Shakespeare or Cervantes or Conrad or Dinesen and recreating them, taking over from the original creator.

After Elmyr introduces himself, Welles reverts to autobiography, with some excerpts from a low-budget 1950s science-fiction film in which spacecraft hover above Washington and pulverise its cardboard monuments. He is recalling the fakery in his *War of the Worlds* broadcast. But why should Elmyr's falsifications have called up this doomsday scenario? Because the faker is a nihilist, undermining the notions of uniqueness or identity on which the art market and humanist philosophy both depend; his work has the same effect as the splintering ray guns that lay waste to Washington. He looks ahead to a world of simulacra and simulations, where people and what passes for art are industrially manufactured, duplicated indefinitely like copies of a photograph or a film. Irving goes on to describe an experiment that proves the point. He took some fakes by Elmyr to galleries and museums for appraisals; in all cases they were authenticated. 'After that I lost my faith', he says, leaving a brief pause before he completes the sentence with the phrase 'in the concept of expertise.' Loss of faith is indeed at issue in *F for Fake*, which is why it ends – just before the time-limit on veracity expires – with Welles's contemplation of Chartres. Despite this pilgrimage, which he undertakes in the hope of absolution, Welles's own artistic technique was based on guile and deception. 'The thing about film', he told Baxter, 'is that you can get away with a great deal more than people think. Confidence is all that matters.' Or confidence trickery? Welles dreaded Gielgud's arrival in Spain for *Chimes at Midnight*. 'I don't want him to think me just a trickster,' he said to Baxter. In *Don Quixote*, the knight rails against a camera that films him in the street. Sancho explains that photography is blameless white magic, but Quixote is not pacified. He sees in it the subversion of his crusade: this machine, he declares, insidiously turns truth into falsehood and falsehood into truth.

Though Welles later venerated stories as receptacles of human experience, stores of wisdom, in *The Magnificent Ambersons* he was happy to equate storytelling with falsification. George, castigated after his fight with a neighbour, reviles the boy's father as 'an ole liar!' When told he must not use that word, he adroitly selects a synonym and calls him 'that ole storyteller'. *F for Fake* notices the similarity between the stratagems of its fakers and Welles's own evasions. Montage, the editorial art he practised with such brilliance, relies on the hand to move faster than the eye. It coaxes us to make subliminal associations for which there might be no reasonable evidence, to see a whole when there is only a quick succession of ill-fitting parts. Even the costumes for Welles's films were assembled on this principle. The extras in *Othello* wore armour hammered from sardine cans, and for the battle in *Chimes at Midnight* Baxter scavenged cast-offs from a warehouse: 'knitted chain-mail pants and a soldier's tunic from *El Cid*', the Anthony Mann film in which Welles had been offered a role, and a suede jerkin 'embroidered with piping from Stephen Boyd's horse's harness from *The Fall of the Roman Empire*', which Mann had also recently made in Madrid. In the same way, it is by glueing fragments of film together that Welles incriminates Elmyr and Irving. On the soundtrack, he discusses the signatures of both forgers, illustrating his comments with glimpses of their silent, shifty body language. Elmyr flutters nervously. Irving, his blink-rate speeding up, gives the camera a remorseful glance when Welles, off-screen, mentions that he is being sued for 55 million dollars. Though the two men look as if they are being arraigned together, they were filmed separately, and are not reacting to Welles's comments at all. Images and words have been artifically joined to produce that flustered semblance of guilt. Because Welles narrates from his Moviola table, the seat of editorial and judicial power, there is no appeal from his verdict. In an aside he reveals how peremptory and opportunistic his procedures are. Some film snaps as it is being rewound. Welles shrugs as he notices the accident: it can easily be spliced together again.

The Soviet theorist Lev Kuleshov, who defended Eisenstein against Stalin, taught his students how to fabricate narratives from scraps of film, tenuously linking action and reaction. Hitchcock admired Kuleshov's cunning, and illustrated it with a coincidental narrative of his own. Take a shot of James Stewart grinning, follow it with a close-up of a baby, and his smile will look benign and paternal. Replace the baby with a shot of a girl in a bikini, and the smile will look lecherous. The two smiles, of course, are the same: we retroactively choose to alter the expression on Stewart's face. Whole sequences in *F for Fake* rely on Kuleshov's principle. Welles manipulates visual and verbal testimony as trickily – and, perhaps, as illegitimately – as the investigators in *The Trial* when they impugn K with the help of arbitrary evidence. On the sound-track, Elmyr inconsequentially prattles about his move to the United States. He needed a change of landscape, he says, and hoped to meet newer, more attractive people. On the screen, his hand flaps, and then is frozen by Welles as it approaches the backside, clad in tight red trousers, of the young American admirer who has volunteered to be his body-guard. No contact is made, because the hand and the buttocks it seems to be magnetised towards are separated in space; but the superimposition, and the way a passing gesture is arrested as if it were a caress, acts out the fantasy and imputes a motive to Elmyr. Immediately afterwards, Irving is heard explaining why Elmyr actually embarked on his travels. The FBI and police from four different states were 'on his tail', Irving says, contributing to Welles's double-entendre. While Irving talks, a small pet monkey frisks around him, scratching itself or exploring his ear and fondling his hair. By cutting so often to the creature, Welles makes it a commentator: mischievous, disrespectful, it apes human actions and is therefore a physiological forger. At another point, Welles is heard musing about the complicity of Irving's Swiss wife Edith, who renamed herself Helga R. Hughes and opened a Swiss bank account into which fees for the false memoir were paid. Could she be the mastermind? Here Welles inserts a quick shot of a cuckoo clock: a metonym for Switzerland and also, because of its allusion to *The Third Man*, a stand-in for Welles himself. Perhaps Harry Lime was wrong to deride the cuckoo clock. It is a playful machine, an automaton that pretends to be alive, like the film we are watching.

Kuleshov explained that 'thanks to montage it is possible to create . . . a new geography, a new place of action'. During the examination of the Hughes hoax, Welles gives the appearance of reporting from Las Vegas or Beverly Hills, though these inserts were filmed at Orvilliers, near Paris, and matched with American footage contributed by his helper at home, Gary Graver (who does some faking of his own in the film when he appears as a newsreader and declaims bulletins about Hughes). We are meant to notice the joins, and to be mistrustful. After labouring to construct a semblance of geographical cohesion in *Othello*, Welles picked apart the film's disparate locations in a German television documentary about the film, completed in 1979. A Tuscan staircase, he pointed out, had been insecurely welded on to a Moroccan battlement. Iago quit a church on Torcello in the Venetian lagoon and walked straight into a Portuguese cistern on the African coast. Roderigo struck Cassio in Mazagan, while Cassio hit back a thousand miles away in Orvieto. The documentary is an exercise in ironic self-destruction, like Prospero's curtailment of his masque. Yet by exposing the unreality or untruthfulness of his trick, the magician – in an even more ironic reversal – has drawn attention to his own cleverness as an artificer.

As he prowls through an art gallery in *F for Fake*, wearing his magician's cape, Welles pauses to recite some lines from a poem by Kipling.

Though he doesn't give its title, it is called, very significantly, 'The Conundrum of the Workshops'. *F for Fake* is about the conundrums of Welles's own workshop; it incorporates the skills Kuleshov taught in his workshop at the State School of Cinema during the 1920s, as well as looking into the shady workshops of Elmyr and Irving. Kipling's poem covers all these cases, because it goes back to the earliest artistic work-shop of all. Adam in Eden takes a stick and scratches a drawing in the mould:

> . . . the first rude sketch that the world had seen was joy to his
> mighty heart,
> Till the devil whispered behind the leaves, 'It's pretty, but is Art?'

The poem summarises the history of subsequent aesthetic endeavours, and repeatedly introduces the devil to disparage the artist and ridicule the conceit of human creation. When he quotes the question, Welles plays devil's advocate, sabotaging his own case. Among the lines he chooses from Kipling is a rousing testament that recalls his own youth-ful boldness:

> . . . each man knows as his lip-thatch grows he is master of
> Art and Truth.

Still, now much older, Welles cannot suppress a last twinge of doubt. As he dies, the man in the poem has to suffer the devil's ultimate sneering interrogation: 'You did it, but was it Art?' To this, Welles adds another vexing philosophical query. Whether or not it was art, did it tell the truth? He can only answer by employing a paradox. 'What we professional liars hope to serve is truth,' he says while he pretends to levitate the shrouded figure of Kodar's grandfather. 'I'm afraid the pompous word for that is art.' Irony once again allows him room for manoeuvre. Is he being complacent in assessing his life, or – since the sheet after all contains no body – has he grown tired of his own feigning?

In a scene that recurs several times during *F for Fake*, Elmyr burns one of his phony Matisse drawings in the fireplace. It is not an act of penitence, since he can scribble a dozen more Matisses in a morning, but perhaps Welles – who brings it back so often – saw a more personal meaning in the incident. He abandoned many of his films, or left others to chop them up and discard leftover footage. Watching Elmyr incinerate his own art, Welles perhaps admired his courage. No work of art, as he knew, is ever worthy of our initial hopes for it; no matter how relatively worthy it might be, it will, as he says at Chartres, in the end be destroyed or forgotten. Elmyr speeds up the process, and smiles as he feeds the flames. Prospero's shimmering dreams fade into air, those of Welles and Elmyr sift into soot.

In the first scene of Shakespeare's play, Prospero stages a tempest, staying out of sight while the mariners are battered by wet and windy special effects. In the second scene, he appears in person and tells a story about the tempest to a single, entranced auditor. First we see the storm happening, then we are given a spoken description of it. Prospero alternates between drama and narrative. He puts on shows, but will not let them speak for themselves; he reserves the right to comment, analyse, extrapolate, and to go on doing so – as in his monologues about the renunciation of magic at the end of the play – even after the show is over.

Welles shared this dualism. He dramatised scenes by fragmenting them into what MacLíammóir, vexed by the discontinuity of *Othello*, called 'snippets'. However, he also employed long, stealthy tracking shots that respect the continuity of narrative. In *The Lady from Shanghai* he laid tracks extending three-quarters of a mile for the dolly shot that follows Elsa's carriage through Central Park. Later, he had the camera close in on the Bannisters as they conspire outside the court room: moving with imperceptible slowness through their long conversation, it tentatively edges near enough to eavesdrop on them. Sometimes Welles cramps us in a 'huis clos', an enclosed stage where the dramatic unities of time and place are concentrated and grimly enforced, as when he squeezes his camera into the hotel elevator in *Touch of Evil*. But with the revolving turntables of *Five Kings* or *Around the World*, he explored the amplitude of narrative and showed how the earth serenely revolves, restoring losses and ending sorrows. Drama whips up climaxes, while narrative is about duration, endurance. Like Prospero, Welles in *The Immortal Story* and *F for Fake* is both an actor in a drama and a narrator observing events from a judicious distance, a subject of the story and the story's supposedly objective teller.

Given a choice between roles and forms, Welles preferred narrative to drama. When introducing his radio version of Daphne du Maurier's *Rebecca* in 1938, he corrected the announcer by insisting that his adaptation – which he narrated, and in which he played Maxim – was 'not a play, it's a story'. 'Everybody loves a story,' he added, 'and radio is the best storyteller.' Much later he decided that television suited his 'predilection for telling stories'. The time-limit of thirty minutes or an hour did not bother him: 'I prefer stories to dramas or plays,' he told André Bazin. 'I read "great novels" with extreme difficulty. I prefer stories.' Appearing as himself in *Someone to Love*, which is set in a derelict Santa Monica playhouse, Welles describes the theatre as 'the temple of the story'. It is a doubly odd remark. Drama stages actions rather than telling stories; and theatres are usually proud to be worldly, ribald, rather than aspiring to sacredness. But for Welles, stories were offshoots or remnants of myth, so the place where they were retold has a claim to sanctity. 'Tell me your story,' he says to the friends Henry Jaglom has assembled.

After his broadcast of *Dracula* in 1938, Welles returned for an epilogue in which he tried to convene a community held together by narrative: 'Ladies and gentlemen, what are your favourite stories? If there is one you are particularly fond of and would like to hear on the air, would you please write me about it?' He meant it when he described himself on the radio as the audience's 'obedient servant', a bard available for hire. And he assumed that a conversational exchange could occur between himself and his auditors. Narrating *The Magnificent Ambersons*, he engages in dialogue with the citizens on the screen, who overhear his commentary. A gossip predicts that Wilbur and Isabel will have many children and spoil them all; Welles records the fact that they have just one, which provokes the unseen busybody to snap that George was 'spoiled enough for a whole car load'. When the townspeople hope that school will knock the stuffing out of George, the narrator adds that it didn't. The soundtrack is a forum, a marketplace like that where – as Welles said to Bazin – 'Arabian storytellers' set up shop. Pooling experiences and viewpoints as they exchange anecdotes, he and his fellow citizens hope to arrive at a consensus. Only later in the film, having gained the trust of those he is obediently serving, does he exercise the narrator's novelistic privilege of omniscience and tell us what goes on behind the faces of the characters, as when he comments on the Major's dying meditation or George's prayer. The conversation between narrator and actor, each of whom properly belongs in his own incommunicable world, continues in Welles's *Don Quixote*. Introducing an episode in which Sancho is sent to Dulcinea with a love letter, Welles as narrator remarks that the author would have preferred to pass over what happened next, because he will surely not be believed. The Sancho of Tamiroff then steps forward to assure Cervantes and his spokesman Welles that truth will rise above falsehood like oil floating on water. 'Thank you, Sancho,' says Welles, offscreen. 'Not at all,' replies Sancho. Welles resumes the story with the words 'This history goes on to state . . .', well aware that history is just a story, its statements of fact actually fictitious.

The week after his *Dracula*, Welles promised his listeners that he would 'tell you Robert Louis Stevenson's exciting yarn about pirates and the sea': tell, not dramatise. He dispensed with scene-setting illusion in his *Rebecca*, explaining that 'the only illusion I want to create is the illusion of the story'. Though it is through the activity of play that human beings discover their freedom and inventiveness, plays are provisional, ephemeral, uncontrollable, since actors are likely to run away with them. A story, whether written down or inscribed on celluloid or tape, is more fixed and permanent – immortal, as Dinesen declared. Discussing *Citizen Kane* in a BBC television interview in 1960, Welles agreed that it was a fable about the acquisitive society, but argued that he did not have the polemical idea first and then design a character to fit it. He might have been paying homage to Dinesen when he added 'The storyteller's duty is always to the story.' It was a nimble revision of the record, since in *Citizen Kane* the various storytellers feel no such duty. None of Kane's former friends understand him, so the stories they tell are either self-vindications or, like Bernstein's reverie about the girl in the white dress on the ferry back in 1896, irrelevant personal memoirs. The journalist, researching a story about Kane, scouts for gossip and pays bribes to informants, but is no wiser by the end. Welles had brought his first film up to date with his current reverence for what Dinesen called 'the storyteller of all the ages', who carries with him a 'big bag of tales' summarising 'our classic Western civilisation'.

Interviewed in hospital in *Citizen Kane*, Leland calculates the weight of that big bag of tales. 'I remember everything,' he says; memory for him is a curse. But it is also a solemn obligation, because how else will the stories on which civilisation is founded be kept alive? This duty, as Welles saw it, gives a personal force to some dialogue in *The Magnificent Ambersons*, even though the words were taken from Tarkington's novel. Greeting strangers at the ball, George says to everyone with slick, formulaic politeness 'Remember you very well!' He is twice challenged, once by Eugene and then by his mother, who says to him when he meets Lucy 'You don't remember her either . . . , but of course you will.' It's a poignant comment: our present happiness is just an investment set aside for a future when we will only possess the memory of happiness, like the contents of a photographic album. And in this case, there may actually be no happiness to remember. Near the end of the film, walking in the garden with her father, Lucy retells the story of the Indian chieftain Vendonah, who once lived on the site of their house and was banished by his tribe. This is her way of recalling George, though she only summons him up in order to expunge him from her memory. When Eugene cross-questions her about the story, she claims not to remember Vendonah's name, despite having uttered it seconds before. Eugene hopes that she will one day truly be able to forget the other, unspoken name. Welles makes his own prologue to the film sound as if it too had been salvaged from oblivion, retrieved from the past like the wispy remnants of Prospero's dream. He begins to speak about the Ambersons in the darkness, over a black screen. With eyes closed, he might be conjuring up this vanished world, whose ghosts wriggle into bodies again. Then, as the seasons change, the camera watches people on the street stray into transparency. Social progress, like death, entails obliteration, erasure. To remember is to care for our collective history by tending the graves of our predecessors.

The culture we share is based on stories, which become myths by being told over and over again. In 1946, David O. Selznick relied on the portentous voice of the unseen Welles to effect that transformation in his Western *Duel in the Sun*. Welles, with a down-home twang, introduces the film's luridly operatic characters in a prologue showing scorched dusk in a literally painted desert, with a crag sculpted into the likeness of a squaw's head. The myth in this case is cobbled together from mimicry of Shelley's poem 'Ozymandias' mixed with Enobarbus's tribute to Cleopatra in Shakespeare's play: 'Deep among the lonely sun-baked hills of Texas, the ancient weather-beaten rock still stands . . . Time cannot change its impassive face, nor dim the legend of the wild young lovers who found heaven and hell in the shadows of the rock.' Welles recited the metrical rhetoric, but prudently took no credit for his contribution.

'This is what the legend says,' he mutters as *Duel in the Sun* begins. Stories that are legendary predate us and will outlast us; a play depends on the presence of players. Welles liked to show how plays derive from stories or are absorbed into history. He therefore inserted a spoken narrative at the beginning of his *Othello*, filling in the Moor's courtship of Desdemona and their elopement, just as *Chimes at Midnight* is framed by Ralph Richardson's quotations from Holinshed's chronicle. Welles coaxed Shakespeare himself to acknowledge the primacy of narrative in the prologue he wrote for his 1938 recording of *Twelfth Night*. As the actor Richard Burbage, he chides Shakespeare for interrupting work on *Hamlet* to write a comedy: 'What's the story? You stole the story, I know you did. You all do now, you versemakers.' Shakespeare, who indeed made up none of his own stories, nonchalantly replies 'The world is full of stories, Dickie.' Why bother to invent new ones, even if it were possible to augment the modicum of six or eight compulsory, archetypal plots? Old stories are best, because they narrate the course of all our lives. Repetition hallows them, gives them a patina, confirms their pertinence to us. The ghost story *Return to Glennascaul*, filmed by MacLíammóir's Gate company in 1951 with a prologue in which Welles has a walk-on, is described as 'a tale that is told in Dublin'; Welles is happy to tell it one more time. In *F for Fake* he quotes a line in which Kipling asserts the immortality of his story about Adam, Eve and Satan: 'The tale is as old as the Eden Tree – and new as the new-cut tooth.'

When Welles introduces the recorded performance of *Twelfth Night*, he might be telling the story of *The Tempest*: 'Once upon a time, long, long ago,' he says, 'there was a storm at sea.' Reinforcing the narrative's hypnotic spell, he treats the story as a byproduct of time itself: 'This is long, long ago. This is once upon a time.' The tense of drama is always the present; the action happens as we watch it. Welles made the play retreat into an immemorial past, so that what was lost long ago can be regained – thanks to the leisurely unfurling of romance – in the future. Viola and Sebastian are separated by a shipwreck in *Twelfth Night*. Another shipwreck in *The Tempest*, which turns out not to have wrecked the ship at all, brings about reunion and reconciliation. These eternal retellings can be oppressive. By reciting Kafka's parable about the law at the start of *The Trial*, Welles told K's story in advance. In Kafka's novel, K hears the parable at the end, as he is on his way to his execution. He questions the priest who narrates it, and disputes its interpretation. But the priest insists that 'The written word is unalterable, and opinions are often only expressions of despair.' In the film, Welles's Advocate emerges from the shadows of the cathedral and retells the story, making a con-cession to film by using what he calls 'visual aids': projected slides of A. Alexeieff's pin-hole illustrations. Perkins's K cuts him off, saying 'I've heard it all before. We've all heard it.'

That, of course, merely confirms its truth. In 1961, Welles was engaged to retell another story we have all heard before in Nicholas Ray's biopic about Christ, *King of Kings*. Unseen and again uncredited as if he were an absent god, he delivered a narration derived from the Gospels. At the start, he asserts the predestinate power of the tale by saying 'And it is written that in the year 63 BC the Roman legions like a scourge of locusts poured through the east.' Like Kafka's priest, he assumes that writing is an unalterable fate. But though the story was written long ago in the past, it is being spoken now in the present. At the voice's command, we see the invasion taking place: scripture serves as a film script. In the early stages of the film, the narrator has the monopoly of speech. Welles identifies the silent characters and supplies them with motives; he animates and directs them, as if he were their creator. Muting his trombonal register, he whispers a world into being through the microphone. When Pilate asks why there are no statues of Caesar in his new province, a centurion replies that 'the Jews have only one god, and their law forbids the presence of any image'. Images of Christ risk sacrilege, which is why the film is so coy about showing the face of Jeffrey Hunter, who plays the part; the word, declaimed by Welles on the soundtrack, is sacrosanct. Visually, we are restricted to what happens in the present, but words can foretell the future. Welles the narrator must cope with a doomed foreknowledge, which Christ shares. When his preaching angers the scribes and pharisees, Welles says that they 'numbered his days, and knowing the sum thereof, Jesus came to spend time with his mother'.

Such forethought is typical of Welles's narrators, who inflect the stories they tell with a post-mortem mood of retrospection. Sartre commented on the 'intellective order' of *Citizen Kane*, which subordinates 'the order of events to the order of causes: everything is dead'. This narrative is at odds with the immediacy of journalism, which is the film's subject and which suggests its form. The reporters scramble to piece together a story which, like K, we know already. They are at the beginning, and never get far beyond it; we, having witnessed Kane's death, look back at them from the vantage point of the end. Othello's funeral inaugurates the film: he is dead before his dramatic life begins. Welles's characters live on the assumption that they have already died, or that they soon will. In *The Lady from Shanghai*, Bannister ask Elsa if she is glad that O'Hara signed on for the voyage. She is, and says he must have changed his mind about her. O'Hara then makes a curious remark: 'Faith, Mr Bannister, I've already told your wife I never make up my mind about anything until it's over and done with.' Is he himself already over and done with? Did he die while trying to forget the story that he retells as he sails through limbo? Prospero's storm is a repetition of the one that wrecked his ship a generation ago, just as his entire life is summarised and abbreviated within the single day that elapses during *The Tempest*. All stories are mortal, because their subject is mortality. 'Death', as Walter Benjamin said, 'is the sanction of everything that the storyteller can tell. He has borrowed his authority from death.'

Perhaps because his beginnings were so precocious, Welles anticipated a premature ending. He played old men in his adolescence: how much life could he possibly have left? While he was still in his twenties, wits described him as America's youngest living has-been.

Stories usually begin at a precise point in time and end a little while later. Welles complicated this chronology. The story of his own life hints at remoter, more primordial beginnings, as the newsreel does in *Citizen Kane* when it declares 'Famed in American legend was the origin of the Kane fortune.' How did Welles originate? Did fairies deposit him on a doorstep in Kenosha, Wisconsin, as arbitrarily as the lodger who left Kane's mother 'the supposedly worthless deed to an abandoned mine shaft'? The myth which Welles elaborated also flirted with an apocalyptic ending. Hence his interest in the last man: he dared the world to survive after his departure from it. Bernstein adopts the limitless time scheme of myth when he tells the journalist about his friendship with Kane. 'I got nothing but time,' he says. Thompson prompts him by remarking: 'You were with him from the beginning.' Bernstein insists on a correction: 'From *before* the beginning . . . And now it's after the end.' The myth, comprising all the short stories told about Kane by his former friends, begins and ends nowhere. Its multiple versions reach varying conclusions, but nothing can be concluded. Thompson asks Bernstein about Kane's first marriage: 'It didn't end well, did it?' Bernstein replies 'It ended. Then there was Susie. That ended too.' Kane's marriages end, but he never does, and he is still alive – as an insoluble puzzle – after the end. From his earliest years, Welles had to contend with people who wanted him to end once and for all, rather than contriving a series of resilient resurrections. When *The Magnificent Ambersons* was first previewed, his narration – spoken as if posthumously – announced 'Ladies and gentlemen, that's the end of the story.' Members of the audience yelped for joy when they heard that the ordeal was over: they had no patience with the tempo of Welles's storytelling, which brought the Ambersons back from the dead, followed them slowly through life and then interred them once more. The studio snipped out the provocative phrase, so in the truncated version the narrator went straight on to recite the credits. Unhappy with the set for the crazy house in *The Lady from Shanghai*, Welles broke into the studio after hours and repainted it. The head of production was infuriated by the extra expense, and unfurled a banner outside the sound stage announcing ALL'S WELL THAT ENDS WELLES. The intended victim laughed at the murderous jest.

The end is meant to justify the means, to crown the life, to arrive at a victory. The endings to Welles's stories never manage such uplifting certainty, and he did not envisage that kind of end for his own life. 'Well, it's time to close,' he remarks at the end of his television film about the Basques. As he says this, he gazes up at fireworks that fitfully illuminate his face, like Harry Lime flushed out of his hiding-place by the glare from a window across the way. The pyrotechnics symbolise brief, brilliant lives, the premature fizzling of youthful incandescence. Welles goes on to explain that he intends to give the programme 'a Basque ending', which will, he warns, be 'a little tough, . . . not a bit sentimental'. Local storytellers, having conducted their characters to the end, 'don't say "And they *lived* happily ever after". No, here in the Basque country they say "And *if* they lived well, they died well".' That proviso discounts the prospect or even the possibility of happiness, and leaves the characters free to live well or badly. It also accepts that stories – even though they might pause for a wedding, or a fiesta like the one Welles filmed in the Basque village – only end when the characters in them die. Welles spent his life awaiting this end, and disapproved of those who thought they could evade it. He knew that there was no way to challenge the nullification of our dreams and ambitions, to stop Kane's globe smashing on the floor. As Faulkner's Will Varner in *The Long, Hot Summer*, Welles played a Lear who schemes to prevent tragedy. The dynastic plantation-owner Varner does not surrender power or crawl towards death, as Lear says he wants to do. Concerned with self-perpetuation, he recruits a spunky hired hand (played by Paul Newman) to fertilise his spinster daughter. 'I'm talking', he says in a drawl as unctuous as molasses, 'about the e-stablishment of my im-mortality.' Mr Clay mistakenly believes that his million dollars will live on after his death because of the child he has helped to engender by bringing Paul and Virginie together. Varner suffers no such disillusionment. At the end of *The Long, Hot Summer*, while his children and their partners romp and snigger coitally upstairs, he lays meaty hands on his mistress (Angela

Lansbury) and says 'I like life, Minnie. I like it so much I just might live forever.' That, for Welles, was the voice of Faust.

He even worried about characters who enjoy an endless life in fiction. The narrator in the *Third Man* radio series introduced Harry Lime as an 'immortal character', even though each episode began with the gun shots that killed him. So how could Welles explain away his own demise in his spoken prologue? A logical evasion made him pretend that these were stories about Lime's doings before his death in the sewer. But Lime was still alive after that supposedly terminal event, because the spiel always concluded with Welles declaring in a present-tense whisper 'I am Harry Lime.'

There is an ironic discussion of the same issue in Welles's *Don Quixote*, as Sancho washes his master in a rooftop bathtub. Such ablutions were a traditional induction into knighthood, purifying the aspirant: hence, in England, the Order of the Bath. During the ceremony, newcomers were instructed in the obligations of chivalry by more senior knights. Welles turns the ritual upside down. Sancho, looking at the scrawny physique he swabs, questions the legacy of Quixote's knightly predecessors. What value do their exploits have, since they are all dead? 'Great deeds', avers Quixote, 'confer on men a portion of immortality.' It is a moment when, in Welles's estimation, he is truly mad. The wise Sancho instantly corrects him. He cites the case of 'a humble little barefoot friar', recently canonised by the church. Isn't such a man, entirely lacking heroic pretensions, worthier of admiration than a knight errant? Behind Quixote is a neon sign for Quijote Cerveza. He is only immortal because his name can be taken in vain and used to sell someone else's merchandise.

Stories may indeed be immortal, but the storytellers and the men about whom they tell their stories are not. Welles, whether as a father or an artist, disavowed any pretension to go on living through his daughters or his brainchildren. He told Kathleen Tynan that he considered speculations about artistic immortality to be in poor taste. When Bogdanovich bemoaned the loss of Welles's personal archive – burned, supposedly, in a fire at his house in Madrid in 1970 – he shrugged, disparaging the preoccupation with posterity as just 'another form of worldly success'. All the same, he then instructed Bogdanovich to 'jot that down . . . on a slab of marble'. The irony deftly enabled him to contradict himself. He did expect an epitaph, and preferred to compose it himself.

Before the detour to Chartres in *F for Fake*, Welles remarks that, because Elmyr's paintings are in so many important collections, 'it must

be said he has achieved a certain immortality, under various other signatures'. He pauses before 'immortality', to make sure that the word has an
ironic inflection. Then at Chartres – a work of art signed by no one,
without an auteur – he praises anonymity, humbly conceding that 'Maybe
a man's name doesn't matter that much.' Again he pauses, this time before
'that much'. What follows is a qualification, not an outright denial that
one's identity and achievements are negligible. He murmurs 'that much'
in an undertone, hoping we will not notice the slight retraction. This, late
in the day, is a scene from the performance he might have given as
Hamlet, brooding over the skull of Yorick. But though the cathedral like
the skull reminds him of 'a fact of life – we're going to die', he is not
entirely reconciled to Hamlet's pessimism.

Suddenly, after the camera has glanced aside to study the cathedral,
Welles reappears, looking strangely cheerful as he pronounces our collective obituary. He resembles Arkadin congratulating himself on his
fake amnesia, which he calls 'a merciful affliction'. If Arkadin does not
know who he is, he cannot be held responsible for the crimes he has
committed. Welles likewise pleads the future's forgetfulness in his own
defence: centuries from now, no one will know who he is, so why bother
rebuking him for failed hopes, broken promises, incomplete films?
Despite the permanence of Chartres, he acknowledges that 'our works in
stone, in paint, in print' will only be 'spared, some of them, for a few
decades or a millennium or two'. Prospero, having renounced magic,
says that 'my ending is despair / Unless I be relieved by prayer.' His last-
minute bid for salvation is unconvincing; Welles seems more genuinely
consoled by the cathedral – though not for religious reasons, since he does
not enter it. The obsequy in *F for Fake* concludes bravely, buoyantly, as
he imagines an admonition delivered by 'dead artists out of the living
past'. 'Be of good cheer,' they tell him. 'Our songs will all be silenced.
But what of it? Go on singing.' Again he confidentially lowers the
vocal volume. Though the dead artists sing or cry or chant their 'grand
choiring shout of affirmation', all Welles can do, paraphrasing them, is
hollowly whisper. Is the world's end, or an individual's death, really such
a cause for jubilation?

An end cannot congeal into a tableau that prolongs happiness indefinitely, because time itself never stops. The end must accept the eventual
extinction of whatever we leave behind, and (as Welles says at Chartres)
the disposability of the earth itself, which will soon 'wear away into the
ultimate and universal ash'. He then turns himself into the living, dying

exemplification of his sonorous metaphor. After the comment on our ashen residue, he changes the subject to Picasso and his estate, valued at 758 million dollars. Introducing the anecdote about Picasso and Kodar, he strides into view in silhouette, hatted, caped, and preceded by his cigar, whose tip glows, although his face is blurred by a blue fog. Smoking, Welles makes his own meagre contribution to the crematorial pile. But he smiles as he puffs and the cinders drop from the cigar. In *Winter's Tales*, Dinesen proposes that 'the true art of the gods is comedy', because they are immune to the lowly miseries and grinding necessities that make tragedy the unique 'right of human beings'. For all his gloom, Welles sees our tragic decay as a joke, and this lifts him above it, giving him the demeanour that Dinesen called aristocratic: 'The very same fatality which, in striking the burgher or the peasant, will become tragedy, with the aristocrat is exalted to the comic. By the grace and wit of our acceptance thereof, our aristocracy is known.'

Your life is a tragedy if you choose to take it seriously, bothering like the bourgeois about progeny and patrimony. If you live nonchalantly, performing in an existential comedy, you stand a chance of outwitting death. In *The V.I.P.s*, Welles as the tax-evading film director announces that his next project will be an adaptation of Schiller's *Mary Stuart*. To secure an investment from the backers, he is obliged to give the role of the martyred queen to the vacuous starlet Elsa Martinelli. 'Is a tragedy?' she asks, never having heard of Schiller's play. 'Is a tragedy!' intones Welles, sepulchrally sorry for himself – though of course, to the lookers-on, the situation is comic. The difference between the genres depends on your point of view, or where you decide to position the camera. Chaplin thought that the tragedian demands a close-up. Welles disagreed: tragedy looks at the world in long shot, registering the little-ness of individuals and making room for life's indifferent continuation. Again and again in *Chimes at Midnight*, human history is effaced by views of a landscape that has no history except its vegetative cycle of death and rebirth. Corpses on rickety gallows decompose in the air. Churned mud gobbles up the soldiers in a collective grave. Seen from a high angle, Falstaff's coffin is dragged away into the open country. Freeze the frame at a certain point and the outcome might look comic. Allow time to resume and tragedy, sooner or later, takes over. After that, does comedy recur as the cycle proceeds? In the last scene of *The Big Brass Ring*, a fast train enables Menakar and Pellarin to escape their pursuers. Yet will their boyish happiness last any longer than the time it takes for the train to travel from Spain to France? The script calculates that they 'have six more hours together'. At some point during the trip, Pellarin will probably realise his error. As Welles said, he is 'a great man' who – assailed by '*cosmic* doubt' or by 'the devil of self-destruction that lives in every genius' – runs away, plays truant to his vocation. The self-accusing comment twists Pellarin's momentary delight into a symptom of moral cowardice or suicidal self-indulgence. A parenthesis at the bottom of the script's last page leaves the choice between tragedy and comedy open, like the dubious, conditional Basque ending in the television programme: '(If you want a happy ending, that depends, of course, on where you stop your story.)'

The stories Welles retold and applied to himself all dealt with insoluble problems, contradictions that could not be resolved by a formulaic closure. Does Faustus deserve damnation? Should Marlow have told the truth about Kurtz? Has Iago, who refuses to comment on the deaths of Othello and Desdemona, succeeded or failed? Is Hal's rejection of Falstaff justifiable? Is K a rebel or a meek, sheepish victim? Did Kane die happily, or was he reproaching himself when he last held that globe? Can Quinlan be at once a great detective and a lousy cop – that is, a brilliant artist and a flawed human being?

In *Someone to Love*, adjudicating the emotional disputes of Jaglom's friends, Welles rates the value of stories according to the intractability of the problems they present. 'All stories are about men and women,' he opines (although most of his own stories were about the friendship, rivalry and treachery between men). He goes on to declare that 'Mohammedans cannot make a good story', because their endings are too painlessly glib. A man only has to say to a woman 'I divorce you' three times, and he is rid of her. 'Where's their problem?' chortles Welles. Jaglom, having accumulated footage randomly, consults Welles about how to tie up the loose ends of these nascent or fraying relationships. Welles offers his advice from the cheap seats at the back of the theatre, not – as he warns Jaglom – from Mount Sinai, and he skirts the issue by philosophising about it rather than issuing a prophetic decree. 'Endings', he says, 'are a great American preoccupation.' It is, as usual, a startling idea. Surely the American preoccupation is with beginnings, since the country offered a new start to humanity by rescinding all previous history? But Welles knew that America needed to make good its myth of a second creation by ruling out the possibility of destruction; it had to control the future and convince Americans that they lived in a world without end, a rich, hedonistic heaven on earth.

Earlier in *Someone to Love*, he interrupts the anxious Californian chit-chat about personal growth and fulfillment to deride America's obsession with pursuing happiness, and wishes that the founding fathers had not burdened the country with that expectation. To the consternation of his fellow citizens, he calls happiness a piece of luck, not a right guaranteed by the constitution. He wonders if the feminists – who seem so pleased with their lives, despite their difficulty in finding someone to love – are secretly miserable. Only one person admits to being less than blissful: Oja Kodar, who as a European is inured to unhappiness. Welles remonstrates with Jaglom in similar terms when asked how the film should end, and paraphrases the bracketed afterthought he appended to *The Big Brass Ring*. 'Happy endings – which is what you're after because you're a sentimentalist – depend on stopping the story before it's over,' he says. 'Comedies end in marriage, and tragedies end in death. Those are your choices.' Immediately Jaglom, showing how right Welles is to call him a sentimentalist, asks whether he should kill himself. He is unlucky in love, and can't finish his film. Why go on? 'It didn't work in *Hamlet*,' grunts Welles, and he rebukes Jaglom by noting that Hamlet at least asked such puling, immature questions in blank verse. He also got over his quandary during the third act, whereas Jaglom is still agonising on the last day of shooting. Hamlet, Welles points out, 'gave it up and went on for two more acts'. But as they ineffectually talk, life solves their artistic problem by carrying them a little closer towards their quietus. 'You've got your ending,' Welles tells Jaglom, 'because we have come to the end.' Jaglom therefore asks Welles to say 'Cut', and then coaxes him to do so a second time. A director again, he gives the order to terminate the story and the film.

His own abrupt ending followed a few months later, on the night of 9 October, after a day spent appearing on one more pointless television talk show, followed by a last meal at Ma Maison. Rather than an end, it was an interruption, foreseeable – since he had been looking haggard, despite his bulk – but all the same unexpected. Welles was at his typewriter when the heart attack happened, still working, or at least still having ideas. He had sat down to plan the next day's scenes for the magic show he was filming. He was alone, as he had been all along. In *Someone to Love* he chides Jaglom for defining happiness as cohabitation with a woman, and casts a desolate look back across the centuries, reviewing an even longer history than he contemplated at Chartres. 'For twenty thousand years', he asserts, 'all the generations that have passed through all the civilisations of the world have been totally alone. We come into the world alone, we die alone, we live alone.' Significantly he rearranges the usual order of birth, copulation and death: dying here precedes living. 'We've always been alone,' he repeats, though he admits that love and friendship allow us periodically to forget the bleak truth. He then suggests that what Jaglom thinks of as 'a contemporary crisis' is in fact 'an eternal condition'. Sedentary and therefore unable to take part in the film's final dance, cordoned off in a row of empty seats, he embodies that condition. Welles, of whom there were supposedly so many, is singular and therefore solitary.

The Basques would have asked if he died well. At least it was not a showy, dramatised death, like Kindler's plunge from the tower in *The Stranger* or Othello's self-glorifying suicide. It could be called a fortunate death, because with luck he would not have known that it was happening. And had he lived well? As a son, brother, husband, father, employee, businessman, taxpayer and citizen, probably not. But, in his view, he had little choice. As a genius, possessed by a gift he did not ask for and could not control, he lived the only way he could – ingeniously, recklessly, and inconclusively, never reaching the point of satisfied stasis that is fatal to Goethe's Faust, who dies only when he decides that his quest is over and his achievement complete.

Welles twice calls 'Cut' in *Someone to Love*, barking the order directly into the view-finder the second time. Even so, he is not permitted to cut himself off. The camera continues to run, awarding him – since the film was not released until two years after his death – a posthumous return. After the end, he chortles, chuckles, laughs, guffaws and applauds, looking more and more unconvinced and uneasy. He is obliged to go on being himself, living up to his legend. Despite the pretence of mirth, his abiding self-mistrust is apparent in his sad, fearful eyes, and the forced laughter leaves him short of breath. The story is over, though the film refuses to stop.

Index